TRAUMA, TRANSFORMATION, AND HEALING

An Integrative Approach
to Theory, Research, and
Post-Traumatic Therapy

Brunner/Mazel Psychosocial Stress Series

Charles R. Figley, Ph.D., Series Editor

1. *Stress Disorders Among Vietnam Veterans,* Edited by Charles R. Figley, Ph.D.
2. *Stress and the Family Vol. 1: Coping with Normative Transitions,* Edited by Hamilton I. McCubbin, Ph.D., and Charles R. Figley, Ph.D.
3. *Stress and the Family Vol. 2: Coping with Catastrophe,* Edited by Charles R. Figley, Ph.D., and Hamilton I. McCubbin, Ph.D.
4. *Trauma and Its Wake: The Study and Treatment of Post-Traumatic Stress Disorder,* Edited by Charles R. Figley, Ph.D.
5. *Post-Traumatic Stress Disorder and the War Veteran Patient,* Edited by William E. Kelly, M.D.
6. *The Crime Victim's Book, Second Edition,* By Morton Bard, Ph.D., and Dawn Sangrey
7. *Stress and Coping in Time of War: Generalizations from the Israeli Experience,* Edited by Norman A. Milgram, Ph.D.
8. *Trauma and Its Wake Vol. 2: Traumatic Stress Theory, Research, and Intervention,* Edited by Charles R. Figley, Ph.D.
9. *Stress and Addiction,* Edited by Edward Gottheil, M.D., Ph.D., Keith A. Druley, Ph.D., Steven Pashko, Ph.D., and Stephen P. Weinstein, Ph.D.
10. *Vietnam: A Casebook,* By Jacob D. Lindy, M.D., in collaboration with Bonnie L. Green, Ph.D., Mary C. Grace, M.Ed., M.S., John A. MacLeod, M.D., and Louis Spitz, M.D.
11. *Post-Traumatic Therapy and Victims of Violence,* Edited by Frank M. Ochberg, M.D.
12. *Mental Health Response to Mass Emergencies: Theory and Practice,* Edited by Mary Lystad, Ph.D.
13. *Treating Stress in Families,* Edited by Charles R. Figley, Ph.D.

BRUNNER/MAZEL PSYCHOSOCIAL STRESS SERIES No. 14

TRAUMA, TRANSFORMATION, AND HEALING

An Integrative Approach to Theory, Research, and Post-Traumatic Therapy

By

John P. Wilson, Ph.D.

BRUNNER/MAZEL, *Publishers* • New York

Library of Congress Cataloging-in-Publication Data

Wilson, John P. (John Preston)
    Trauma, transformation, and healing : an integrative approach to
theory, research, and post-traumatic therapy / by John P. Wilson.
    p. cm.—(Brunner/Mazel Psychosocial stress series ; no. 14)
    Bibliography: p.
    Includes indexes.
    ISBN 0-87630-540-0
    1. Post-traumatic stress disorder. I. Title. II. Series.
    [DNLM: 1. Crisis Intervention. 2. Stress, Disorders, Post
-Traumatic. 3. Veterans—psychology. W1 BR917TB no. 14 / WM 170
W6863t]
RC552.P67W55 1989
616.85′21—dc19
DNLM/DLC
for Library of Congress
                                              89-639
                                            CIP

Copyright © 1989 by John P. Wilson

Published by
BRUNNER/MAZEL, INC.
19 Union Square
New York, New York 10003

MANUFACTURED IN THE UNITED STATES OF AMERICA

10 9 8 7 6 5 4 3 2 1

This book is dedicated
to the memory of
Ann Alhadeff

Foreword

This rich and exciting book draws together a wide range of theoretical conceptualizations, current research, and clinical understanding to provide the most up-to-date and comprehensive account yet available of traumatic stress and its consequences. John Wilson integrates complex theoretical frameworks from Freud to Seligman, Horowitz to Selye, to paint a powerful explanatory picture of the interaction between trauma, person, and post-trauma environment. By incorporating current concepts of neurotransmitter systems in relation to intrusive, avoidant, and hyperarousal symptom patterns, he is able to provide an attractive set of hypotheses for the interaction of psychological and biological processes in reaction to stress and in the development of the adaptations that may follow.

Also of great interest is the linking of cultural with psychological and biological themes. From his own experience of the Native American Sweat Lodge Ritual and his work with Native healers dealing with post-traumatic stress disorders in warriors, Vietnam veterans, Wilson is able to show that such processes probably involve mechanisms that will counteract many of the pathological physiological processes, such as hyperarousal, and may thus promote healing and recovery.

Following on these well-argued psychological, biological, and cultural concepts, a number of valuable research studies are presented. These explore the construct of post-traumatic stress; issues of the relationships between stressor and post-traumatic outcomes; the nature of stress sensitivity; the variables that contribute, especially among veterans to the persistence of post-traumatic phenomena and the development of disability in relation to these. These empirical studies introduce many exciting research questions that Wilson, his colleagues, and many others will answer in the future.

One of the general challenges in the area of traumatic stress relates to the relationship between the severe life experience and the outcomes—the nature of the modulating factors. It is quite clear that whatever the contribution to variance made by premorbid variables, both clinically and empirically it is the reaction to the severe trauma itself and its integration that are the most important factors. Victims from Vietnam to Pearl Harbor, from death to divorce, from rape to child abuse, attest to the nature of the threat and its severity, in the consequences that follow. Grief and loss, encounters with death, threat and destruction are the most powerful of the stressor components, but dislocation, moral conflict, and other traumata also play their part.

Our understanding of traumatic stresses and individual reactions to them is only just emerging. Yet, because of the ubiquity of traumatically stressful experiences, be they the consequences of war or urban violence, domestic unhappiness or community disaster, it is vital to expand knowledge in this field. This also offers the opportunity to examine, in development, the specific phenomenology of illness and may thus offer a unique opportunity to explore the etiology of psychiatric disorder and, hopefully, its prevention. For these reasons this integrative volume is even more timely and will provide an excellent starting point for researchers and clinicians alike.

Therapy for post-traumatic stress disorder is a particularly difficult area. The severity of illness, the pervasiveness of its effects, especially those that impinge powerfully on interpersonal relationships and the capacity for trust, which is so necessary for any therapeutic efficacy, all mean that treatment is complex and limited and may not be efficacious. The sensitive and powerful adaptation of cultural ritual to intensive treatment experience as presented in this book is a wise innovation and a careful attempt to extend the limits of the current therapeutic armamentarium; it offers in its effectiveness a potential model for post-traumatic stress disorder and other disorders in the future.

It is not easy to work clinically with those who have been severely traumatized. The pain of empathy, the burden of knowing and hearing of human suffering, the willingness to ask of and share the stories of the trauma take a special commitment. Transference and countertransference themes are especially powerful in this work, yet it is only with real empathy, with real sharing of the victim's experience in the therapy that healing can occur. The discussion of therapeutic processes in this volume summarizes the important contributions to the field of Ochberg and Horowitz, while adding the author's own experience and understanding. Of special value is his delineation of the countertransference themes that will beset those who work with the traumatized. For all of us who have dealt with the victims of catastrophe, violence, warfare, and personal disaster, these insights have a truth and validity that are unquestionable, yet which must be constantly reiterated. Only then can the distress be shared, and the capacity for empathy and healing be maintained.

This fine volume ends with the "Arms of Justice," highlighting the inevitability with which so many victims find themselves involved with the legal system—whether on seeking compensation, support for disability, in family relations, or as a defense when actions bringing legal sanctions may have been carried out in a traumatized state. Justice is not only a real and legal requirement for many of the victimized, but also a very powerful symbolic motive which demands some resolution. As Wilson wisely indicates, much further research is required to expand our understanding of this field.

This rich and excellent volume warms the heart and excites the mind. For it is clear that the author brings a wealth of compassionate and human concern to his explorations and care of those who have been traumatized; as well as a sharp, critical, broad-ranging and challenging set of conceptualizations and empirical studies to expand our knowledge of this vitally important field.

Beverley Raphael, M.D.
University of Queensland
Brisbane, Australia

Contents

Preface

Today the field of traumatic stress studies is rapidly becoming a unique, multidisciplinary area in the medical and behavioral sciences. From the days of my initial research projects on Vietnam veterans over a decade ago, the field of traumatic stress studies has undergone a profound transformation that has pleasantly surprised many clinicians and researchers who work with traumatized persons. Moreover, with the advent of PTSD as a mental disorder in DSM-III of the American Psychiatric Association in 1980, the recognition and acceptance of traumatic stress syndromes have increased greatly among professionals in the field and stimulated major programs of research in the United States and in many other countries in the world.

It is my belief that the study of traumatic stress is here to stay and will eventually occupy an important place in the field of psychiatry, psychology, and sociology. This is so because traumatic stress reactions are human responses to extraordinarily stressful societal and life events. To study and treat post-traumatic stress syndromes is to come face to face with the very harsh realities of what victimization and survivorship mean. The experience of trauma can transform the human spirit in a variety of ways, which range from extreme diminution of the will to an existential transcendence which is spiritual in nature.

At this time we are just beginning to understand these alternative pathways of post-traumatic personality alteration and adaptation. We know even less about the successful treatment of post-traumatic stress disorders and the stress recovery process. Yet, it is a fact of history that individuals do triumph over seemingly insurmountable adversities, such as the Holocaust, and live healthy and productive lives. I believe that it is important for future research to understand the processes of healthy coping following traumatic life events. To understand the nature of human resiliency and recovery from extreme stress would teach us much about pathological forms of stress response syndromes. Knowledge of the psychic mechanisms that enable positive coping, ego vitality, and continued growth throughout the life cycle will help us to identify the processes of maladaptive coping and psychopathology. The field of traumatic stress research will inevitably require holistic and integrative theories which can account for healthy and pathological forms of adaptation. Based on our current level of knowledge, such theories will of necessity, have to specify the complex linkage between neurophysiological, cultural, and psychological bases that determine the unique nature of the phenomena. *Ultimately, we seek to understand trauma, transformation, and healing as the core processes of victimization and survivorship.*

The chapters of the book concern different aspects of traumatic stress reactions and include discussion of the psychobiology of trauma, cross-cultural healing rituals, stress sensitivity, psychometric assessment, prolonged stress effects in Pearl Harbor survivors, forensic considerations, and issues in treatment and the recovery from trauma. By and large these chapters reflect my research program in post-traumatic stress for the past decade and are the product of work with my graduate students and colleagues at Cleveland State University—in particular, Suzanne Johnson, Gus Krauss, Ken Prabucki, W. Ken Smith, and Alice Walker, whose Master's level work in recent years has continued a tradition begun with the Forgotten Warrior project 15 years ago.

Chapter 1 presents a person-environment approach to traumatic stress reactions. This conceptual orientation expands an earlier theory of social action (Aronoff & Wilson, 1985) to the field of traumatic stress research. The interactional framework attempts to delineate the elements necessary to make predictions of both pathological and nonpathological forms of post-traumatic adaptation.

Chapter 2, co-authored with Alice Walker, discusses the psychobiology of trauma. It contains a set of premises regarding the mind-body relationship as affected by traumatic events. Included here is an analysis of how trauma disrupts physical and psychological equilibrium and leads to the symptoms of post-traumatic stress disorder at four interrelated levels of organismic functioning.

Chapter 3 looks at culture and trauma and examines the role of healing rituals in the stress recovery process. In particular, the Native American sweat lodge ceremony is discussed as a therapeutic technique that has many unique features that can facilitate natural, organismically based healing by altering the psychobiology of post-traumatic stress disorder. This study began in 1985 when I attended the Fourth Annual National Vietnam Veteran Inter-Tribal Association traditional pow-wow on the Sioux Indian reservation in Sisseton, South Dakota. It was at that time that I experienced my first sweat lodge, an unforgettable and extraordinary experience. During the next three years I had the opportunity to learn much about Native American rituals for healing, purification, and growth from several medicine persons. In the Pacific Northwest, on the Olympic Peninsula, I have learned a great deal from Andy Callicum, a gifted healer from the Mawatchaht Tribe, for whom I have the deepest appreciation and respect for all that he has shared with me.

In Chapter 4, co-authored with Ken Prabucki, we extend the use of an interactional model of post-traumatic stress disorder (PTSD) to an examination of the concept of *stress sensitivity*, a personality dimension that refers to an individual's vulnerability to be affected by an array of stressor dimensions that could lead to post-traumatic stress disorder or some other form of adaptation following a traumatic event.

Chapter 5 concerns the assessment of post-traumatic stress disorders. Specifically, the chapter explores the prediction of the dimensions of PTSD by use of an MMPI PTSD subscale, originally constructed by Terrance Keane and his associates. The results of this study are especially interesting in terms of current theories about the dynamics of post-traumatic stress syndromes.

Chapter 6, co-authored with Zev Harel and Boaz Kahana, explores the long-term effects of stress on aging and adaptation among the survivors of the Japanese attack on Pearl Harbor in 1941. This study was begun in 1985 with Col. Dan Devaris, M.D., who was then Chief of Liaison Psychiatry at Tripler Army Hospital in Honolulu, Hawaii. As a visiting scholar in residence at Tripler Hospital in 1985 and 1986, I learned that there had been no study of the possible psychological sequelae of the Pearl Harbor attack. Through Col. Devaris, I discovered the existence of the Pearl Harbor Survivor Association (PHSA), an organization with a membership of about 11,000 veterans. In 1986 I contacted the President of the PHSA, Mr. Tom Stockett, and arranged to attend the 45th reunion of the PHSA in Honolulu. With the approval of the executive board of the PHSA, my colleagues Boaz Kahana, Zev Harel, and I conducted interviews and administered questionnaires to about 800 Pearl Harbor survivors. The preliminary results of this study are presented in the chapter. Among the most interesting results is the discovery of what I have termed *contextual* post-traumatic stress reactions, in which the survivors will freely report stress disorder symptoms in the context of an historically important and heroic event that both justifies and validates the symptoms' existence. It is also interesting that the men who report these symptoms (e.g., intrusive images in 1986 of the attack in 1941) tend not to think of them as pathological. The Cleveland Foundation generously provided financial support to conduct the research in Hawaii.

Chapter 7, co-authored with Alice Walker and Bruce Webster, presents the results of a one-week intensive, experimental treatment program for Vietnam veterans suffering from PTSD. Bruce and I developed an eclectic, therapeutic milieu approach to treatment and stress recovery that occurred in the wilderness of the Olympic National Park. Although multifaceted in design, the treatment program utilized a daily sweat lodge ritual as part of the overall program. The results of the treatment program and the follow-up study are summarized in the chapter and point to the potential long-term effectiveness of this form of psychotherapy.

Chapter 8 discusses some of the general principles of treatment and intervention for post-traumatic stress disorder from the perspective of the interactional person-environment model presented in Chapter 1 and the psychobiology discussed in Chapter 2. Included here is an extensive discussion of countertransference reactions in post-traumatic therapy.

The last chapter concerns the role of PTSD in the forensic process. The purpose of the chapter is to present both conceptual and empirical information about PTSD in the legal arena. In particular, research data are presented for the "trauma profile" as discerned psychometrically from the MMPI, SCL-90, and Impact of Event Scale, and from the 16-Personality Factor measures of personality and psychopathology in civilian- and military-related traumatic events.

Acknowledgments

Since I began my work in the field of traumatic stress studies over a decade ago, there have been many individuals who have personally influenced my thinking and contributed, in one form or another, to my understanding of post-traumatic stress disorder. In addition, many of them have become valued friends and colleagues. Special thanks are extended to Dr. Charles R. Figley, founding President of the Society for Traumatic Stress Studies, who was instrumental as the series editor of the Brunner/Mazel Psychosocial Stress Series in making this book a reality. Charles encouraged me to pull together in one place some of my most recent work on post-traumatic stress disorder, and I am grateful for the opportunity.

My appreciation and thanks also extend to my friends and colleagues in the field of traumatic stress during the last 15 years: David Addlestone, Joel and Marilyn Aronoff, Art Blank, Jr., Yael Danieli, C. Peter Erlinder, Bonnie Green, Fred Gusman, Sarah Haley, Edna J. Hunter, Harry Kormos, Henry Krystal, Robert S. Laufer, Robert J. Lifton, Jack Lindy, Charles Marmar, Bill Mehedy, Shad Meshad, Robert Muller, Frank Ochberg, Erwin Parson, Ray Scurfield, Chaim Shatan, Steve Silver, Bessel van der Kolk, Lynda M. Van Devanter, Bruce and Char Webster, Tom Williams, and Patty and S. D. (Ziggy) Zigelbaum.

At Cleveland State University I have received support from Deans Georgia Lesh-Laurie and Harry Andrist for my research efforts in recent years. My colleagues Zev Harel and Boaz Kahana, former chairperson of the department of psychology, have provided many hours of stimulating conversation, helped to create a scholarly milieu in which to work, and contributed significantly to the study of Pearl Harbor survivors. As gerontologists, Zev and Boaz have taught me a great deal. I also wish to thank Alice J. Walker, who has been a graduate student in the Department of Psychology for the last two years. On many occasions she went well beyond the call of duty to make sure that all of the research was complete. Her hard work and dedication are enormously appreciated. Finally, a special thank you to Ann Alhadeff, executive editor at Brunner/Mazel, and her staff for the outstanding job in the production of the book.

Cleveland, 1989   *J. P. W.*

Series Note

John P. Wilson has worked for many years in the area of traumatic stress and has gained a national reputation for his contributions, particularly studying and treating Vietnam veterans. In many ways this book serves as an important bench mark for the Wilsonian views of the traumatic stress. Perhaps more important, this book will make a significant contribution to the emerging field of traumatic stress through Wilson's theoretical perspectives. Thus, the Editorial Board of the Psychosocial Stress Book Series is proud to welcome *TRAUMA, TRANS-FORMATION, AND HEALING* as the fourteenth book in the Series.

The Series was established many years ago to develop and publish books that in some way make a significant contribution to the understanding and management of the psychosocial stress reaction paradigm. These books are designed to advance the work of clinicians, researchers, and other professionals involved in the varied aspects of human services who confront issues of psychosocial stress reactions.

The Psychosocial Stress Book Series is among the few that are "refereed." The quality and significance of the Series is guided by a nationally and internationally respected group of scholars who compose the Editorial Board. The Board must review and approve each book that is published in the Series. Like the readership, the Board is represented by the fields of general medicine, pediatrics, psychiatry, nursing, psychology, sociology, social work, family therapy, political science, and anthropology.

Books in the Series focus on the stress associated with a wide variety of psychosocial stressors. Collectively, the books in the Series have focused on the immediate and long-term psychosocial consequences of extraordinary stressors such as war, divorce, parenting, separation, racism, social isolation, acute illness, drug addiction, death, sudden unemployment, rape, natural disasters, incest, crime victimization, job stress, and many others.

Together with *TRAUMA, TRANSFORMATION, AND HEALING*, these Series books form a new orientation for thinking about human behavior under extraordinary conditions. They provide an integrated set of source books for scholars and practitioners interested in how and why some individuals and social systems thrive under stressful situations, while others do not. Certainly, this latest contribution to the Series and field, by John P. Wilson, helps us understand and appreciate our capacity as humans to survive and endure. As Wilson states in his epilogue, "To study traumatic stress is to learn a great deal about the extremes of human nature in terms of life, death, and the transformation of the spirit."

Charles R. Figley, Ph.D.
Series Editor
Purdue University
West Lafayette, Indiana

TRAUMA, TRANSFORMATION, AND HEALING

An Integrative Approach
to Theory, Research, and
Post-Traumatic Therapy

SECTION I
Theory

1

A Person-Environment Approach to Traumatic Stress Reactions

In recent years theoretical approaches to the study of human behavior have recognized the need for interactional models that specify how many variables work together to create social-psychological and psychobiological processes (Aronoff & Wilson, 1985; Kenrick & Funder, 1988; Rossi, 1986). Interactional models of behavior attempt to identify the central elements necessary for theoretical hypotheses that specify patterns of interactions that codetermine different forms of adaptive behavior. In the area of research on stress and coping, an interactional approach to the understanding of stress response syndromes has been suggested, at least implicitly, by clinicians and theorists for many years.

Trimble (1981, 1985) has reviewed the concept of traumatic neurosis and noted that early explanations of the syndrome tended to focus on *physiological* causation as the determinant of a symptom pattern or change in personality. In these approaches, clinicians speculated that concussions to the head, injury to the spinal cord, or small cerebral hemorrhages altered psychic functioning either acutely or in a prolonged way.

Later, toward the beginning of the 20th century, Freudian influence postulated a model of traumatic neurosis based on *intrapsychic* mechanisms in which the "protective shield" of the ego was overwhelmed by an excessive influx of stimulation produced by a stressful life event.

Once the ego was traumatized, however, other stimuli could function so as to become equivalent to the original stressor. Freud's model, explicated in different works, is interesting because his original theory (i.e., seduction theory) was an early formulation of post-traumatic stress disorder. Later, of course, Freud developed the Oedipal theory of neurosis and abandoned the model of trauma in which an external event led to neurotic symptoms. Nevertheless, Freud did state that constitutional factors were important in determining how the ego would react to stressful life events (Freud, 1966). Other psychoanalytic explanations (Winnicott, 1950) speculated that traumatic war neurosis, in particular, was caused by neurotic separation anxiety which lay dormant in the unconscious of the person until reactivated by the stresses of warfare. In this view, the vulnerability to a traumatic neurosis was the result of early infantile problems of attachment to parental figures. Consequently, the stressors of war led to regression in the face of unmanageable anxiety. Later theories, which developed out of the study of war veterans (Grinker & Spiegel, 1945; Kardiner, 1959), emphasized both the nature of combat stress and predispositional variables as determinants of personality alteration and post-combat adjustment.

Since World War II a number of researchers have proposed models of stress, coping, and adaptation. These models were developed from studies of different populations of victims as well as laboratory-based experimental work. For example, Hocking (1965, 1970) proposed a theoretical model that views the onset of psychopathology as an interactive effect of the severity and duration of extreme stress and the personality attributes of the individual. In a similar way, Horowitz (1986) has proposed a model of stressful life events in which psychopathology results from incongruency between self-schemata and unassimilated information (affect and imagery) from the trauma. To Horowitz and his associates, dispositional variables are seen as personality styles which moderate the cognitive processing of the trauma. Marmar and Horowitz (1988) suggest that coping or defensive mechanisms modulate the extent to which new information is integrated with pre-trauma cognitive schema. Thus, the stress syndrome includes a cycle of oscillation between episodes of intrusive imagery and avoidance of the trauma-laden affect and imagery.

In his seminal and pioneering contributions, Lifton (1976, 1979, 1988) suggests that traumatic events affect psychoformative processes. These processes include changes in the self-structure of the individual such that the traumatized person may experience himself or herself as suffering from a sense of stasis, separation, disintegration, a loss of continuity, decentering, numbing, and a changed view of the world. Similar to other dynamically oriented theorists, Lifton considers defensive processes as mechanisms that affect the extent to which the individual restructures and reformulates the traumatic experiences.

In the last decade, explicit interactional paradigms of stress and coping have been put forth by Lazarus and Folkman (1984) (see also Appley & Trumbull, 1986; Dohrenwend & Shrout, 1984; Green, Wilson, & Lindy, 1985; and Raphael, 1987). In these models it is proposed that post-traumatic adaptation is determined by several classes of variables and include: (1) the nature and dimensions of the trauma; (2) personality attributes; (3) the nature of the recovery environment; and (4) the coping resources of the person. It is believed that these variables interact in influencing both pathological and nonpathological forms of adaptation to stressful life events.

Figure 1.1 presents a model of the elements for a theory of traumatic stress reactions. This model builds on those previously discussed in the literature and is an attempt to develop a potential framework that will eventually lead to a detailed interactional model of traumatic stress reactions. Moreover, the model is generic in nature and provides an organized framework for the other chapters in this book.

A POTENTIAL FRAMEWORK FOR A THEORY OF TRAUMATIC STRESS REACTIONS

Traumatic events occur inside the psyche of individuals. The *subjective* experience of a traumatic event varies from person to person and from one event to another. It is also the case that there are levels of objective severity to traumatic events and it is possible to conceptualize stressors as falling along a continuum of stressfulness of different dimensions, such as the threat to life and physical integrity to a more purely psychological focus, for example, the witnessing of an atrocity or the infliction of harm to a loved one. As noted in DSM-III-R (APA, 1987), traumatic events can be either man-made or the result of a natural disaster or environmental event. Moreover, it is also true that individual difference variables, such as personality traits, cognitive style, gender, and intelligence, affect the way in which stressful events are perceived, appraised, and processed. An interactional model of traumatic stress reactions must also specify how excessive stress *alters* personality functioning in pathological and nonpathological ways as well as its influence on life-course development. Further, traumatic events are never "culture free," and it is important to understand how cultural differences affect how a person perceives, interprets, and assimilates such experiences.

As a general principle, an interactional theory assumes that: (1) individuals with differing personality propensities seek out reinforcers from situations, including traumatic ones, that will gratify their prepotent need states (Aronoff & Wilson, 1985); (2) the propensities of the person interact in a dynamic way with the environmental and situational elements of the traumatic stressor to (3) set up both individual subjective reactions to the trauma and (4) patterns of post-traumatic adaptation which can be acute or prolonged in nature. Figure 1.1 summarizes these relationships.

ELEMENTS FOR A THEORY OF TRAUMATIC STRESS REACTIONS

Person Variables

An interactive theory of traumatic stress recognizes implicitly the importance of personality variables in determining reactions to traumatic events. These personality dimensions include the major variables studied by clinicians and researchers in the field of personality and social psychology: motives, traits, beliefs, values, abilities, cognitive structure, mood, defensive and coping styles, as well as genetic propensities. Moreover, as discussed by Aronoff and Wilson (1985), personality traits are directly associated with cognitive styles of information processing, especially in the acquisition, processing, and goal-setting dimensions of encoding information from situations. More specifically, the acquisition of information includes the cognitive processes of selective attention, search flexibility, and search persistence. The outcome of these two major components of information processing is the development of a *schema for enactment* which includes setting a level of aspiration and risk taking as well as problem-solving behavior. *When the personality characteristics of the individual are organized around safety-oriented needs (i.e., insecurity, anxiety, dependence, authoritarianism, approval seeking, etc.), the cognitive style of information processing under conditions of stress results in a tendency toward the reduction or constriction of information from the stimulus field, which, in turn, directly affects the processing of encoded information and the formulation of a schema for enactment. On the other hand, personality characteristics concerned with enhancing self-*

INPUTS TO THE PROCESSING OF TRAUMA

FORMS OF STRESS RESPONSE DETERMINED BY PERSON-ENVIRONMENT INTERACTION

PERSON VARIABLES $\Longleftrightarrow$ (P x E) $\Longrightarrow$ ENVIRONMENTAL AND $\longrightarrow$ INDIVIDUAL SUBJECTIVE $\longrightarrow$ POST-TRAUMA ADAPTATION
(P)　　　　　　　　　　　　SITUATIONAL VARIABLES　　RESPONSE TO TRAUMA
　　　　　　　　　　　　　　(E)

Motives
Traits
Beliefs
Values
Abilities
Cognitive Structure
Mood
Coping Style
Defensive Style
Genetic Propensities

I. Dimensions of the Trauma
   a. Bereavement/Loss
   b. Imminence
   c. Duration/Severity
   d. Displacement
   e. Exposure to death, dying, etc.
   f. Moral conflict
   g. Role in trauma
   h. Location
   i. Potential for re-occurence
   j. Life-threat
   k. Complexity of stressor
   l. Impact on community

II. Experience of Trauma
   a. alone
   b. with others
   c. community based (collective)

III. Structure of Trauma
   a. single stressor
   b. multiple stressor
   c. complex vs. simple
   d. natural vs. man made

IV. Post-Trauma Milieu
   a. level of support
   b. cultural rituals for recovery
   c. societal attitudes towards event
   d. opportunity structures

I. Emotional
   a. Affective distress
   b. Affective numbing
   c. Affective balance

II. Cognition
   a. denial/avoidance
   b. distortion
   c. accurate appraisal
   d. dissociation
   e. intrusion

III. Motivational
   a. aroused
   b. non-aroused

IV. Neurophysiological
   a. hyperarousal
   b. depression-avoidant
   c. balanced

V. Coping
   a. instrumental
   b. emotional
   c. cognitive re-structure
      1. positive
      2. negative
   d. resilient

I. Acute
   a. Pathological
      1. PTSD
      2. Other disorders
   b. Non-Pathological

II. Chronic
   a. Pathological
      1. PTSD
      2. Other disorders
   b. Non-Pathological
      1. Personality alteration
      2. Character change

III. Life-course development
   a. Intensification of developmental stages
   b. Retrogression
   c. Psychological acceleration

Figure 1.1. Elements for a theory of traumatic stress reactions.

esteem and competency (i.e., need for achievement, dominance, internal locus of control, nurturance, etc.) tend to be associated with a cognitive style that augments and expands the search of the stimulus field under conditions of stress. As a result, there is vigilance in processing the material encoded which can lead to effective problem solving or excessive hyper-vigilance, depending on how the stressor was perceived and initially appraised during the trauma.

An interactionist perspective of traumatic stress implies that person-ality processes affect and dynamically interact with all four categories of environmental variables to influence the specific nature of the in-dividual subjective response to the trauma (see Figure 1.1). A person with rigid moral beliefs in a situation of high moral conflict, for example, who commits an atrocity in warfare may have a subjective response that includes strong affective distress, cognitive distortion as to his role in the event, the arousal of guilt feelings, physiological hyperarousal, and emotional-laden coping actions. As a consequence of this form of individual subjective response to the situation, pathological symptoms might be manifest immediately or after a period of latency.

Theoretically, it is possible to suggest that many different personality dimensions could be crossed with the four environmental dimensions (stressor attributes, experience of trauma, structure of trauma, and post-trauma milieu) to create a matrix of predictions regarding the five dimensions of individual subjective response and the different forms of post-trauma adaptation. Such a set of tables of predictions would, of necessity, be quite complex since there are many subdimensions which form interaction possibilities. Although such an analysis is beyond the scope of this chapter, it is noteworthy that the outcome of such an effort would yield: (1) a specific set of testable hypotheses; (2) higher-order predictive explanations; and, (3) the evolution of new conceptual possibilities pertaining to the explanation of traumatic stress response syndromes. It is crucial to a theory of traumatic stress that such a systematic effort be undertaken to move the field beyond models that simply assume that personality variables moderate the relationship between stressor dimensions and outcome variables.

ENVIRONMENTAL AND SITUATIONAL VARIABLES

The Dimensions of Traumatic Experiences

Traumatic events differ on many different dimensions. As Figure 1.1 indicates, it is possible to identify these dimensions as follows: (1) the degree of life threat; (2) the degree of bereavement or loss of significant others; (3) imminence or the rate of onset and offset of the stressors; (4) the duration and severity of the stressors; (5) the level of displacement and dislodging of persons from their community; (6) the exposure to death, dying, injury, destruction, and social chaos; (7) the degree of moral conflict inherent in the situation; (8) the role in the trauma (agent versus victim); (9) the location of the trauma (e.g., home versus elsewhere); (10) the complexity of the stressor (single versus multiple); and, (11) the impact of the trauma in the community (e.g., a natural disaster). Traumatic events can be classified according to the level to which these 11 dimensions exist in the trauma. The more these dimensions are present in any particular trauma, the greater the potential for producing a pathological outcome. However, consistent with the general principle of an interactional theory, personality and situational variables (e.g., social support and economic resources) will interact with the stressor dimensions in determining post-trauma adaptation. Finally, each of these stressor dimensions can be linked to post-traumatic symptomatology independent of the personality traits of the person that might moderate different outcome processes.

Experience of the Trauma

Clinicians and researchers have long observed that traumatic events can be experienced either alone, with other persons, or in the context of a community-based experience. When the trauma is experienced alone, the individual may feel helpless, terrorized, fearful, vulnerable, and at the mercy of fate. In groups, the effect of a trauma may be different, as in the case of the Chowchilla incident in which children were kidnapped in a school bus (Terr, 1985). In the context of a group, well-known social-psychological processes may operate, such as contagion, rumors and myths, social pressure and norms of regulation, and identification with the perpetrator, as recently identified in the Stockholm syndrome (Ochberg, 1988). When a trauma affects an entire community, it can produce many secondary stressor experiences if the destruction or devastation is severe enough. Indeed, Erikson (1976) coined the term *loss of communality* to describe the massive social and individual trauma in the Buffalo Creek Dam disaster. The disaster not only exposed the survivors to high degrees of death, dying, and destruction, it eliminated many sociocultural support systems so necessary for recovery.

The Structure of Trauma

Since traumas are psychological events, they possess an inherent structure similar to many other social-psychological phenomena. We can think of traumas as containing a single stressor or multiple stressor experiences. Single-stressor events are rare and typically involve an accident, such as a chemical explosion, which produces physical injury. Most traumatic experiences contain multiple stressors, such as combat in warfare, which may include such dimensions as life threat and exposure to death and injury. Moreover, the psychological structure of a traumatic event may be thought of as complex or relatively simple. Complexity refers to the number of subcomponents inherent in a trauma, the number of competing or conflicting choices to be made and the ambiguity as to possible alternative actions in the event. On the other hand, a simple traumatic event is typically unidimensional and clear with respect to the nature of the event and the possible behaviors one could enact. For example, the atomic bombing of Hiroshima and the Cambodian holocaust of the Khmer Rouge were complex events that involved massive destruction and killing for reasons that were not clear to the victims. In both situations there were many competing alternatives, e.g., whether to help others or protect oneself in order to survive. Moral dilemmas were indigenous to these events which affected virtually every aspect of society. Beyond these dimensions, both events were of such an immensity that ideological perspectives and beliefs about human nature and life itself were profoundly altered (e.g., Kinzie, 1988; Lifton, 1967). As noted in DSM-III-R, traumatic events can be man-made or the result of a natural disaster. At present it is thought that these causes of traumatic episodes have important implications for both attributions of causality in stress response syndromes as well as post-traumatic adaptation.

Post-Traumatic Milieu

An interactional theory of traumatic stress must attempt to delineate the important dimensions of the recovery environment that affect post-traumatic adaptation. Broadly conceived, the milieu that exists following an excessively stressful event can be classified in four major dimensions. (1) First is the level of social, economic, and personal support present. This has been conceived as the trauma membrane by Lindy (1988) since there is a tendency for significant others to form a protective membrane of support around the victim to insulate them from further stress or harm. It is assumed that the greater the level of supportive mechanisms and opportunities after a traumatic event, the more positive will be the stress recovery process, especially if there is rapid clinical intervention and nurturing support.

(2) As noted by van der Hart (1983), cultures develop rituals to aid persons suffering from emotional distress. It is possible to delineate the various ritualistic and culturally evolved mechanisms that concern the legacy of the trauma. Further, some rituals (e.g., Memorial Day parades for war veterans) are collective expressions concerned with the event whereas other rituals are highly specific and idiosyncratic (e.g., the sweat lodge purification ritual of Native American groups). Cultures also differ on the number, kind, and frequency of the rituals that are designed to heal traumatized persons (Silver & Wilson, 1988). To date, there are no systematic cross-cultural analyses of healing rituals for stress recovery as determined by the human relations area files (HRAF). However, studies of shamanistic rituals have produced important information on rituals, trance states, and their larger function in different cultures (Winkelman, 1986). Clearly, the anthropological study of various facets of traumatic stress would generate a wealth of useful information necessary for an integrative and holistic theory of traumatic stress reactions.

(3) Included in such a set of studies would be an analysis of the sociocultural attitudes and responses toward the victimized individual and the stressful event itself. For example, it has been widely noted that the U.S. ambivalence toward and rejection of Vietnam veterans contributed to their post-war problems of adjustment (e.g., Figley & Leventman, 1980). Societal and political attitudes toward traumatized persons are important aspects of the recovery environment because they determine how resources will be allocated to provide the services that are needed by the victim.

(4) Beyond the resources that aid in the recovery from traumatic stress, it is possible to speak of the *opportunity structures* which exist or are created to facilitate an integration within the culture in terms of a career, assuming personal responsibilities, and establishing viable personal identity that has meaning and significance within the culture.

INDIVIDUAL SUBJECTIVE RESPONSE TO TRAUMA

Individual subjective response to trauma refers to the initial responses that occur in the wake of stressful experiences. There are five separate, but interrelated dimensions to adaptive behavior, which can be classified as: (1) emotional; (2) cognitive; (3) motivational; (4) neurophysiological; and (5) coping resources.

Emotional

By their very nature traumatic events upset the psychic equilibrium of the individuals affected by them. Traumatic events inevitably produce powerful emotional reactions in persons because they disrupt normal homeostatic functioning on the physiological level and radically alter the optimal levels of arousal on the psychological level (see Chapter 2). Persons vary in how they subjectively experience and cope with the excessive autonomic nervous system arousal and endocrine secretions triggered by threatening and overwhelming traumatic experiences. In *affective distress* the person feels overwhelmed emotionally, fearful, flooded with distressing affect, extremely anxious, and may be unable to mobilize intellectual and personal resources to effectively problem-solve in the face of what has happened. Alternatively, some persons shut down emotionally when confronted with an intense and upsetting event and experience *affective numbing*, a state in which the capacity to feel is greatly reduced. The term *psychic numbing* was coined by Lifton (1967). Affective or psychic numbing has a continuum which ranges from a stuporous, zombielike daze and psychomotor retardation to very subtle manifestations, such as impacted sensuality and difficulties in giving and receiving affection. Lifton (1988) has suggested that psychic numbing involves several ego-defense processes, including the mechanisms of splitting, repression, and forms of dissociation. It is also the case, at least clinically, that when affective numbing is reduced, alleviated, or suddenly 'lifted' by a failure in ego defenses, the person may experience affective distress, forms of vulnerability, or a fear of loss of control.

Affect Balance

Affect balance refers to the third category of emotional reaction to a traumatic event. As implied by the term, affect balance indicates that the person is able to successfully modulate affective states, both positive and negative, which naturally occur in unusually stressful situations. To a large degree, affect balance is a healthy response to trauma and is associated with the cognitive ability to realistically appraise what has happened and to respond with instrumental coping which is efficacious in meeting the immediate demands of the situation.

Cognitive

The cognitive responses that occur in the immediate and long-term aftermath of a trauma refer to modalities of information processing or ways of understanding the event that has occurred. In an interactional theory of traumatic stress reactions, cognitive processes are especially important because they are multidimensional and include the following: (1) perception of the event(s); (2) appraisal of the situation; (3) attributions of causality; and, (4) a schema for enactment of a response. There are, in turn, at least five major cognitive styles of information processing that characterize how individuals encode and process the four dimensions listed above.

Cognitive denial or avoidance refers to the tendency to deny or avoid what has happened by blocking the perception of the event; appraising the situation as one that does not require help; forming an attribution of causality that minimizes responsibility or involvement in the larger context of the situation and leads to a schema for enactment that includes denial in fantasy; avoidance of situations that trigger reminders of the experience or survivor guilt for a failed enactment.

Cognitive distortion is similar to psychic denial except that the person engages in extensive distortion in perception, appraisal, attribution, and enactment. Cognitive distortion is a mechanism that seems to ward off the intense anxiety and fear that the individual experiences so acutely in the immediate context of the event. Distortion, like denial, is a cognitive style whose effect is to *reduce* rather than augment internal stimuli. It can be thought of as a safety mechanism which prematurely terminates a search of the stimulus field for additional information that could lead to problem-solving behavior. As such, there is a high degree of selective attention, a narrow search of the stimulus field, an intolerance of ambiguity due to affective arousal, and a low level of search persistence for information that pertains to the processes of appraisal, attribution, and enactment.

Accurate appraisal is a third cognitive process that characterizes an information-processing ability to accurately perceive what has happened in the trauma, realistically appraise the situation in terms of the persons and events involved, make a correct or adequate assessment about causality, and initiate attempts to respond effectively and adaptively. The person who can accurately appraise the nature of a traumatic event is more likely to *augment* internal stimuli, actively scan the stimulus field, engage in a search of new or necessary information, and persist in such attempts, since the outcome of this mode of cognitive functioning is the ability to act competently in terms of personal needs and the demands of the situation.

As reviewed by Lifton (1988), much of the early thinking about reactions to trauma involved the concept of *dissociation*. As traditionally conceived, the concept of dissociation refers to an alteration in consciousness, identity, or behavior (DSM-III-R, APA, 1987). As a cognitive mechanism, dissociation is an alternative way to cope with extreme emotional distress by altering the nature of perception, appraisal, attribution, and the schema for enactment. Single episodes of dissociation in response to trauma can be thought of as severe reactions to a state of psychic overload and thus constitute a kind of hysterical reaction to overwhelming affect (cf. Braun, 1986; Freud, 1966). However, repeated episodes of dissociation as a cognitive modality of information processing probably reflect a learned approach to situations that are perceived to be potentially threatening. In response to the perception of threat, the individual fears being vulnerable and helpless and engages in a dissociative reaction which could be an alteration in level of consciousness, the expression of personality, or unconscious behavioral expressions such as fugue states. Similar to denial and distortion, dissociation is a safety-oriented cognitive mechanism in which the individual is attempting to avoid situations of conflict or threat that disrupt the psychic equilibrium.

The concept of reexperiencing in imagery and affect some element of the traumatic event is the *sine qua non* of post-traumatic stress disorder. *Intrusion* as a cognitive mechanism refers to the sudden, unbidden, and involuntary presence of visual images or distressing affect associated with the traumatic event. Intrusive images or memories may occur with or without distressing affect. When intrusion occurs without affect, it is presumed that some form of splitting, dissociation, or numbing has occurred as a defense against feelings that would overwhelm the individual. Similarly, it is possible for the individual to experience affective flooding without visual imagery or memory. In this case there is a repression, blocking, or unconscious avoidance of the catastrophic imagery. Intrusion as an acute or prolonged response to stress refers to a state of psychic overload in which the person is immersed in the wake of the trauma. In this state, the distressing affect and imagery overwhelm the individual and absorb a great deal of psychic energy. As a consequence, the result is a state of fatigue, excessive autonomic nervous system arousal, and anxiety in preparation for the next anticipated episode of reexperiencing the trauma.

Motivation

Traumatic events can affect the motivational propensities of a person. Motivational propensities refer to individual differences in the strength of various motives that have emerged from psychosocial development (e.g., the need for affiliation, the power motive, the need for safety and predictability). From the perspective of an interactional theory, these motives may be activated by the trauma or remain dormant. For example, the unexpected death of a loved one may arouse a motive of nurturance and lead to the active initiation of generativity, caring for others, or involvement with organizations or groups with prosocial goals and values. On the other hand, it is also possible for motives of safety (Aronoff & Wilson, 1985) to be activated and lead to behaviors designed to defend against anxiety by constructing highly predictable, structured, and ordered activities. Such a phenomenon was observed by Goldstein (1963) in brain-injured individuals and led him to formulate the construct of catastrophic anxiety which the individual experienced when an expected routine or order was disrupted. Finally, it may be the case that traumatic events can either give birth to new motives or transform old motives in new directions. When new motives are born from the trauma, they represent a form of personality alteration, as in the case of psychosocial acceleration in ego development (Wilson, 1980a). The transformation of motives seems to occur when the trauma produces a rapid change in the cognitive structure of the person in terms of the organization of the belief structure. For example, when a great deal of *deillusionment* is produced by a stressful life event, the person may let go of belief systems that now seem inoperative in light of what has happened. In this process of cognitive disequilibration, there then emerges a new set of beliefs and values which may facilitate a change in the nature, prepotency, and organization of basic needs.

Neurophysiology

In the next chapter the psychobiology of post-traumatic stress disorder is discussed. In terms of individual subjective response to trauma, there are variations in neurochemical and endocrine secretion which result from exposure to traumatic events. In an overly simplified way these neurophysiological processes can be classified as states of: (1) hyperarousal, (2) avoidance-depression, or (3) balance. In hyperarousal, it is believed that the catecholaminergic substances of noradrenalin, serotonin, and dopamine are extremely elevated to the point that their use eventually exceeds synthesis and leads to an avoidance cycle. In this state, cholinergic substances such as cortisol and acetylcholine are elevated and result in depression, avoidance behaviors, and blocked awareness of the emotions of fear, anger, and aggression. In a balanced state, there is a relative balance in ergotropic and trophotropic neural subsystems which does not result in a pathological response to trauma. Clearly, these neurophysiological states can vary in duration, severity, and periodicity depending on their activation by external stimuli or through associative learning. In the extreme form, chronic activation of the hyperarousal-avoidance cycle can be thought of as the neurophysiological substrate of post-traumatic stress disorder.

Coping

Lazarus and Folkman (1984) define coping as a process and state such that it is a "constantly changing cognitive and behavioral effort to manage specific external and/or internal demands that are appraised as taxing or exceeding the resources of the person" (p. 141). Building on their seminal work as well as that of Kahana, Harel, Kahana, and Rosner (1988), it is possible to identify four types of coping responses to traumatic events: (1) instrumental, (2) expressive, (3) cognitive restructuring, and (4) resilient. Each of these forms of coping is thought of as an active psychological process which can be employed by individuals and varies in use from one situation to another. It is also believed that these forms of coping are associated with personality processes (i.e., traits and cognitive style) which affect the predominance in use of a particular coping style. However, an interactional model of traumatic stress syndromes assumes that coping is affected by the complex interplay of situational variables and personality processes. Similarly, Lazarus and Folkman (1984) write that "the dynamics and change that characterize coping as a process are not random; they are a function of continuous appraisals and re-appraisals of the shifting person-environment relationship" (p. 142).

The four forms of coping refer to the efforts made by the individual to manage the challenges or demands presented by the stressors that exist in a situation. Although these stressors are often external to the person (e.g., a natural disaster), they may be internal as well. Internal stressors are psychological states of psychic overload in which the person feels unable to manage or process decision choices in terms of role responsibilities or other behavioral alternatives.

Instrumental coping is defined by problem-solving attempts to directly manage the demands posed by the stressors in the situation. It refers to the active initiation of either short- or long-term goal-directed behavior and contains either an implicit or explicit schema for enactment. Instrumental coping may be accompanied by different affective states and cognitive expectancies regarding the anticipated outcome of the effort. As defined here, this form of coping is similar to problem-solving coping identified by Lazarus and Folkman (1984) and many others.

Expressive coping is characterized by attempts to reduce distress and emotional arousal through a variety of cognitive and emotional strategies. At one end of the continuum are raw emotional expressions, such as anger, rage, fear, apprehensiveness, whining, and complaining. Accompanying these emotional outbursts are often the cognitive mechanisms discussed above, such as denial, distortion, dissociation, or intrusion, which attempt to reduce distress by reducing or augmenting information through safety-oriented responses to threat and vulnerability. In cognitive reducing modes of information processing, there is selective attention, a low search of the stimulus field for additional information, low search persistence, and a narrow and limited schema for enactment. As a consequence of this style of coping, the four major cognitive tasks of perception, appraisal, attribution of causality, and the schema for enactment are negatively affected. Generally, the negative outcome includes feelings of helplessness, hopelessness, and vulnerability and the defensive operations of denial, minimalization, repression, or psychic numbing. On the other hand, the individual may augment information from the stressor and lead to states of intrusion or dissociation induced by *psychic overload*, which may result in the same set of negative outcomes.

Cognitive restructuring refers to coping by reappraising and restructuring thoughts and feelings pertaining to the stressors experienced. As defined by Lazarus and Folkman (1984), cognitive reappraisal includes "cognitive maneuvers that change the meaning of a situation without changing it objectively, whether the changed construal is based on a realistic interpretation of cues or a distortion of reality" (p. 151). In positive cognitive restructuring the individual engages in cognition that augments information processing either by: (1) wide-scope attention to the properties and elements of the stimulus field, (2) active and persistent search for new data relevant to problem solving, and (3) the formulation of alternative schemas for enactment. Similarly, positive restructuring may involve complex forms of processing persistence that is strictly internal, i.e., rational and intuitive modalities of rethinking ways to manage the stressor experience. In negative restructuring or reappraisal, the person employs defensive operations such as denial or distortion to cope with the stressful event. Negative restructuring alters the processes of perception, appraisal, attributions of causality, and the schema for enactment and serves to reduce the level of distress and emotional arousal. Extreme forms of negative restructuring may result in grossly impaired adaptive functioning since there is a potential failure to process and assimilate information necessary for efficacious action and attempts at mastery of the situation.

Resilient coping refers to the capacity of the individual to continually manifest flexibility and mastery of stressful events without a disruption in psychic equilibrium. Resilient coping is different from instrumental coping because the individual's resources are not taxed or exceeded. Resiliency as a construct is similar to that of the hardy coper (Kobasa, 1979), who is characterized as having an internal locus of control, a strong sense of commitment to personal goals, and substantial capacity to meet difficult and challenging situations. In terms of cognitive processes, the resilient coper engages in accurate perception, appraisal, and attribution of the traumatic event. As a result, there is developed an effective schema for enactment which may be either a behavioral strategy or a form of cognitive reappraisal.

Post-Traumatic Adaptation

There are many diverse ways that individuals adapt to traumatic life events. As noted by Green, Wilson, and Lindy (1985), the cognitive processing of stressful life events is affected by personality variables, the nature of the stressors experienced, coping resources, and the nature of the recovery environment. These classes of variables interact with one another to codetermine both pathological and nonpathological forms of post-traumatic adaptation. As Figure 1.1 indicates, it is possible to classify post-traumatic adaptation into acute and chronic forms that are either pathological or nonpathological and which occur at some stage of life-course development.

The pathological outcome possibilities are theoretically unlimited and include, of course, all the major mental and personality disorders, depending on the nature, severity, and developmental onset of a traumatic event. Clinically, however, the most common pathological outcome of traumatic experiences is the development of post-traumatic stress disorder or other disorders that one would expect to occur in response to life threat, bereavement, loss, or the witnessing of horrible events. These include dysthymia or major depression, dissociative reactions, anxiety disorders, adjustment reactions, substance abuse as self-medication, and personality alteration.

The nonpathological responses to trauma also can be classified into several subcategories, including: (1) no change in personality or behavior, (2) positive personality alteration and character change, (3) intensification of specific stages of ego development, (4) psychosocial acceleration in ego development, (5) changes in prepotency in the motive (need) hierarchy, and (6) alteration in beliefs, attitudes, and values. An interactional theory of traumatic stress assumes that there is a range of variability in the strength and degree of nonpathological outcomes. However, it is assumed here that when positive changes in personality occur, they are relatively permanent and likely to be associated with resilient coping styles, greater levels of ego strength, and strong tendencies toward self-actualizing behavior (Maslow, 1970). Positive forms of character change following trauma may be construed, at least theoretically, as higher forms of psychological functioning which are organized in the wake of the trauma.

The effects of trauma are also age related and have, at least potentially, a number of effects on life-course development. In terms of the epigenetic development of personality and identity, three major effects are discernible: (1) the intensification or aggravation of the current stage of ego development; (2) retrogression in development, which includes not only actual regressive behavior but the reactivation of previous unresolved conflicts, distressing feelings, and prior episodes of vulnerability to stress or trauma; and (3) psychosocial acceleration, in which there is a premature emergence of cognitive capacities, qualities of awareness, modes of valuing, and philosophical outlook. Psychosocial acceleration also refers to the capacity for unusually autonomous behavior, independence from cultural norms and expectancies, a capacity for existential transcendence, and a deep sense of human spirituality that appreciates the interrelatedness of mankind and his environment.

In summary, Figure 1.1 illustrates the core elements for a theory of traumatic stress reactions. As a model, it assumes that there are dynamic person-environment interactions of great complexity that determine how individuals subjectively react to traumatic events that can lead to either acute or chronic forms of adaptation which are, in turn, either pathological or nonpathological.

The person inputs to the model include all dimensions of personality processes, such as traits, needs, cognitive style, values, and genetic propensities to stressful experiences. The environmental inputs to the processing of trauma include four major categories: (1) the dimensions of the trauma, (2) the experience of the trauma, (3) the structure of the trauma, and (4) the post-traumatic milieu. The features of the person and the environmental dimensions of the trauma codetermine the individual subjective responses to the stressors, of which there are five categories: (1) emotional reactivity, (2) cognitive processes, (3) motivational, (4) neurophysiological, and (5) coping patterns. These five dimensions occur simultaneously within a person at different levels of awareness and ultimately determine the post-traumatic pattern of adaptation, which can range from severe psychopathology and diminution of humanness to self-actualizing transcendence, positive character change, and altruism toward others. To study and treat victims of extreme stress is to understand the psychic struggle that begins with trauma and ends with a transformation of the spirit. An interactional approach to trauma is a template by which to approach an understanding of these human processes.

2

The Psychobiology of Trauma

with ALICE J. WALKER

Traumatic events are experiences that impact on organismic functioning and human adaptation. Extreme stress affects organismic functioning directly on four interrelated levels: physiological, psychological, social-interpersonal, and cultural. Although the immediate and long-term effects of a trauma may impact on one level more severely than another (e.g., a disabling physical injury), they are, in fact, interrelated processes which influence each other in direct and subtle ways that constitute the essence of the mind-body relationship. For purposes of scientific inquiry we necessarily separate these systems in order to understand how complex psychobiological processes influence behavior. However, an integrated theory of traumatic stress ultimately must be holistic and be capable of specifying the nature of integrative organismic functioning and the mind-body relationship. Nowhere is this more important than in discovering the psychobiology of healing. When a traumatic event produces changes in physical and psychological well-being that we label as pathological, it fundamentally alters the mind-body relationship in ways that counter organismic striving toward effectance motivation and self-actualization (Maslow, 1970; White, 1959). For this reason it is important that we understand some of the basic aspects of the psychobiology of traumatic stress in order to broaden our conceptual knowledge of maladaptive responses to stress and the techniques that are developed to alleviate the adverse effects which result from such experiences.

21

BASIC ASSUMPTIONS

In order to develop a general perspective of the psychobiology of traumatic stress reactions, a set of basic assumptions will be presented to organize a discussion of the mind-body relationship in post-traumatic adaptation.

1. Traumatically stressful experiences disrupt the physiological and psychological equilibrium of the person. The disequilibration of organismic functioning includes both physical levels of homeostasis and optimal levels of psychological arousal.
2. Traumatically stressful experiences produce state-dependent learning that has both physiological and psychological correlates. (2a) In some persons, especially those who have endured extremely prolonged and physically arduous experiences, there may be relatively permanent changes in nervous system functioning that result in chronic hyperarousal and a cognitive information-processing style that functions in trauma-associated ways in nearly all situations.
3. The disequilibrium that occurs in response to traumatic events affects all four levels of organismic functioning: physiological, psychological, social-interpersonal, and cultural. (3a) A corollary of this assumption is that organismic functioning is holistic and systemic in nature and an effect to one level produces an associated effect on another level.
4. The altered psychobiological state produced by traumatic events can be reversed to restore normal organismic functioning and healthy growth and development. (4a) The physical and psychological disequilibrium produced by a trauma can be changed by deconditioning the altered psychobiological state through various intervention strategies, including medication, exercise, and transformative cultural rituals.
5. Culture-specific and transcultural ritualistic practice can effectively decondition altered psychobiological states and restore vitality and emotional well-being.

We will discuss some of the specific ways that cultural rituals can significantly affect such states as post-traumatic stress disorder in Chapter 3.

APPROACHES TO THE PSYCHOBIOLOGY
OF STRESS AND WELL-BEING

The evolution of the psychobiological study of behavior, especially in terms of understanding mental disorders, is currently in its infancy, but accelerating so rapidly that it may soon develop into a discipline of its own (Andreasen, 1984). More recently, however, Rossi (1986) has succinctly reviewed the major approaches to the psychobiology of mind-body healing and proposed his own theory of how psychological processes modulate four interconnected organismic processes of the immune, endocrine, neuropeptide, and autonomic nervous systems.

In terms of traumatic stress responses, there is beginning to be a convergence of knowledge accumulated from different areas of psychobiological research that is starting to illuminate the exquisitely intricate but coherent mind-body structure of post-traumatic stress disorder (PTSD). These areas of biological research include: (1) neuroscientific studies of neurochemical transmitters and cell function; (2) psychiatric studies of the relationship of brain chemistry to mental disorders (e.g., depression, alcoholism, schizophrenia, etc.); (3) the study of somatic therapies (i.e., pharmacological interventions to alleviate the symptoms of mental disorders); (4) the study of the psychobiology of state-dependent learning; and, (5) the analysis of PTSD as a unique phenomenon which has features that overlap with other disorders, especially depression, anxiety, and dissociative syndromes.

In any field of research there exist major theoretical paradigms which influence thinking and hypothesis generation. In a recent review of the research on the brain and behavior relationship, Groves and Young (1986) have stated that:

In our research for the biological basis of behavior and cognition, conceptual models of brain function have nearly always been based on ideas developed first in the older, more established physical and engineering sciences. For example, ideas in Freudian drive theory derive, in part, from the field of thermodynamics and the notions of free and bound energy. The field of cybernetics with its feedback control systems theory has been applied to understanding sensory and motor control systems in the brain. Ideas from the exploding field of computer science dominate concepts of information processing in the behavioral and brain sciences. More recently, the physical and engineering sciences have found it necessary to describe the behavior of complex, nonideal systems, such as turbulence, climatic change, wave motion and exhibiting instabilities that are, at times, almost chaotic or quasi-random. . . . These ideas appear to more closely approximate the analyses and descriptions that will be required for our understanding of brain and behavior. . . . An exciting feature of this approach is that the properties of nonlinear dynamic models may be applicable across the many levels of analysis, from the molecular to the behavioral, and cognitive domain that must be considered in understanding brain functioning and behavior. (p. 18)

This perspective is quite informative because it recognizes, implicitly, that there is a complex mind-body relationship. Mental states can dynamically affect neurochemical processes in the nervous system which, in turn, produce responses that alter mental processes as well. From the perspective of psychic trauma, it is quite apparent that a powerful external stressor will exert an effect on personality, cognition, and coping that will subsequently lead to several alternative behavioral outcomes, some of which may ultimately have deleterious effects physically and psychiatrically. On the other hand, how the individual modulates a traumatic stressor may lead to a nondeleterious outcome. As with many other phenomena, there is a range of reactions to traumatic stressors, and it is highly probable that the mind can and does modulate facets of the endocrine and autonomic nervous systems. In writing on this relationship, Rossi (1986) stated:

> In general, mind influences of the cerebral cortex reach the hypothalamus via its associated limbic system structures, the hippocampus, amygdala, and thalamus. The hypothalamus then mediates these mind influences to the autonomic nervous system via the lower brain stem control centers, which serve as relay stations to the sympathetic and parasympathetic nervous systems. . . . The vital processes of all the organs regulated by the autonomic nervous system are subject to the influences of state-dependent learning via their association with the hypothalamic-limbic system, which feeds our life histories of experiential learning into them. . . . During times of stress, state-bound patterns of information may be generated in the regulation of any organ or combination of them. These patterns may then become manifest as the unfortunate responses that we call "psychosomatic problems." (p. 105)

In situations of extreme stress the state-bound patterns of information may be quite strongly associated with powerful autonomic nervous system activity, primarily in the secretion and depletion of neurotransmitters. Stated simply and phenomenologically, the victim of a traumatic event may encode in all sensory channels the imprint of the stressors in a psychobiological state of hyperarousability. Thus, there is state-dependent learning and the patterning of information associated with the nature of the stimuli inherent in the event itself. Moreover, in extreme stress experiences involving direct or indirect life threat or the witnessing of such events, the state-dependent learning may supplant the previous nonhyperaroused optimal level of stimulation, become the new baseline of mental functioning, and lead to a set of symptoms that we call post-traumatic stress disorder. This, then, is the essence of the mind-body psychobiology of traumatic stress reactions, especially when they are severe and chronic. However, in order for this to occur, there must be a neural substrate and set of mechanisms that could trigger the activation and deactivation of such a conditioned set of state-dependent responses (see also Chapter 7).

Andreasen (1984) has indicated that in terms of the biological revolution in brain-behavior studies, three classes of neurotransmitters have been identified as playing a central role in the four major syndromes of mental disorders. These neurotransmitters include cholinergic agents (acetylcholine [ACh]), biogenic amines (dopamine [DA], norepinephrine [NE], serotonin [5-HT], histamine), and amino acids (gama-aminobutyric acid [GABA], glycine, and glutamate). Additionally, other research has identified the neuropeptides of endogenous opioids (beta-endorphin and enkephalin) as importantly associated with altered states of consciousness and stress response syndromes (Janowsky, Risch, & Neborsky, 1986). But how do neurotransmitters work in response to stress and threat?* In a lucid and analytical paper, Ciaranello (1983) writes:

> At the molecular level, similar differential response capabilities exist. In general, the various components of the catecholamine system respond to stress at different rates. Activation of adrenergic neurons and release of catecholamines from nerve terminals and the adrenal medulla occur virtually instantaneously after exposure

---

* In terms of biogenic amines, Schildkraut, Green, and Mooney (1985) have succinctly summarized as follows: "The neuronal systems utilizing both norepinephrine (NE) and serotonin (5-hydroxytryptamine (5-HT)) originate as [a] relatively small collection of cell groups located mainly in the brain stem. From there, the cell groups project into other centers. Such widespread projection makes these neuronal systems logical targets for psychiatric research; small changes in them can have widespread behavioral effects" (p. 770).

to a stressor. Response of cellular target organs varies from very fast (contraction of muscles) to somewhat slower (fat breakdown). Doubtless this has something to do with the biologic function being served by the metabolic process. The most slowly responding part of the catecholamine system seems to be replenishment of the spent neurotransmitter by enzyme action.

Thus, at all levels, differential response capability exist[s] to modulate, amplify, or attenuate responses to stress. The function of this system is quite basic: it serves to keep the animal alive.

Depending on the organism's perception of the threatening nature of a stimulus, it will activate one or another central neuronal pathway, utilizing different neurotransmitters, resulting in different sympathetic and hormonal responses. We know from much animal data that the development, basal functioning, and ability of these systems to respond is subject to genetic regulation. The gene controls on these functions are varied and complex. Their effect is to place natural limits on the ability of an organism to respond to environmental stimuli. (pp. 100–101)

Ciaranello's analysis that the perception of threatening stimuli will activate central neuronal pathways is especially germane to understanding the psychobiology of post-traumatic stress disorder since, as DSM-III-R (APA, 1987) notes, stressors that produce the syndrome often involve ". . . serious threat to one's life or physical integrity; serious threat or harm to one's children, spouse, or other close relatives and friends; sudden destruction of one's home or community; or seeing another person who has recently been, or is being, seriously injured or killed as the result of an accident or physical violence" (p. 250). Clearly, these types of stressors are sufficient to activate psychobiological responses, which include the fight-flight mechanisms, endogenous peptides, endocrine secretions, and increases in catecholamines and adrenergic substances. If such neurochemical processes occur in conjunction with state-dependent learning and conditioning, it is possible to understand that a mind-body relationship could develop such that internal or external stimuli could trigger the neurological system and produce a set of symptoms that involve three interrelated symptom clusters associated with PTSD: (1) reexperience and intrusive imagery; (2) avoidance, detachment, emotional constriction, and depression; and, (3) physiological hyperarousal and "overdriven" motor activity and nervous system functioning. These symptom clusters are, of course, the central feature of PTSD and are also common to anxiety and depressive and dissociative disorders as well.

BIOGENIC HYPOTHESES RELATED TO TRAUMATIC STRESS RESPONSES

The accumulated body of research on the neurophysiology of these disorders has been reviewed by Andreasen (1984), Britton (1986), Ciaranello (1983), Costa (1985), Gray (1985), Janowsky, Risch, and Neborsky (1986), and van der Kolk (1987). These reviews are detailed and beyond the scope of this chapter. Nevertheless, they all converge in four sets of hypotheses that are important in their implications for analyzing the psychobiology of PTSD. In an overly simplified form, these hypotheses are as follows:

The Catecholamine Hypothesis

This hypothesis argues that PTSD symptoms of avoidance, detachment, emotional constriction, and depression result from a decrease in norepinephrine (NE) and that increased catecholamine production (NE, 5-HT, DA) results in feelings of well-being, self-control, and higher energy levels. As we discuss below, disruption in the production and depletion of catecholamines (i.e., a change in steady state) is thought to be associated with intrusive episodes of reexperiencing or reenacting elements of the traumatic experience.

The Balance Hypothesis

This hypothesis postulates that a balance between adrenergic and catecholaminergic levels is associated with positive mood states. On the other hand, an imbalanced condition, especially a disruption of the steady state due to increased cholinergic production, leads to the symptoms of avoidance, detachment, emotional constriction, and depression. As a neural substrate of PTSD, an imbalance is thought to be a part of the avoidance cycle described above, whereas the restoration of balance modulates the severity of the avoidance, intrusion, and physiological symptom expression. As we discuss in the next chapter, some cultural rituals, such as the Native American sweat lodge, may succeed therapeutically by producing a balanced condition and a temporary deconditioning of the state-dependent learning and hyperarousal state.

The Serotonin Hypothesis

A decrease in serotonin (5-HT) is thought to result in the avoidance-depression set of symptoms, whereas increases in this catecholamine reverses this effect and leads to a sense of well-being. An implication of this logic is that decreased serotonin levels would be associated with avoidance, emotional constriction, and depressive symptoms of PTSD.

The Opioid Hypothesis

Similar to the other hypotheses, a decrease in endogenous opioid production is thought to result in depressive-avoidant symptoms, whereas increased levels restore a sense of well-being and are anxiolytic in nature.

In summarizing some of the recent brain behavior evidence pertaining to mental disorders, especially the affective disorders, Janowsky, Risch, and Neborsky (1986) conclude:

> It is important to stress that, at this time, although much is known about the phenomenology of affective disorders, knowledge of their biochemical and psychological etiologies, or how treatment actually works, is uncertain, although multiple explanations exist. *A final common pathway hypothesis represents an excellent way to integrate disparate etiologic hypotheses and treatment techniques with respect to depression. However, it remains a future goal to decide if this holistic explanation, as seductive as it is, is actually valid.* (p. 186, emphasis added)

It is our belief that it is highly likely that a common neural-endocrine pathway does exist and that the recovery from PTSD entails a recognition of the powerful interplay between the mind and body. A similar position has been stated by Rossi (1986):

> The neurotransmitters of the autonomic nervous system, the immunotransmitters of the immune system, all function as "messenger molecules" or keys that open the receptor locks on the surface of the cells. This messenger molecule and cell-receptor communication system is the psychobiological basis of mind-body healing, therapeutic hypothesis, and holistic medicine in general. If each cell of the body is like a miniature factory, its receptors are locks on the doors. The autonomic, immune, and neuropeptide

systems are communication channels whereby mind may activate genes and the internal cellular machinery. The genes, of course, are the ultimate blueprint for building, organizing, and regulating how the cellular machinery works. (p. 129)

THE NEUROPHYSIOLOGICAL PROCESSES OF PTSD

As discussed earlier, PTSD can be thought of as a human reaction to abnormally stressful life experiences which disrupt the physical and psychological equilibrium of the person. As a result, a set of interrelated symptoms develop and cluster into at least three major groups: intrusion and reexperience; avoidance, emotional constriction, detachment, and depression; and physiological hyperarousal. To further explain our conception of the psychobiology of PTSD, we will organize our discussion by each symptom cluster.

The Neurophysiological Processes of the Intrusion Cycle of PTSD

Exposure to inescapable and unavoidable aversive or traumatic events is accompanied by intense fear, terror, and feelings of helplessness in most individuals (APA, 1987). Increased autonomic arousal mediated through central adrenergic pathways prepares the person for active confrontation of the situation by either fight or flight responses that increase heart rate and blood pressure as well as mobilizing bodily resources (Cannon, 1932; Kolb & Multipassi, 1982). As illustrated in Figure 2.1, physiologically, norepinephrine (NE) turnover and plasma catecholamine levels (NE, dopamine [DA], and serotonin [5-HT]) are increased, resulting in intense stimulation of noradrenergic neurons in the central nervous system (van der Kolk, Krystal, & Greenberg, 1984). Enhanced memory retention, particularly visually associated information, occurs as a result of this increased stimulation (Brende, 1984; Delaney, Tussi, & Gold, 1983).

When exposure to the traumatic event is prolonged or repeated, catecholamine use eventually exceeds synthesis (van der Kolk & Greenberg, 1987). Consequently, NE and DA are depleted and levels of 5-HT are decreased (van der Kolk, Greenberg, Boyd, et al., 1985). In addition, increased levels of acetylcholine (ACh) have been noted (van der Kolk, Krystal, & Greenberg, 1984). This pattern of chronic cate-

Exposure to Inescapable and Unvoidable Aversive Events

↓

Increased Autonomic Arousal
      Increased NE turnover
      Increased plasma catecholamine levels
      Depeletion of brain NE
      Enhanced memory retention

PROLONGED   REPEATED

                      ↓

Catecholamine Use Exceeds Synthesis
   Depletion of NE
      Decreased motivation
      Decreased functioning
      Decreased memory storage
   Depletion of DA
      Decreased readiness to approach novel stimuli
   Decreased level of Serotonin
      Anxiety
      Increased sensitivity to pain
      Enhanced reaction to incoming stimuli
Increased levels of Acetylcholine
   May include dissociation
Escape deficits

                      ↓

Chronic Noradrenergic Hypersensitivity
      All-or-None Phenomena
   Decreased tolerance for arousal
      Hyperalert
      Difficulty modulating affect
      Re-experiencing
      Subjective sense of loss of control
      Compensatory symptoms:
         Estrangement
         Detachment
         Emotional constriction

Adapted From: Anisman et al. (1978, 1979, 1981)
                    Delaney, Tussi & Gold (1983)
                    Maier & Seligman (1976)
                    Seligman (1974)
                    Stein (1978)
                    van der Kolk et al. (1987, 1985, 1984)
                    Zuckerman (1983)

Figure 2.1. Model inescapable shock and conditioned response: intrusion.

cholamine depletion produces enduring changes in noradrenergic receptor sensitivity, such that these receptors become hypersensitive to subsequent stimulation in response to stress or arousal (Anisman, Ritch, & Sklar, 1981).

Behaviorally, van der Kolk (1985) has observed a type of global constriction as a result of NE depletion characterized by depressed functioning, reduced memory storage, and a lack of motivation. As levels of 5-HT decrease, symptoms of anxiety become evident. Increased sensitivity to pain and enhanced reaction to incoming stimuli appear to influence the individual's perception of the surrounding environment (Ellison, 1977; Zuckerman, 1983). Depletion of both NE and 5-HT results in underresponsiveness to positive reinforcement and overresponsiveness to negative reinforcement (Ellison, 1977). DA depletion results in a decreased readiness to approach novel stimulation (Stein, 1978). The overall effect appears to be one of anxiety, escape deficits, and reluctance to leave a secure environment. These findings are consistent with Anisman and colleagues' (1978, 1979, 1981) animal studies on inescapable shock which noted deficits in learning to escape from novel aversive stimuli, decreased motivation to learn new contingencies, and a pervasive sense of chronic subjective distress. Traumatized individuals may also manifest some of these same behavioral characteristics (van der Kolk, Krystal, & Greenberg, 1984).

Current research suggests that chronic NE depletion results in noradrenergic hypersensitivity such that the traumatized individual has a decreased tolerance for arousal (Dobbs & Wilson, 1960; Kolb & Multipassi, 1982; van der Kolk & Greenberg, 1987). From this conceptual perspective, the intensity of autonomic arousal induced by subsequent threat far exceeds that which is necessary for adaptive functioning. The individual thus appears to respond to any threat with the same qualitative, high-intensity, physiological arousal that was produced by the original trauma. Dobbs and Wilson (1960) and Kolb and Multipassi (1982) propose that this all-or-none phenomenon of responding is a conditioned emotional response governed by long-term alterations in noradrenergic neuronal receptor sensitivity.

In terms of PTSD symptomatology, decreased tolerance for arousal results in hyperalertness, hypervigilance, irritability, explosive anger, and exaggerated startle response. The individual is sensitized to incoming stimulation such that seemingly minor stresses can trigger overwhelming autonomic arousal, a hypothesis originally put forth by Freud (1957). Moreover, as suggested by state-dependent learning theory, information encoded in a state of heightened autonomic nervous system arousal will be retrieved (i.e., relived) when that state is once again induced. Therefore, the vivid imagery associated with the trauma that was rapidly and efficiently encoded into memory during the trauma is released (Brende, 1984; van der Kolk & Greenberg, 1987; van der Kolk, Krystal, & Greenberg, 1984). Intrusive imagery in the form of nightmares and reexperiencing aspects of the trauma creates a sense of recurrence such that the individual may experience difficulty distinguishing the elements of reliving the trauma from what is occurring in the environment. In addition, increased levels of acetylcholine (ACh) may induce a dissociative state or "flashbacks" (Braun, 1984) whereby the individual thinks and responds as if he/she is immersed in the original trauma with complete lack of awareness of the current situation. Due to NE depletion and subsequent reduction of memory storage capabilities, in most cases the dissociated individual in this altered state of consciousness typically has no recall for the "flashback" incident.

The Neurophysiological Processes of the Avoidance Cycle of PTSD

Trauma victims experience intrusive symptoms with a subjective sense of fear of loss of control. They are often unaware of what triggers the reexperiencing and become fearful that they may be flooded with intrusive imagery unexpectedly. Modulating affect is often subjectively experienced as a difficult task. Consequently, the individual may develop compensatory symptoms of estrangement, detachment, and emotional constriction in an attempt to avoid stimuli that may produce the previously conditioned all-or-none physiological-emotional response (van der Kolk, Krystal, & Greenberg, 1984). In this sense, overcontrol, isolation, and numbing evolve into elaborate defenses against the unexpected and unpredictable onset of distressing affect and imagery.

Van der Kolk, Krystal, and Greenberg's conceptualization of compensatory responses appears to be a parsimonious explanation for the characteristic avoidance symptoms of PTSD. However, as Figure 2.2 illustrates, distinct physiological mechanisms, apart from those involved in intrusive symptoms, may be responsible for the avoidance response.

Autonomic arousal is mediated by the sympathetic-adrenal-medullary system through release of NE. This adrenergic response is nonspecific; that is, both positive and negative stimuli (emotional and situational) induce catecholamine release (Frankenhaeuser, 1986). As discussed above, in traumatized individuals chronic NE depletion due to involvement in the original trauma creates a conditioned noradrenergic hyperactivity resulting in decreased tolerance for arousal. Due to the nonspecific nature of catecholamine release, symptoms of reexperiencing can be induced by pleasant or aversive stimuli that trigger the conditioned response. Intrusive symptoms are experienced as distressing and unpredictable. Consequently, in an effort to establish a sense of control, the individual may isolate and detach from normal activity. However, denial is a tenuous adaptive mechanism restricting social and emotional interaction and is easily overwhelmed in intrusive imagery. Therefore, both intrusion and compensatory avoidance are experienced with a

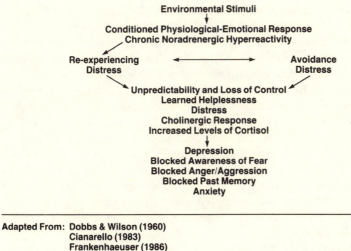

Adapted From: Dobbs & Wilson (1960)
                        Cianarello (1983)
                        Frankenhaeuser (1986)
                        Kolb & Mutalipassi (1982)
                        Rose (1985)
                        Sachar (1975)
                        Seligman (1974)
                        Selye (1950)
                        van der Kolk & Greenberg (1987)

Figure 2.2. Model of inescapable shock and conditioned response: avoidance.

subjective sense of loss of control and unpredictability not unlike Seligman's (1974) learned helplessness.

Feelings of loss of control, unpredictability, and learned helplessness have all been associated with depression (Frankenhaeuser, 1986; Mason, 1975; Seligman, 1974; Selye, 1950). The common link appears to be the pituitary-adrenal-cortical system, specifically, cortisol release in response to uncertainty (Rose, 1985) or helplessness (Frankenhaeuser, 1986). Behaviorally, the cholinergic response is manifest as depression (Brende, 1984; Frankenhaeuser, 1986), blocked awareness of fear, blocked expression of anger/aggression, and blocked memory (Brende, 1984). Combined with the global constriction and learning deficits associated with NE depletion, the avoidance phase of PTSD becomes evident. Cognitive and affective constriction, withdrawal, detachment, selective inattention, and amnesia may be related to NE depletion and cholinergic response.

Biphasic Response in PTSD

Gellhorn and Kiely (1972) noted the probability of synchronization between the excitatory (ergotropic) and inhibitory (trophotropic) systems that provides a basis for the observed cyclic alternation between intrusion and avoidance characteristic of PTSD noted by Horowitz (1986) and others (Laufer, Frey-Wouters, & Gallops, 1985). Although current research on the intricacies of such an integrated system of physiological responding is extremely limited, literature on dissociative phenomena provides a basis for the construction of a viable model.

As discussed earlier, and as shown in Figure 2.3, intrusive symptoms are mediated by the excitatory sympathetic-adrenal-medullary system and catecholamine activity. Symptoms of avoidance are mediated by the inhibitory pituitary-adrenal-cortical system and cholinergic activity. The mechanisms responsible for the interaction between the two systems are, however, unclear at this time. Current research suggests that the cyclic alternation ("kindling") of the two systems may be due to a peptide-mediated dissociation involving endorphin release (Braun, 1984; Brende, 1984; van der Kolk & Greenberg, 1987; van der Kolk, Krystal, & Greenberg, 1984).

Figure 2.4 continues the sequence of responding outlined in Figures 2.1–2.3. Endorphin release is stimulated by the subjective sense of anxiety felt by the individual. Endorphins have a natural anxiolytic-

INTRUSION	AVOIDANCE
PHYSIOLOGICAL MECHANISMS	
Right Hemisphere	Left Hemisphere
Under-Control	Over-Control
Re-enactment	Protective
Visual Associated Memory	Verbal/Auditory Memory
Ergotropic (Excitatory)	Trophotropic (Inhibitory)
Amygdala	Hippocampus
Sympathetic-Adrenal-Medullary	Pituitary-Adrenal-Cortical
Catecholaminergic (NE, 5-HT, DA)	Cholinergic (ACh, Cortisol)
Increased Arousal	Depression
Fight-Flight	Block awareness of fear
	Block anger/aggression
	Block past memory
PATHOLOGICAL RESPONSE	
Intrusive Imagery	Denial
Disturbing Emotion	Emotional Detachment
Hypervigilance	Numbing
Startle Reactions	Depression
Sensation of Recurrence	Inability to Visualize Memories
Overgeneralization of Associations	Selective Inattention
Flashbacks	Amenesia
	Cognitive Constriction

Adapted From: Braun (1984)
            Davidson, Fleming & Baum (1986)
            Frankenhaeuser (1986)
            Horowitz (1986)
            Lex (1979)

Figure 2.3. Post-traumatic stress disorder as a bi-phasic physiological response.

tranquilizing action that decreases rage, aggression, and paranoia, as well as an antidepressant action that increases a sense of well-being and control (van der Kolk, Krystal, & Greenberg, 1984; Vereby, Volvavka, & Clouet, 1978). Production of conditioned analgesia in response to repeated or prolonged exposure to inescapable stress mediated by endorphins is well documented, is blocked with naloxone (Kelly, 1982), and shows cross-tolerance with morphine (Maier, Sherman, Lewis, et al., 1983). Although endorphin release and subsequent analgesia may bring relief from chronic anxiety and depression, palliation is only temporary. Furthermore, due to the interaction of opioid and noradrenergic systems, the cycle of physiological and psychological loss of control is exacerbated. Decreased opioid receptor binding in the brain associated with central noradrenergic hyperreactivity results in an opiate-withdrawal-like syndrome that includes symptoms of anxiety, irritability, explosive outbursts, insomnia, hyperalertness, and emotional lability (Jaffe & Martin, 1980) that are qualitatively identical to the intrusive symptoms observed in PTSD.

In addition, dissociation has been linked to increased levels of ACTH (Braun, 1984). ACTH and endorphins share a common precursor (Mains, Eipper, & Ling, 1977) and exert effects on the limbic system through

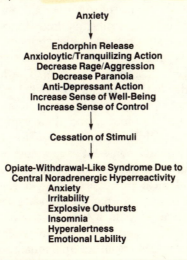

Adapted From: Braun (1984)
Jaffe & Martin (1980)
Redmond & Krystal (1984)
Verebey (1978)
van der Kolk, Krystal & Greenberg (1984)
van der Kolk, Greenberg & Boyd (1985)
van der Kolk & Greenberg (1987)

Figure 2.4. Model of addiction (condition analgesia).

the locus ceruleus, which mediates NE and 5-HT release to the amygdala and hippocampus. Therefore, it appears that increased levels of endorphins stimulated by anxiety may be accompanied by increased levels of ACTH. Dissociation ("kindling") between the excitatory mechanism of the amygdala and the inhibitory mechanism of the hippocampus may be facilitated by increased levels of ACTH that share a common pathway with the endorphins in the limbic system, namely the locus ceruleus (Braun, 1984; Brende, 1984). As a result, cyclic alternation between ergotropic and trophotropic functioning may occur, thereby influencing the manifestation of symptoms of intrusion and avoidance. Furthermore, due to state-dependent learning and the dissociation between the two systems, elements of the trauma and subsequent patterns of adaptation may remain disjuncted and disconnected with the individual. This cycle may be induced repeatedly by environmental stimuli or reflective ideation about the trauma.

CONCLUSION

Understanding the psychobiology of post-traumatic stress disorder is especially important in terms of discovering effective modalities of treatment. At this point in our collective knowledge, it seems clear that PTSD has a neurological substrate which possesses its own structure and process which is analogous to a set of commands that govern a complex set of steps in a computer program. The neurological program of PTSD based in the brain governs the switching on and off of the ergotropic and trophotropic subsystems, catecholamine and cholinergic secretions, neuropeptides (opioids), and their expressions as affect and imagery in the right and left hemispheres of the brain.

In the most fundamental sense, it is possible to think of the psychobiology of trauma as an imbalanced condition, one in which physiological and psychological processes are in a state of disequilibrium because the vitality of the normal steady-state functioning has been severely altered by immersion in a traumatic event. The impact of the trauma on the organism extends to four interrelated levels of being: physiological, psychological, social-interpersonal, and cultural. The major symptoms of PTSD are manifestations of the disequilibrium that exists at each of the four levels. Physiologically there are degrees of overdriven hyperarousability (e.g., hypervigilance) that result from state-dependent learning. Psychologically, the individual may suffer from distressing intrusive imagery (visual reliving/flashbacks) or distressing affect (depression, anger, rage, grief, sadness). The overt symptoms of excessive autonomic nervous system arousal and the more florid symptoms of the syndrome may then lead to difficulties in interpersonal relationships and attempts at intimacy. These difficulties include emotional constriction, detachment, alienation, depression, and isolation, which often impair the capacity to bond with others in loving relationships. Finally, these interacting levels of being may affect the individual's relationship to his or her culture, depending on how it responds to those who have been victimized. In the absence of cultural rituals and opportunities to heal after a traumatic event, the individual may become alienated from the mainstream of society and experience anomie or some other form of estrangement.

One of the most exciting consequences of the converging information on the psychobiology of trauma stems from the recognition that the organism is an integrated system, a mind-body whole with different levels of information intersecting in complex ways. The psychological experience of reliving a trauma not only has a neurological program running the symptom presentation, but occurs in a sociocultural context. Indeed, as will be discussed in the next chapter, many cultures have evolved rituals to aid traumatized persons in the recovery from stress and recognize explicitly that psychic trauma can alter ego vitality and a sense of well-being. Moreover, as Rossi (1986) concludes, "Information transduction is emerging as the key concept in our psychobiological theory of mind-body communication and healing. The basic laws of biology, psychology, and cultural anthropology are all essentially descriptions of different levels of information transduction" (p. 203). Clearly, if the concept of information transduction proves to be a valid characterization of the intricate neurochemical exchanges occurring in the brain, it becomes possible to discover how the mind-body relationship can promote organismically based natural healing by the transduction of information that will restore psychic and physiological well-being.

3

Culture and Trauma: The Sacred Pipe Revisited

INTRODUCTION

An Indian Myth on the Origin of Curing
Ceremonies (White Mountain Apache)

This is how ceremonies started among us for the curing of sick people. Long, long ago, the earth was made. Then the One Who Made the Earth also planned for each person to have a piece of land that he could live on and call his own. Our people were living in one such place, but they didn't like that particular spot. So the One Who Made the Earth told them to move to a new location, and when they did, they slept well, and liked it, and lived in a good way.

Then two men among them became sick and grew weaker day by day. The people didn't do anything for them because no one knew then about illnesses and how to cure them. The One Who Made the Earth said, "Why don't you do something for those two men? Why don't you say some words over them?" But the people had no knowledge of curing ceremonies.

Four men among the people happened to be standing, one to the east, one to the south, one to the west, and one to the north. The One Who Made the Earth spoke to one of these men, telling him, "Everything on earth has power to cause its own kind of sickness, make its own trouble. There is a way to cure all these

This chapter was prepared with the assistance of Alice J. Walker and Bruce Webster.

things." Now this man understood that knowledge was available. Then those four stood there. On the first night, the one standing on the east side began to chant a set prayer all by himself. On the second night, the one on the south started to drum and sing lightning songs. On the third night, the one on the west chanted a set prayer. On the fourth night, the one on the north began to drum and sing lightning songs. They did not conceive this pattern in their own minds; it was bestowed upon them by the One Who Made the Earth. It was as if the knowledge of what they should chant or sing had suddenly been transmitted to them from outside.

Then the One Who Made the Earth said to these four, "Why don't you go to the two sick men and say some words over them and make them well?: So those four went to where the two sick men were and worked over them, and they were cured. From that time on, we had curing ceremonies and knowledge of the different kinds of sickness that may be caused by various things. That's the way all curing ceremonies started (Erdoes & Ortiz, 1987, p. 37).

How do traumatized persons heal? In this chapter attention is focused on cultural rituals for healing, growth, and psychic integration. In particular, the sweat lodge ceremony will be discussed as a technique of treatment with important implications for the treatment of psychic trauma and PTSD.

The study of shamanistic healing is not new and has been reviewed by Harner (1982), Henry (1982), Jilek (1982), Ludwig (1966), Prince (1980), and Winkelman (1986). However, the study of shamanistic practices and ritualized group ceremonies that may have therapeutic effects on stress disorders is presently an uncharted area of scientific research. It is important for social scientists to learn about these techniques of healing and treatment since they have been in existence for centuries in many cultures in the world, a fact that points to their psychological and sociobiological value in many respects.

It is the purpose of this chapter to develop a conceptual framework to explore shamanistic rituals as therapeutic tools for the treatment of stress disorders. Initially, we present a discussion of one specific Native American ritual, the sweat lodge, as a *cultural* practice with a variety of functions. After describing the sweat lodge ritual, we present an analysis of its common *psychological* processes and their relationship to the potential treatment of anxiety and depressive disorders, especially post-traumatic stress disorder (PTSD). Moreover, because of the extreme heat, sensory deprivation, and physical properties of the sweat lodge ceremony, we found it necessary to ascertain its possible *psychobiological* effects, particularly in the production of altered states of consciousness (ASC), biogenic amine production, including endogenous opiate pro- duction (neuropeptides), and changes in neurophysiological functioning, especially catecholamine production (e.g., noradrenalin and serotonin). We conclude the analysis of Native American healing rituals with some speculations about the complex interrelationships between the psycho- biological mechanisms of PTSD and the amelioration of the disorder by cultural rituals that appear designed to facilitate a positive change in mental state leading to a form of natural organismically based healing. Chapter 7 presents research findings on an experimental treatment program that used the sweat lodge ritual as a therapeutic intervention for 15 Vietnam combat veterans suffering from PTSD. This study used a number of standard psychiatric measures (e.g., SCL-90) to evaluate the long-term effects of the treatment procedure.

WAR TRAUMA AND RITUALS

Throughout the centuries societies have recognized the need to pro- vide rituals that welcome home those who served as warriors in battle (Silver & Wilson, 1988). Although the psychological nature of what it means to be a combatant varies a great deal owing to historical cir- cumstances and ideological values, many cultures seem to have rec- ognized the importance of facilitating the transition from the role and identity of a warrior to that of a productive member of society who attains a new status and set of responsibilities. At a minimum, warfare requires a different psychological state of being from that typical of civilian life. Many Native American rituals implicitly recognize this fact and are designed to transform the warrior mode of being into a different one that is congruent with the needs of the culture.

It is also interesting to note that in the United States and Western Europe there do not appear to be culturally specific and highly ritualized mechanisms to facilitate the transition from the role of soldier to that of civilian. Only during World War II were widespread public, private, and governmental efforts made to celebrate the end of the war and to honor those who served in the military forces. At that time the victory parades, priority in jobs, and highly adequate educational, occupational, and economic benefits essentially assured that the transition into civilian life could proceed with a minimum of disruption of adult life-course development. Stated simply, the culture created a good opportunity structure that facilitated a smooth and rapid course of post-war readjustment.

When viewed in this way, these benefits were primarily psychosocial in nature and recent research confirms their benefit to the readjustment process in post-war civilian life (Elder & Clipp, 1988). It must also be recognized that these economic benefits represent a powerful psychological meaning of gratitude and reparation for sacrifices made during the war as well as an implicit promise of a place of importance in the society. On the other hand, Elder and Clipp's (1988) study revealed that 56% of a sample of aging World War II combat veterans had dreams, anxiety, and other negative emotions 40 years after the war. Similar results are reported for Pearl Harbor survivors in Chapter 6. This finding may well indicate that while some celebrations, benefits, and opportunities help individuals to find a niche in society, they may not fully address the question of how to heal the psychic wounds of war.

In Western civilization one of the clearest and best examples of ritualized ceremonies for returning warriors can be found among different Native American tribes who have evolved, over hundreds of years, very complex social-psychological and religious processes to reintegrate warriors within the matrix of their society. While it is important to recognize that these ceremonial events differ among tribes and often have specific tribal or cultural significance, their general function is to reaffirm and assure the individual mental health of the warrior and the continuity of the group identity of the tribe itself (Erikson, 1950). To accomplish this aim, a variety of individual tasks (e.g., the Sioux Vision Quest) or group ceremonies (e.g., Honoring Ceremonies, the Ceremonial Fire, the Gourd Dance, Sweat Lodge, Sun Dance, Red Feather Ceremony) may be enacted at different intervals throughout the year to facilitate the process of gaining spiritual strength and recovering from trauma (Silver & Wilson, 1988). Although diverse in function, these rituals have a common purpose of building inner strength and reaffirming individual identity and a sense of connectedness and continuity with a meaningful community.

NATIVE AMERICAN HEALING AND PURIFICATION RITUALS: CULTURE-SPECIFIC TREATMENT FOR MENTAL ILLNESS, STRESS REACTIONS, AND ENHANCED SELF-AWARENESS

In different cultures throughout the world religious and ritualistic practices have been developed to treat emotional illness, anxiety, and states of "dispiritedness," including war-related stress reactions. These rituals have, of course, both specific and general purposes in terms of cultural values and psychological adaptation (see van der Hart, 1983, for a review). Elsewhere, I have presented earlier formulations of the specific psychological functions of some rituals as a form of stress reduction and methods of gaining psychological insight into emotional problems (Wilson, 1988b, pp. 262–268; Silver & Wilson, 1988, pp. 337–354). However, there are rituals surrounding death which are designed to facilitate the expression of grief and the loss of a loved one. In various rites of passage the ritual serves to change status and identity within a group, such as the confirmation of adulthood. Similarly, there are rituals that prepare men for battle and return from it. Among some Native American groups, war is regarded as an abnormal condition and aberration of the harmonious order of the universe (Silver & Wilson, 1988). Thus, those who become warriors must of necessity assume a changed psychological state in order to kill the enemy and win victory so as to restore harmony and balance in nature. After battle, the community may recognize the need to return the warrior to a new role and identity in the culture. To do so, the culture honors the warrior's acts of bravery and provides rituals to purge, purify, and heal the physical and psychological wounds of war. In addition to providing a supportive and caring milieu for the warrior, there is the awareness, often tacit and intrinsic to the group, that the warrior identity must be transformed into a new identity that demands maturity and responsibility. Failure to achieve this transformation of the warrior identity may lead to alienation and the assumption of a victimized state, with debilitating psychological consequences (e.g., alcoholism, depression, self-despair, and suicide).

In most tribal groups the shaman of the culture assumes the role of healer or medicine person and performs rituals of various types designed to cure suffering and restore good health and spirituality to the victim. Anthony F. C. Wallace (1966), the distinguished anthropologist, has written that:

> Efforts to induce an ecstatic spiritual state by crudely and directly manipulating physiological processes are found in every religious system. Such manipulations may be classified under four major headings: (1) drugs, (2) sensory deprivation, (3) mortification of the flesh by pain, sleeplessness and fatigue, (4) deprivation of food, water and air. (p. 55)

The last three dimensions are commonly employed by various Native American groups as part of healing and purification rituals, especially in their sweat lodge ceremonies. The sweat lodge ceremony is widely used by many tribal groups and has physical, psychological, group-oriented, and spiritual dimensions that are potentially useful in alleviating emotional symptoms. As it pertains to war veterans in particular, the sweat lodge ritual has several major purposes: (1) to transform the warrior identity into a more nurturing and mature form of adaptation (generativity) (Erikson, 1968); (2) to establish individual and cultural continuity; (3) to promote self-disclosure while physically and emotionally bonded to others in an environment of intense heat, sensory deprivation, and shared collective pain. Later in this chapter we will discuss how these functions are achieved in the ceremonial ritual.

In writing about various cultural and religious practices as a form of psychotherapy for the mentally ill, Wallace (1966) observes that they are designed to transform identity crises and maladaptive behavior.

> These rituals of salvation are, in a sense, similar to rites of passage because they seek to effect a change in the career line of their subject; conversely, rites of passage, much as the Plains Indians' vision quest, may involve mystical phenomena in the course of identity change. The justification for setting aside a special category of salvation rituals lies in the fact that some identity crises are not universally anticipated in a society and are not treated with universally applied rites of passage, but rather are more or less ad hoc ceremonies performed by and upon only those persons who "spontaneously" enter into the experience for the sake of spiritual enrichment or salvation. . . The function of ritual, in these cases, is undoubtedly to provide a pattern for a process in remission of psychopathology which will bring the victim of severe mental illness out "on the other side." . . . If the ritual is effective, he will arrive at a condition that will permit him to take care of himself and perform useful services (often ritual services) for the other members of the community. (pp. 206–207)

Considering the perspective of ritual transformations, we can ask how the sweat lodge ceremony facilitates a remission of symptoms and a new vision of the self in society.

THE SWEAT LODGE PURIFICATION RITUAL (INIPI ONIKARE)

The sweat lodge purification ritual is a Native American religious event of thanksgiving and forgiveness which is typically led by a medicine person of the tribe. It is regarded as a serious and sacred occasion in which spiritual insights, personal growth, and physical and emotional healing may take place. The process of purification is experienced on many levels of awareness, including the physical, psychological, social, and spiritual.

THE SWEAT LODGE*

The Structure of the Lodge

The Sweat Lodge is a dome-shaped tent which has a frame constructed of tree branches. The lodges vary in size and can hold between 4 and 20 or more persons. The frame is covered with layers of blankets and topped with heavy canvas. In the Pacific Northwest, the dome is layered and laced with cedar boughs. In this tradition cedar is thought to be symbolic of the feminine, the one who listens with care and receives what is being given. The ground floor inside the dome is sometimes covered with old carpeting or soft cedar boughs to make the seating more comfortable. However, some medicine persons prefer that the lodge be built only over "mother earth" and have no ground cover. In the center of the floor is a shallow pit that has been dug out to a depth of about 4 to 8 inches. The pit holds rocks or firebrick that have been heated in a fire located next to the sweat lodge. The opening to the lodge consists of a small entranceway which is covered by a canvas flap and is attended by a "door keeper," who also attends the fire. To enter the lodge the participants must kneel down and are instructed to crawl into the tent in a clockwise fashion. At the apex of the dome may hang different colored cloth strips (red, black, yellow, white) which may be thought of as symbolic element(s) of unity and integration.

Preliminary Activities for the Ceremony

Prior to the arrival of the participants, a fire is made by placing rocks for the ritual into a mound which is encased by logs stacked upright in a conical shape. The fire is heated to a very hot temperature in preparation for the ceremony. Directly in front of the lodge the medicine

---

* The author gratefully acknowledges his appreciation to Andy Callicum, Roland Ryan, Vivian Sandy, Susy Bear, David Fourlines, Marvin Stevens, Rod MacAfee, and other Native Americans who have taught him about their ways of healing.

person may place the ceremonial instruments, which include the sacred pipe, an eagle wing, or other religious artifacts.

When it is time to begin the ceremony, the medicine person lights a small amount of sage in a bowl. The smoke is fanned by the participants over the head and chest to purify the body before entering the sweat lodge. Then the medicine person takes an abalone shell or bowl to the ceremonial fire, places a few red hot coals into it, and then stands before the door of the lodge. He or she then asks the Great Spirit for help with the ceremony prior to walking around the outside of the lodge one time in a clockwise direction. The lodge is then entered in a similar clockwise way, with the final resting position being next to the entrance.

Once inside the lodge, the shaman may add medicine to the glowing embers, usually sage, sweet grass, or cedar, or sometimes a bundle made of all three. As the smoke from the medicine rises and purifies the lodge, the guidance of the Great Spirit is requested and the lodge is prepared for the coming of the Grandfathers and Grandmothers (spiritual powers). When the shaman feels the sanctuary of the lodge is ready and the Spirit Help has been assembled, the medicine person then calls the participants by name in the order he or she wants them to enter. Each individual stands before the doorway and silently requests the aid of the Spirit Helpers before circling the exterior in a clockwise fashion. Once inside, each participant sits to the right of the shaman. Prior to the arrival of the heated stones, each participant pulls the medicine smoke from the shell over his body in a personal act of cleansing and purification. As the ceremony begins inside the lodge, the medicine person may instruct the celebrants about the nature and purpose of the sacred ritual. In a warriors' sweat the first round is generally focused on the release and catharsis of painful emotions, i.e., anger, guilt, grief, sorrow, remorse, cowardice, etc. The sanctuary of the lodge offers a comforting environment for the release of emotional distress.

THE SWEAT LODGE RITUAL*

Functional Purpose

The sweat lodge may be used for different purposes. Generally, the religious purpose is to promote healing and purification; to aid in the

---

* The author (J.W.) has participated in over 20 sweat lodge ceremonies. The views expressed here are a reflection of these experiences.

release of pain from whatever origin; and to facilitate a sense of the self as connected, living harmoniously with the earth in a pure, un-contaminated, and natural way of being. There are also special occasions in which the sweat lodge is used in preparation for marriage or another ceremony such as the Sun Dance. There are also medicinal sweats in which the therapeutic properties of certain plants are well known and these are used accordingly. A variety of herbs, roots, and plants may be administered externally or internally. Herbs such as sweet grass, sage, and/or cedar needles may be used during the ceremony. Tradi-tionally, tobacco has also been used as a way of sending prayers to the Great Spirit. Occasionally, there may be conducted a "power" sweat in which the medicine men and/or women gather together to help a particular individual make a difficult transition in life or to increase spiritual strength needed to meet personal challenges and responsibil-ities.

The Initial Stage of the Four Doors

Inside the sweat lodge the participants sit cross-legged in a tightly packed circle. In the traditional way the medicine man uses the antlers of a deer to place the first set of heated stones into the pit. The door keeper may use a shovel to remove the rocks from the fire and place them into the pit under the medicine person's direction. Although the number of rocks used ceremonially varies according to the wisdom of the shaman, in some traditions either four or six stones are initially placed into the pit. These rocks represent the "Six Grandfathers/Grand-mothers" or the different powers of the universe (the Four Winds, Earth, and Sky). Additional rocks may then be added before the flap to the door is closed. The inside of the tent is now completely dark except for the dim glow from the red-hot rocks. The medicine person speaks in a calm and soothing voice about how good things can happen if all participants put their minds together. If necessary, a brief ori-entation and explanation of the ritual may be provided. During the orientation the medicine person may state that healing and purification can happen and that the participants can grow stronger by praying and overcoming pain and suffering. An explanation is given that all of the participants will suffer together in the intense heat and that all of life is a struggle with pain and suffering. Water is then splashed onto the rocks for each of the Grandfathers/Grandmothers (six times) as the medicine person sings a song of prayer in the native language, which, in turn, is sung collectively by the participants.

One by one, in a clockwise manner, each of the participants offers his or her individual prayer, which often begins with the words "Thank you, Grandfather/Grandmother" and ends with the phrase "all my relations." During the ceremony there are "four doors," or four brief intervals during which the flap to the lodge is opened. These four intervals have symbolic meaning of unity in the sacred directions and provide relief from the intense heat. At the beginning of each round of the ceremony, more stones are added to the circular pit and the ritual continues as water is poured or splashed onto the rocks. In some ceremonies as many as 40 or more stones may be used during the four intervals of the ritual and create extremely hot temperatures. And although there is some variability in custom, each of the four rounds typically has a specific purpose: purification, healing, thanksgiving and revitalization, rejoicing and celebration. At the end of the "fourth door," the ceremony concludes as the individuals emerge into the cool air after spending between one and three hours in the sweat tent. At this point the sacred pipe may be passed around in a closing ritual. When participating in lodges on the Olympic Peninsula in Washington State or in other parts of the Pacific Northwest, individuals usually immerse themselves four times in the cold waters of the straits of Juan deFuca or the rivers and glacial lakes in the forests.

"BLACK ELK SPEAKS": A DESCRIPTION OF INIPI ONIKARE—THE RITE OF PURIFICATION

Table 3.1 summarizes the symbolic and sacred aspects of the Sioux Indian sweat lodge ritual—Inipi Onikare—as described by Black Elk, one of the holiest and most revered medicine men of the Sioux tribe, in the book *The Sacred Pipe* (Brown, 1986).

In keeping with the religious cosmology of the Sioux, all things in life are in relation to each other, and this, of course, pertains to the actual and symbolic elements used in the sweat lodge rite of purification, Inipi. Black Elk's account of the rite of purification is a beautiful, almost poetic presentation of the symbolic meaning of the ritual. A careful reading of his account reveals a deep inner structure of the mystical cosmology of the Sioux Indians (Mails, 1972).

According to Black Elk, the willow branches used to construct the lodge are pliant, supple, and young. They represent the season of spring, renewal, and the cycle of life in which things are born and die,

TABLE 3.1
Symbolic Elements of the Lakota Sioux
Sweat Lodge Ritual—Inipi Onikare—Adapted from Black Elk

ELEMENT	SYMBOLIC MEANING
Sweat Lodge (Onikare)	All powers of Grandfathers
Door to the East	Direction of wisdom and light
Water	Thunderbeings
	Goodness
Willow branches	Spring; rejuvenation
	Cycle of life
Circular pit for stones	Center of the Universe
Rocks for heat	Grandmother Earth
	Great Spirit
Heated stones	Fire without end;
(Peta-owihonkeshni)	power to heal
Sweet grass-sage	Purification
Clockwise entry	Sunwise movement; Natural Order
Darkness	Ignorance
Four Intervals	Four Ages of Man
("Doors")	Knowledge
Function of the Four	Purification
Doors/Intervals	Healing
	Thanksgiving, Affirmation
Order of the Rocks	1 = Center of the Universe
	2-5 = Sacred Directions
	6 = Power of Universe
Sacred Directions	North = Purity
	South = Source of Life
	East = Light, Wisdom
	West = Setting Sun
Sacred Pipe	Gift of Wisdom

Source: Black Elk. Compiled by John P. Wilson.

a repetitive, ever-lasting cycle of nature. The rocks symbolize Grand-mother earth and the Great Spirit because they are indestructible and give "life" when heated for the sweat lodge. Water, which comes from the Thunder Beings, represents the Great Spirit, who is always flowing, giving power and life to everything, i.e., "all the relations of beings on earth."

The pit into which the rocks are placed is round and symbolizes the center of the universe from which the power of the Great Spirit will emanate from the four sacred directions (north = purity; south = source of life; east = light, wisdom; west = sun sets, ending). The heated stones (Peta-Owihankeshni) are the "fire without end" and come from a heated pile which is always built to the east of the lodge. Likewise, the door to the lodge always faces the direction of wisdom. The hot rocks, one for each Grandfather/Grandmother, are placed into the pit in ritual order. The first stone is placed into the "center of the universe" and the next four are placed according to the sacred directions (north, east, south, and west). The additional stones symbolize the other powers of the universe (sky, earth, Great Spirit).

The lodge itself represents all the powers of the Grandfathers and the power of "all relations to each other." The sage smoke and sweet grass which is fanned over the body symbolize purity and cleansing, which must occur prior to entry into the lodge in a "sunwise" movement (clockwise) through the door. Thus, entry proceeds from the east (source of wisdom), to the south (source of life), to the north (purity) and west (cycle ending).

The darkness of the lodge symbolizes ignorance, which is counterpointed by the light (wisdom) obtained each of the four times the door is opened. The four intervals of the lodge also represent the sacred directions. Thus, the four rounds of the ritual, juxtaposed over the four sacred directions, the "fire without end," and the goodness of the Thunder Beings (water), directly concern purification, healing, thanksgiving, and affirmation of all that is good and comes from the "Creator of all good things" and "all the relations on Mother Earth." Thus, the sharing of the sacred pipe at the end of the ritual collectively and individually celebrates the gift of wisdom and healing obtained in the Inipi Onikare. As Black Elk spoke:

> When we leave the sweat lodge we are as the souls which are kept, as we have described, and which return to Wakan-Tanka after they have been purified; for we, too, leave behind in the Inipi lodge all that is impure, that we may live as the Great Spirit wishes, and that we may know something, of that real world of the spirit, which is behind this one. (Brown, 1986, p. 43)

PSYCHOLOGICAL DIMENSIONS OF THE SWEAT LODGE RITUAL

There appear to be many diverse functions of the sweat lodge ritual. Lopatin (1960) has reviewed the literature on the origin, variation, and prevalence of the sweat lodge. He notes that the sweat tent ceremony and similar procedures have existed for centuries and were found in ancient Russia, the Scandinavian countries, and among Indian tribes in North and South America. Lopatin notes that the sweat lodge procedures were employed for therapeutic, ritualistic, and social purposes. Henshaw (1910), writing for the Smithsonian Bureau of American Ethnology, noted that among the various Native American tribes, the sweat lodge was used to: (1) prepare warriors by propitiating spirits; (2) invoke spirits to cure those who were sick and suffering; and (3) reinvigorate the body after physical exertion, a custom that was common among the Kiowa, Arapaho, Sioux, and Cheyenne. More recently, Hall (1985) surveyed the use of the sweat lodges ritual among tribal groups throughout the United States and found that it is widely used as a technique for the treatment of alcoholism.

From our perspective, it must be recognized that each participant's perception and experience of the event will be affected by his personality characteristics, religious orientation, and cultural values. Nevertheless, the ceremony does have its own process and internal structure which bonds the participants together in a common group experience. In this regard, then, the sweat lodge ceremony contains a set of implicit psychological processes which involve group dynamics and individual modes of experience that are facilitated by the leadership skill of the medicine person.

Table 3.2 summarizes the core psychological dimensions of the sweat lodge ritual and their associated psychological effect. Each of these dimensions is discussed below.

Extreme Heat/Sensory Deprivation and Physical Space

The first dimension of the ceremony that impacts on the members of the group is the sheer physical intensity of the lodge itself. The lodge is small and compact, with an interior height of less than 5 feet. Once the flap covering the door is closed, the lodge is totally dark except for the soft, dim glow of the hot rocks in the pit. It is difficult to see one's own hand in front of the eyes. The heat is extreme and oppressive since there is no air circulation or any form of ventilation. When the water is ladled onto the rocks, the steam rises like a wave, penetrating and engulfing the entire body surface as if a steaming, smoking sheet had been wrapped around one's skin. The combination of the heat, steam, and lack of ventilation creates a suffocating effect in which it is difficult to breathe with comfort. As a result, attention is focused on one's *inner state* and *simultaneously on the words of others.* There is a struggle with pain induced by the heat and cramped conditions. There is often a reported loss of time and near or actual

TABLE 3.2
Psychological Dimensions of the Sweat Lodge Ritual

DIMENSIONS OF RITUAL	PSYCHOLOGICAL EFFECT
Sensory deprivation, lack of light	Attention focused on inner state and word of others; lack of social cues and external stimuli; loss of time
Extreme heat and lack of oxygen	Struggle with pain, dehydration; altered states of consciousness
Encapsulated interior space	Womblike atmosphere; claustrophobic, urge to leave; no physical movement
Participants seated tightly in circle	Collectively joined and physically bonded
Individual prayers	Self-disclosure of personal concerns and needs; catharsis; acceptance of others; release
Four "Doors" or rounds of prayer	Unity thema; collective suffering; collective sharing; enhanced sense of inner strength
Leadership of medicine person	Create expectations for healing; share wisdom of ritual; provide sense of continuity; role model of spiritual strength
Crawl in and out of tent in clockwise fashion	Humbleness; smallness; release; renewal

Source; Wilson, 1988, p. 268

dehydration, and many members described altered states of consciousness (see Harner, 1980, and Jilek, 1982, for a discussion).

The Circle of Unity and Bonding

The interior of the lodge creates an encapsulated environment that produces feelings of claustrophobia and an urge to escape. The lodge is crowded since the members sit knee to knee in cross-legged fashion. There is not enough room to stretch out or alter one's posture of facing the pit. *The space is configured in a circle which links the group together; there is both physical and symbolic unity.* The group is bonded together in a common environment that is simultaneously a dark space void of light but full of stress and pressure generated by the heat, steam, and smoke. The early stages of the ceremony, especially prior to the first "door," are painful, distressing, and trying. The urge to escape to find relief is strong, yet there is nowhere to move and only one door to exit at, which is stationed near the medicine person. In response to these conditions the individual becomes acutely aware of his or her physical and psychological state. Physically, the body is attempting to adapt to the change in temperature and humidity. The heart beats rapidly; the breathing is shallow and quick, and sweating is profuse. There is an inner struggle to overcome the powerful urge to escape. Each participant must find a way to overcome the pain, suffering, and distress, while at the same time concentrating on the prayers and words of the leader and the other members. Perhaps because of the environmental condition, attention *alternates* between being self-focused in a *seemingly isolated state* of discomfort and listening carefully to the concerns, needs, pains, hopes, and emotions of the other members, who are *collectively joined* in the common task of enduring the heat in order that, according to tradition, a sacrifice will be made which will bring greater personal strength. One way this is accomplished is by the *individual subordination* of personal desire (to leave) and the simultaneous act of "drawing power" from the prayers of the other members. Hence there is created a circle of unity and bonding.

Self-Disclosure/Catharsis/Release

During the four rounds of the sweat lodge ceremony, each participant has the opportunity to speak honestly and openly about himself, although there is no coercion to do so and a minimum of group pressure. Typically, the environment is conducive to self-disclosure, which serves to create a sense of cohesion and bonding among the members (Chelune, 1979). In the lodge, each individual experiences self-confrontation and listens to others in the security provided by the darkness. Further, the darkness eliminates external stimuli, particularly facial and nonverbal cues in the other members, and demands an inner self-focus in order to find one's own "light" and vision of the self-in-the-present. The darkness comes to symbolize many things, including ignorance, uncertainty in life, pain, aloneness, fear, death, as well as the absence of external cues to aid adaptation in a shared encapsulated inner space. Further, the reduction of external stimuli also facilitates powerful unconscious processes, including primary process thinking and repressed affect, so that the individual can speak of these terrors and images more freely in the darkness of the lodge.

Encapsulated, Womblike Inner Space

It is important to recognize that the "womblike" quality of the lodge directly concerns a psychological "inner space." (See Erikson, 1968, and McClelland, 1974, for a discussion of inner space.) First, the lodge can be regarded as maternal in nature since the small, dark space encapsulates the members in a manner that makes it difficult to move and change positions. Second, the "business" of the lodge is purification, healing, and strengthening of character through emotional release. The ritual forces awareness of one's psychological state. Third, many participants report a kind of maternal reattachment through the ceremony. This maternal reattachment is typically described as feelings of being connected in deeper ways to "mother earth." Individuals state that they have a heightened sensory awareness of the environment as the living earth which not only permits a good existence but which also can be harmed in many ways ranging from chemical pollution to the destructive effects of warfare. The reported increase in *sensory awareness* may be environmentally stimulated since the lodge has its own unique smell that comes from a combination of the wet earth, the steam, and herbs permeating the branches cut to construct and adorn the structure of the lodge. Finally, as will be discussed later, there is the sense of release and rebirth as the participants leave the hot, damp lodge at the end of the ceremony. It is clearly possible to speculate that the lodge contains multiple symbolic, sensory, and neuropsychological effects. In terms of maternal inner space, the lodge symbolizes the possibility of the self being created in a new form, one that emerged from the process of the ceremony and envisions a new life beyond.

The Four Doors and the Leadership Role of the Medicine Person

In individual and group psychotherapy the skill and experience of the therapist are crucial to an effective outcome. So, too, is the competency of the medicine person to conduct a sweat ritual. Indeed, it is a right and privilege to lead a sweat lodge ceremony and to use one's shamanic powers. The good medicine person, much like a good psychotherapist, is a caring and sensitive guide who is responsible for the proper spiritual setting of the ceremony, particularly since each round of the "four doors" has its unique characteristics which develop out of the group process and the personalities of the participants. For example, in several of the sweat lodge ceremonies in which I have participated, the medicine person stated that each time the door was opened (bringing with it a sense of temporary relief and movement toward some end state) we would be able to see the world and ourselves more clearly, to recognize and understand more things "out there" (the world and environment) and "in here" (one's psychological processes). By his or her leadership and direction, the medicine person helps the participants to "see" more fully the symbolic nature of the ritual as a paradigm of life's central human struggles. The juxtaposition of darkness and light may then take on deeper symbolic values of the paradigms life versus death; insight versus ignorance; growth versus stagnation; hope versus despair; relief versus suffering; renewal versus stasis; connection versus separation; communality versus aloneness; and will versus resignation. Moreover, these thematic concerns, so indigenous to the process of epigenetic development, may vary in clarity, predominance, saliency, and level of consciousness during each of the "four doors." Perhaps for this reason the ceremony is often regarded as a purifying ritual since the intensity of the sweat lodge creates the conditions that induce emotional and cognitive reappraisal which may result in an altered perception of the self-in-the-world.

Individual and Cultural Continuity

Another major dimension of the sweat lodge ceremony centers around the issue of the *continuity of the community and the continuity of the individual in the culture.* In one of the sweat lodge ceremonies in which I participated, the spiritual leader of the group spoke about the importance of "passing on" tribal traditions that concerned spiritual strength and continuity. He spoke of real grandfathers (relatives) as well as the Spiritual Grandfathers and how the traditions of the "native way" had been passed down from generation to generation. In these talks, the leader made clear reference to the continuity of the culture, its sacred rituals and practices, as it affects the individual's ability to live successfully with inner strength in today's world. Therefore, the sweat lodge ceremony, with its songs and prayers of thanksgiving, further solidifies the sense of continuity by virtue of the physical and interpersonal bonding. The unity achieved during the ceremony reinforces the historical reality of the tribe while enhancing a sense of group identity and the individual's attempt at a successful variation within it (Erikson, 1950, 1968).

For Native American war veterans with PTSD the issue of continuity in ego identity and group identity is especially significant because of the warrior ethos in many tribes. Specifically, the greatest risk to a firm sense of ego vitality *after* returning home from the war rests in the inability to reestablish continuity in the community due to isolation and the recognition that it may be difficult to attain full-warrior status if the acts of battle do not meet with cultural sanction or further opportunities to actualize the tribally defined and historically shaped meaning of being a warrior. Moreover, the sweat lodge experience helps the veteran to transform the warrior-like attributes of persistence, perseverance, patience, stamina, and aggression into new modalities of coping. The ceremony recognizes the warrior's deeds in battle but also ritually forgives and reassures that he will have the power to properly modulate and transform these hostile tendencies in accordance with tribal custom.

In a very tangible way, however, the sweat lodge ceremony is one of many Native American rituals that ensures ego vitality and a sense of continuity. The sweat lodge creates an atmosphere in which the members contemplate their individual lives in common suffering and physical bonding. The process of the ritual also alternates between *group* and *individual* modes of participation. There is group song and prayer and individual acts of thanksgiving which are multifaceted in nature. Similar to group psychotherapy, the members make statements of self-disclosure, confessions, admissions of personal suffering, imperfection, weaknesses, and addictions, as well as expressions of faith, hope, concern for others in the community, and the desire for greater personal and spiritual strength.

Release, Rebirth, and Renewal

By the end of the fourth round there may emerge an enhanced sense of inner strength that one has overcome the pain, extreme heat, and darkness of the lodge to see new "light" in the self. The ritual is its own symbol and process: the members enter naked and crawl in a humble and diminished position into the sweat tent. Then, through the guidance of the medicine person and the process of the four rounds of prayer, emerge again from the interior of the "womb" with a profound sense of release, relief, and personal renewal. At different levels of awareness and bodily functions, many individuals report a strong sense of peace, calmness, clarity of mind, and rebirth. The sweat that flowed so profusely has cleansed the skin and symbolically represents the shedding of unhealthy aspects of the self. Upon leaving the lodge and emerging into the cool air and light outside, there is an immediate and acute sense of release from the compact womb of darkness. One by one the members emerge and stand, a welcome posture after the long, cramped sit in the lodge. The members exchange ideas and feelings about some of the aspects of the ceremony. There are expressions of well-being and enjoyment of the air as it feels soothing and refreshing against the hot skin. Finally, the medicine person may light the sacred pipe and pass it among the members in a last act of sharing and unity.

THE SWEAT LODGE AS A FORM OF TREATMENT FOR POST-TRAUMATIC STRESS DISORDER

The sweat lodge ritual contains a set of procedures that bear at least a superficial resemblance to many forms of modern psychotherapy: group counseling, hypnosis, transcendental meditation, client-centered therapy, and cognitive behavior modification. Nevertheless, the sweat lodge ritual grows out of a different culture which has evolved its own methods and principles for helping persons with physical ailments and psychic distress. Achterberg (1985), Harner (1982), Jilek (1982), and Wallace (1966) have noted that in shamanic practices there is often an attempt to produce an altered (ASC) or shamanic state of consciousness (SSC) by: (1) extreme temperature conditions (hot or cold); (2) physical and sensory deprivation; (3) use of drugs and sacred plants; (4) sleep deprivation; (5) fasting; (6) dehydration; (7) hypoxemia; (8) mortification of the flesh; (9) rhythmic music, singing, drumming, and dancing; and (10) prolonged vigilance states. In commenting on shamanic practices in different cultures Harner (1982) states:

> The widespread similarities in shamanic methods and beliefs throughout much of the world have been extensively documented by Eliade in his classic work, *Shamanism*. It is precisely because of the consistency of this ancient power and healing system that Eliade and others can speak with confidence of the occurrence of shamanism among peoples long isolated from one another. . . . Both shamans and scientists personally pursue research into the mysteries of the universe, and both believe that the underlying causal processes of the universe are hidden from ordinary view. And neither master shaman nor master scientists allow the dogma of ecclesiastical and political authorities to interfere with their explorations. (pp. 57–58)

It can be argued, of course, that the role of the shaman is not unlike the role of the psychiatrist, psychologist, or other health care providers who seek to help people with emotional or physical pain. What does differ, of course, is the cultural context, language system, and symbolic aspects in which the ritualized practice of healing takes place. *But is it possible that the sweat lodge ritual contains an archetypal form of human experience that in some way transcends cultural diversity in producing a psychobiological state that is associated with a reduction of pain and of emotional distress and with changes in modalities of perceiving, evaluating, and thinking about oneself in relation to others and the world?* Is the sweat lodge a potentially valuable technique for the treatment of persons suffering from PTSD or other mental disorders, such as depression or addiction to alcohol and drugs?

PTSD SYMPTOM REDUCTION: THE EFFICACY OF THE SWEAT LODGE

This section examines how the sweat lodge may function as a form of treatment for anxiety, depression, and stress-related disorders. To organize the possible therapeutic effects of the sweat lodge ritual, the common symptom clusters of PTSD will be discussed and illustrated separately in terms of the changes produced by the purification ritual. Table 3.3 summarizes this discussion.

Depression

In terms of the salutary effects of the sweat lodge ritual, it is expected that there will be an immediate elevation in positive mood state, a reduced sense of helplessness, and a strongly enhanced sense of centering and ego identity. Through the individual acts of prayer, self-disclosure, atonement, and hope for personal strength, a nonjudgmental environment is created which permits both self-effacement and self-acceptance without the fear of stigmatization or misunderstanding. As we discuss later, the extreme heat of the lodge may also induce high levels of endogenous opioid production and a balance in catecholamine-adrenergic neurochemical states and result in increased feelings of well-being and a decrease in depression.

Physical Symptoms, Memory Impairment, Problems of Concentration

The darkness and heat of the lodge cause both physical discomfort as well as a heightened awareness of one's internal physical state and

TABLE 3.3
The Effects of Sweat Lodge Purification Rituals on PTSD

PTSD DIMENSIONS AND DSM-III-R CRITERIA	CHANGE IN SYMPTOM CLUSTER PRODUCED BY PURIFICATION RITUAL
Depression, search for meaning, identity diffusion (C)	Reformation of the self, positive mood, enhanced sense of centering and identity
Physical symptoms, memory impairment (B,D)	Tension release, relaxation, awareness focused on internal states, ability to concentrate
Stigmatization/alienation (C)	Sense of unity, bonding, communality and continuity
Anger/rage (B,D)	Inner calmness, acceptance of fate, release of destructive thoughts
Sensation seeking/hyperarousal (B,D)	Creative channeling of need to enhance feeling of vitality
Intrusive imagery/affective flooding (B,D)	Reformulation of reason to enter ritual, transformation of imagery in less distressing direction, emotional calm
Intimacy conflict (C)	Strong physical, psychological and spiritual bonding
Isolation (C)	Enhanced sense of unity, bonding which contravenes isolation and aloneness
Emotional constriction/avoidance (C)	Emotional expressive, reduced numbing, counterphobic tendency reduced, interpersonal trust

Source: Wilson, 1988, P. 264
Note: DSM-III-R Criteria B, C, D refer to category of symptoms

level of psychic tension. Eventually, through the process of the "four doors," physical tension is greatly reduced by profuse sweating and the need to concentrate to overcome personal discomfort and to attend empathically to the prayers of the other group members. Second, part of PTSD is the somatization of psychic conflict, and thus the ritual reduces the physical symptoms, partly by cognitive restructuring of the imagery and affect associated with the disorder. Moreover, emergence from the lodge provides a great contrast effect of the oppressing heat of the lodge with the freedom and enjoyment of the cool air outside. The members are literally released from claustrophobic encapsulation and may emerge with new insights and feelings about living in new and perhaps healthier ways of being.

Stigmatization/Alienation

Many survivors or victims of traumatic events have a changed view of society and its value (e.g., Janoff-Bulman, 1985; Lifton, 1967; Wilson,

1980a). Existentially, survivors often feel like "outsiders" who carry with them the taint of the trauma or, alternatively, the need to bear witness to it. A common consequence is that the survivors often have a changed sense of identity and ideology which is beyond conventional modes of valuing. As a result many experience alienation from mainstream cultural values, especially materialism as an end in itself.

The sweat lodge ritual overcomes individual alienation and stigmatization in a number of ways. First, there is immediate and direct physical bonding among the members. Second, the group leader provides guidance that points to the *long-term continuity* of the culture and "its ways" which is carried into the immediate present inside the tent. Third, the process of the ritual creates *a sense of communality* (Erikson, 1976) by the individual acts of thanksgiving, prayer, and humility. Fourth, the darkness forces an awareness of aloneness in life and the subsequent need to bond with others for strength and guidance. Finally, the completion of the ceremony leads to a sense of accomplishment in overcoming adversity and pain which was shared by the group as a whole. Stated simply, there is an implicit cohesion and unity born of commitment to the ritual itself.

Anger/Rage

It is common for individuals with PTSD to experience what Horowitz (1979) has termed "rage at the source" of their distress in life. The source of this anger and rage stems from being victimized, exploited, or poorly understood after a stressful life event because of the difficulties associated with PTSD, e.g., reliving the trauma in painful and distressing ways. The sweat lodge helps to reduce feelings of both anger and rage through the release of destructive and self-defeating forms of thinking. The feeling of inner calmness and vitality at the end of the ceremony helps the individual with a stress disorder to learn that there are alternative modalities of coping with difficult feelings produced by events in the past. Additionally, the process of listening to the self-disclosure of others facilitates the acceptance of fate and the realization, guided by the thoughtful words of the medicine man, that personal strength is tantamount to assuming personal responsibility for one's life through sacrifice, discipline, and commitment to those processes which reaffirm a growing sense of ego vitality, selfhood, and integrity. In different Native American groups there are many rituals designed for this purpose (see, for example, *The Peyote Hunt*, by Meyeroff, 1974).

Sensation Seeking/Hyperarousal

In the last chapter sensation seeking was described as one of many psychobiological patterns of adaption to stressful life events. In this syndrome individuals actively seek out high levels of intensity, excitement, arousal, and stimulation in order to recreate the mental state experienced during the trauma in which there was a heightening of sensory and perceptual systems. As noted in Chapter 2, the syndrome is also defensive in nature because the high levels of activity block awareness of memories, images, and emotions that would produce distress, anxiety, and depression. In another way, stimulus seeking is a reenactment of the psychic state of arousal during the trauma and therefore a subtle form of searching for meaning by exploring the pain that exists within, through external activities that create heightened arousal.

The sweat lodge ritual has a built-in appeal for those survivors who crave intensity, novelty, and optimal levels of arousal. First, the lodge is a challenge to be met which contains much ambiguity and uncertainty. Paradoxically, however, the process of the ritual reduces physical arousal by virtue of the heat and steam while at the same time offering new insight on how to creatively channel the compulsive need to seek out situations that increase physiological arousal. In this way, then, *the ritual reduces the tendency to seek external sources of stimulation in compensation for painful emotions or internal fears of nothingness, death, or the loss of ego identity* by engaging the participants in an intensely interesting process that creates "sensation" by the task of "seeking" within oneself. As will be discussed later, the sweat lodge ritual produces the same neurophysiological changes as sensation-seeking activities (e.g., increased opioid levels) but without the often dangerous physical activities; which may become addictive.

Intrusive Imagery/Affective Flooding

Intrusive imagery constitutes the core process in PTSD and is the single greatest source of anxiety, depression, and affective flooding. Marmar and Horowitz (1988) have commented that it is quite common for persons with PTSD to experience a cyclical alternation between the symptoms of avoidance and intrusive recollection.

Although the sweat lodge ceremony offers no way to excise the process of reliving a painful life trauma, it serves as a transitional experience that helps the individual to reformulate the meaning of it. The lodge provides a kinesthetic grounding, a safe space for beginning emotional healing and detachment. In the darkness of the lodge, bonded to the other group members, a supportive atmosphere exists which permits the individual to request help in dealing with unresolved aspects of the trauma. In this regard the person can face the ghosts of the past in a group that is suffering together but ends with less pain and a greater sense of relief, calmness, and inner peace. This enhanced sense of individual vitality may now represent a psychoformative style in which there is a stronger sense of personal integrity, integration, and connection as opposed to feelings of disintegration, stasis, and separation (see Lifton, 1976, for a discussion of these modes of psychological experience). Additionally, the ritual helps to both "name" and "contain" traumatic imagery and affect; it limits the power of the trauma to affect present life; it limits a sense of guilt and helps to integrate the past events into a present personal identity. One potential outcome of this change in psychoformative processes is a greater sense of internality in locus of control which staves off feelings of helplessness and vulnerability associated with the experience of unbidden imagery of the trauma.

Intimacy Conflict, Avoidance, Emotional
Constriction

The last two dimensions of PTSD that may be affected by the sweat lodge ceremony are intimacy conflict and isolation. As stated earlier, the physical dimensions of the lodge create person-to-person contact. There is physical, psychological, and spiritual intimacy created by the group and individual prayers of thanksgiving. Although the darkness intensifies a sense of aloneness, it simultaneously creates a need to reduce uncertainty and anxiety by participating silently and empathically with the other members. Gradually, as the process of the "four doors" shapes the nature of a sweat lodge on any occasion, the members build a special sense of unity out of their efforts to overcome their discomfort. The success of this process is symbolized by the sharing of the sacred pipe at the end of the ceremony and by the words repeated throughout: "All my relations." This response affirms the individual's act of purification and release.

THERAPEUTIC EFFECTS OF THE SWEAT LODGE

In summary, Table 3.3 indicates the different ways that PTSD might be affected by the sweat lodge ritual. Based on the analysis presented above, it is possible to see how the emotional, cognitive, and inter-

personal components of the stress syndrome can be positively ameliorated by such a seemingly simple ceremony. However, a deeper analysis
into the implicit structure and process of the group dynamics suggests
that a complex form of interaction occurs as a product of the physical
setting, cultural tradition, the personality characteristics of the members,
and the emergent process which involves both individual self-disclosure
and communal participation. The therapeutic benefit of this process
derives from the meditative reflections, the guidance provided by the
group leader, and the difficult task of overcoming personal pain and
discomfort which occur on many levels of psychological awareness.
When the ceremony is repeated or combined with other ritual forms
of healing, purification, or self-confrontation, it is possible to speculate
that very specific and sophisticated psychosocial, neurophysiological,
and behavioral mechanisms may be successful in restoring, maintaining,
or enhancing optimal and adaptive states of psychological well-being.
A comparative study of these practices across Native American groups
would probably yield an interesting set of findings on the different
ways that cultures deal with post-traumatic stress and other forms of
psychic pain.

PSYCHOBIOLOGICAL ASPECTS OF THE SWEAT LODGE RITUAL

In Chapter 2 we discussed the psychobiology of PTSD and reviewed
the four major hypotheses regarding the neurochemical changes in brain
chemistry that affect symptom presentation: (1) the catecholamine hypothesis; (2) the balance hypothesis; (3) the serotonin hypothesis; and,
(4) the opioid hypothesis. We believe that the conditions of the sweat
lodge have a direct effect on these neurochemical processes in several
basic ways.

First, the conditions in the sweat lodge are conducive to inducing an
altered state of consciousness (ASC), a mind-body state that is sometimes
associated with changes in mental functioning and levels of well-being
(Tart, 1969). Second, the conditions of the sweat lodge are likely to
affect production of neuropeptides (endogenous opioids), which are
commonly associated with both ASC and psychological reports of calmness, euphoria, energy, and well-being. Third, it is possible that the
conditions of the sweat lodge may *decondition* the overdriven hyperaroused state inherent in PTSD and lead to a temporary balance (steady
state) in the catecholaminergic-cholinergic systems in the autonomic

nervous system. This deconditioning effect is a mind-body form of organismically based natural healing.

To facilitate the discussion of these issues, which build quite substantially on the material presented in Chapter 2, the following will be considered: (1) rituals and altered states of consciousness; (2) shifts in hemispheric dominance in the ergotropic and trophotropic neural subsystems; and (3) the deconditioning of the overdriven hyperarousal condition of PTSD that results from state-dependent learning.

Rituals and Altered States of Consciousness

In recent years there has been a growing interest in the relationship of altered states of consciousness to their possible induction by ritualistic practices (Winkelman, 1986). As defined by Tart (1969):

> An altered state of consciousness for a given individual is one in which he clearly feels a qualitative shift in his pattern of mental functioning, that he feels not just a quantitative shift, but also that some quality or qualities of his mental processes are different. (p. 2)

Thus, with the discovery of endogenous opioid peptides (endorphins) in the brain in the mid-1970s, speculation began as to whether or not various shamanistic healing practices might produce ASCs that were therapeutic in nature. Moreover, if such a relationship could be demonstrated between ritual practices and ASC, a logical hypothesis followed which took form as to the possible changes in brain chemistry and levels of consciousness that might be associated with a natural form of healing emotional distress. For example, if one thinks of PTSD as a *chronic hyperaroused neurophysiological state* developed in response to a traumatic and threatening environment or life event, a condition that is easily intensified and biologically activated by a broad range of stimuli (van der Kolk, 1987), then it is clear that in severe cases this state does not easily decondition or extinguish according to the principles of learning theory. Moreover, given that this is so, it is possible to speculate that a change in the neurophysiology of the brain, such as an increase in endorphin production and an associated change in EEG pattern, may decondition the pathological state and produce a different, "healthier" condition in which new modalities of thinking and experiencing can occur. *Thus, it is quite possible that certain ritualistic experiences could, in effect, reverse a neurophysiologically based state of PTSD by supplanting*

*it with one that promotes a sense of well-being through endorphin pro-
duction, altered states of consciousness, and a deconditioning of the chron-
ically hyperaroused pathological state of the autonomic nervous system.* But
is there any evidence to support such a hypothesis? The answer is not
as much as rigorous scientific standards would require, but enough to
suggest the probable validity of the larger relationship of PTSD to
psychobiologically based hyperaroused states that can be altered in
positive, healing directions by such rituals as the sweat lodge.

In reviewing some of the major research studies on the relationship
of ASC, neurophysiology, and ritualistic practice, it is necessary to first
understand the nature of the brain mechanisms associated with endogenous opioid production and then show how certain conditions can
produce a changed neurophysiological state, one that leads to a balanced
and integrated neurophysiological basis of mental functioning.

In an important paper on endorphins in altered states of consciousness,
Henry (1982) stated that four essential conditions had to be met to
explain ASC and ritual behavior:

1. a mechanism in the body to reduce pain;
2. a mechanism to activate the pain reducing process;
3. the mechanism for activation is a normal part of neurophysiology, and
4. certain classes of behavior are associated with the activation of
   the endorphin mechanism.

Henry reviews a series of experiments that identified the existence of
beta-endorphins and enkephalin and their loci in the brain as well as
the mechanism which would establish that ASC are associated with
endorphin production. As to the fourth criterion he concludes:

> Could other conditions associated with altered states of conscious-
> ness also provoke the release of endorphins by the pituitary into
> the blood? These conditions, as described above, were principally
> the participation in group activity with the understanding that this
> would result in a trance-like state for the individual concerned.

He continues by saying:

> It is reasonable to suggest that the ritualistic dance associated with
> the altered states of consciousness . . . might be physiologically
> and/or emotionally stressful enough, or might activate propri-

oceptive inputs so as to raise circulating levels of endorphins to levels that could result in states of relative analgesia. Besides these analgesic properties, morphine and other opiates are known for their euphoric effects. Thus, the conjecture seems reasonable that if the transfer of beta-endorphin through the blood-brain barrier at supraspinal levels, perhaps most importantly in limbic structures, is the same as that in the spinal cord, these altered states of consciousness might be due to the activation of this same pituitary mechanism by stress. (pp. 404–405)

In a similar review of anthropological evidence, Jilek (1982) compared the Sun Dance ceremony of Native Americans with the Spirit Dance of the Pacific Northwest Salish Indians. Both ceremonies involve rhythmic movement, focused attention, acoustic and pain stimulation, some degree of exposure to extreme temperature, and other factors commonly associated with the production of ASC. Jilek (1982) proposes that both sets of rituals have therapeutic effects within the cultural context which give the participant a spiritual, supernatural, and social framework by which to establish a firmer sense of ego identity without depression, anxiety, or self-condemning thoughts. In regard to the neurophysiological mechanisms associated with the specific tribal ritual, Jilek (1982) states:

We may propose that these therapeutic results could in part be due to the antidysphoric, antidepressant and anxiolytic effects of endogenous opioid peptides released through specific treatment modalities during the initiation process. We may further propose that the release of these substances could be triggered by the same conditions known to induce altered states of consciousness, notably pain, acoustic and kinetic stimulation, hypoglycemia, and dehydration, in combination with physical exertion. (p. 340)

Hemispheric Dominance Shifts: The Ergotropic
and Trophotropic Neural Subsystems

In one of the most comprehensive analyses of the neurobiology of ritual trance, Barbara Lex (1979) argues that various rituals that lead to ASC or trance states involve a distinct and discernible neural mechanism in which there is a change in hemispheric dominance and a "tuning" of the central nervous system. Lex identifies two integrated neural subsystems as ergotropic and trophotropic mechanisms which characterize the attempt of the organism to expend or conserve energy. She states:

> Ergotropic response consists of augmented sympathetic discharge, increased muscle tonus, and excitation in the cerebral cortex manifested as "desynchronized" resting rhythms; the trophotropic pattern includes heightened parasympathetic discharges, relaxed skeletal muscles, and synchronized cortical rhythm points to an interconnected "tripartite" hub—the limbic system, hypothalamus, and reticular formation of the paleocortex are its members—as comprising the mechanism that integrates purposive, foresighted behavior in man by mediating subcortical responses in the ergotropic and trophotropic systems. (p. 135)

In the phenomenon described as tuning there is a shift in the predominance of the ergotropic and trophotropic systems. Associated with this shift is a tendency for right-hemispheric dominance which is generally produced by auditory driving through dance, song, or rhythmic drumming (Neher, 1961, 1962). According to Lex's theory (1979), the shift to right-hemispheric dominance renders the person vulnerable to:

> . . . spatial and tonal perception, recognition of patterns—including those constituting emotion and other states in internal milieu—and holistic, synthetic thought, but linguistic capability is limited and the temporal capacity is believed absent. (p. 125)

In effect, one consequence of the shift in the neural subsystem produced by some rituals is to change the physical state and to alter the psychological state so that new modalities of thinking occur, those which are more holistic and integrative in nature. Lex (1979) suggests that the therapeutic value of abreaction response for emotionally distressed persons is that it:

> . . . helps the individual to reexperience, under controlled conditions, intense emotional responses to stress-provoking stimuli, permitting discharge of affect with accompanying physiological readjustments. The heightened tension excites the ergotropic system to the extent that trophotropic rebound results, establishing a new configuration of internal functioning. (p. 142)

In this view, then, the two neural subsystems tend to "balance" each other's effects, resulting in a psychological state in which new integrations are possible, both cognitively and neurophysiologically.

The Deconditioning of PTSD by the Sweat Lodge Ritual

It is quite possible that the conditions of the sweat lodge (extreme heat, sensory deprivation, singing, restricted mobility, etc.) could produce a shift from ergotropic to trophotropic functioning, right-hemisphere dominance, endogenous opioid production, an ASC, and a balance in the catecholaminergic-cholinergic systems, all of which are the physical and psychological antithesis of the pathological state of hyperarousability and the state-dependent condition of reliving the trauma (i.e., the effects are antidepressant, anxiolytic, analgesic, euphoric, and holistic-integrative cognitive processing). Moreover, the shift from ergotropic to trophotropic functioning does create a changed neural state, if only temporarily. *However, the therapeutic significance is that for the person with post-traumatic stress disorder the awareness of the shifts in physical and psychological state may lead to the perception that there are other nonpathological states of being besides the chronic tension and hyperarousability associated with the anxiety disorder. Thus, the awareness and experience of the changed psychobiological state may be the beginning of organismically based healing. The person in the nonpathological state can begin to integrate and assimilate previously traumatic material in a new form.*
Viewed from another perspective, it is possible to think of these changes in neurophysiological states as a shift in lateralization in hemispheric dominance. Recently, Dean (1986) has reviewed the literature on the lateralized functions of the right and left hemispheres and noted that "it seems that the right hemisphere more efficiently serves tasks that require the holistic, or simultaneous, processing of nonverbal gestalts and the complex transformations of complex visual patterns" (p. 82). In contrast, he states that "the left hemisphere has been more closely linked to processing involving speech, language, and calculation" (p. 121). In the context of our analysis, the shift in hemispheric lateralization, along with the aforementioned neurophysiological changes in catecholaminergic functioning, may permit greater holistic integration of traumatic *visual* images, but in a nonaroused, calm state of being which is, in itself, therapeutic in nature (see Anisman, Kokkinidis, & Sklar, 1985, for a review of these neurological mechanisms).

The idea of a neurophysiological link between certain rituals and positive therapeutic consequences is both parsimonious and appealing from the perspective of their adaptive function to human behavior, especially in the treatment of emotional distress or as techniques designed to facilitate greater "spiritual" strength. However, to show that the sweat lodge is a ritual of therapeutic value determined by the interaction of psychobiological, cultural, and social factors, it is necessary to demonstrate that:

1. There are conditions present in the sweat lodge ritual to produce an ASC;
2. These conditions are of the type commonly identified with the production of endorphins and changes in ergotropic and trophotropic neural systems leading to a shift in hemispheric dominance; and
3. The participants in the ritual characteristically report behaviors commonly associated with ASC.

Based on the work of Jilek (1982), Ludwig (1966), and Tart (1969), Table 3.4 presents the set of physical and psychological factors commonly associated with the production of ASC. Of the 13 factors listed, nine are indigenous to the sweat lodge ritual:

1. extreme heat for prolonged period of time;
2. visual sensory deprivation in the darkness of the lodge;
3. restricted motor activity caused by the cramped seating conditions in the small lodge;
4. seclusion from other members during the ceremony;
5. dehydration caused by the profuse sweating in the lodge;
6. directed attention through the guidance and suggestion of the medicine person;
7. acoustic stimulation produced by the songs of the medicine person and the collective singing by the members of the group;
8. hyperventilation caused by the extreme heat, steam, and lack of oxygen in the lodge; and
9. pain stimulation by virtue of overcoming extreme heat and the compactness of the lodge.

Thus, there are more than enough conditions present to induce an ASC. When they are combined together in the typical sweat lodge ritual, it is highly likely that an ASC is an expected outcome of the ritual process.

TABLE 3.4

Factors Associated with the Production of Altered States of Consciousness (ASC) Commonly Found in Sweat Lodge

PHYSICAL AND PSYCHOLOGICAL FACTORS ASSOCIATED WITH THE PRODUCTION OF ALTERED STATES OF CONSCIOUSNESS (ASC)	ASC FACTOR COMMONLY FOUND IN SWEAT LODGE RITUAL
Exposure to extreme temperatures	Yes
Sleep deprivation	No
Sensory deprivation	Yes
Restricted motor activity	Yes
Seclusion	Yes
Acoustic stimulation (auditory driving)	Yes
Pain stimulation	Yes
Increased motor activity; hypermobility	No
Dehydration	Yes
Hypoglycemia	Variable
Suggestion; directed attention trance state	Yes
Hyperventilation	Yes
Pharmacological substances (e.g., peyote)	Variable

Note: Adapted from Ludwig (1966), Jilek (1982) & Tart (1969).

While it is clearly the case that the necessary conditions exist to produce an ASC and with it changes in neural subsystems, do the participants routinely report the characteristic behaviors that define a qualitative shift in this pattern of mental functioning? Table 3.5 lists the nine major criteria of ASCs identified by Ludwig (1966). As the table illustrates, nearly all of the characteristics are commonly found in the sweat lodge ritual, the exception being a sense of change in body image. Although there are many possible reasons for this, the most cogent explanation is that the stability of body imagery is strongly affected by individual differences in personality.

In summary, it appears that the neurophysiological mechanisms of PTSD may be altered by the sweat lodge ritual in several ways that are theoretically discernible. First, the extreme temperature of the lodge and the conditions present to induce an altered state of consciousness point to a changed state of neurophysiology in the brain. As Figure 3.1 suggests catecholaminergic (NE, 5-HT, DA) and cholinergic (ACh, cortisol) levels are reduced to promote a neurological condition that results in a greater balance in the ergotropic and trophotropic subsys-

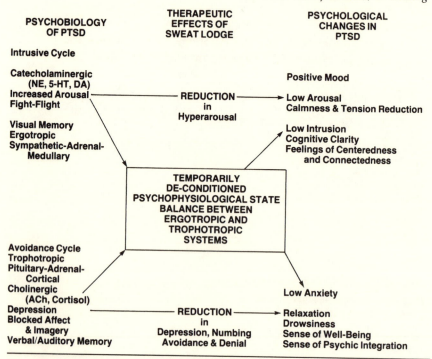

Figure 3.1. Psychobiology of PTSD and its partial de-conditioning by the sweat lodge ritual. (Source: John P. Wilson and Alice J. Walker.)

tems. The psychological and behavioral result is a reduction in both intrusive and avoidance symptoms of PTSD. Specifically, there is a positive mood state; a greater sense of emotional stability and expressiveness; low levels of anger, anxiety, fear, and depression; and an increased sense of well-being that is experienced as being calm and relaxed and having a greatly enhanced sense of ego vitality. More important, the traumatized individual is able at this point to begin new forms of integration of previously traumatic affect and imagery. In this way the effect of the ritual is allosteric and a form of natural healing.

In conclusion, it seems apparent upon closer analysis of the various dimensions of the sweat lodge ritual that this seemingly simple rite of purification is indeed very complex. It is a phenomenon that occurs on many levels of psychological reality. It is an integrated and holistic form of ritual with its own symbolism which is strongly colored by

TABLE 3.5
Characteristics of Altered States of Consciousness
Commonly Found in Sweat Lodge Ritual

CHARACTERISTICS OF ALTERED STATES OF CONSCIOUSNESS (ASC)	ASC CHARACTERISTIC COMMONLY FOUND IN SWEAT LODGE RITUAL
Alteration in normal cognition	Yes
Changed sense of time	Yes
Loss of control	Yes
Change in emotional expressiveness	Yes
Change in body image	Variable
Change in meaning or significance	Yes
Sense of the Ineffable	Yes
Feelings of rejuvenation	Yes
Hypersuggestibility	Yes

Note: Adapted from Ludwig (1966).

cultural practices of Native Americans. It creates a physical environment that can lead to neurophysiological changes in the brain and nervous system. It is a group process with its own social-psychological mechanisms. What might appear mystical to individuals unfamiliar with these types of rituals is, in reality, a long-evolved human process of healing and transformation—a mind-body relationship. In conclusion, it appears that this simple ceremony, conducted in an earthy environment, can restore a sense of well-being, connectedness, and continuity with meaningful forms of personal and cultural integration.

SECTION II

Empirical Support

4

Stress Sensitivity and Psychopathology

with KEN PRABUCKI

A person-environment model of human responsivity to stressful life events implicitly recognizes that there are differential stress response thresholds. Traumatically stressful events do not necessarily have a uniform effect on all people, and for this reason theorists have postulated that various psychological processes (e.g., stress appraisal) determine how these experiences are perceived, processed, and integrated into the self-structure.

Antonovsky (1979), for example, has argued that the ability to successfully manage and cope with different types of stressors (i.e., traumatic versus mundane) is contingent on a "sense of coherence" which he defines as "the extent to which one has a pervasive, enduring though dynamic feeling of confidence that one's internal and external environments are predictable and that there is a high probability that things will work out as well as can reasonably be expected" (p. 123). Antonovsky's concept of a sense of coherence is similar to Kobasa's concept of the hardy-coper personality type, which characterizes a person who enjoys challenges and handles stressful life events by maintaining an internal locus of control and a sense of commitment to a well-formed value system. Kobasa's research with her associates (1979, 1981, 1982) has indicated that the hardy coper is resilient to the types of stresses that produce deleterious effects in others. Common to both Antonovsky's and Kobasa's concept of stress sensitivity is the idea that there is a complex mind-body relationship which is affected by many factors such as culture, learned patterns of stress management, cognitive coping styles, and autonomic nervous system functioning.

As noted in Chapter 1, many other theorists from Freud to the present have postulated concepts of vulnerability and sensitivity to stressful life events (e.g., Anthony & Koupernick, 1974; Coyne & Lazarus, 1980; Dohrenwend & Dohrenwend, 1974; Garmezy, 1981; Gleser, Green, & Winget, 1981; Lazarus & Folkman, 1984). In an explicit person-environment formulation of stress sensitivity, Appley and Trumbull (1967) state:

> It is consistently found that these [stress] reactions vary in intensity from person to person under exposure to the same environmental event. . . . It has also been noted that, with few exceptions, the kind of situation which arouses a stress response in a particular individual must be related to significant events in that person's life. Many people have used the terms "ego strength," "stress tolerance," and "frustration tolerance." It is perhaps doubtful that there is such a thing as a general stress-tolerance in people. There is more likely to be a greater or lesser insulation from the effects of certain kinds of stress producers rather than others. . . . It seems more likely that there are differing thresholds, depending upon the kinds of threats that are encountered and that individuals must be differentially vulnerable to different kinds of stressors. . . . To know what conditions of the environment are likely to be effective for the particular person the motivational structure and prior history of the individual would have to be taken into account. Where the particular motives are known . . . what kinds of goals have for him been likely to increase anxiety or lead to aversive or defensive behavior . . . a reasonable prediction of stress proneness might be made. (pp. 10–11)

In a 19-year update from their original formulation on stress sensitivity, Appley and Trumbull (1986) summarize as follows:

> In our view *stress vulnerability profiles* (cf. Appley, 1962) are determined by underlying motivational patterns that identify particular areas of relatively greater or lesser susceptibility, thus influencing the appraisal processes in different ways for different individuals. (p. 13)

The various conceptions of sensitivity or vulnerability to stress presented above are dynamic explanations that assume that person and environmental variables codetermine whether or not a stressor will produce psychic overloading and distress or be effectively managed by the individual in ways that do not adversely affect adaptive functioning. Clearly, some persons are especially likely to manifest pathological stress response to some stressors which would have little effect on others. Conversely, some stressors (e.g., torture) would produce post-traumatic stress in nearly everyone.

There is, of course, a large literature on the concept of stress vulnerability and stress invulnerability (e.g., Anthony & Koupernik, 1974; Block & Block, 1980; Coelho, Hamburg, & Adams, 1974; Garmezy, 1981; Garmezy & Rutter, 1983; Kahana, Harel, Kahana, & Rosner, 1988). The review of these studies, while important, is beyond the specific scope of this chapter. It is clear from the results of these studies and many others (e.g., Archibald & Tuddenham, 1965; Danieli, 1988; Lindy, 1988; Laufer, Frey-Wouters, & Gallops, 1985; Nefzger, 1970; Ochberg, 1988; Wilson, Harel, & Kahana, 1988) that situations of extreme stress, such as high levels of combat in warfare or prolonged internment in concentration camps (Eitinger & Strom, 1973), produce consequences that diminish some individuals' ability to tolerate stressors later in life whereas other persons appear to develop even greater levels of resiliency in managing inevitable stressors associated with life-course development (Kahana, Harel, Kahana, & Rosner, 1988). What we seek to understand in this chapter is the concept of *stress sensitivity* as it relates to the formation of psychopathology and psychiatric symptom formation, especially post-traumatic stress disorder among Vietnam war veterans, for whom an extensive data set exists (Wilson & Krauss, 1985). This data set allows us to test hypotheses on stress sensitivity and psychopathology.

The well-formulated general theories discussed above, as well as clinical insights concerned with more specific relationships between personality processes and traumatic experiences, provide strong support for the contention that research in this area should attempt to identify the complex relationships between relevant dispositional and situation variables as they influence post-traumatic adaptation. Unfortunately, these complex interactional approaches have not, for the most part, been widely used in research paradigms on PTSD. For a variety of reasons many investigators have examined the relationship between stress and psychopathology through bivariate correlational procedures or simple group comparisons which do not tease out the more complex interactions between variables (Denny, Robinowitz, & Penk, 1987). Moreover, studies that use appropriate multivariate statistical procedures have primarily emphasized the main effects of important independent variables while giving less attention to interactive effects. Further, researchers have often pointed to studies that have found no relationship between dispositional variables and post-traumatic psychological problems to support interpretations that pre-trauma personality is unrelated to post-traumatic adaptation. However, there need not be a strong main effect of dispositional attributes for these variables to have an impact on psychosocial adaptation. Understanding the effects of pre-trauma disposition is quite likely to involve experimental designs that include various interactions between personality variables and severity of different types of stressors as added independent variables.

APPROACHES TO ASSESSING PTSD AND STRESS SENSITIVITY IN VIETNAM VETERANS

DeFazio, Rustin, and Diamond (1975) used a univariate statistical analysis to assess the effects of combat stress on subsequent psychosocial problems. This study compared a group of Vietnam combat veterans to noncombat veterans on the existence of several psychosocial problems thought to be related to combat stress. They found that combat veterans tended to exhibit more problems with intimacy, somatic tension, and frequent nightmares than did their noncombat counterparts.

Denny, Robinowitz, and Penk (1987) also used group comparisons to determine relationships between combat stress and various psychological problems (e.g., emotional numbing, sleep problems, and difficulty controlling anger). Their findings suggest that combat veterans who were involved in "heavy" combat exhibited more of these symptoms than those who reported "light" combat duty. Additional findings suggest that self-reported premilitary background was not related to the symptoms measured.

Helzer and associates (1974) compared Vietnam combat veterans to "matched controls" on depressive symptoms and found that while the combat veterans as a group exhibited more of these symptoms than did the controls, these differences disappeared after preservice variables were taken into account. When any one of four preservice variables (i.e., antisocial behavior, education, parental psychiatric problems, or parental arrest) was accounted for, the differences became statistically nonsignificant.

Solkoff and associates (1986) also used a group comparison design in a study of 50 Vietnam combat veterans with a diagnosis of PTSD who were compared to 50 Vietnam combat veterans without PTSD on selected variables related to prewar experiences and homecoming experiences. The results indicated that only their measure of combat experiences, and the perception of homecoming experiences, significantly differentiated the two groups. None of the preservice variables were found to be related to the diagnosis of PTSD for this sample. These results are similar to those found by Wilson and Krauss (1985).

Other studies have used multivariate statistical procedures to assess the relationships between combat stress, predispositional variables, and subsequent psychosocial problems. Frye and Stockton (1982) and Foy and associates (1984) used discriminant analysis to predict group membership (i.e., positive diagnosis of PTSD versus negative) with both preservice and combat stress measures as the predictor variables. These studies report that the preservice measures failed to significantly distinguish between the two groups. However, the combat stress measures were positively related to a diagnosis of PTSD. Frye and Stockton also found that family support at homecoming was negatively related to the diagnosis.

Laufer, Gallops, and Frey-Wouters (1984) used multiple-regression procedures to assess the relationships between dispositional and situational variables, and subsequent psychosocial problems. Regressions of three dimensions of war stress (i.e., a general combat stress measure, the witnessing of abusive violence in combat, and the participation in atrocities) and several dispositional variables (e.g., preservice education, race, early antisocial behavior, etc.) on stress symptom measures yielded support for the inclusion of interactional terms in multivariate designs. A central finding of this study which is relevant to the present discussion has to do with the interaction between race and abusive violence. Laufer found that whites who participated in abusive violence scored lower on feelings of demoralization, guilt, and anger than those who only witnessed these events. For blacks, participation was strongly related to feelings of demoralization, guilt, and active hostility, while the witnessing of abusive violence had no significant relationships with these variables.

THE INTERRELATIONSHIPS BETWEEN STRESSOR DIMENSIONS AND THE SYMPTOMS OF PTSD

An area of research in the dynamics of post-traumatic stress disorder (PTSD) which has not been studied extensively concerns the interrelationships between symptom clusters and their relationships to the variables associated with them. As noted previously, the *Diagnostic and Statistical Manual of Mental Disorders,* Third Edition, Revised (DSM-III-R) suggests that the diagnosis of PTSD involves three basic clusters of symptoms: (1) intrusive reexperiencing of the trauma in a variety of ways, (2) avoidance and numbing responses to ward off painful imagery and affect associated with the trauma, and (3) physiological states of hyperarousal. The avoidance symptoms include psychogenic amnesia, detachment, estrangement, restricted range of affect, a loss of interest in significant activities, a foreshortened sense of the future, and active avoidance of situations that would arouse recollections of the stressful life event.

Many researchers have begun to question the utility of viewing these symptoms as unidimensional and specific to the diagnosis of PTSD. Brett and Ostroff (1985) argue that a two-dimensional model has been implicitly suggested by several theorists (Freud, 1920; Horowitz, 1986; Kardiner and Spiegel, 1947; Kolb and Multipassi, 1982; Krystal, 1968; Lifton, 1976). The two-dimensional theories posited by most of these theorists predict that trauma victims will respond initially with affective and/or somatic symptoms which involve reliving the traumatic experience. Reexperiencing of the trauma coexists with defensive attempts to deny the trauma, such as psychogenic amnesia, emotional numbing, and avoidance behaviors. Brett and Ostroff (1985) note that a number of questions regarding the interrelationships between these symptom dimensions and their natural sequelae need to be studied.

Laufer and his associates (1985) have attempted to make use of this two-dimensional model in their recent research. The results indicated that while the *numbing dimension* was found to be significantly related to the combat stress and witnessing of abusive violence measures, the *reexperiencing* cluster was associated only with participation in abusive violence. These results suggest that post-traumatic stress reactions involve at least two dimensions of symptoms which must be considered separately in experimental designs. Moreover, since war stressors are multidimensional in nature, it is important to understand how they interact together in determining different symptom clusters. However, if the correlation between the combat stress measure and participation in abusive violence were too high, problems with multicolinearity might prevent a valid assessment of the interactive effects of these two stressors.

WAR STRESS AND PSYCHIATRIC SYMPTOM PATTERNS

There are several potentially important and interesting stressor dimensions which have not been adequately explored. One which has been suggested by Vietnam veterans who have written books about their personal experiences is the exposure to an aversive environment (Ketwig, 1985; Mangold & Penycate, 1985; Shook, 1986; Wright, 1983). These accounts strongly suggest that the soldiers in Vietnam were concerned about the threat of disease, snakes, leeches, red ants, various insects, extremely oppressive heat, monsoons, and dense jungle terrain. The exposure to these conditions may have psychological consequences, which include: (1) an additive effect when combined with other combat-related stressors, (2) production of patterns of symptoms which are altogether different than those produced by combat, or (3) a negligible influence on coping with an adverse environment or in terms of post-traumatic adaptation.

It is important to note that while these stressors cannot be considered catastrophically traumatic, the *subjective reactions* of those exposed to these aversive environmental stressors (i.e., the extent to which they thought about or were bothered by them) may indicate a heightened *sensitivity* to certain types of stressors. Determining the relationships between these subjective reactions and later symptom development may result in a more concise understanding of which types of stressors can be expected to affect "stress-sensitive" individuals. Additionally, the symptoms which are considered to be clear indications of PTSD—as opposed to those which may occur as a result of interactions between traumatic experiences and dispositional variables—may be found by identifying those who have a heightened sensitivity to many stressors.

Attempting to identify the post-traumatic symptoms that relate differentially to, for example, exposure to injury and death, and the environmental stressors mentioned above, may lead to positing a more precise definition of post-traumatic stress disorder and identifying those who were at risk prior to the trauma. It may also help to determine whether dispositional variables predict an increase in the severity of PTSD symptoms or are associated with psychopathology other than PTSD (Wilson and Krauss, 1985).

As noted above, the approach taken in DSM-III-R views PTSD as a symptom cluster with three unique subgroupings: intrusive reexperiencing, avoidance and numbing, and physiological hyperactivity. Many of the symptoms listed in the DSM-III-R as criteria for PTSD overlap with criteria for major depression disorder, dysthymic disorder, anxiety disorders, and several personality disorders (Wilson, 1988a). An interactional model attempts to differentiate among stressor dimensions and their effects in terms of symptom patterns. Since combat consists of a *multidimensional* set of stressors (e.g., mortar attacks, booby traps, scenes of death/dying, ambushes), "stress-sensitive" individuals may develop different patterns of stress response after combat than persons without this vulnerability.

EXPERIMENTAL DESIGNS AND METHODOLOGICAL STRATEGIES

The conceptual issues we have considered give rise to questions of method. To the extent possible, the measurement of key variables that may be associated with post-traumatic adaptation is an ideal goal. However, measures of pre-traumatic dispositional variables are typically retrospective and subject to the effects of time as well as the traumatic event itself. Nonetheless, they are important factors relevant to the study of PTSD. In terms of research, the variability in these measures which is due to the trauma may be explored by including the stressors as independent variables in a multivariate design. Dispositional measures must also be included in order to assess their effects on post-traumatic adaptation as they *interact* with combat stressors if hypotheses based on current theory are to be adequately tested.

As noted in Chapter 1, identification of dimensions and subdimensions of stressors and symptoms is necessary for the prediction of PTSD. General responses to combat stressors are likely to be strongly influenced by the nature of the event, whereas idiosyncratic and diverse patterns of responses may be due primarily to predispositional tendencies or exposure to different types of stressors. There is no doubt that we have begun to understand the general patterns by which individuals respond to extreme stress (Raphael, 1987). What is far less transparent are individual differences in response to trauma. Ultimately, of course, knowledge of both universal and idiosyncratic responses will provide a fuller view of how humans respond to traumatic stress. Attempts to focus on one or the other in isolation often result in confusion and inconsistency with regard to the specification of combat stress–related symptomatology.

STRESS SENSITIVITY AND PTSD

The focus in this chapter is on assessment of the relationships between dispositional personality tendencies, stress sensitivity, and combat stressors as they relate directly to PTSD and to other psychiatric symptom clusters. In addition, an attempt will be made to determine whether these variables or the interactions between them are associated with different patterns of psychopathology.

As in previous research efforts, it is hypothesized that the combat stressor measure will be found to correlate primarily with PTSD symptomatology. It is expected that these associations will remain relatively constant even when the measures of environmental stress and dispositional personality tendencies are included as independent variables in the regression model. Moreover, it is hypothesized that the measure of environmental stress used in this study relates to a *dispositional sensitivity to stress* which will correlate primarily with symptoms that are not specific to PTSD. Further, when this stress-sensitive variable is included with the other combat stressors as a predictor of the symptom clusters in the regression analysis, the combat stressor will retain its relationships with the PTSD symptoms but will not be found to correlate with other psychiatric symptoms. Assessment of the interrelationships between dispositional personality *and* combat stress as they relate to various symptom clusters is examined in a separate set of analyses. It is hypothesized that the dispositional personality measures will be found to *interact* with the stressor measures to produce *different* patterns of responses. These patterns of symptoms are thought to reflect individual differences in cognitive styles as they affect reactions to traumatic combat experiences. The relationships between the combat stressor dimension and the severity of PTSD symptoms should not be substantially modified by the addition of these dispositional personality measures to the regression model.

Overall, these predictions are based on theoretical formulations which suggest that persons exposed to extreme trauma will manifest some of the symptoms of PTSD (Lifton, 1988). The *severity* of these symptoms will be related primarily to the degree of exposure to combat stressors.

The *patterns* of PTSD symptoms exhibited will be related both to the type of stressors to which the person was exposed and to his *level of stress sensitivity*. The severity of symptoms that are not specific to PTSD will be associated with the degree of stress sensitivity.

METHOD

Subjects

The subjects used in the present study are 114 Vietnam combat veterans seeking treatment at Veterans Administration readjustment counseling centers throughout the United States. Relevant demographic and other information is contained in Wilson and Krauss (1985).

Measurement of PTSD and Stress Sensitivity

The Vietnam Era Stress Inventory (VESI) was used in the present study (Wilson & Krauss, 1985). However, in order to test the hypotheses, the VESI was modified in several ways. Two subscales were constructed which separated combat stressors from environmental stressors in Part III of the VESI, which measures exposure to specific stressors indigenous to the Vietnam War (see Appendix A). Table 4.1 lists the items that comprise the subscales.

Part IV of the VESI was also modified in order to separate PTSD-specific symptoms from general psychiatric complaints. Symptom clusters of scales were constructed both by utilizing DSM-III-R criteria for diagnostic classification, and by using current clinical and theoretical insight. The mean values for items were used as the measure for each cluster. In addition, three items (depression, suicidal concerns, anxiety) were used as measures of post-traumatic psychosocial problems. These items which make up the symptom scales and the single items are listed in Table 4.2.

Statistical Analysis

The statistical procedures used in the current study progress from simple bivariate correlational analyses to regression analyses with dispositional, situational, and *dispositional-by-situational* interaction terms to predict post-traumatic symptoms. Each set of analyses builds on the previous set in a hierarchical fashion. The regression procedure chosen

TABLE 4.1
Stressor Dimensions Derived from
Vietnam Era Stress Inventory

SCALE NAME	VESI ITEM	CONTENTS
Combat stress	#1	How often did you fire your weapon at the enemy
	#2	How often did you kill the enemy
	#3	How often did you see someone killed
	#4	How often did you see enemy wounded
	#5	How often did you see our guys wounded
	#6	How often did you see dead enemy
	#7	How often did you see dead Vietnamese
	#8	How often did you see our own dead
	#10	How often were you directly involved as a participant in hurting Vietnamese
	#18	How often did you participate in a body count of enemy dead
	#20	How often did you see our guys wounded by antipersonnel devices (booby traps, trip wires, etc.)
	#39	How often were you directly involved as a participant in killing Vietnamese
	#44	How often were you directly involved in mutilating bodies of Vietnamese
Environmental Stress	#25	How often were you bothered by bad climate
	#26	How often were you bothered by bad food
	#31	How often were you bothered by insects and filth
	#38	How often were you bothered by the threat of disease.

for the current study involves the simultaneous entry of independent variables into the regression model such that each predictor variable's independent relationship with the dependent variable is assessed while considering the relationships of the other variables in the model as well. This was chosen as an alternative to a stepwise procedure which necessitates either a determination of the order in which the independent variables should be entered or a determination of the basis by which these variables will be ordered for entry (Cohen & Cohen, 1975).

Bivariate Correlations

Premilitary personality propensities. Initial analyses involved the correlations between the two stressor measures and premilitary personality and demographics. Both Pearson and Spearman correlations were used to assess these relationships because many of the premilitary measures were not normally distributed. The tables show only the Pearson cor-

TABLE 4.2
Present Symptom Clusters Derived
from Vietnam Era Stress Inventory

SCALE NAME	VESI ITEM	CONTENTS
Reexperiencing	# 5	Thoughts of a buddy killed in Vietnam
	# 10	Reexperiencing nightmares
	# 15	Getting rid of unpleasant thoughts about Vietnam when they come into your head
	# 20	Memories of Vietnam which just seem to pop into your head
	# 24	War-related thoughts (i.e. memories of Vietnam)
Detachment	# 8	Feeling like isolating or withdrawing yourself from others
	# 26	Feeling an inability to be close to someone you care about
	# 29	Feeling alienated from other people
	# 42	Experiencing problems being close to your mother
	# 43	Experiencing problems being close to your father
Constricted Affect	# 16	Feeling numb or nothing
	# 35	Feeling unable to express your real feelings to others
Hypervigilance	# 23	Using military self defense tactics when under stress
	# 77	Feeling jumpy or jittery especially when sudden noises occur
	# 78	Feeling nervous when you hear a helicopter
	# 79	Driving down a highway and searching for ambush spots
	# 80	Walking in the woods and listening carefully to sounds around you
	# 84	Feeling the need to have a weapon on or near you
Survivor guilt	# 6	Asking yourself why a buddy was killed in Vietnam and not you
	# 7	Feeling guilt that a buddy was killed and not you
Denial	# 81	Thoughts that it is hard to believe that Vietnam happened to you
	# 82	Thoughts that Vietnam is something you still cannot accept in your life
	# 83	Thoughts that Vietnam was just one big nightmare.

TABLE 4.2 *(continued)*

SCALE NAME	VESI ITEM	CONTENTS
Anger and Rage	# 11	Experiencing anger
	# 12	Experiencing rage
	# 36	"Flying off the handle" in frustration when things don't go right
	# 37	Losing your temper and getting out of control
Conflicts with other	# 33	Getting into fights or conflicts with loved ones
	# 34	Getting into fights with others
	# 38	Experiencing problems with your wife or lover
	# 39	Arguing with your wife or lover
	# 44	Your wife or lover complaining that Vietnam has messed up your relationship with her
	# 72	Experiencing problems with co-workers
Externality	# 17	Feeling that all your problems are caused by other people.
	# 52	Feeling that you cannot control the important events in your life
	# 88	The feeling that you are not free to make your own decisions
Self-esteem problems	# 46	Feeling that you are are no good and worthless
	# 51	Experiencing self-doubt and uncertainty
	# 54	Not feeling really satisfied with yourself
	# 55	Not feeling proud of the kind of person you are
	# 56	Feeling that you are not a person of worth
	# 60	Feeling like you've been a failure since leaving military service
Autonomic hyperarousal	# 93	Faintness or dizziness
	# 98	Heart pounding or racing
	# 101	Hot or cold spells
	# 102	Numbness or tingling in parts of your body
	# 103	A lump in your throat
Motor tension	# 92	Nervousness or shakiness inside
	# 96	Trembling

ITEM NAME	VESI ITEM	CONTENTS
Depressed Mood	# 4	Feeling depressed (Down, bummed out)
Suicidal Thoughts	# 2	Suicidal Thoughts
Feeling Anxious	# 1	Feeling anxious or nervous

relations because few inconsistencies between the two approaches were found.

Table 4.3 reveals no significant associations between the premorbid personality measures and the two stressor measures, indicating that those who scored *higher* on premorbid personality tendencies were *no more likely* to report being exposed to a greater amount of any of the stressors measured than were those who scored lower on premilitary personality tendencies.

Similarly, few significant correlations were found between premilitary demographics and the stressor measures. The only significant correlation was between the size of the town or city raised in and the environmental stress measure ($r = .24$, $p < .01$).

TABLE 4.3
Correlations of Combat Stressors with
Premorbid Personality Measures and
Demographics

Personality Disorder	Combat Total		Environmental Stress	
	R	p	R	p
Early Antisocial	.10	ns	.12	ns
Late Antisocial	.10	ns	.06	ns
Paranoid Mistrust	.09	ns	.10	ns
Paranoid Hypersensitivity	.08	ns	.10	ns
Restricted Affect	-.08	ns	-.002	ns
Narcissistic Grandiosity	-.08	ns	.008	ns
Narcissistic Ideology	-.04	ns	.07	ns
Demographics:				
Number of Siblings	.13	ns	.05	ns
Birth Order	-.01	ns	-.08	ns
Size of town Raised in	-.02	ns	-.24	**
Number of towns lived in	.08	ns	.02	ns
Married versus Not Married	-.14	ns	-.10	ns
Age when sent to Vietnam	-.04	ns	-.09	ns

* p<.05
** p<.01

There was also a positive relationship between environmental stress measure and being divorced after military service ($r = .25$, $p < .01$) and a negative correlation with educational level ($r = -.21$, $p < .05$). These results indicate that the environmental stress variable is measuring something different than the combat stress measure, since the latter was not found to correlate significantly with either divorce or education. Additional support for this contention comes from the intercorrelations between the two stressor measures. Although the environmental stressor variable correlates significantly with combat stress ($r = .25$, $p < .01$), this correlation shares only about five percent of the total variance in the combat stress measures.

Table 4.4 lists the correlations between the symptom clusters and premilitary personality tendencies. The first six symptom clusters are those which have been suggested as indications of PTSD, while the second set of measures are generally thought to be more closely associated with other psychiatric disorders. Taken together these results suggest that the measures of antisocial behavior after the age of 15, paranoid interpersonal sensitivity, and narcissistic ideology are strongly related to many of the symptoms measured. None of the other personality variables, except antisocial behavior prior to age 15, appears to be strongly correlated with the symptoms measured. Early antisocial behavior, however, correlates strongly with the measure of later antisocial behavior ($r = .62$, $p < .0001$) and overlaps the pattern of associations between the later measures and the symptom clusters. It was therefore decided to leave out the measure of earlier antisocial behavior to reduce the number of variables to be used in the analyses that follow.

It is interesting that none of the premorbid personality measures, with the exception of paranoid interpersonal sensitivity, are strongly correlated with the PTSD-related symptoms, a finding similar to that of Wilson and Krauss (1985). In contrast, many of the correlations between the symptom measures related to other disorders and the personality variables were found to be significant. Table 4.4 shows that *late antisocial* behavior was correlated with autonomic hyperactivity, explosive anger and rage, conflicts with others, problems with self-esteem, externality, and denial. The *paranoid mistrust* measure was correlated to the measure of autonomic hyperactivity and motor tension. The *narcissistic ideology* scale was significantly associated with depressed mood, problems with self-esteem, explosive anger and rage, conflicts with others, and externality. Similarly, *narcissistic grandiosity* was also associated with symptoms of depression. *Paranoid interpersonal sensi-*

TABLE 4.4
Correlations of Premorbid Personality with Post-traumatic Symptom Measures

	Early Antisocial		Late Antisocial		Paranoid Mistrust		Paranoid Sensitive		Restricted Affect	
	P	p	P	p	P	p	P	p	P	p
PTSD Symptoms;										
Reexperiencing	.12	ns	.13	ns	.17	ns	.13	ns	-.01	ns
Detachment	.09	ns	.15	ns	.12	ns	.22	**	.11	ns
Constricted Affect	.11	ns	.12	ns	.14	ns	.19	*	.06	ns
Denial	.21	*	.18	*	.17	ns	.17	ns	.02	ns
Survivor Guilt	.13	ns	.12	ns	.14	ns	.19	*	.05	ns
Hypervigilance	.16	ns	.21	*	.17	ns	.23	**	-.01	ns
Not Specific to PTSD:										
Autonomic Hyperarousal	.22	**	.23	**	.18	*	.17	ns	-.03	ns
Motor Tension	.16	ns	.14	ns	.18	*	.25	**	-.01	ns
Self-Esteem Problems	.15	ns	.19	*	.16	ns	.26	**	.06	ns
Anger and Rage	.25	**	.25	**	.13	ns	.23	**	.01	ns
Conflicts with Others	.05	ns	.20	*	.15	ns	.21	*	.04	ns
External Locus of Control	.05	ns	.25	**	.17	ns	.25	**	.02	ns
Single Items:										
Depressed mood	-.01	ns	.03	ns	.02	ns	.13	ns	.04	ns
Suicidal Thoughts	.08	ns	.02	ns	.04	ns	.11	ns	.02	ns
Feeling Anxious	.16	ns	.08	ns	.13	ns	.29	**	.03	ns

* p < .05
** p < .01
ns: not significant

TABLE 4.4 (continued)

	Narcissistic Grandiosity		Narcissistic Ideology	
	R	p	R	p
PTSD Symptoms:				
Reexperiencing	.06	ns	.02	ns
Detachment	.15	ns	.17	ns
Constricted Affect	.14	ns	.23	**
Denial	.08	ns	.08	ns
Survivor Guilt	.06	ns	-.10	ns
Hypervigilance	.04	ns	.13	ns
Not Specific to PTSD:				
Autonomic Hyperarousal	-.03	ns	.15	ns
Motor Tension	.04	ns	.15	ns
Self Esteem Problems	.21	*	.28	**
Anger and Rage	.05	ns	.21	*
Conflict with Others	.13	ns	.21	*
External Locus of Control	.11	ns	.31	***
Single Items:				
Depressed mood	.22	*	.27	**
Suicidal Thoughts	.02	ns	.06	ns
Feeling Anxious	.06	ns	.15	ns

* p<.05
** p<.01
*** p<.001

tivity was correlated significantly with detachment, constricted affect, survivor guilt, Vietnam-related hypervigilance, motor tension, problems with self-esteem, explosive anger and rage, conflicts with others, externality, and anxiety. Of the five symptom measures for which this variable did not reach conventional significance, two (autonomic hyperactivity and denial) were found to relate marginally ($r = .17$, $p < .06$). The results suggest that this personality dimension may indicate a *particular propensity* to be strongly affected by extreme stress situations. This finding indicates the need to control for the effects of personality in order to assess the associations between combat stress and patterns of post-traumatic adaptation.

Demographics. Correlations between the premilitary demographic variables and the symptom measures produced few significant results (see Table 4.5). The negative significant correlations between the size of community in which the veteran was raised and the measures of survivor guilt and anxiety, together with the earlier finding of this variable with stress sensitivity, may suggest the possibility that individuals from smaller communities are at greater risk than those from larger communities for certain kinds of problems. The only other significant correlation between the premilitary demographics and the symptom measures is survivor guilt with being married prior to military service ($r = .18$, $p < .05$).

The last set of bivariate correlations is outlined in Table 4.6. These analyses indicate the relationships between the two stressor measures and the symptom clusters. The measure of combat stress correlates significantly with the PTSD symptoms of: (1) reexperience, (2) constricted affect, (3) denial, (4) survivor guilt, and (5) hypervigilance. The combat stress variable was also significantly correlated with all of the other symptoms except autonomic hyperarousal, self-esteem problems, depressed mood, and suicidal ideation. The environmental stress variable, on the other hand, was correlated with all of the symptom measures.

Regression Analyses

The next set of analyses involve a series of regressions that progress from relatively simple to complex in a hierarchical fashion. This approach allows us to see how the addition of a variable to the model modifies or adds to the relationships between the variables already entered into the equation. By exploring a series of analyses, we are able to see distinct patterns emerge from within the data set.

The first set of regressions go one step beyond the bivariate correlations between the combat stressors and the symptom measures. Regressing each of the symptom clusters on the two stressor measures will indicate the extent to which each of them is related to the symptom clusters, independent of the association of the other.

Combat stress and PTSD. The regression results in Table 4.7 suggest that combat stress, independent of the environmental stress measure, is associated with reexperiencing war trauma, constricted affect, denial, survivor guilt, hypervigilance, autonomic hyperarousal, motor tension, and conflicts with others. The environmental stress measure continues to be strongly correlated with all of the symptoms measured, suggesting

TABLE 4.5
Correlations of Premilitary Demographics with Post-traumatic Symptom Measures

	Number of Sibs		Birth Order		Community Size		Number of towns		Married vs. not		Age Sent to Nam	
	P	p	P	p	P	p	P	p	P	p	P	p
PTSD Symptoms												
Reexperiencing	.19	*	-.03	ns	-.11	ns	.02	ns	-.14	ns	-.02	ns
Detachment	.05	ns	-.04	ns	-.10	ns	.04	ns	-.02	ns	.05	ns
Constricted Affect	.01	ns	-.01	ns	.01	ns	-.03	ns	.02	ns	.01	ns
Denial	.15	ns	.09	ns	-.01	ns	-.01	ns	-.15	ns	-.01	ns
Survivor Guilt	.15	ns	.12	ns	-.20	*	.04	ns	-.18	*	.05	ns
Hypervigilance	.05	ns	-.04	ns	-.11	ns	.09	ns	-.12	ns	.01	ns
Not Specific to PTSD:												
Autonomic Hyperarousal	.11	ns	-.06	ns	-.14	ns	.08	ns	-.05	ns	.14	ns
Motor Tension	.01	ns	-.01	ns	-.11	ns	.02	ns	-.05	ns	.01	ns
Self Esteem Problems	-.05	ns	.01	ns	-.03	ns	.10	ns	-.01	ns	.05	ns
Anger and Rage	.02	ns	-.04	ns	.01	ns	.10	ns	-.10	ns	-.01	ns
Conflicts with Others	.01	ns	-.05	ns	-.05	ns	.13	ns	-.10	ns	.08	ns
External Locus of Control	.09	ns	.05	ns	-.01	ns	.17	ns	-.01	ns	-.01	ns
Single Items:												
Depressed mood	.07	ns	-.08	ns	-.06	ns	-.06	ns	-.10	ns	.06	ns
Suicidal Thoughts	.09	ns	-.04	ns	-.15	ns	-.02	ns	-.14	ns	-.01	ns
Feeling	.14	ns	.01	ns	-.20	*	-.06	ns	.03	ns	.06	ns

*p < .05; **p < .01

TABLE 4.6
Correlations of Combat Stressors
with Symptom Measures

	Combat Total		Environmental Stress	
	R	p	R	p
PTSD Symptoms:				
Reexperiencing	.57	***	.47	***
Detachment	.13	ns	.33	***
Constricted Affect	.23	**	.25	**
Denial	.44	***	.43	***
Survivor Guilt	.42	***	.43	***
Hypervigilance	.39	***	.36	***
Not Specific to PTSD:				
Autonomic Hyperarousal	.33	***	.31	***
Motor Tension	.31	***	.29	***
Self Esteem Problems	.14	ns	.33	***
Anger and Rage	.23	**	.35	***
Conflicts with Others	.27	**	.30	***
External Locus of Control	.19	*	.32	***
Single Items:				
Depressed Mood	.12	ns	.38	***
Suicidal Thoughts	.06	ns	.36	***
Feeling Anxious	.18	*	.37	***

* $p < .05$
** $p < .01$
*** $p < .001$

that this stressor measure is somewhat independent of the combat stressor measure as it relates to both PTSD and non-PTSD symptom measures.

In terms of the ability of each of these stressor measures to account for the variance in the symptom measures, the results indicate the following. *Combat stress* is found to be more strongly associated with reexperiencing, hypervigilance, autonomic hyperactivity, motor tension, and denial of Vietnam stress than is the environmental stress measure. Conversely, *environmental stress* is more strongly correlated with the

TABLE 4.7
Regressions of Combat Stressors and Environmental Stress on Each Symptom Measure

SYMPTOM MEASURE	COMBAT STRESS		ENVIRONMENTAL STRESS		R-SQUARE
	*Beta	p	*Beta	p	
PTSD Symptoms:					
Reexperiencing	.46	.0001	.34	.0001	.41
Detachment	.05	ns	.31	.0001	.09
Constricted Affect	.17	.07	.20	.03	.07
Denial	.34	.0001	.34	.0001	.28
Survivor Guilt	.34	.0001	.32	.0002	.27
Hypervigilance	.32	.0004	.27	.002	.21
Not Specific to PTSD:					
Autonomic Hyperarousal	.26	.005	.24	.009	.14
Motor Tension	.24	.009	.22	.02	.12
Self Esteem Problems	.05	ns	.31	.001	.09
Anger and Rage	.14	ns	.31	.0008	.13
Conflicts with Others	.20	.03	.25	.008	.11
Externality	.11	ns	.29	.002	.10
Depressed Mood	.01	ns	.38	.0001	.13
Suicidal Thoughts	-.05	ns	.37	.0001	.12
Feeling Anxious	.08	ns	.35	.0001	.13

*Standardized regression coefficient

symptom measures of detachment, constricted affect, problems with self-esteem, externality, explosive anger and rage, interpersonal conflict, anxiety, depressed mood, and suicidal ideation.

Since the independent relationships of each of the stressors with the symptom measures has been assessed, the interaction between combat stress and environmental stress may be added to the model. This *interaction term, which is simply the product of the combat stress measure times the environmental stress measure,* will be used to determine whether the relationships between the two stressor measures and the symptom clusters are significantly different at lower or higher levels of the other stressor variable. Regressions of each of the symptom measures on combat stress, environmental stress, and the interaction between the two yielded the results shown in Table 4.8.

The interaction term accounted for a significant amount of variance for the symptom measures of survivor guilt, suicidal thoughts, autonomic hyperactivity, and motor tension. Plots of residuals suggest that the relationships between the interaction term and survivor guilt, autonomic hyperactivity, and motor tension are due to the stronger relationship

TABLE 4.8
Regressions of "Combat Stress," "Environmental Stress," and Combat/Environment on Each Symptom Measure

SYMPTOM MEASURE	*R-SQUARE	**VARIANCE ADDED	***p
REEXPERIENCING	.41	.004	ns
DETACHMENT	.09	.001	ns
CONSTRICTED AFFECT	.07	0	ns
DENIAL	.28	.002	ns
SURVIVOR GUILT	.31	.04	.01
HYPERVIGILANCE	.21	0	ns
AUTONOMIC HYPERAROUSAL	.19	.05	.009
MOTOR TENSION	.14	.03	.09
SELF-ESTEEM PROBLEMS	.09	0	ns
ANGER AND RAGE	.12	.002	ns
CONFLICTS WITH OTHERS	.12	.005	ns
EXTERNALITY	.09	0	ns
DEPRESSED MOOD	.12	0	ns
SUICIDAL THOUGHTS	.15	.04	.01
FEELING ANXIOUS	.12	0	ns

*R-square: Refers to the variance in each symptom measure explained by the regression model with the interaction term included.

**Variance added: Refers to the added variance explained in each symptom measure when the interaction term is added to the model.

*** p: The level of significance associated with the interaction term regression coefficient.

of combat stress with these symptoms as environmental stress increases. At *lower* levels of environmental stress there appears to be only weak, if any, association between combat stress and these three symptom measures. The significant relationship between the interaction term and the measure of suicidal thoughts is explained by the positive relationship of combat stress with this symptom at higher levels of environmental stress and the negative association at lower levels. In order to better represent these relationships, subjects were divided into three groups of "low," "medium," and "high" based on their environmental stress scores. Correlations between the combat stress measure and the four symptom clusters found to be significantly related to the interaction term were then performed separately for each of the three groups. These correlations, which are shown in Table 4.9, support the interpretations suggested by the residual plots. Significantly, at *high* levels of environmental stress, the combat measure is strongly correlated with survivor guilt, autonomic hyperarousal, and motor tension.

Personality Disorders and Stress Measures

In the next set of analyses the relationships between the prewar personality tendencies, war stressors, and the symptom clusters were explored. Only the personality measures "late antisocial behavior," "paranoid interpersonal sensitivity," and "narcissistic ideology" were used in the regression analyses that follow since the other personality measures were not found to be associated with different patterns of symptoms in the bivariate correlational analyses.

Antisocial personality tendencies. The first set of regressions explored the interactions between the symptom clusters, personality, and stressor

TABLE 4.9
Correlations of "Combat Stress" with
Symptom Measures at Three Levels of
Environmental Stress

SYMPTOM MEASURE	ENVIRONMENTAL STRESS LEVEL		
	LOW (N = 46) R(p)	MEDIUM (N = 44) R(p)	HIGH (N = 25) R(p)
Survivor guilt	.18 (ns)	.40 (.007)	.59 (.002)
Suicidal thoughts	-.27 (.07)	-.04 (ns)	.28 (ns)
Autonomic hyperarousal	.08 (ns)	.21 (ns)	.45 (.02)

measures. The results of this set of regressions (see Table 4.10) indicated that the relationships between the antisocial personality measure and the symptom clusters were consistent with the results from the bivariate correlational analyses. This suggests that the associations between this premorbid measure of antisocial behavior and the symptoms measured are independent of the relationships of these symptoms with either of the stressor dimensions. Further support for this interpretation can be found by studying how the relationships between the two stressor variables and the symptom clusters are modified by the addition of the antisocial behavior measure. These associations were unchanged when the measure of antisocial behavior was added to the model, lending further support to the contention that antisocial behavior and the stressor measures are independent as they relate to these symptom measures.

Paranoid interpersonal sensitivity. The results for the interactive effects of paranoid interpersonal sensitivity and the other variables are shown in Table 4.11. The findings appear to be similar to the analyses that included antisocial behavior as an additional predictor variable in that the associations between paranoid interpersonal sensitivity did not significantly change the relationships between the stressor dimensions and the symptom measures.

Narcissistic ideology. The last analyses explored the relationships of the premilitary measure of narcissistic ideology to the two stressors to predict each of the symptom clusters. The results from these regressions can be found in Table 4.12.

These results suggest that the relationships between narcissistic ideology and the symptoms measured are, with one exception, similar to those indicated by the bivariate correlations. However, narcissistic ideology was significantly associated with *constricted affect.* Since the strength of the associations between the stressor measures and constricted affect is not modified by the addition of narcissistic ideology to the regression equation, we believe that this personality measure is related significantly only to the variance which is left unaccounted for by the two stressor measures. This suggests that narcissistic ideology is related to constricted affect, but that this association is obscured by the relationships of the two stressor measures with this symptom cluster.

Overall, these sets of regression analyses suggest that the single effects of the two stressor measures, as well as the premilitary measures of personality tendencies, account for different parts of the variability in the symptoms measured. Clearly, premilitary personality is related

TABLE 4.10
Regressions of "Combat Stress," "Environmental Stress," and "Late Antisocial" on Each Symptom Measure

SYMPTOM	COMBAT STRESS		ENVIRONMENTAL STRESS		LATE ANTISOCIAL		R-SQUARE
	*Beta	p	*Beta	p	*Beta	p	
PTSD Symptoms:							
Reexperiencing	.45	.0001	.34	.0001	.07	ns	.41
Detachment	.04	ns	.31	.001	.13	ns	.10
Constricted Affect	.16	.09	.20	.03	.09	ns	.07
Denial	.33	.001	.33	.0001	.13	ns	.29
Survivor Guilt	.32	.0002	.34	.0001	.07	ns	.27
Hypervigilance	.30	.0006	.26	.003	.17	.04	.23
Not Specific to PTSD:							
Autonomic Hyper.	.24	.008	.23	.01	.20	.02	.17
Motor Tension	.23	.01	.22	.02	.11	ns	.13
Self Esteem Problem	.30	ns	.31	.001	.17	.05	.11
Anger and Rage	.12	ns	.30	.0009	.22	.01	.17
Conflicts	.19	.04	.24	.009	.16	.06	.13
Externality	.09	ns	.28	.002	.22	.01	.14
Depressed Mood	.01	ns	.38	.0001	.01	ns	.12
Suicidal Thoughts	-.05	ns	.37	.0001	.01	ns	.11
Feeling Anxious	.08	ns	.34	.0003	.05	ns	.12

*Standardized regression coefficient

TABLE 4.11

Regressions of "Combat Stress," "Environmental Stress," and "Paranoid Hypersensitivity" on Each Symptom Measure

SYMPTOM MEASURE	COMBAT STRESS		ENVIRONMENTAL STRESS		PARANOID HYPERSENS.		R-SQUARE
	*Beta	p	*Beta	p	*Beta	p	
PTSD Symptoms:							
Reexperiencing	.46	.0001	.34	.0001	.06	ns	.41
Detachment	.04	ns	.30	.002	.19	.03	.12
Constricted Affect	.16	.09	.19	.04	.15	.09	.09
Denial	.33	.0001	.32	.0001	.18	ns	.29
Survivor Guilt	.32	.0002	.33	.0001	.13	ns	.28
Hypervigilance	.31	.0005	.25	.003	.17	.04	.23
Not Specific to PTSD:							
Autonomic Hyper.	.25	.006	.23	.01	.12	ns	.15
Motor Tension	.23	.01	.20	.02	.21	.02	.16
Self Esteem Problem	.03	ns	.29	.001	.22	.01	.14
Anger and Rage	.13	ns	.30	.001	.19	.03	.15
Conflicts	.19	.04	.23	.01	.17	.06	.13
Externality	.10	ns	.27	.003	.21	.02	.13
Depressed Mood	.01	ns	.37	.0001	.09	ns	.13
Suicidal Thoughts	-.05	ns	.37	.0001	.08	ns	.11
Feeling Anxious	.07	ns	.33	.0004	.25	.004	.18

*Standardized regression coefficient

TABLE 4.12
Regressions of "Combat Stress," "Environmental Stress," and "Narcissistic Ideology" on Each Symptom Measure

SYMPTOM MEASURE	COMBAT STRESS *Beta	p	ENVIRONMENTAL STRESS *Beta	p	NARCISSISTIC IDEOLOGY *Beta	p	R-SQUARE
PTSD Symptoms:							
Reexperiencing	.46	.0001	.34	.0001	.02	ns	.40
Detachment	.06	ns	.30	.002	.15	.10	.11
Constricted Affect	.19	.04	.18	.05	.23	.01	.12
Denial	.35	.0001	.33	.0001	.07	ns	.28
Survivor Guilt	.32	.0002	.35	.0001	-.11	ns	.27
Hypervigilance	.33	.0002	.26	.003	.13	ns	.22
Not specific to PTSD:							
Autonomic Hyper.	.27	.003	.22	.01	.14	ns	.16
Motor Tension	.25	.006	.21	.02	.14	ns	.14
Self Esteem Problem	.07	ns	.29	.002	.27	.003	.16
Anger and Rage	.15	.09	.29	.001	.19	.03	.16
Conflicts	.22	.02	.23	.01	.20	.02	.15
Externality	.13	ns	.26	.003	.30	.0007	.18
Depressed Mood	.03	ns	.35	.0001	.24	.005	.18
Suicidal Thoughts	-.04	ns	.37	.0001	.03	ns	.11
Feeling Anxious	.09	ns	.33	.0004	.12	ns	.14

*Standardized regression coefficient

to some post-traumatic symptoms. However, these relationships are independent of the single effects of the two stressor measures used.

The Interaction of Personality Propensities and Stressor Measures

To explore the possibility that premorbid personality may modify the relationships of the stressor measures to the symptom clusters, or vice versa, additional regression analyses were performed which included the interactions between each of the personality measures and the stressor measures as independent variables in the model. In order to do this in an organized fashion, six sets of regression analyses were executed. The first set of regressions used the two stressor measures, antisocial personality, and a combat stress by antisocial personality *interaction term* to predict each of the symptom clusters. The next two sets of regressions assessed the relationships of paranoid interpersonal sensitivity by combat stress and narcissistic ideology by combat stress with the symptom measures in a similar fashion. The major focus of these analyses was to determine if combat stress is associated with the symptoms of PTSD irrespective of pre-trauma personality style, or if this measure of combat stress is better understood as being related to PTSD symptomatology only when one or more dispositional tendencies are present. An additional question involves whether or not pre-trauma personality tendencies, as they interact with combat stress, are associated with patterns of symptoms that cannot be considered specific to PTSD.

Overall, these analyses suggest that interactions between combat stress and premorbid personality tendencies, as measured by the VESI, are essentially unrelated to *all* of the symptom clusters. *Although both the combat stress and the dispositional personality measures are related to post-traumatic problems, neither independent variable modifies the associations of the other with the symptom clusters.* However, the only combat stress by dispositional personality interaction term that was found to explain a significant amount of variance in any of the symptom measures was paranoid interpersonal sensitivity. This variable was found to be associated with the measure of suicidal thoughts ($p < .03$).

Three similar sets of analyses were also performed to determine whether the interactions between dispositional personality attributes and the environmental stress measure related to the symptom clusters. Similar to the previous analysis, interactions between the stress measure and each personality variable were assessed in separate regression models. The first set of analyses used the two stressor measures, antisocial behavior, and an environmental stress by antisocial personality interaction term to predict each of the symptom measures. The second and third sets included the same stressor measures but used paranoid interpersonal sensitivity and narcissistic ideology, respectively, as well as their interactions with environmental stress, as independent variables. The results of these analyses reveal few significant relationships that would not be predicted by chance. None of the terms which represent the interactions between environmental stress and premorbid personality were found to be associated with any of the symptom measures.

The Interaction of Demographic Variables and Stressor Measures

Two final sets of regressions were explored in order to further examine the relationship of childhood size of community with the symptom clusters. Since this premilitary demographic variable was found to correlate significantly both with the environmental stress measure and with the measures of survivor guilt and anxiety, it may indicate a sensitivity to certain types of war stress for those who were raised in small communities. The first set of analyses regresses each of the symptom measures on the two stressor measures and childhood community size.

The results of these regressions indicate that when the two stressor variables are included in the model, the associations of community size with anxiety and suicidal thoughts become statistically nonsignificant. This suggests the possibility that the variance shared by this premilitary demographic variable and the environmental stress measure is also shared by these two symptom measures. This may mean that both findings indicate a similar type of pre-traumatic stress sensitivity which, in turn, is associated with increased anxiety and suicidal thoughts.

The interaction between childhood community size and the combat stress measure was included in a separate set of regression equations to determine if these relationships were consistently evidenced across all levels of combat stress, or if this "stress sensitivity" predicted more problems only at higher levels of combat stress. Results suggest that the interaction between combat stress and size of childhood community is significantly associated only with suicidal thoughts. Plots of residuals and correlations of community size with suicidal thoughts at two levels of combat stress indicate that being raised in a smaller community was associated with suicidal thoughts only when the individual reported being exposed to a "high" combat level. At lower levels of combat exposure this relationship disappeared. These results indicate that the environmental stress and size of childhood community measures share a common relationship with self-report of suicidal ideation since the combat stress by environmental stress interaction term was found to be related to this symptom as well.

DISCUSSION

Limitations of the Study

This study was a preliminary attempt to explore the relationship between combat stress, stress sensitivity, personality propensities, and post-traumatic adaptation using the VESI. Clearly, the treatment-seeking nature of the sample places constraints on the external validity of the study, but nevertheless it uncovered a number of interesting findings that can be tested in future research. The large number of statistical analyses performed also limits the validity of the study, and caution must be taken when attempting to meaningfully interpret the significant results. Yet, the availability of the national sample taken from the Veterans Administration readjustment counseling program afforded us the opportunity to test hypotheses derived from the interactional model of traumatic stress presented in Chapter 1.

Combat Stress and Post-Traumatic
Symptomatology

In recent years there has been a growing awareness that war stress is multidimensional and complex. In Vietnam, war stress included combat exposure, witnessing or participating in atrocities, exposure to injury, death, dying, destruction, social chaos, and extremes of ecological stress which include high temperature, dense jungles, snakes, leeches, rats, and insects. The results of this study are consistent with earlier findings (Schnaier, 1986; Wilson & Krauss, 1985) since exposure to injury, death, and dying in combat is strongly associated with the symptoms that define PTSD. However, without the inclusion of other important variables in the predictive model, the ability to differentiate PTSD symptoms from other patterns of adaptation is difficult and could result in inaccurate identification of subtypes of the syndrome. The advantage of an interactional model, as noted in Chapter 1, is that it permits us to specify some of the ways that person, situation, and recovery environment variables codetermine the psychological processing of traumatic events.

Environmental Stress and Stress Sensitivity

The measure that was found to be strongly associated with all PTSD symptoms was "environmental stress." This variable may reflect a dimension which has its greatest influence on the severity of the symptoms manifested. The measure of sensitivity to environmental stressors is likely to reflect the degree to which the individual was sensitive to and distressed by the environment in Vietnam. Since most persons in our sample would have been exposed to roughly similar geographical environments during the war, the variability of scores due to actual exposure to environmental stress should be more restricted than that of the variability due to individual sensitivity. We believe that variability among environmental stress measures will be influenced by *subjective responses* to the environment. If the variability of these scores was due to differences in actual exposure, then we would expect this measure to be highly correlated with the other combat stress measures, which it is not. Given the relatively low correlations of this measure with the combat stress measures, and the high correlation with all of the symptom measures, this variable may be considered an indication of *sensitivity to environmental stress*. Further, since environmental stress was not found to correlate significantly with the measures of premorbid personality tendencies but was strongly associated with all current mental health problems, it is likely that this measure is indicative of a general sensitivity which is not necessarily related to personality type or to specific patterns of symptoms. Rather, it is related to increased problems in all areas of psychological functioning, as well as to reports of physiological hyperarousal.

The analyses that included environmental stress in the model indicate that this measure is strongly related to all of the symptom clusters even when the effects of exposure to injury and death are controlled for. *This result suggests that sensitivity to environmental discomforts is not related to a specific set of symptoms. Rather, it may be considered a more general sensitivity to a stressful environment.* The negative correlation between this stressor dimension and the size of community in which the veteran was raised supports the contention that this measure is associated with a dispositional trait. As such, it may reflect the kind of prewar vulnerability found by Elder and Clipp (1988) that predicted current PTSD symptoms in aging World War II veterans who were part of the original Oakland Growth Study. Their findings indicated that at high levels of combat exposure, men who were somewhat introverted, obsessional, and sensitive were predisposed to PTSD in the postwar aging process.

If the measure of "environmental stress" is indeed indicative of a dispositional vulnerability which affects the severity, rather than the pattern of symptoms, then how might this dimension relate to the combat stressor dimensions and their associations with psychological problems? In the present study, it was predicted that the measure of exposure to death and injury was the dimension of primary importance in terms of its generic effects on the development of PTSD symptoms. This result suggests that this variable should be found to relate only to PTSD symptoms when important differences in stressor type and dispositional attributes are included in the predictive model.

*The Interactive Effects of Stress Sensitivity and
Combat Stress*

The analyses that include both the combat and environmental stressor dimensions to predict the symptom clusters provide some support for the hypotheses. When the environmental stressor measure is added to the model, *combat stress* is found to be significantly associated only with the symptoms of reexperiencing, hypervigilance, survivor guilt, denial of the trauma, interpersonal conflicts, autonomic hyperarousal, and motor tension. On the other hand, the environmental stress measure was found to be related to all of the symptoms measured. However, there was no systematic pattern of symptoms found to be associated with this measure. Thus, the interactive effects of stress sensitivity and combat predict the core symptom clusters of PTSD listed in DSM-III-R.

With the exception of interpersonal conflict and the two anxiety-related physiological symptoms, *exposure to the injury and death of others is found to be associated with PTSD symptoms when the environmental stress measure is included as an additional independent variable in the model*. It is curious, however, that the symptoms which reflect numbing of responsiveness (restricted affect and detachment) are not found to be associated with the combat stress measure after environmental stress is added to the model. We believe that this may reflect the stress evaporation phenomenon described by Figley (1985). Other researchers (e.g., Horowitz, 1986; Lifton, 1979) have suggested that the working through and acceptance of a traumatic event must include the processing of the distressing affect associated with the event. This painful process usually occurs over time and in a cyclical fashion as the person oscillates between the denial and intrusive stages of stress recovery (Marmar & Horowitz, 1988). This may suggest that numbing of responsiveness is a psychological defense which modulates the person's attempts to assimilate the experience into existing cognitive schema. In the stress recovery process a healthy resolution would include a progression toward a diminishing need for psychic numbing. If this is the case, then one would expect the independent association between combat stress and numbing to weaken over time. Furthermore, it may be the case that those who seek treatment are experiencing emotional pain to a greater degree than those who do not. If so, then the level of psychic numbing may indicate the degree to which the war trauma is unresolved.

Overall, the results of analyses that include the measure of stress sensitivity suggest that this dimension is indicative of a predispositional vulnerability to certain types of stressors. Moreover, stress sensitivity does not appear to relate specifically to any pattern of symptoms. Rather, it is correlated with increased problems in several areas of functioning. However, when the interaction term is added to the regression model, new information is found in terms of symptom patterns. Combat stress, as measured in this study, was found to be associated with reported physiological hyperarousal and conflicts with others as well as core symptoms of PTSD. Autonomic hyperarousal and motor tension, while related to PTSD, are also associated with other anxiety disorders and may represent the manifestation of an underlying predispositional sensitivity to stressors. This interpretation is supported by the relationship of the combat by environmental interaction term with these two measures of physiological symptoms. *The finding that combat stress is significantly related to autonomic hyperarousal and motor tension only at higher levels of environmental stress may indicate that chronic hyperarousability is a possible sequela of trauma for stress-sensitive persons.* Indeed, Ciaranello (1983) speculated that there might be a genetic basis for such a relationship.

Finally, the two survivor symptoms that correlated with the interaction term are survivor guilt and suicidal thoughts. Similar to the two measures of reported physiological symptoms, these symptoms are found to correlate positively with combat stress at *lower* levels of environmental stress. Unexpectedly, depressed affect, which is often assumed to accompany these two cognitive symptoms, was not found to share their relationships with the combat by environmental stressor interaction term.

Personality Characteristics and Combat Stress

The results also provided yet another way of exploring the relationship of dispositional and situational variables to patterns of post-traumatic symptomatology. The addition of each of the premorbid personality disorder measures to the model makes it possible to determine whether these variables are related to the severity of PTSD-specific symptoms, other psychiatric symptoms, or different patterns of both. It was hypothesized that premorbid personality style interacts with exposure to trauma to produce different patterns of symptoms among Vietnam combat veterans. Although there is some indication that the premorbid personality measures used do relate to different patterns of psychological problems, there is no support for the hypothesis that these different patterns are also dependent on exposure to injury and death, or to the measure of environmental sensitivity.

Antisocial Personality

The measure of antisocial personality was found to be related to a pattern of symptoms indicating *hyperarousal, denial, excessive anger, externality, and interpersonal conflicts.* This pattern of symptoms is consistent with the DSM-III-R conceptualization of antisocial personality disorder and is remarkable in that it: (1) provides some validation for the dispositional measure and (2) is consistent with research on the core features of sociopathic personalities (Hare, 1970; Reid, Dorr, Walker, & Bonner, 1986). The fact that this pattern of relationships remains even when the combat and environmental stress measures are included in the model suggests that this premorbid personality dimension is independently associated with these symptoms, and exposure to the traumatic stress measure has little or no impact on them. It is also important to note that the associations of the stressor measures with post-traumatic symptomatology are unchanged by the addition of the antisocial personality scores and that the interaction between combat stress and antisocial personality was not found to be significantly related to any of the symptoms measured. Overall, this suggests that premorbid antisocial tendencies and the two stressors measures are independent of one another in terms of their relationships with post-traumatic symptomatology.

Paranoid Personality

When the measure of paranoid interpersonal sensitivity was included in the regression model, it was unrelated to the stressor measures in terms of post-traumatic symptomatology. While this personality measure was found to correlate with a pattern of symptoms normally associated with paranoid personality disorder (e.g., detachment, restricted affect, hyperarousal, motor tension, projection, etc.), neither these relationships nor the associations between the stressor measures and post-traumatic symptoms were altered by including both the dispositional and situational variables in the regression model. Moreover, it is surprising that the measures of paranoid interpersonal sensitivity and of environmental sensitivity are not significantly correlated. Although both appear to be tapping a form of sensitivity, they may be measuring different types of sensitivity to situations. Sensitivity to relationships with other people, as commonly found in the self-consciousness of paranoid individuals, differs from sensitivity to environmental stressors. The nature of this difference is that sensitivity to ecological stress seems to reflect a limitation in cognitive structure and personality-mediated styles of information processing (i.e., low tolerance for uncertainty), whereas paranoid sensitivity concerns emotional mistrust and suspicion (see Chapter 1 for a discussion of personality and information processing).

Narcissistic Personality

The pattern of symptoms found to correlate with this personality measure includes problems with self-esteem, depressed mood, excessive anger, interpersonal conflict, and externality. This pattern of symptoms is consistent with those described in the works of Kernberg (1975), Kohut (1971), and Morrison (1986) and as characterized in DSM-III-R as a personality disorder. As Parson (1988) has written, it is possible that trauma may produce post-traumatic *self-disorders* in which there is narcissistic scarring. As noted elsewhere (Wilson, 1980a), most soldiers in Vietnam were 19 years old and in the normal crisis of identity formation. Thus, combat stress could very well produce fragmentation in the self-structure of a narcissistic type by creating identity diffusion. Further, the significant correlation between the measures of narcissism and a pattern of depressive symptoms also suggests that this personality tendency may predispose individuals toward depressed affect after the war. Moreover, the analyses that included both of the stressor measures and narcissistic ideology as independent variables indicate that the dispositional personality measure retains its strong association with a pattern of depressive symptoms even after controlling for the effects of the stressor dimensions. The measures of survivor guilt and suicidal thoughts, however, were not found to be related to narcissistic ideology.

This suggests that there may be dispositional attributes which increase the likelihood that an individual will be depressed, but are not as likely to affect cognitive content. These results support the argument that depressed affect may vary as a function of predispositional characteristics (e.g., narcissistic tendencies), while the *cognitive content* is affected to a greater extent by the nature of the traumatic experience (e.g., intrusive imagery).

Taken together, the results from the analyses that include the dispositional personality and stressor measures, as well as the interactions between the two, indicate that the premorbid personality tendencies measured are related only to post-traumatic symptomatology consistent with what one would expect to find based on the DSM-III-R conceptualizations of the personality disorders themselves, rather than on consideration of how different types of individuals would respond to exposure to the stressors of war. However, these findings must be qualified, since only the three premorbid personality measures from the VESI were used in this study. In future research it will be interesting to explore the effects of many different dimensions of personality as they interact with other classes of variables in determining PTSD.

In conclusion, the specification of which symptoms can be considered specific to the differential diagnosis of PTSD is likely to improve our understanding of this syndrome and the type of person most likely to develop relatively "pure" forms of the stress response and those who might develop other symptom patterns.

Perhaps the most important findings of this study involve the relationships between the dimensions called "environmental stress" and post-traumatic adaptation. The *stress sensitivity concept* probably reflects both a dispositional and situational influence and has been shown to be associated with a large number of psychiatric symptoms, including PTSD. The concept of "stress sensitivity" may be important in determining the nature of the stressors and the threshold level in stressful experiences that lead to PTSD or other alternative forms of human adaptation to extreme stress.

5

Assessing the Construct of Post-Traumatic Stress Disorder

As the literature on the dynamics and vicissitudes of traumatic stress reactions has grown in recent years, the need for psychological measures of stress response syndromes and associated forms of adaptation has also assumed an important place in research, treatment, and diagnosis. Until recently, there were very few generic or specific measures of PTSD available for researchers and clinicians to use in their professional work. However, when one looks retrospectively at the cumulative body of knowledge on traumatic stress reactions, such traditional psychological measures as the MMPI have produced results suggestive of profile patterns for PTSD (e.g., Archibald & Tuddenham, 1965).

Clearly, of course, the rapidly expanding field of post-traumatic stress and victimology is currently witnessing an extraordinary growth in which survivors and victims of various stressful life events are being studied through the traditional methodological approaches indigenous to epidemiological research, retrospective and longitudinal studies of victim populations, as well as more basic physiological approaches to the understanding of the acute and chronic effects of extreme stress experiences (Green & Grace, 1988; Raphael, 1987; van der Kolk, 1987). Moreover, in the near future we will have available normative data on the psychological profiles of trauma victims. At present, there is a paucity of knowledge in this area, despite several important studies on

The author expresses his appreciation to W. Ken Smith and Gus Krauss for their statistical analysis.

war veterans (e.g., Fairbank, Keane, & Malloy, 1983; Lindy, 1988). Further, the issue of the psychometric properties of psychological tests designed to measure PTSD is clearly germane here as well. As new tests are developed to measure traumatic stress syndromes, their reliability and validity will be important in terms of carrying out important laboratory, field, and naturalistic studies of human response to traumatizing experiences. The importance of such data cannot be underestimated in terms of their relevance to diagnosis and to such forensic and legal issues as personal injury, disability claims, and criminal litigation proceedings (see Chapter 9 for a discussion of these points).

Ultimately, the convergence of accumulated information from different traumatic events and disasters will enable us to have a clearer sense of the diverse patterns of adaptation to extreme stress, both pathological and nonpathological. Such inquiry raises many important issues for the field of traumatic stress. For example, is PTSD a single entity or a complex pattern of personality alteration and adaptation that has subtypes, both pathological and normal? What is the range of symptom patterns for individuals with post-traumatic stress? What are the positive changes in ideology, identity, values, moral reasoning, and perception that are shared by survivors and victims? In prolonged and severely stressful life situations, is there a permanent change in psychobiological systems (hyperarousal) that leads to new levels of optimal stimulation? What are the limitations of traditional scales of psychopathology to measure the subtle and central features of post-traumatic stress reactions? These and other questions await future research efforts as the study of psychological trauma evolves into a distinct discipline of its own.

The purpose of this chapter is to present two studies that build on the findings reported in earlier studies (Wilson, 1988a; Wilson & Krauss, 1985). The first study is an initial attempt to partially validate the Vietnam Era Stress Inventory (VESI) (Wilson & Krauss, 1980). In this study the scores on the VESI were correlated with the scores obtained on the Beck Depression Inventory (BDI), the Sensation Seeking Scale (SSS) (Zuckerman, 1979), and the Impact of Event Scale (IES) (Zilberg, Weiss, & Horowitz, 1982). The second study explores the relationship of the factors of PTSD measured by the VESI to the MMPI PTSD subscale constructed by Keane and his associates (Keane, Malloy, & Fairbank, 1984). The results of these two studies demonstrate substantial empirical support of the VESI as a specific measure of PTSD for Vietnam veterans and show areas of convergence among the measures used in these two studies.

STUDY I

Subjects

The volunteer subjects in the first study were 74 combat veterans who were selected from each of the counties that constitute the catchment area of the VA hospitals located in Cleveland and Brecksville, Ohio. The age range was 31 to 41 years, with a mean of 35 years. The men were contacted through the cooperation of the VA Outpatient Mental Health Clinic, the VA readjustment counseling program, and the Northern Ohio Veterans Association. As noted above, the subjects were administered the BDI, SSS, IES, and VESI scales (see Wilson, Smith, and Johnson, 1985). Bivariate Pearson-Product Moment correlations were computed and are summarized in Table 5.1.

Results

Beck Depression and Vietnam Era Stress Inventory. As shown in Table 5.1, all of the VESI dimensions of PTSD are significantly associated with the BDI ($r = .65$ to $.83$, $p < .001$). The highest correlation, as expected, is between the two measures of depression ($r = .83$), a fact which supports the symptoms of depression as a component of PTSD.

Sensation Seeking Scale and Vietnam Era Stress Inventory. The correlations between the SSS subscales and the VESI PTSD dimensions indicated that there were significant correlations ($p < .05$) between the VESI measure of sensation seeking and each of the four subscales of the SSS: thrill and adventure seeking, $r = .36$; experience seeking, $r = .25$; disinhibition, $r = .40$; and boredom susceptibility, $r = .55$). Additionally, the SSS disinhibition subscale was significantly correlated with all of the VESI PTSD dimensions except intrusive imagery ($r = .22$ to $.40$, $p < .05$). Similarly, the SSS boredom susceptibility subscale was significantly correlated with *all* of the VESI PTSD subscales ($r = .35$ to $.47$, $p < .05$). Thus, these results strongly bolster the VESI PTSD factor of sensation seeking as a component of PTSD among Vietnam veterans.

Impact of Event Scale and Vietnam Era Stress Inventory. The correlations between the IES as a generic measure of PTSD and the VESI as a specific measure of PTSD for Vietnam veterans were all highly significant and positive ($r = .52$ to $.74$, $p < .0001$). Specifically, the IES avoidance

TABLE 5.1

Intercorrelations Between the VESI PTSD Dimensions with the Beck Depression Inventory (BDI), Sensation Seeking Scale (SSS), and the Impact of Event Scale (IES)

SUBSCALES	VESI							SSS				BDI	IES		
	2	3	4	5	6	7	8	9	10	11	12	13	14	15	16
VIETNAM COMBAT VETERANS (N = 74)															
VESI PTSD DIMENSION															
1. DEP	.85***	.87***	.83***	.81***	.81***	.83***	.97***	.15	.20	.30*	.45***	.83***	.67***	.57***	.67***
2. PHYS		.85***	.82***	.83***	.81***	.84***	.94***	.15	.13	.27*	.43**	.73***	.77***	.57***	.73***
3. STIG			.79***	.82***	.86***	.76***	.93***	.17	.13	.22*	.41**	.72***	.75***	.54***	.70***
4. SEN				.81***	.76***	.70***	.88***	.36*	.25*	.40***	.55***	.73***	.61***	.54***	.62***
5. RAGE					.73***	.71***	.88***	.18	.16	.34*	.46***	.70***	.68***	.57***	.67***
6. IMAG						.72	.88***	.14	.06	.14	.35*	.65***	.72***	.57***	.70***
7. INTIM							.86***	.04	.10	.24*	.44***	.74***	.64***	.52***	.63***
8. TOTAL								.18	.17	.29*	.47***	.81***	.75***	.61***	.74***
SENSATION SEEKING SCALE															
9. TAS									.37***	.24***	.19	.14	.08	.02	.05
10. ES										.43***	.19	.20	.01	.01	.004
11. DIS											.53***	.32*	.11	.10	.12
12. BS												.42**	.21	.24*	.25*
BECK DEPRESSION INVENTORY													.59***	.53***	.61***
IMPACT OF EVENTS SCALE															
14. INTRUS														.69***	.91***
15. AVOID															.93***
16. TOTAL															

***p < .0001
**p < .001
*p < .05

measure correlated .57 with the measure of depression, whereas the two measures of intrusive imagery were correlated at .72. These findings, especially considered in the perspective of the widespread use of the IES in traumatic stress research (Horowitz, 1986), add additional evidence to the construct validity of the VESI as a measure of PTSD in Vietnam veterans.

Discussion

The results of Study I provide preliminary evidence in support of the construct validity of the VESI as a measure of PTSD among Vietnam combat veterans. Both the BDI and the IES were strongly and significantly associated with all of the VESI dimensions of PTSD, which include depression, somatization, stigmatization/alienation, anger/rage, intrusive imagery, intimacy conflict, and the total PTSD measure.

The Zuckerman SSS scale produced a different but interesting pattern of association with the VESI PTSD scales. First, the VESI dimension of sensation seeking was moderately correlated with each of the subscales of the SSS, thrill and adventure seeking ($r = .36$), experience seeking ($r = .25$), disinhibition ($r = .40$), and boredom susceptibility ($r = .55$). However, the boredom susceptibility was strongly correlated with all of the VESI PTSD dimensions, as was the disinhibition subscale with the exception of the VESI PTSD subscale intrusive imagery. Although these results are subject to many interpretations, perhaps the most parsimonious explanation contains two interrelated elements. First, after a one-year tour of duty that involved heavy combat and the exposure to multiple life-threatening and traumatic stressors, the individual soldier adapted to such an environment through states of physiological hyperarousal which altered the prewar level of optimal stimulation for effective functioning. Thus, on reentry to civilian status this war-conditioned, hyperaroused state could potentially be activated by a broad range of environmental and internal, ideational stimuli (see Chapter 2 for a discussion). The consequences of survival of combat, in the present context of sensation seeking, include a propensity toward a disinhibition of ego controls and a susceptibility to boredom since the normal challenges of daily living rarely, if ever, match the level of stimulation generated by life-death combat situations.

Second, as noted elsewhere (Wilson, 1988a; Wilson & Zigelbaum, 1983), it is possible to consider sensation seeking as a motive, biosocial in origin, which serves a defensive function in persons suffering from PTSD. By this we mean that sensation seeking behaviors recreate and parallel the level of arousal experienced during combat. In this regard, the individual then employs a "survivor mode" of functioning which produces feelings of competency and efficacy since actions, tactics, feeling states, perception, and cognitive processing are largely those learned during the traumatic event. In this state (hyperarousal) the individual may produce increased levels of catecholamines and endogenous opioids (endorphins) which lead to elevated mood and feelings of well-being that are antagonistic to the typical avoidance-intrusion cycle that characterizes PTSD (Horowitz, 1986; van der Kolk, 1987). Viewed in this way, sensation seeking can be considered to be a neurologically conditioned cycle which has as its reinforcement the temporary alleviation of anxiety, depression, irritability, and intrusive imagery, symptoms that return in distressing ways when the sensation behaviors are terminated.

STUDY II

The primary purpose of Study II was to examine the relationship between the VESI dimensions of PTSD and the MMPI PTSD subscale developed initially by Fairbank, Keane, and Malloy (1983). As noted earlier, PTSD has become an important mental disorder in many areas of society that involve either traumatization or victimization. Thus, the issue of diagnosis and assessment is particularly important in terms of clinical treatment, compensation for personal injury, and the determination of pension claims (see Chapter 9). Moreover, since the MMPI is such a widely used and relied upon psychological measure of psychopathology in clinical work, research, and forensic settings, it is important that we understand the limitations of this instrument to measure PTSD since the MMPI was not constructed to measure the unique and idiosyncratic features of traumatic stress syndromes (e.g., intrusive imagery, survivor guilt, psychic numbing, dissociative reenactment, etc.). Stated differently, at present we do not have specific MMPI profiles or norms for different types of traumatized persons. For example, is the profile for combat veterans with PTSD the same as or similar to that for other groups who have endured a trauma (e.g., rape victims, disaster victims, torture victims, POW's, or abused children)? Further, do some of the MMPI clinical and validity scales measure certain aspects of PTSD?

On face validity alone, for example, we might expect Scale 1 of the MMPI (Hypochondriasis) to pick up the tendencies of somatization of psychic trauma; Scale 2 (Depression) to assess feelings of helplessness, depression, and restricted affect; Scale 3 (Hysteria) to assess stress-related physical symptoms; Scale 4 (Psychopathic Deviance) to discern feelings of anger and rage concerning the consequences of victimization; Scale 6 (Paranoia) to differentiate the victims' state of mistrust, suspicion, and feelings of having been "persecuted" by the trauma; Scale 7 (Psychasthenia) to encompass ruminative and obsessive qualities of the attempts to assimilate trauma-related imagery and affect; Scale 8 (Schizophrenia) to assess aspects of intrusive, unbidden imagery and bizarre sensory experience; Scale 9 (Hypomania) to reflect a tendency to reenact unassimilated distressing elements of the trauma; and Scale 0 (Social Introversion) to detect patterns of isolation and withdrawal. However, as logical, if simplistic, this approach may be as a starting point, it does not address the answer of what *profile configuration* on the MMPI is specific to PTSD for different types of traumatic events. Yet, despite the lack of a substantive body of literature on these questions, there are several studies which give us partial answers to some questions and point to future directions for more sophisticated MMPI studies of post-traumatic adaptation.

Research Studies Using the MMPI

Among the best-known studies to use the MMPI in the evaluation of World War II veterans was that of Archibald and Tuddenham (1965). They evaluated 57 combat veterans and 48 controls in a 20-year follow-up study and found at least two important results. First, the traumatic effects of combat were persistent over a 20-year span of time with relatively little decrease in symptom levels during this time period. Second, the combat veterans had a significantly higher score only on the Hypochondriasis Scale in a profile similar to that for known hysterical and anxiety neuroses.

More recently, there have been a number of studies on Vietnam War veterans, most of whom were patients at VA medical facilities. These studies are summarized in Table 5.2. Penk, Robinowitz, Roberts, Paterson, Dolan, and Atkinson (1981) compared veterans with high and low combat exposure. The veterans with heavy combat exposure had elevated scores on the MMPI Scales F, 8, 4, 7, 2, and 9 (T scores = 70–80). Somewhat similar results were obtained by Fairbank, Keane, and Malloy (1983) for 36 Vietnam Veterans diagnosed as suffering from PTSD. They found elevations on Scales F, 8, 2, 1, 7, 6, 4, and 3 and suggested that the two-point code 8–2 with a moderately elevated F-

Scale score may be suggestive of a PTSD profile. Additionally, they found that the PTSD-positive group were more depressed and anxious than the controls as measured by the Beck and Zung Depression Scales and the state-trait measures of anxiety. These results are similar to those found in Study I. In a follow-up study, Keane, Malloy, and Fairbank (1984) studied 100 Vietnam veterans and found that those with PTSD generated the profile produced in the earlier study (F, 8, 2).

Several other studies of Vietnam veterans have replicated the results of Keane and his associates in terms of the MMPI profile elevations on Scales F, 8, 2, 7, 9, 1, 4, and 6 (Burke & Mayer, 1985; Chaney, Williams, Cohn, & Vincent, 1984; Hyer, O'Leary, Saucer, Blount, Harrison, & Boudewyn, 1986). However, several other studies have suggested caution in using the 49-item MMPI subscale developed by Fairbank, Keane, and Malloy (1983) (see also Keane, Malloy, & Fairbank, 1984) since they were unable to replicate the earlier findings that a mean score of 35 or above was diagnostic of PTSD among World War II and Vietnam combat veterans (Gayton, Burchstead, & Matthews, 1986; Hyer, Fallon, Harrison, & Boudewyn, 1987; Query, Megran, & McDonald, 1986; Watson, Kucala, & Manifold, 1986).

TABLE 5.2
MMPI Studies of Post-Traumatic Stress Disorder

AUTHORS	DATE	SUBJECTS	2-POINT CODE
Archibald & Tuddenham	1962	WW II Veterans	2-3
Merbaum & Hefez	1976	Israeli & American Soldiers	8-2 & 8-7
Penk, Robinowitz, Roberts Patterson, Dolan, Atkinson	1981	Vietnam Veterans	8-4
Fairbank, Keane, Malloy	1983	Vietnam Veterans	8-2
Keane, Malloy, Fairbank	1984	Vietnam Veterans	8-2
Burke & Mayer	1985	Vietnam Veterans	8-2
Chaney, Williams, Cohn, Vincent	1984	Trauma Patients	8-9
Hyer, O'Leary, Saucer, Blount, Harrison, Boudewyn	1986	Vietnam Veterans	8-2
Gayton, Burchstead, Matthews	1986	Vietnam Veterans	PTSD Subscale
Hyer, Fallon, Harrison, Boudewyn	1987	Vietnam Veterans	PTSD Subscale
Query, Megram, McDonald	1986	Vietnam Veterans	PTSD Subscale
Frederick	1985	Child Trauma Victims	8-2
Watson, Kucala, Manifold	1986	Vietnam Veterans	PTSD Subscale
Wilson & Walker	1988	Civilian & Military Trauma	8-2

Finally, additional evidence of the potential utility of the MMPI in assessing PTSD can be found in Merbaum and Hefez's (1976) study of Israeli and American soldiers who had elevations of Scales F, 8, 2, 7, 1, 6, 4 (*T* scores = 70–90), although the patterning of the profiles differed somewhat for the two groups. In a study of MMPI profiles of adults and children after natural disasters and after sexual and physical abuse, the most common two-point code showed elevations on Scales F, 8, and 2 (Frederick, 1985). In our most recent work (see Chapter 9) we have found the F, 8, 2 elevation to be common among different trauma victims.

In summary, the studies currently available using the MMPI to assess PTSD in war veterans and other traumatized persons appear to be identifying both a profile configuration and a specific subscale that is indicative of traumatic stress syndrome. First, the profile configuration suggests that the Fake Scale is elevated (*T* scores = 70–90s), indicating, perhaps, *genuine distress* rather than symptom exaggeration or "faking bad." Second, the two-point code of 8-2/2-8 seems to reflect the core dimensions of PTSD in terms of *intrusive recollections* (8) and *restricted affect* (2). Further, elevations on Scales 1, 4, 6, and 7 also seem to be measuring some aspects of PTSD, including somatization, anger, mistrust, and obsessive fixation to the traumatic event. In terms of the specific MMPI PTSD subscale, Keane's 49-item scale, constructed on the basis of face validity and empirical methodology, holds promise as a shorter, more economical measure of PTSD. Thus, the purpose of Study II is to examine the relationship of Keane's 49-item, six-factor MMPI subscale to the eight PTSD dimensions assessed by the VESI as a means of determining the construct validity of each set of scales as well as their predictive validity in terms of specific PTSD symptom clusters.

Method

The subjects of this study were 59 Vietnam combat veterans who were seeking treatment at a VA readjustment counseling center or at a VA mental hygiene clinic in Cleveland, Ohio. The sample was predominately white (86%) and the age range was from 30 to 45 years, with a mean age of 36. About two-thirds of the sample were high school graduates and about 20% were college graduates. In terms of marital status, about one-third were divorced at the time of the study. Forty-four percent of the men were unemployed and mean income level for the sample was $14,000 a year. Seventy-eight percent of the veterans had enlisted in the military. The distribution by branch of service was: 63% Army; 29% Marine Corps; 5% Air Force; and 3% Navy. Ninety-eight percent of the men were honorably discharged.

Design

The VESI (Appendix A) and the Keane MMPI subscale were the two measures of PTSD. The MMPI subscale was developed by Keane, Malloy, and Fairbank (1984), who gave the MMPI to 200 male veterans at a VA hospital. A validation sample consisted of 100 men who had a positive diagnosis of PTSD and the control group consisted of 100 individuals without a PTSD diagnosis. A chi-square analysis was used to differentiate between the groups and resulted in the identification of 49 items. A "cutting score" was then applied to the PTSD subscale scores to ascertain the correct classification rate. The result indicated that a score of 30–35 identified the PTSD-positive group and was suggested as a decision rule for possible classification. However, as noted above, subsequent research has challenged the validity of the mean score method as a way to classify PTSD-positive subjects.

To assess the relationship between the Keane MMPI PTSD subscale and the VESI PTSD scales, it was decided to perform bivariate correlations between the variables comprising each of the scales. Second, the Keane PTSD subscale was subjected to a Varimax solution factor analysis, which produced four orthogonal dimensions. Finally, both the original Keane six-factor, 49-item MMPI subscale and our four-factor model were regressed onto the eight PTSD dimensions of the VESI using a stepwise multiple regression technique.

Results

Correlations between MMPI PTSD subscale and VESI PTSD score. Table 5.3 summarizes the results of the correlation between Keane's MMPI PTSD subscale and the VESI total PTSD score. As shown in Table 5.3, all six of the Keane MMPI PTSD subscales are significantly correlated with the VESI total PTSD score ($r = .46$ to $.66$, $p < .005$).

Factor analysis of Keane's 49-item MMPI PTSD subscale. Tables 5.4 to 5.7 present the results of the factor analysis of Keane's MMPI PTSD subscales using the Varimax solution for our sample of combat veterans. Contrary to the findings of Keane et al. (1984), we find that only four factors emerged from the analysis of 49 MMPI items: (1) anxiety,

TABLE 5.3
Relation Between Keane's MMPI PTSD Subscale
and VESI Total PTSD Score

KEANE'S MMPI PTSD SUBSCALE	VESI PTSD TOTAL SCORE (N = 59)	p VALUE
Survivor Guilt and Depression (B, C)[a]	.66	.0001
Hyperarousal and Sleep Disturbance (D)	.53	.0001
Numbing and Alienation (C)	.64	.0001
Re-Experiencing, Intrusive Thoughts and Dreams (B)	.46	.005
Memory and Concentration Problems (D)	.66	.0001
Fear of Loss of Control (D)	.58	.0001

[a] Letters refer to DSM-III-R diagnostic categories

depression, and guilt; (2) intrusive imagery and dissociation; (3) demoralization; and, (4) fear of loss of control.

Correlations between Wilson and Krauss MMPI subscale and VESI PTSD score. Table 5.8 presents the correlations between the VESI total PTSD score and the four factors of the MMPI PTSD subscales derived from the factor analysis. All four MMPI subscales are significantly correlated with the VESI total PTSD score ($r = .47$ to $.63$, $p < .0002$). The results parallel those found using Keane's six-factor model and are of a similar magnitude of association with the VESI measure of total PTSD.

Multivariate Analysis of MMPI Subscale Predictors of the VESI PTSD Dimensions. Table 5.9 summarizes the relationship of Keane's MMPI PTSD subscales to the prediction of each of the PTSD dimensions measured by the VESI. The results of the regression analysis are all highly significant ($R^2 = .23$ to $.55$, $p < .0001$). Specifically, however, the subscale *survivor guilt/depression* was predictive of the VESI PTSD factors of depression, sensation seeking, and intimacy conflict. The *numbing/alienation* subscale predicted the PTSD dimensions of stigmatization, alienation, anger/rage, intrusive imagery, and the total PTSD score. The remaining VESI PTSD factor, physical symptoms, was predicted by the Keane subscale *hyperarousal/sleep disturbance.*

Table 5.10 presents a replication of the previous regression model using the four-factor model of the MMPI PTSD subscales. Once again, the results of the analysis are all highly significant ($R^2 = .19$ to $.42$, $p < .0001$). As shown in Table 5.10, the pattern of results is different than that obtained with the Keane subscales. The *anxiety, depression,*

TABLE 5.4
Wilson and Krauss Factor Analysis of Keane's MMPI PTSD Subscale Varimax Solution—4 Factors

Factor 1: Anxiety, Depression, and Guilt

MMPI Item	LOADING
8. My daily life is full of things that keep me interested. (*)	.59
39. At times I feel like smashing things.	.58
57. I am a good mixer. (*)	.53
67. I wish I could be as happy as others seem to be.	.70
76. Most of the time I feel blue.	.59
94. I regret things more often than others seem to.	.46
107. I am happy most of the time. (*)	.49
137. I believe my home life is as pleasant as that of most people I know. (*)	.59
147. I have often lost out on things because I couldn't make up my mind soon enough.	.69
152. Most nights I go to sleep without thoughts or ideas bothering me. (*)	.46
217. I frequently find myself worrying about something.	.40
336. I easily become impatient with people.	.47
338. I have certainly had more than my share of things to worry about.	.44
359. Sometimes some unimportant thought will run through my mind and bother me for days.	.39
366. Even when I am with people I feel lonely much of the time.	.46
372. I have sometimes felt that difficulties were piling up so high that I could not overcome them.	.67
376. It makes me feel like a failure when I hear the success of someone I know well.	.55

% of Variance = 6.51

* Answered False

guilt subscale predicted four of the VESI dimensions of PTSD: (1) depression; (2) physical symptoms; (3) sensation seeking; and (4) total PTSD score. The remaining four dimensions of PTSD measured by the VESI (stigmatization/alienation, anger/rage, intrusive imagery, and intimacy conflict) were all predicted by the MMPI subscale *intrusive imagery/dissociation*. Thus, of the four subscale factors we identified, only two were predictive of the VESI dimensions of PTSD.

Discussion

The results of Study II have provided additional support regarding the construct validity of the VESI as an objective, self-report measure of PTSD in Vietnam veterans and in further differentiating the factors that predict the different symptoms of the stress response syndrome.

TABLE 5.5

Factor 2: Intrusive Imagery and Dissociation

MMPI Item	Loading
2. I have a good appetite.	.41
3. I wake up fresh and rested each morning. (*)	.24
15. Once in a while I think of things too bad to talk about.	.42
33. I have had very peculiar and strange experiences.	.81
72. I am troubled by discomfort in the pit of my stomach.	.52
114. Often I feel as if there were a tight band about my head.	.41
156. I have had periods in which I carried on activities without knowing later what I had been doing.	.60
241. I dream frequently about things that are best kept to myself.	.53
286. I am never happier than when I am alone.	.33
303. I am so touchy on some subjects that I can't talk about them.	.57
314. Once in a while I think of things too bad to talk about.	.48
323. I have had very peculiar and strange experiences.	.75
349. I have strange and peculiar thoughts.	.54
350. I hear strange things when I am alone.	.48
384. Whenever possible I avoid being in a crowd.	.50
% of Variance = 7.51	

* Answered False

TABLE 5.6

Factor 3: Demoralization

MMPI Item	Loading
16. I am sure I get a raw deal out of life.	.75
24. No one seem to understand me.	.41
32. I find it hard to keep my mind on a task or job.	.44
61. I have not led the right kind of life.	.53
88. I usually feel that life is worthwhile. (*)	.62
104. I don't seem to care what happens to me.	.60
106. Much of the time I feel as if I have done something wrong or evil.	.43
339. Most of the time I wish I were dead.	.61
358. Bad words, often terrible words, come into my mind and I cannot get rid of them.	.55
% of Variance = 4.73	

* Answered False

First, both Keane's six-factor MMPI subscale and our four-factor model of the scale show strong correlations to the VESI total PTSD score. When both sets of results are combined, the following subscale factors of PTSD emerge as bivariate associations to the VESI PTSD scale: survivor guilt and depression; intrusive imagery; fear of loss of control; hyperarousal and sleep disturbance; numbing and alienation; memory

TABLE 5.7

Factor 4: Fear of Loss of Control	
MMPI Item	Loading
22. At times I have fits of laughing and crying that I cannot control	.77
31. I have nightmares every few nights.	.48
40. Most of the time I would rather sit and daydream than do anything else.	.40
43. My sleep is fitful and disturbed	.53
97. At times I have the strong urge to do something harmful or shocking.	.55
139. Sometimes I feel as if I must injure either myself or someone else.	.66
182. I am afraid of losing my mind.	.59
326. At times I have fits of laughing or crying that I cannot control.	.81
% of Variance = 4.63	

TABLE 5.8
Correlation Between Wilson and Krauss MMPI PTSD Subscale and VESI Total PTSD Score

WILSON AND KRAUS MMPI PTSD SUBSCALE	VESI PTSD TOTAL SCORE (N = 59)	p VALUE
Anxiety, Depression, Guilt (B, C)[a]	.63	.0001
Intrusive Imagery/Dissociation (B)	.57	.0001
Demoralization (C)	.59	.0001
Fear of Loss of Control (D)	.47	.0002

[a] Letters refer to DSM-III-R diagnostic criteria

loss and problems of concentration; and demoralization. Clearly, these distinct factors closely correspond to the diagnostic criteria in the DSM-III-R, which contains a four-category classificatory scheme that includes three clusters of symptoms: (B) intrusive reexperiencing or reenactment; (C) avoidance and numbing responses; and, (D) physiological hyper-reactivity. As noted in Tables 5.3 and 5.8, both MMPI PTSD subscales represent symptoms in each of the diagnostic categories and lend support to the concept of the stress syndrome as cyclical in nature, i.e., alternating between cycles of intrusion and avoidance (Horowitz, 1986). This also supports a dual stress model (Laufer, Frey-Wouters, & Gallops, 1985) in which the nature of the traumatization (e.g., atrocities) and of the ego defenses determines the particular pattern of symptom expression,

TABLE 5.9
Stepwise Multiple Regression Analysis of Keane's
MMPI Subscale and VESI PTSD Dimensions

VESI PTSD DIMENSION	KEANE MMPI PTSD SUBSCALE BEST PREDICTOR	F	R²	p
Depression	Survivor Guilt/Depression	52.96	.48	.0001
Physical Symptoms	Hyperarousal & Sleep Disturbance	32.87	.37	.0001
Stigmatization/Alienation	Numbing/Alienation	34.89	.38	.0001
Sensation Seeking	Survivor Guilt/Depression	28.57	.33	.0001
Anger/Rage	Numbing/Alienation	23.16	.29	.0001
Intrusive Imagery	Numbing/Alienation	39.86	.41	.0001
Intimacy Conflict	Survivor Guilt/Depression	16.65	.23	.0001
Total PTSD Score	Numbing/Alienation	34.17	.55	.0001

TABLE 5.10
Stepwise Multiple Regression Analysis of Wilson and Krauss
MMPI PTSD Subscale and VESI PTSD Dimensions

VESI PTSD SUBSCALE	WILSON AND KRAUSS MMPI SUBSCALE BEST PREDICTOR	F	R²	p
Depression	Anxiety, Depression, Guilt	44.33	.42	.0001
Physical Symptoms	Anxiety, Depression, Guilt	23.54	.29	.0001
Stigmatization/Alienation	Intrusive Imagery/Dissociation	26.65	.32	.0001
Sensation Seeking	Anxiety, Depression, Guilt	21.45	.27	.0001
Anger/Rage	Intrusive Imagery/Dissociation	16.10	.22	.0001
Intrusive Imagery	Intrusive Imagery/Dissociation	33.06	.37	.0001
Intimacy Conflict	Intrusive Imagery/Dissociation	13.32	.19	.0006
Total PTSD Score	Anxiety, Depression, Guilt	37.81	.40	.0001

i.e., reexperiencing versus denial. Although both conceptual models have coherent theoretical formulations which can organize the empirical findings, the results of the multivariate analysis are most thought provoking since they generated somewhat different predictors of the eight VESI dimensions of PTSD.

In the Keane six-factor MMPI subscale of PTSD, the *numbing of responsiveness and alienation* measure was the best predictor of the VESI PTSD dimensions of: (1) stigmatization/alienation; (2) anger/rage; (3) intrusive imagery; and, (4) total PTSD. In contrast, the Wilson and Krauss four-factor model found that the subscale of *intrusive imagery/ dissociation* predicted the same dimensions of PTSD, including intimacy conflict but minus the total PTSD score. This finding is especially interesting since the data are based on the same sample of veterans but with different factor structures. Yet it is possible to argue that strong *avoidance* tendencies, as evidenced by the factor numbing of responsiveness, could lead to feelings of alienation, anger over one's emotional condition, states of affective flooding, and intrusive imagery as well as high levels of distress. Similarly, a person with frequent episodes of *reexperiencing* trauma, as implied by the factor intrusion/dissociation, may also develop this same cluster of symptoms.

As noted in Chapter 1, it is possible to understand these differences in symptom pattern expression as a function of *cognitive style*, i.e., how the individual attempts to assimilate traumatic material stored in memory. If the person employs a cognitive style which reduces information processing, one characterized by constriction of attention (selective attention), rigid and narrow bands of search persistence, and category width utilization in problem solving and thinking, then this form of avoidance can be thought of as a control operation designed to enhance a psychological sense of security and to ward off upsetting thoughts and feelings which disrupt the equilibrium produced by the cognitive style of information processing. Thus, when ego controls modulating this process fail, the person may develop a self-image as victimized and tainted by the trauma (stigmatization) and subsequently feel angry and flooded with distressing imagery. Clearly, this model of cognitive style could readily account for the result produced by Keane's six-factor MMPI PTSD subscale and is consistent with the literature on cognitive style and personality processes (e.g., Aronoff & Wilson, 1985; Goldstein & Blackman, 1978).

If one extends the model of cognitive styles of information processing of traumatic material to the other set of findings from the four-factor predictive model of the VESI dimensions of PTSD, an alternative form of assimilation may be discerned. Where the factor intrusive imagery/ dissociation predicts the cluster of symptoms described above, it may be the case that the individual engages in the *augmenting* of the averaged evoked potential (AEP) of stimuli in the brain produced by internal or external stimuli (Aronoff & Wilson, 1985; Byrne, 1961; Gardner, Jackson, & Messick, 1960; Wilson et al., 1988). As noted by Zuckerman (1983),

the difference between augmenters and reducers is produced by their different responses to high intensities of stimulation. At these high intensities, the augmenter shows additional increase in magnitude of AEP, and the reducer shows an inhibition of response relative to responses to stimuli of lesser intensity. (p. 51)

In the context of the present discussion, persons with augmenting tendencies are more likely to have a cognitive style in which there is *more* attention paid to internal thoughts and imagery, greater rumination and reflection over traumatic episodes, and less ability to impose controls over the influx of imagery and affect that is distressing. Thus, given this modality of processing traumatic material, it is also possible that the individual would feel stigmatized by what happened in the trauma, angry and periodically flooded with intrusive imagery, and prone to interpersonal conflict, as found by the predictor variable in the four-factor model.

What about the results from the multivariate analysis? In what ways are they consistent with or contrary to the conceptual framework presented above? First, both Keane's scale and the four-factor model predicted the VESI PTSD dimensions *depression* and *sensation seeking* from the MMPI subscales of depression and guilt. It is expected, of course, that the VESI measure of depression would be predicted by the MMPI subscale of depression since both are similar constructs of psychopathology and therefore share a common variance. As found in Study I and also by Fairbank, Keane, and Malloy (1983), veterans with PTSD had higher scores on depression and anxiety. Since combat in warfare commonly involves *loss* (buddies, ideology, sense of self, witnessing atrocity) and *life threat*, it is expected that depression would be a component of PTSD, which may also have a biological component that results from decreased levels of catecholamines, serotonin, and endogenous opioid production (Janowsky, Risch, & Neborsky, 1986). As discussed in Chapter 2, a psychobiological model of PTSD includes a chronic overactivation of these neurophysiological mechanisms which may, in turn, create depressive states as well as the motive of sensation seeking which is associated with the inverse effect of depression, i.e., anxiolytic, euphoric, relaxed, calm, and sedate (Janowsky, Risch, & Neborsky, 1986; van der Kolk, 1987).

As noted earlier, sensation seeking can be considered a form of coping with PTSD that induces hyperaroused states that parallel the level of arousal experienced in combat and leads to sensation-seeking activities that block the onset of distressing intrusive imagery and painful affect associated with the trauma. However, when the sensation-seeking behaviors are terminated, the person may undergo opiate withdrawal caused by an excessive noradrenergic hyperactivity (Braun, 1984; van der Kolk, Krystal, & Greenberg, 1984; van der Kolk, 1987). Consistent with this model of the relationship between depression and hyperarousal states, the results also indicated that Keane's MMPI subscale *hyperarousal and sleep disturbance* and our four-factor variable of *anxiety, depression, and guilt* predicted the VESI PTSD dimension of physical symptoms. Viewed from the conceptual perspective of the cognitive and biological components of the avoidance and intrusion cycles of PTSD, these results suggest that there are alternative pathways by which psychological symptoms can be expressed in somatic and psychological ways as part of the disorder.

In conclusion, the combined results from Study I and Study II have provided additional support for the VESI as a measure of PTSD among Vietnam veterans. The results of Study I show strong correlations between the eight dimensions of PTSD assessed by the VESI and the Beck Depression Inventory, the Zuckerman Sensation Seeking Scales, and the Impact of Event Scale. In Study II both the Keane six-factor, 49-item MMPI PTSD subscale and the four-factor model of it were highly correlated with the VESI dimension of PTSD. Moreover, the results of the factor analysis of the MMPI subscale produced sets of symptom clusters that are consistent with the DSM-III-R classificatory schema: (1) anxiety, depression, guilt; (2) intrusive imagery/dissociation; (3) demoralization; and, (4) fear of loss of control. The results of the regression analysis indicated that the VESI PTSD dimensions of depression and sensation seeking were predicted from the MMPI subscales of depression and guilt.

It was suggested that both depression and sensation seeking have a neurophysiological *and* a psychological basis that are interrelated. The precipitating trauma is an external, environmental cause that, in turn, alters the internal brain chemistry that regulates affect, especially the emotional states of anxiety and depression (Janowsky, Risch, & Neborsky, 1986). It was further argued that a psychobiological model of PTSD could readily account for the disparate findings produced by Keane's six-factor model versus the four-factor model obtained by this study. It was suggested that Keane's MMPI subscale was associated with the prediction of PTSD symptoms in a cognitively reducing style of information processing. On the other hand, the four-factor MMPI subscale *intrusive imagery/dissociation* was related to a cognitive style that *augmented* the attempts to assimilate traumatic material incongruent with self-schemata. Thus, consistent with conceptions of PTSD as a dual stress response syndrome (denial vs. reexperiencing), a psychobiological model, and an information-processing model (Horowitz, 1986; Laufer et al., 1985; van der Kolk, 1987; Wilson, 1988a), the results of this study suggest that alternative pathways of adaptation may be discerned by the interactive effects of cognitive style and underlying psychological processes.

6

The Day of Infamy:
The Legacy of
Pearl Harbor

with ZEV HAREL and BOAZ KAHANA

The history of war is characterized by critical events which influence and shape the future of nations in different directions. Nowhere was this more evident than on December 7, 1941, when Japan attacked the United States at Pearl Harbor in Hawaii and began America's involvement in World War II. The "Day of Infamy," as President Roosevelt called it, was the result of a carefully planned military strategy designed by the Japanese Naval Fleet Commander Admiral Isoroku Yamamota. The surprise attack, launched from a fleet of Japanese ships located 200 miles north of the Hawaiian island of Oahu under the command of Admiral Chuichi Nagumo, was a brilliant military success.

This Day of Infamy, forever recorded in history, has also caught the minds and souls of over 11,000 Pearl Harbor survivors and their families, who to this day recall with remarkable accuracy the scenes of that momentous occasion. This chapter will describe the findings regarding post-war adaptation and related results based on both survey data and personal interviews with the survivors.

In order to better understand Pearl Harbor survivors both in terms of post-traumatic stress and as human beings in their elderly years, a brief description of the attack on Pearl Harbor and its sequelae on the

---

This chapter was prepared with the assistance of Alice J. Walker.

survivors is useful. This description is, of necessity, a general portrayal of the attack; detailed historical analyses (e.g., Wallin, 1968) provide a more complete understanding.

The central objectives of the attack were twofold. First, to immobilize U.S. airbases located at Ford Island, Wheeler Field, Pearl Harbor and at other bases on Oahu, including Hickam, Ewa, Bellows, and Kaneohe. Second, to destroy the U.S. Pacific naval fleet moored in the cloverleaf-shaped inlet of Pearl Harbor. The Japanese plan called for two tandem aerial assaults on the military objectives. The first wave of 189 planes was led by commander Mitsuo Fuchida and attacked at 7:55 A.M at Ford Island and Wheeler Field. The second wave, at 8:50 A.M., consisted of 171 planes; it was led by commander Shigekazu Shimazaki and included horizontal dive bombers, fighters, and torpedo planes (Wallin, 1968). When the attack was finished there were 2,251 U.S. military personnel killed in action. An additional 1,119 Navy, Army, and Marines were wounded in the surprise attack. The result of the air seize was extensive damage to the airbases on Oahu and the ships moored at Pearl Harbor: *Pennsylvania, Helena, Utah, Nevada, Arizona, California, West Virginia, Raleigh, Maryland, Tennessee, Honolulu, Vestal, Oglala, Shaw, Floating Dry Dock Number Two, Cassin, Downes, Curtiss,* and others (Wallin, 1968).

In the chaotic confusion which reigned throughout the attack, the U.S. military forces were directly and indirectly exposed to many traumatically stressful events. On the U.S.S. *Arizona,* Lt. Commander S.G. Fuqua stated:

> I was in the ward room eating breakfast about 0755 when a short signal on the ship's air raid alarm was made. I immediately went to the phone and called the Officer-of-the-Deck to sound general quarters and then shortly thereafter ran up to the starboard side of the quarter deck to see if he had received word. On coming out of the war room hatch on the port side, I saw a Japanese plane go by, the machine guns firing, at an altitude of about 100 feet. As I was running forward on the starboard side of the quarter deck, approximately by the starboard gangway, I was apparently knocked out by the blast of a bomb which I learned later had struck the face plate of #4 turret on the starboard side and had glanced off and gone through the deck just forward of the captain's hatch, penetrating the decks and exploding on the third deck. When I came to and got up off the deck, the ship was a mass of flames amidships on the boat deck and the deck aft was awash

to about frame 90. The anti-aircraft battery and machine guns apparently were still firing at this time. Some of the ARIZONA boats had pulled clear of the oil and were lying off the stern. (Wallin, 1968, p. 304)

On the U.S.S. *West Virginia*, Lt. Commander T.T. Beattie described his experiences in poignant detail.

About five minutes to eight I was in the wardroom just finishing breakfast, when word came over the loud speaker from the officer-of-the-deck, "away fire and rescue party." This was followed immediately by a second announcement over the loud speaker, "Japanese are attacking, all hands General Quarters," and the general alarm was rung.

I heard several dull explosions coming from other battleships. Immediately I left the wardroom and ran up the starboard passageway to the bridge. The Captain was just ahead of me and proceeding in the same direction.

At this time the ship listed at least five or six degrees and was steadily listing more to port. The Captain and I went to the conning tower, our battle stations, and at this time dive bombing attacks started to take place and numerous explosions were felt throughout the ship. Upon testing our communications with central station and to the guns we found they were disrupted. I suggested to the Captain as long as no communications were in the battle conning tower that we leave there and attempt to establish messenger communication and try to save the ship. We went out on the starboard side of the bridge discussing what to do. During all this time extremely heavy bombing and strafing attacks occurred. The ship was constantly shaken by bomb hits.

The Captain doubled up with a groan and stated that he had been wounded. I saw that he had been hit in the stomach probably by a large piece of shrapnel and was very seriously wounded. He then sank to the deck and I loosened his collar. I then sent a messenger for a pharmacist's mate to assist the Captain.

Just then the U.S.S. ARIZONA's forward magazines blew up with a tremendous explosion and large sheets of flame shot skyward, and I began to wonder about our own magazines and whether they were being flooded. I posted a man with the Captain and went down to the forecastle where a number of the crew and officers had gathered. I got hold of a chief turret captain to check immediately on the magazines and to flood them if they were not flooded at this time. Large sheets of flame and several fires started aft. Burning fuel oil from the U.S.S. ARIZONA floated down on the stern of the ship. Just then the gunnery officer, Lieutenant Commander Berthold, came aboard and I asked him to try to flood the forward magazines. Shortly thereafter I was informed that the after magazines were completely flooded but that they were unable to flood the forward magazines as the water was now almost to the main deck. (Wallin, 1968, p. 297)

These two vignettes provide us with an indication of how extreme the stressors were during the attack, which lasted a total of about two hours. The enemy attack was sudden, effective, well planned, and deadly. It caught the U.S. forces in a moment of vulnerability during a quiet, tropical dawn on a sleepy Sunday morning. The torpedoes, 800-kilogram armor-piercing bombs dropped from an altitude of 10,000 feet, made the damaged ships look like discarded and junked salvage. Oil and gasoline fires burned on many of the ships and the wounded had to be evacuated. Wherever possible, antiaircraft fire was directed at the attacking planes, 29 of which were shot down. When it was all over, several of the U.S. ships were sunk, including the U.S.S. *Arizona,* which became a permanent tomb for 1,100 men who went down in the azure waters of the harbor.

The Japanese attack on Pearl Harbor was instrumental in shaping the U.S. military involvement in World War II. But apart from the historical questions, there are critical questions to be explored concerning the effects of this experience on the lives of survivors of the Pearl Harbor attack.

What was the psychic legacy of the survivors of Pearl Harbor? What impact did the Day of Infamy have on their lives afterward? Are the images and emotions of that day still alive in memory and being? Does such a special historical experience serve to organize the self-structure in ways that shape life-course development, including adjustment to aging?

The questions raised above were explored in a pilot study conducted at the 45th reunion of the Pearl Harbor Survivors Association (PHSA) in Honolulu, Hawaii, the week of December 2–9, 1986. The decision to conduct this study was made for several reasons pertaining to interest in post-traumatic syndromes and aging. First, the survivors of the attack are a unique historical group who went from being victims of an act of war to heroic victors who defeated the enemy in the waters and islands of the South Pacific. Second, there is surprisingly little research on this population of survivors and virtually no published data on traumatic stress reactions for this group of veterans. Third, the study permitted us to explore a new conceptual approach to PTSD, one that I have termed *contextual PTSD*. Stated differently, will survivors of a historically profound event (e.g., Pearl Harbor) freely report symptom levels of PTSD in the *context* of a heroic national event from which they ultimately emerged in World War II as victorious and celebrated? Does such a historical, heroic context permit the admission of symptoms of PTSD (e.g., nightmares of the attack) which the survivor would be less willing to express without such a psychohistorical context by which to organize the experience.

BACKGROUND TO THE STUDY

In 1985, I had the opportunity to be a visiting scholar and consultant to the U.S. Army Medical Center in Honolulu, Hawaii. During my visit there and in collaboration with Col. Dionisious ("Dan") Devaris, M.D., then Chief of Liaison Consulting Psychiatry, I learned that there had been no systematic follow-up study on the psychiatric sequelae of the survivors of the Japanese attack at Pearl Harbor in 1941. Through Col. Devaris and his efforts I learned of the existence of the Pearl Harbor Survivors Association (PHSA), a national organization made up of approximately 11,000 members. Subsequent contacts were then made with Mr. Tom Stockett, past president of PHSA, who learned of my interest in conducting a study of the membership. In 1986, the 45th reunion of the attack was held in Hawaii and afforded the opportunity to survey the 800 members who traveled to the conference. Together with my colleagues Zev Harel and Boaz Kahana, we developed a 16-page questionnaire that would provide information for a series of research questions and hypotheses designed to measure combat experiences in World War II; reactions to the Pearl Harbor attack; and the impact of their experiences on coping and the aging process (see Appendix B). We received about 300 completed questionnaires within two months of the reunion and performed statistical analyses on the first wave of responses, a sample of 250. This chapter reports on the first set of analyses from this sample and is generally limited to an examination of (1) PTSD symptoms in this population; (2) predictors of stress response syndromes; and, (3) predictors of affect balance in this population. Future publications will contain more detailed and elaborate multivariate analyses of the data.

METHOD

The Pearl Harbor Research Questionnaire (PHRQ)

The PHRQ was developed specifically for the 45th reunion of the Pearl Harbor Survivors Association and was approved by the board of directors of the PHSA. The questionnaire built on the seminal works of Elder and Clipp (1988) on aging World War II veterans; Laufer's (1985) work with war stress measures among Vietnam veterans; Wilson and Krauss' (1985) Vietnam Era Stress Inventory; and the research of Kahana, Harel, and Kahana (1988) on Holocaust survivors. The PHRQ contains three parts (see Appendix B). Part I was designed to measure combat and military service in World War II and included sections on (A) general military information (e.g., branch of service, years of active duty, military occupational specialty); (B) the personal experiences on December 7, 1941; (C) locations of World War II duty; (D) recollections of the attack at Pearl Harbor; and, (E) military duty after Pearl Harbor. Several measures of war stress were incorporated in Part I: (1) combat exposure; (2) exposure to war-related stress; (3) type of service; (4) internment in prisoner of war camps; and, (5) subjective stress in combat and military roles.

Combat Exposure measures the extent and intensity of actual combat exposure the veteran encountered, such as firing a weapon, participating in the killing of enemy soldiers, and being placed in life-or-death situations. This variable reflects active participation in "traditional" warfare situations. *Exposure to Stress* is based on Wilson and Krauss' (1985) stressor dimension of exposure to death, dying, and destruction as well as on Laufer's (1985) measure of witnessing or participating in atrocities. *Type of Service* indicates the length of time the individual was involved in military service, his primary military occupational specialty, place(s) of service, and rank. *War Stress* refers to the subjective perception of war stress and assessed the veterans' rating of duty assignment in the theater served on a four-point Likert scale ranging from "not at all stressful" to "extremely stressful."

Additionally, *The Pearl Harbor Post-Traumatic Stress Disorder Symptom Checklist* is a 17-item, "yes-no" format questionnaire designed to assess the diagnostic criteria for PTSD *specifically* in the context of the Japanese attack on Pearl Harbor on December 7, 1941. The instructions ask the veteran to indicate whether he had recollections of the 1941 event during the last year (1986). The 17 items were divided into five groups of PTSD symptoms: (1) intrusion; (2) avoidance; (3) survivor guilt; (4) hyperarousal; and, (5) associated features. The purpose of including this *context-specific* measure of PTSD was to attempt to determine whether the veteran would report higher symptom levels of PTSD within the framework of a psychohistorical event that was viewed as heroic as compared to a generic measure of the stress syndrome.

Part II of the PHRQ was constructed to assess different aspects of the reentry into civilian life following World War II and included measures of health appraisal, contacts with fellow servicemen, locus of control, affect balance (consists of two sets of items measuring positive and negative affect), self-disclosure of war experiences to significant others, and measures of PTSD at reentry and during 1986. Additionally, there were open-ended items that permitted the veteran to comment in a personal way on the meaning of his experiences in World War II and at Pearl Harbor. Finally, Part III of the PHRQ elicited standard demographic characteristics. In all, the questionnaire contained 175 items and took about one hour to complete, including writing descriptive free-response material to seven questions.

Sample Characteristics

The sample of 250 members of the PHSA is unique in several ways. First, it represents those who volunteered to complete the questionnaire and return it to us. At present, there is no way of knowing whether or not this wave of respondents is representative of the larger membership of the PHSA or of other survivors who do not belong to the organization. Second, this sample represents only those who were healthy enough to attend the 45th reunion in Hawaii. Thus, it is possible that this group of survivors may be different in important ways from other veterans who could not make the long trip to Honolulu to attend this historic meeting. However, within the cohort group, the first 50 sets were compared with the next four sets of 50 questionnaires and no significant differences were found on any of the variables, a fact which gives some confidence in the representativeness of the sample in terms of those who attended the reunion. And in another set of data obtained on 30 survivors who did not attend the reunion and were members of a local chapter located in Ohio, no significant differences were found in the responses, a fact which bolsters the strength of the findings. I am currently conducting a survey of those Pearl Harbor survivors who did not participate in the 45th reunion to determine any possible differences between the two populations.

In 1986 the mean age of the survivors was 65, with a range of 62 to 85 years. The average age of the veterans at the time of the attack in 1941 was 19 years. Seventy-two percent of our sample served duty in the U.S. Navy and 18% were in the Army. The others, representing less than 15% of the sample, were in the Marine and Air Corps. Nearly all of the men (93%) enlisted for military service and 71% had graduated from high school or had higher education. In terms of demographic variables, 92% of the men are married and only 17% have been divorced. In terms of religious affiliation, the majority of the veterans (61%) were Protestant and 28% were Catholic. Interestingly, only half of the survivors used the G.I. Bill after the war.

RESULTS

Degree of Combat Exposure

Table 6.1 describes the types and degrees of combat exposure. As evidenced from the table, the veterans reported high levels of combat exposure, which includes firing weapons at the enemy; being subjected to enemy fire; seeing unit members killed and wounded in action; seeing towns destroyed by combat; and experiencing life-and-death situations.

Contextual PTSD

Table 6.2 summarizes the results of the descriptive analysis of PTSD symptoms reported in 1986 within the context of the Japanese attack at Pearl Harbor. The results are organized according to the diagnostic categories for PTSD in the DSM-III-R manual (APA, 1987). The table shows the results for PTSD in terms of a psychohistorical context. In 1986, 65% of the veterans reported experiencing some type of intrusive imagery related to the attack in 1941. Recurring thoughts and memories which sometimes "just pop into my mind" were most prevalent (i.e. = 79%). Dreams of the attack were reported by 29% of the veterans. Intrusive symptoms of PTSD were reported four times as often as were symptoms characteristic of avoidance. Yet, 45 years later one-third of the veterans reported difficulty in expressing their feelings about what

TABLE 6.1
Degree of Combat Exposure in World War II

TYPE OF COMBAT EXPOSURE IN WORLD WAR II	PERCENTAGE OF SAMPLE (N = 250)
Fired a weapon at the enemy	61%
Killed someone	46%
Under enemy fire	95%
Wounded by enemy action	17%
Hospitalized due to a wound	8%
Received life-threatening wound	2%
Received a wound which left me impaired	6%
Received a wound which led to discharge	3%
Unit members killed	8%
Unit members wounded	7%
Unit members killed and wounded	58%
Friends, family or relatives killed	23%
Friends, family or relatives wounded	5%
Friends, family or relatives killed and wounded	36%
Saw allies killed	5%
Saw allies wounded	8%
Saw allies killed and wounded	54%
Saw enemy killed	20%
Saw enemy wounded	3%
Saw enemy killed and wounded	32%
Saw allies tortured	3%
Saw allies mutilated	2%
Saw allies tortured and mutilated	2%
Saw enemy tortured	4%
Saw and participated in enemy torture	1%
Saw towns destroyed by combat	68%
Saw civilians killed	2%
Saw civilians wounded	4%
Saw civilians killed and wounded	20%
Under direct attack by enemy	
Once or twice	25%
Some	20%
Many times	50%
Experienced a war incident that was so awful that it changed views on life	23%
Experienced a life-or-death situation	66%
Experienced unbearable combat fatigue	28%

happened at Pearl Harbor. Thirteen percent indicated that they do not remember much of what happened at Pearl Harbor and 6% found it difficult to be close to people after the attack. On the average, 17% of the Pearl Harbor survivors reported avoidance of some or all aspects of the Japanese attack at Pearl Harbor. Hyperarousal and startle responses are still present in one-quarter of the veterans. Survivor guilt was reported by 42% of the veterans. Approximately 42% of the veterans reported having anger or bad feelings toward the Japanese and avoid them when possible. Twenty-seven percent reported having difficulty going to sleep or staying asleep. Two-thirds of the veterans believed that the Pearl Harbor experience had a deep influence on the course of their life. Almost all of the veterans (89%) had returned to Hawaii to visit Pearl Harbor and reported having special feelings on December 7, the day of the attack.

PTSD Symptoms Reported at Reentry
and in 1986

Table 6.3 presents the percentage of PTSD symptoms reported at reentry and within the last year (1986). As expected in terms of the context-specific hypothesis, symptoms of PTSD were reported less often at these periods than symptoms reported specific to the attack at Pearl Harbor. Intrusive imagery was the most frequently reported symptom. On the average, 23% of the veterans reported some type of reexperiencing at reentry, which decreased to 12% reporting within the last year. One-quarter of the veterans reported "nightmares in which I relive my World War II experiences" at reentry. Seven percent reported nightmares related to war experiences within the last year. On the average, intrusive symptoms decreased by 48% from reentry to 1986. However, "anger at what actually happened during the war" was one of the symptoms most resistant to change. At reentry 35% of the veterans reported anger, which decreased to only 29% in 1986. One-quarter of the survivors still feel angry at what happened during the war.

On the average, avoidance symptoms were reported half as frequently as intrusive symptoms at reentry and in 1986. About 20% of the veterans reported that it was "hard to express my feelings" and "avoided talking about the war" at reentry and half as many reported those symptoms in 1986. On the whole, symptoms of avoidance were the most resistant to change.

TABLE 6.2
PTSD Symptoms in 1986 Reported Specific to Japanese Attack at Pearl Harbor

PTSD SYMPTOM DIMENSION	PERCENT (N = 250)
INTRUSION (DSM-III-R-B)	
I have had, at times, recurring thoughts about "the day of infamy" (December 7, 1941) and what happened at Pearl Harbor	87%
I have had, at times, dreams of the attack on Pearl Harbor	29%
Thoughts about the attack at Pearl Harbor sometimes just pop into my mind	73%
I have had, at times, memories of the bombed ships and airfields at Pearl Harbor	77%
I have had, at times, memories of the explosions, screaming and confusion at Pearl Harbor on the Day of Infamy	59%
AVOIDANCE (DSM-III-R-C)	
I sometimes find it difficult to express my feelings about what happened at Pearl Harbor	32%
I can not remember much of what happened at Pearl Harbor	13%
After the attack at Pearl Harbor, I found it difficult to be real close to people	6%
HYPERAROUSAL (DSM-III-R-D)	
When I hear the sounds of certain engine noises, it reminds me of the Pearl Harbor attack	22%
I am easily startled or made "jumpy" by loud or unexpected noises	24%
SURVIVOR GUILT	
Sometimes I wonder why I survived the Japanese attack and my buddies died	42%
ASSOCIATED FEATURES	
On December 7, I have special feelings about the attack on Pearl Harbor	90%
I have, at times, bad feelings toward Japanese people and avoid them when I can	36%
I have, at times, difficulty going to sleep or staying asleep	27%
Even today I still have, at times, anger at the Japanese for the attack on Pearl Harbor	47%
Looking back, I believe that the Pearl Harbor experience had a deep influence on the course of my life	67%
I have returned to Hawaii to visit Pearl Harbor	89%

Symptoms of hyperarousal were reported at approximately the same frequency as intrusion (21% at reentry and 10.5% in 1986). Thirty percent of the veterans reported that they "startled easily" at reentry. In 1986 this number was reduced to 12% reporting a startle response. "Difficulty in sleeping" continued to be a problem for 16% of the veterans, which was only a slight decrease from the 22% reporting sleeping problems at reentry. One-fifth of the veterans reported that at reentry it was "hard to settle-down, get their feet on the ground," which decreased by 85% to only 3% reporting feeling this way in 1986. Twenty-eight percent felt "an urge to catch-up on living" at reentry as compared to half as many reporting this feeling within the last year.

Overall, there was a 47% decrease in the number of veterans reporting symptoms in 1986 as compared with reentry. However, it is unclear whether the veterans reporting symptoms at reentry were now experiencing fewer symptoms or whether some had improved while others had developed symptoms. Alternatively, symptoms may have abated after reentry from World War II into civilian life only to reappear after retirement.

Correlates of the Three Measures of PTSD

Table 6.4 summarizes the bivariate correlations between select demographic measures, war stress, comradeship, personal attributes, and the three measures of PTSD: (1) at reentry; (2) in 1986; and, (3) in the Pearl Harbor context. The results indicate that lower prewar education is significantly correlated with PTSD symptoms at reentry ($r = .21$, $p < .05$). The veteran's use of the G.I. Bill is also significantly correlated with PTSD symptoms at reentry ($r = .25$, $p < .05$) and PTSD symptoms in 1986 ($r = .18$, $p < .05$).

In terms of war stress, all the measures are significantly correlated with the three measures of PTSD ($r = .18$ to $.48$, $p < .05$). However, the measure of *combat stress* produced the highest correlation with PTSD at reentry ($r = .48$), in 1986 ($r = .38$), and in the context of the Pearl Harbor experience ($r = .44$, $p < .001$).

In terms of postwar evaluation of war experiences, a negative attitude toward military service at discharge and the negative evaluation of military duty are significantly correlated with PTSD symptoms at reentry ($r = .20$, $p < .05$). Further, the negative perception of war's effect on current emotions is significantly correlated with all three measures of PTSD ($r = .38$). Membership in veterans' organizations is also significantly correlated with PTSD symptoms reported at reentry ($r = .22$,

TABLE 6.3
PTSD Symptoms at Reentry and Within the Last Year (1986)

PTSD SYMPTOM DIMENSION	PERCENTAGE RE-ENTRY	1986
INTRUSION (DSM-III-R-B)		
Nightmares in which I re-live my World War II experiences	26%	7%
Recurrent upsetting thoughts about the war	21%	10%
Felt upset when things remind me of my WW II experiences	8%	5%
Felt angry at what actually happened in the war	35%	29%
AVOIDANCE (DSM-III-R-C)		
Felt depressed	14%	11%
Felt numb, or unable to feel emotions	9%	2%
Deliberate avoidance of things that remind me of WW II	8%	2%
Problems remembering what happened during the war	7%	9%
Felt distant or estranged from people	11%	4%
Difficulty concentrating	10%	9%
Hard to express my feelings	22%	13%
Avoided talking about the war	20%	7%
Felt isolated	9%	5%
HYPERAROUSAL (DSM-III-R-D)		
Startled easily	30%	12%
Difficulty in sleeping	22%	16%
Felt emotionally overcharged (extremely "hyped up")	13%	9%
Easily irritated	19%	14%
Felt nervous or anxious	22%	9%
Hard to settle down, get "feet on the ground"	20%	3%
ASSOCIATED FEATURES		
Drinking problem	12%	5%
Felt guilty about surviving	10%	7%
Drug addiction	.5%	.5%
Felt mistrustful of people	10%	7%
Problems at work	6%	2%
Marital difficulties	9%	7%
An urge to catch-up on living	28%	14%

$p < .05$) and specific to the attack at Pearl Harbor ($r = .18$, $p < .05$). Finally, veterans with an external locus of control reported more symptoms of PTSD at reentry and in 1986 ($r = -.21$ and $-.32$, $p < .05$).

War Stress and Affect Balance

The Bradburn Affect Balance Scale (Bradburn, 1969) has been widely used in gerontological research to assess affective states in the elderly.

TABLE 6.4
Correlations Between Measures of PTSD (1946 & 1986) and Education, War Stress Measures, Post-war Evaluation of War Experience, Comradeship and Organization Membership, and Personal Resources

VARIABLE	Measures of PTSD		
	PTSD 1946	PTSD 1986	PEARL HARBOR STRESS 1986
EDUCATION			
Pre-War Education	-.21*	-.17	-.15
Use of G.I. Bill	.25**	.18*	.14
WAR STRESSORS			
War Stress	.30**	.23*	.36***
Combat Stress	.48***	.38***	.44***
Exposure to stress	.22*	.18*	.27**
Receive medical treatment	.33***	.31*	.23*
POST-WAR EVALUATION OF WAR EXPERIENCE			
Attitude toward service at discharge	.20*	.17*	.06
Evaluation of military experience	.20*	.13	.08
Training helpful later	-.13	-.04	.02
War's effect on aging	-.10	-.10	-.07
War's effect on current emotions	.38***	.37***	.38***
COMRADESHIP AND VETERAN'S ORGANIZATIONS			
Reserve unit membership	.04	.08	.06
Current contact with service buddies	-.02	-.11	.03
Membership in veteran's organizations	.22*	.08	.18*
PERSONAL RESOURSES			
Locus of control	-.21*	-.32***	-.08
Altruism	-.01	-.16	-.04
Disclosure	-.02	.06	.07

* p < .05; ** p < .01; *** p < .001

The scale contains two five-item subscales which assess positive and negative affect. Table 6.5 summarizes the results. Among the war stress measures, combat stress and receiving medical treatment are significantly correlated with negative affect at present (r = .20 and .28, p < .05). Regarding postwar evaluation of war experience, there is a significant correlation between attitude toward service at discharge and current positive affect (r = −.28, p < .05). Further, those who report that the war had a negative effect on their current emotional state had negative affect at present (r = .25, p < .05). Finally, the locus-of-control measure produced significant correlations with positive affect (internal control) and negative affect (external control) (r = .20 and −.28, p < .05).

Multivariate Analyses of the Measures of PTSD and Affect Balance

PTSD symptoms at reentry. A standard multiple regression was conducted for PTSD symptoms reported at reentry. Table 6.6 indicates that

TABLE 6.5

Correlations Between The Bradburn Affect Balance Scale (Current Positive and Negative Affect) and Education, War Stress Measures, Post-war Evaluation of War Experience, Comradeship and Organizational Membership, and Personal Resources

VARIABLE	BRADBURN AFFECT POSITIVE AFFECT	BALANCE SCALE NEGATIVE AFFECT
EDUCATION		
Pre-war education	.06	-.04
Use of G.I. Bill	-.07	.12
WAR STRESSORS		
War Stress	.01	.16
Combat stress	.01	.20*
Exposure to stress	.07	.02
Receive medical treatment	-.07	.28**
POST-WAR EVALUATION OF WAR EXPERIENCE		
Attitude toward service at discharge	-.28**	.15
Evaluation of military experience	-.06	.08
Training helpful later	.11	-.13
War's effect on aging	.14	-.10
War's effect on current emotions	-.11	.25**
COMRADESHIP AND VETERAN'S ORGANIZATIONS		
Reserve unit membership	.01	.02
Current contact with service buddies	.10	-.11
Membership in veteran's organizations	.07	.06
PERSONAL RESOURCES		
Locus of control	.20*	-.28**
Altruism	.12	-.08
Disclosure	.16	-.02

* p < .05; ** p < .01

there are six variables with significant F values ($p < .05$): (1) combat stress ($F = 15.55$), (2) postwar evaluation of war's effect on current emotions ($F = 8.12$), (3) external locus of control ($F = 7.00$), (4) use of the G.I. Bill ($F = 5.90$), (5) lower prewar education ($F = 4.05$), and (6) altruism ($F = 1.60$). Forty-one percent of the measured variance in PTSD symptoms at reentry was accounted for by the following five variable categories: education, war, postwar evaluation, comradeship, and personal resources ($R^2 = .41$).

PTSD symptoms in 1986. Table 6.7 summarizes the results of the regression analyses for PTSD symptoms in 1986. The variables with

TABLE 6.6
Multiple Regression for PTSD Symptoms
at Reentry—1946

VARIABLE	B	beta	F
EDUCATION			
Pre-war education	-.23	-.11	4.05*
Use of G.I. Bill	1.14	.14	5.90*
WAR STRESSORS			
War Stress	.45	.09	2.18
Combat Stress	.91	.32	15.55*
Exposure to Stress	-.77	-.06	.57
Receive Medical Treatment	.55	.09	2.00
POST-WAR EVALUATION OF WAR EXPERIENCE			
Attitude toward service at discharge	.14	.03	.16
Evaluation of military experience	.33	.06	.84
Training helpful later	-.47	-.08	1.88
War's effect on aging	-.19	-.03	.32
War's effect on current emotions	1.06	.18	8.12*
COMRADESHIP AND VETERAN'S ORGANIZATIONS			
Reserve unit membership	-.44	-.04	.54
Current contact with service buddies	-.64	-.03	.21
Membership in veteran's organizaions	.77	.12	3.43
PERSONAL RESOURCES			
Locus of control	-.97	-.15	7.00*
Altruism	.62	.07	1.60*
Disclosure	-.65	-.08	1.90
$R^2 = .41$			

*$p < .05$

significant F values included: (1) external locus of control ($F = 16.87$), (2) combat stress ($F = 7.98$), (3) postwar evaluation of war's effect on current emotion ($F = 6.51$), and (4) medical treatment received for a combat-related injury ($F = 5.43$). Thirty-five percent of the measured variance in PTSD symptoms in the last year was predicted by the five variable categories ($R^2 = .35$).

Pearl Harbor contextual PTSD. Table 6.8 summarizes the findings for PTSD symptoms in the context of the Pearl Harbor experience reported in 1986. The significant F values are: (1) postwar evaluation of war's effect on current emotion ($F = 12.16$), (2) subjective perception of war

TABLE 6.7
Multiple Regression for PTSD Symptoms in the Last Year (1986)

VARIABLE	B	beta	F
EDUCATION			
Pre-war education	-.10	-.07	1.48
Use of G.I. Bill	.40	.06	.90
WAR STRESSORS			
War stress	.11	.05	.71
Combat stress	.47	.24	7.98*
Exposure to stress	-.21	-.02	.08
Receive medical treatment	.67	.15	5.43*
POST-WAR EVALUATION OF WAR EXPERIENCE			
Attitude toward service at discharge	.94	.02	.14
Evaluation of military experience	-.38	.00	.00
Training helpful later	.48	.01	.04
War's effect on aging	-.21	-.05	.73
War's effect on current emotions	.69	.17	6.51*
COMRADESHIP AND VETERAN'S ORGANIZATIONS			
Reserve unit membership	.24	.03	.31
Current contact with service buddies	-.18	-.11	2.99
Membership in veteran's organizations	.13	.03	.18
PERSONAL RESOURCES			
Locus of control	-1.10	-.25	16.87*
Altruisim	-.12	-.07	1.36
Disclosure	-.40	-.07	1.32
$R^2 = .35$			

*p <.05

stress ($F = 7.49$), and (3) actual combat stress ($F = 6.60$). Thirty-one percent of the measured variance in PTSD symptoms related to the attack at Pearl Harbor was accounted for by the five variable categories ($R^2 = .31$).

Affect balance: Positive affect. Table 6.9 indicates variables with significant F values for positive affect, which are: (1) the postwar evaluation of attitude toward service at discharge ($F = 12.02$), (2) internal locus of control ($F = 5.69$), and (3) self-disclosure of the war experiences ($F = 4.78$). Sixteen percent of measured variance in current positive affect was accounted for by the five variable categories ($R^2 = .16$).

TABLE 6.8
Multiple Regression for PTSD Symptoms Reported
in 1988 Related to Japanese Attack at Pearl Harbor in 1941

VARIABLE	B	beta	F
EDUCATION			
Pre-war education	-.12	-.08	1.71
Use of G.I. Bill	.33	.05	.56
WAR STRESSORS			
War stress	.64	.12	7.49*
Combat stress	.45	.22	6.60*
Exposure to stress	.34	.04	.20
Receive medical treatment	.16	.00	.00
POST-WAR EVALUATION OF WAR EXPERIENCE			
Attitude toward service at discharge	-.20	-.05	.56
Evaluation of military experience	-.54	.00	.00
Training helpful later	.10	.23	.16
War's effect on aging	-.25	-.06	1.05
War's effect on current emotions	.97	.24	12.16*
COMRADESHIP AND VETERAN'S ORGANIZATIONS			
Reserve unit membership	.16	.02	.12
Current contact with service buddies	-.66	-.04	.39
Membership in veteran's organizations	.51	.11	2.64
PERSONAL RESOURCES			
Locus of control	-.52	-.01	.04
Altruism	-.60	-.01	.03
Disclosure	.11	.02	.10
$R^2 = .31$			

*p < .05

Affect balance: Negative affect. Table 6.10 summarizes the findings for current negative affect. The variables with significant F values are: (1) external locus of control ($F = 11.95$), and (2) medical treatment received for a combat-related injury ($F = 7.87$). Twenty-two percent of the variance in current negative affect was accounted for by these five variable categories ($R^2 = .22$).

DISCUSSION

The results of this preliminary study are interesting in several ways despite the limitations of the sample. First, the men in this sample,

TABLE 6.9
Multiple Regression for Current Positive Affect

VARIABLE	BRADBURN AFFECT BALANCE SCALE		
	B	beta	F
EDUCATION			
Pre-war education	.18	.03	.26
Use of G.I. Bill	-.25	-.01	.02
WAR STRESSORS			
War stress	.17	.01	.04
Combat stress	.14	.02	.04
Exposure to stress	.15	.04	-.24
Receive medical treatment	-.11	-.07	.94
POST-WAR EVALUATION OF WAR EXPERIENCE			
Attitude toward service at discharge	-.35	-.26	12.02*
Evaluation of military experience	.14	.10	1.77
Training helpful later	.63	.04	.40
War's effect on aging	.13	.09	1.71
War's effect on current emotions	-.35	-.02	.14
COMRADESHIP AND VETERAN'S ORGANIZATIONS			
Reserve unit membership	.22	.00	.02
Current contact with service buddies	-.92	.00	.00
Membership in veteran's organizations	.65	.04	.29
PERSONAL RESOURCES			
Locus of control	.26	.16	5.69*
Altruism	.81	.04	.32
Disclosure	.30	.15	4.78*
$R^2 = .16$			

*$p < .05$

TABLE 6.10
Multiple Regression for Current Negative Affect

VARIABLE	BRADBURN AFFECT BALANCE SCALE		
	B	beta	F
EDUCATION			
Pre-war education	.20	.04	.33
Use of G.I. Bill	.30	.01	.03
WAR STRESSORS			
War stress	.72	.06	.62
Combat stress	.11	.15	2.60
Exposure to stress	-.45	-.13	2.23
Receive medical treatment	.33	.20	7.87*
POST-WAR EVALUATION OF WAR EXPERIENCE			
Attitude toward service at discharge	.51	.04	.25
Evaluation of military experience	-.23	-.01	.05
Training helpful later	-.15	-.10	2.33
War's effect on aging	-.43	-.03	.19
War's effect on current emotions	.19	.12	2.89
COMRADESHIP AND VETERAN'S ORGANIZATIONS			
Reserve unit membership	-.34	-.01	.04
Current contact with service buddies	-.52	-.08	1.50
Membership in veteran's organizations	.15	.00	.00
PERSONAL RESOURCES			
Locus of control	-.38	-.23	11.95*
Altruism	-.31	-.01	-.05
Disclosure	-.25	-.01	.03
$R^2 = .22$			

*$p < .05$

predominantly veterans who served at Pearl Harbor and in the South Pacific in the Navy during World War II, reported moderate to high levels of combat exposure. More than half of the sample reported the following types of war stress: firing a weapon at the enemy; being subjected to enemy fire; seeing members of their unit or allies wounded; seeing towns or villages destroyed by combat episodes; being under direct enemy attack on many occasions; and, experiencing a life-or-death survival situation. Although these retrospective memories are subject to the problems that are inherent with the passage of time and the cognitive reformulation of these experiences in terms of clarity and meaning, these recollections are nevertheless important. Moreover, in examining the free-response comments about what happened on the Day of Infamy, we have been impressed by the lucidity and detail of the veterans' memory. It is not unwarranted to suggest that momentous events of great historical significance, as in the case of Pearl Harbor, are so important that the emotionally laden imagery is stored in memory in ways that permit accurate recall years later (van der Kolk, 1987). Further, in the face-to-face interviews conducted in Hawaii at the reunion, it was found that the members of the PHSA were proud of their role in World War II. Being a "survivor," as they constantly referred to each other, was a special status and a badge to be worn with pride. It is reasonable to suggest that 45 years of reunions and comradeship have kept their legacy of the Day of Infamy active in their life structure (Levinson, 1978) and psychosocial development (Elder & Clipp, 1988).

If it is granted that the Pearl Harbor experience was salient and powerful to the 19-year-old military personnel stationed on Oahu in 1941, how are we to understand the nature of their survivorship and self-reports of post-traumatic stress–related symptoms? Based on previous research with Holocaust survivors (Kahana, Harel, & Kahana, 1988), it was believed that victims of extreme stress are quite sensitive to issues regarding the psychiatric labeling of pathological states that can result from traumatic experiences. However, for the purposes of this study, it is proposed that if a survivor had a *psychohistorical context* within which to express feelings, images, and behaviors psychodynamically associated with the traumatic event, then post-traumatic stress–related symptoms may not be construed as pathological per se, but rather as normal, expectable patterns of appraisal and assimilation (Lazarus & Folkman, 1984).

Clearly, the data strongly supported this hypothesis of *contextual formulation*, i.e., the reporting of symptoms of post-traumatic stress disorder within an important and heroic historical event. When placed in the perspective that 45 years had elapsed since the Japanese attack at Pearl Harbor, it is impressive that 65% of the men reported symptoms of traumatic intrusive imagery in 1986 and 29% still have recurring dreams of the event, a finding similar to that reported by van der Kolk and associates (1984) for World War II veterans being treated at a VA hospital. Moreover, 73% of the men reported intrusive imagery (Horowitz, 1986) in which "thoughts about the attack at Pearl Harbor just pop into my mind." Those results are unequivocal in their implication: the memories of the Day of Infamy were still very much present in 1986, even if they were made more salient by attendance at the reunion.

However, as noted previously, data from survivors who did not attend the reunion show no significant differences.

The other clusters of symptoms characteristically associated with PTSD also produced interesting results. About one-third reported that it is "sometimes difficult to express feelings about what happened at Pearl Harbor." Although this is a form of emotional constriction which points to areas of difficulty in discussing the attack, only 13% state that they cannot remember what happened on December 7, 1941. And in terms of interpersonal detachment and numbing, only 6% state that it was "difficult to be real close to people" after the attack. Thus, for the Pearl Harbor survivor it appears that the imagery of the attack is still active in memory but that there is less avoidance associated with the experience. Consistent with the hypothesis of *contextual* PTSD, one interpretation of these findings is that the memories and intrusive images of the event are anchored in a psychohistorical context which gave important meaning to the event; the United States was victimized by the aggressive aerial attack that initiated World War II. The survivors ultimately recovered from the attack and went on to play an important role in the eventual defeat of the enemy. Considered from this perspective, there may be less of a need to erect strong defenses of avoidance, denial, or repression. To talk about the experience further validates the historical reality and importance of the event itself.

There are also other features of contextual PTSD that warrant discussion. With regard to reported physiological hyperreactivity, 23% indicated that they startle to loud noises or certain engine noises that remind them of the attack. This finding probably reflects the conditioning effect of traumatic experiences and the resistance to extinction of these learned responses (van der Kolk, 1987).

In terms of symptoms typically associated with PTSD, 42% reported wondering why "they survived when buddies died." In one sense, this is a curious finding in terms of the hypothesis of contextual PTSD. If the experience could be framed in a psychohistorical context that is positive and meaningful, then why is there such a high level of possible survivor guilt being expressed, especially 45 years later? We believe that there is no single answer to this question because it points out the limitations of our current understanding of the deeper levels of what it means to be a survivor. Is the reported survivor guilt associated with sad feelings of helplessness to act to help others injured by the attack? Is it associated with what Lifton (1988) has termed "failed forms of enactment"? Is it part of a long-term grief process in which the memories of comrades invoke guilt feelings that they had a different fate? Or is it a more existential questioning of the total meaning of the experience in terms of life itself?

Finally, the results of the study of contextual PTSD also indicated that the legacy of Pearl Harbor was profound in other ways. Residual anger toward the Japanese was present in 42% of the men. Fully two-thirds of the veterans reported that the Pearl Harbor experience "had a deep influence on the course of my life." Eighty-nine percent of the survivors had returned to Hawaii to visit Pearl Harbor. And 90% of the men reported a form of anniversary reaction on December 7, when they have "special feelings about the attack."

Thus, taken as a set, the data indicate that in the context of this particular historical event, the survivors reported rather high levels of symptoms associated with PTSD some 45 years later. Clearly, of course, these results do not mean that these individuals suffer from post-traumatic stress disorder as defined in DSM-III-R. However, they do suggest that the event is active and important in the lives of these aging veterans. Indeed, 70% of our sample stated that "World War II was the most intense and meaningful experience in my life." For the sample in this study, the first experience occurred on a quiet Sunday morning shortly after dawn had broken over the serene waters on an island that was to be the U.S. chief military base of operations for the western Pacific in World War II and afterward (Wallin, 1968).

PTSD at Reentry

In their retrospective recall of their symptoms at the time of reentry to civilian status after the war, about 23% reported symptoms of intrusive imagery, including nightmares, which were reported by 26% of the sample. Avoidance symptoms of PTSD were reported by only 12% of the men, with the highest endorsement occurring for emotional constriction: over 20% of the men reported that it was "hard to express my feelings" and "avoided talking about the war." Similarly, about one-fifth of the subjects reported symptoms of hyperarousal, which included difficulties in sleeping, startling easily, and difficulties in settling down. In terms of the associated symptoms of PTSD, 12% reported a drinking problem; 10% survivor guilt and mistrust of others; and 28% "an urge to catch up on living."

Current PTSD (1986)

When asked to indicate whether or not any of the same 26 PTSD items were present in 1986, the results were dramatically different. In comparison to their retrospective recall of symptoms 40 years earlier, there was an average reduction of 46% for the PTSD symptom clusters of intrusion, avoidance, hyperarousal, and associated features. However, the level of anger "at what happened in the war" remained at a 25% level in 1986. When the symptom level for 1986 is compared to that reported within the context of Pearl Harbor, these findings are even more striking in terms of the context-specific PTSD hypothesis. Table 6.11 summarizes the comparisons, both assessed by the same questionnaire except that one measure is specific to the attack at Pearl Harbor and the other is generic in nature and adapted from Elder and Clipp's work with aging World War II veterans who were part of the Oakland Growth Study (Elder & Clipp, 1988). As Table 6.11 indicates, the largest decline in the reported symptoms occurred for intrusive imagery (53%) and survivor guilt (35%). The symptoms of hyperarousal and avoidance showed the smallest change between the two measures (10–12%). Clearly, there are multiple explanations for these findings which include inexact comparability of the two measures of PTSD. Yet, the large difference in the report of symptoms in the context of the Pearl Harbor attack cannot be ignored and clearly points to the need in future research to employ multiple measures of self-reports to assess patterns of responses to traumatic events.

The Correlates of PTSD at Reentry, in 1986, and
Pearl Harbor Specific

The results of the bivariate correlates with our three measures of PTSD produced a set of results consistent with those found in previous

TABLE 6.11

Comparison of PTSD Symptom Cluster Reported in the Context of the Pearl Harbor Attack Versus Those Reported Generically in 1986

PTSD SYMPTOM CLUSTER*	PERCENT REPORTING IN 1986 MEASURE OF PTSD		PERCENTAGE DIFFERENCE
	PEARL HARBOR SPECIFIC	GENERIC	
Intrusive imagery	65	12	53
Avoidance	17	7	10
Hyperarousal	23	11	12
Survivor guilt	42	7	35
MEAN	37	9	28

*DSM-III-R Criteria
[a]Adapted from Elder and Clipp (1988)

research (e.g., Archibald & Tuddenham, 1965; Elder & Clipp, 1988; Laufer, 1985). First, the four measures of war stressors were significantly associated with PTSD symptoms on all three measures. Actual reports of combat, subjective perception of the stressfulness of combat, exposure to war trauma, and receiving medical treatment for a war injury produced significant correlations, which ranged from .18 (exposure and PTSD in 1986) to .48 (combat stress and PTSD at reentry). As in previous research, the higher the level of war stress, the more likely the person was to report symptoms of PTSD. Furthermore, membership in a veteran's organization and the use of the G.I. Bill were associated with PTSD symptoms at reentry and in 1986. Veterans with an internal locus of control and more prewar education were less likely to report PTSD symptoms at reentry and in 1986, suggesting the importance of these personal resource factors in the processing of the war experiences. And individuals who stated that their military service had a strong influence in their life and those who evaluated their military experience more negatively had more PTSD at the reentry period. These findings underscore the importance of the appraisal of stressful life events in the determination of post-traumatic coping and adaptation (Kahana, Harel, Kahana, & Rosner, 1988).

The results of the multiple regression analyses for the prediction of PTSD symptoms using the three different measures followed a similar pattern. For the retrospective measure of PTSD symptoms in 1946, the best predictor variables were: less prewar education, the use of the G.I. Bill, combat stress, the perception that the war had a negative effect on current emotions, and an external locus of control. Similarly, for the generic 1986 measure of PTSD symptoms, the best predictor variables were primarily *combat* related: combat stress, receiving medical treatment for a war injury, the negative perception of the war effect on current affect, and an external locus of control. The predictors of Pearl Harbor–specific measures of PTSD symptoms were, in fact, only combat related: war stress, combat stress, and the negative perception of these events on current emotions. These results are interesting since the prediction of PTSD symptoms at reentry includes less education prior to military service and the subsequent use of the G.I. Bill after the war. One plausible interpretation of this finding is that individuals with this profile may have been more vulnerable to acute PTSD in the aftermath of the war. On the other hand, these variables drop out of the predictive equation for the 1986 measures (generic and Pearl Harbor specific) which are determined by war stress variables and an external locus of control for the generic measure of PTSD. Thus, it appears that the reporting of long-term chronicity of PTSD symptoms is more strongly associated with objective measures of combat stress, including being wounded, as well as the subjective perception of how stressful these experiences were for the individual.

Aging and Affect Balance

As noted earlier, the Bradburn Affect Balance Scale has been used successfully in many studies of the elderly. As another measure of current emotional state and its relation to war trauma, the results add to the emerging picture for our sample of Pearl Harbor survivors. Current negative affect was significantly associated with the war stress measures of medical treatment, the negative perception of the war experiences on current affect, and an external locus of control. However, the best predictors of current negative affect only included being injured during the war and having an external locus of control. Clearly, these results point to feelings of vulnerability and helplessness that were, in part, the result of the trauma of war and may have shaped coping patterns from the war to the present time.

Current positive affect was associated with three variables: attitude toward the military at discharge, an internal locus of control, and self-disclosure of the war experience. Unlike veterans with current negative affect, this cluster of predictors suggests that these individuals have a stronger sense of personal efficacy and an ability to share their experiences with others. These variables have also been found to be associated with positive mental health outcome for victims of the Buffalo Creek Dam disaster (Gleser, Green, & Winget, 1981) and survivors of the Holocaust (Kahana, Harel, & Kahana, 1988). Although the precise psychological mechanisms that underlie such transformative processes are unknown at this time, it may be the case that persons with an internal locus of control who can talk about their stressful life experiences develop positive, instrumental coping patterns that lead to healthy adaptation after trauma.

SUMMARY

The Japanese attack on Pearl Harbor on December 7, 1941, initiated the U.S. involvement in World War II. Although the attack had been expected by U.S. military intelligence (Wallin, 1968), it was a surprise that it came early on a Sunday morning. The immediate effects were, of course, devastating and produced significant damage to the U.S. naval fleet moored in the harbor and immobilized the airfields on the island. Over 3,000 men were either killed or wounded in the attack, and the survivors were immersed in chaos, confusion, fires, and explosions during the ordeal, which lasted about two hours. The Day of Infamy became a national rallying cry to go to war against Japan.

The participants in this study were all survivors of the Pearl Harbor attack, 86% of whom went on to fight in the South Pacific theater of war. What the study sought to understand, in a preliminary way, was the psychic legacy of this set of experiences.

The findings were clear and remarkably consistent with those of Elder and Clipp (1988) in their study of aging World War II veterans. In their 1985 survey of men with heavy combat exposure, they found that 54% had symptoms of post-traumatic stress upon exit from the service and 68% had an "undesirable legacy from the service" after age 55 which included "combat anxiety" and "bad memories." In the present study, 65% of the veterans reported symptoms of war-related intrusive imagery in 1986, specifically in the context of the Pearl Harbor attack. Further, 42% of the men reported survivor guilt and residual anger at the Japanese. Nearly one-fourth of the sample stated that they still have startle response to certain stimuli (engine noises) and one-third that it is still difficult to express feelings about what happened at Pearl Harbor. These findings lend strong support to our hypothesis of *context-specific* PTSD, which states that when a trauma occurs in a psycho-historical context, especially one that is profound, heroic, and changes the course of history, the survivors will report symptoms of PTSD more freely than when this is not the situation. Clearly, this is an important finding which merits additional inquiry in future studies. On the average, the subjects reported 28% more symptoms of PTSD in the context of the Pearl Harbor attack than they did for the same symptom clusters on the generic measure of the stress syndrome.

Furthermore, the results of the regression analyses indicated that the war stress measures were the most powerful predictors of our measures of PTSD symptoms in 1986. Men who had high levels of combat exposure, including receiving medical treatment for war injuries, were more likely to report PTSD symptoms, especially if they had an external locus of control. These results clearly point to the complex interaction effects between a personality dimension and war trauma in the development of symptoms that have persisted for 45 years. Moreover, this finding parallels that of Elder and Clipp (1988), who found that the *prewar* personality variables which predicted emotional problems in their sample of World War II veterans were feelings of personal inadequacy; moodiness; over-controlled; introspectiveness; and a tendency to ruminate and express tension in bodily symptoms.

In conclusion, this study has indicated that war stress does have a long-term impact on the survivors of Pearl Harbor. Not only are symptoms of PTSD currently present in this group of survivors, but for some their war experience had a negative outcome in terms of their current affective states. Nevertheless, the men in this sample have lived productive lives, raised families, and found their own unique way to live with the memories of the Day of Infamy. And while we will have to await future analysis of the data to determine how the men utilized environmental, social, and personal resources in coping with war trauma, life-course development, and the aging process, it is clear that the individuals continue to revisit Pearl Harbor in their memories and in their comradeship with fellow survivors, both the living and the dead.

SECTION III

Clinical Applications

7

Reconnecting: Stress Recovery in the Wilderness

with ALICE J. WALKER and BRUCE WEBSTER

In recent years a variety of therapeutic approaches to the treatment of PTSD have been used in both inpatient and outpatient settings (Horowitz, 1986; Lindy, 1986; Parson, 1988; Scurfield, 1985; Silver, 1986; Silver & Wilson, 1988; Smith, 1985; Wilson, 1988a, 1988b). Not surprisingly, these clinical approaches range the full spectrum of intervention techniques and include behavioral techniques (e.g., desensitization), group psychotherapy (e.g., support groups), psychoanalytic approaches (Lindy, 1986, 1988), and milieu therapy (e.g., outward bound in wilderness setting). At present there is a paucity of published research on the efficacy of these various approaches to the treatment of PTSD. However, the research of Horowitz and his associates at the Center for the Study of Neuroses in San Francisco has indicated that time-limited, 12-session, brief psychotherapy can be an effective method of alleviating symptoms of acute PTSD which in some way debilitate the person or interfere with effective functioning (Marmar & Horowitz, 1988). Similarly, inpatient PTSD units for Vietnam veterans in VA hospitals have also achieved success by creating a therapeutic milieu that promotes trust, bonding, and mutual support that facilitates the working through of distressing intrusive imagery and the reduction or elimination of maladaptive self-destructive forms of avoidant behavior (e.g., drug and alcohol abuse, aggressive acting out, social isolation, etc.).

More recently, Atkinson, Reaves, and Maxwell (1988) have reviewed treatment approaches to PTSD in the VA system and argue persuasively that an integrated multidisciplinary, multitherapeutic approach is essential for the successful treatment of PTSD in Vietnam veterans. And as they note, the level of resistance and resentment toward the Veterans Administration is often so great that it is very difficult to establish a therapeutic alliance with Vietnam veterans who suffer from chronic and severe PTSD. Thus, because of the veterans' mistrust of institutionalized forms of treatment for PTSD, we wondered if an intensive program in a natural, wilderness setting would be conducive to creating a comfortable climate in which Vietnam veterans with PTSD would feel safe enough to begin to reestablish the normal stress recovery process (Horowitz, 1986).

Furthermore, our experiences with the sweat lodge (see Chapter 3) and other Native American rituals for healing led us to explore the possibility that an integrated, eclectic approach to treatment that would use individual, group, and Native American practices might facilitate rapid transference reactions, the reduction of defensiveness, and the means to reestablish positive bonding with other veterans who could become a "unit" again for a "mission" of facing together the painful emotional legacy of their combat experiences in the Vietnam War. Stated simply, could they reconnect to themselves and others in the wilderness to recover from prolonged stress?

LOCATION OF THE TREATMENT PROGRAM

The location of the treatment program at Camp David on Lake Crescent in the Olympic National Park provided an ideal setting for the experimental program. Lake Crescent is a deep glacial lake, which is several miles long and totally surrounded by lush green mountains that are densely populated with cedar, fir, and spruce trees. The grounds contain a large main lodge and several other smaller cabins for meetings and sleeping. The camp is isolated from nearby towns and was exclusively available to us for the week-long program. The 15 veterans who volunteered for the experimental program were attending a weekly counseling group and were diagnosed as having PTSD. All of the men were required to be drug and alcohol free prior to the beginning of the treatment program.

THE TREATMENT PLAN

The major goals of the program were as follows: (1) to promote mutual trust and respect; (2) to diffuse and work through unresolved war stress; (3) to learn about PTSD as a syndrome and develop positive coping skills related to it; (4) to identify personal problem areas to work on during the week; (5) to improve self-esteem and self-confidence; (6) to develop better interpersonal communication skills; and (7) to formulate concrete short-term plans for themselves after the treatment program.

The treatment plan involved a combination of Native American healing techniques, primarily the sweat lodge, and traditional clinical approaches to the treatment of PTSD. With the exception of the initial reception and the ceremonial ending of the program, the overall structure of the daily activities was the same although the objectives and treatment focus changed daily. Briefly, each day began with a cold plunge and swim in the lake. Then, after a communal breakfast served in the main lodge, a group session was held from about 8 A.M. to 10:00 A.M. in which a film or other group-oriented experience was conducted. Immediately after the group session the participants were asked to reflect on the experience by writing their reactions to it in a journal that was kept for the entire week's activities. Following the journal entry, each participant was paired with a counselor for 45 minutes of discussion of reactions to the session. The morning activities concluded with a "rap" group which lasted until 12:00 P.M.

A communal luncheon was then served prior to repeating the format in the afternoon with a different set of activities from 1:30 to 5:00 P.M. At the end of the afternoon program, the sweat lodge ritual was led by a Vietnam era veteran and apprentice medicine man until about 7:00 P.M. The focus of the sweat lodge centered around the central thematic issue of treatment for that day (e.g., what happened in Vietnam). In this way, the sweat lodge permitted a unique opportunity and different modality by which to deal with any personal concerns that were stimulated by the events of the day. A communal dinner was shared after the sweat lodge. Following dinner there was the option of individual counseling prior to bedtime, and many chose to continue to the day's activity with peers or staff members.*

---

* A total of 10 staff members volunteered to assist with the program. All were Vietnam era veterans who had previous counseling experience with PTSD.

UNIQUE ASPECTS OF THE TREATMENT PLAN

Native American and Other Rituals Adapted for the Program

After much consideration and consultation with several medicine men from tribes of the Pacific Northwest, we decided to implement some Native American ceremonies as part of the overall treatment plan. These are discussed below.

The Ritual Homecoming Welcome and Warrior Feast

The first ceremony, devised by Bruce Webster and myself, involved the *ritual homecoming* on the first day of the program. Once everyone was registered, the clients and veteran staff members were divided into two "squads." The clients wore an orange armband and the counselors a blue one. The men were taken in two pickup trucks to opposite locations in the wilderness about two miles from the Camp David resort on Lake Crescent. Once there, they were instructed to walk back to the camp as a squad in single file. The purpose of this event was to symbolically recreate the homecoming from Vietnam, i.e., to "rotate" home one by one just as they did years before after their tour of duty had ended.

At the entrance to the campsite, along the dirt road that led to the main lodge, were stationed the family, friends, and other staff members, who waited in a long line to greet the men. We believed it was important to have them present in order to provide an authentic welcome and homecoming ceremony of appreciation for the service in Vietnam. We also thought that a *symbolic reenactment* of walking "back home," one by one, to an extended family was an important beginning to the week-long treatment program. So as the veterans came into the camp, the children would run out to greet their "daddy" and a sentry (BW) shouted out that the veteran was home from Vietnam (e.g., "Hey, Mom, Bill is home from the war"). Then each person greeted the veteran with a handshake and a hug and said, "Welcome home—thanks for serving. I am proud of you."

After the last individual had returned, a warriors' feast was held in the main lodge. The men sat around a long table and were served smoked salmon, nuts, fruits, and other native foods of the Pacific

Northwest. As they ate they were surprisingly solemn. The men were encircled by their families and friends, who later joined them in a communal dinner which honored their sacrifices in the war.

The Ritual of the Ceremonial Fire

On the last day of treatment, the families and significant others returned to the camp in the afternoon to rejoin the men and to participate in a *ceremonial fire*. In this ritual everyone gathered around the fire in a circle. Then one by one, in a clockwise order, each person walked up to the fire and "released" into it an object, actual or symbolic, of something negative and painful that they wished to "let go" from their life. For example, several veterans put their soft "bush" hats from Vietnam into the fire as a symbolic act of "letting go" of war trauma. After the ceremonial fire a special sweat lodge was conducted for the women. While this was in progress, the men prepared a meal to serve to their wives, children, and significant others. The dinner concluded with a traditional potlatch during which gifts were provided for the staff and participants in the program. Finally, a "talking circle" was conducted. Everyone sat around a log fire to continue conversation and dialogue about the week's activities.

The Ritual of Release and Transformation

Another Native American technique adapted for our program involved the planting of two fir trees at the conclusion of the session which addressed the issues of guilt, rage, anger, hatred, sorrow, grief, killing, and destruction as related to the Vietnam experience. Each individual was given two fir saplings and instructed to find a special place to plant them. It was explained that among some Native American groups it is believed that Mother Earth receives that which is given to her in a spirit of harmony, balance, love, and the cycle of the seasons. Thus, by planting the trees one could ask Mother Earth to receive them and in the process take away pain, despair, sadness, hatred, and other negative emotions. It was said that in return, she would nurture the young trees and help them to grow in their natural way.

Alone, and at the place he had chosen, each person was instructed to put his mental focus on the part of his body where he felt tension, pain, or negative feelings. He then placed that part of his body over a hole he dug with his hands and released the negative energy into the earth. The task that followed was to plant the tree and let Mother

Earth transmute the negative emotion into an object of growing beauty. Thus, a "negative" was replaced by a "positive" to complete a cycle which had as its image the act of "getting" by "letting go."

Although it is possible to render various conceptualizations of this simple ceremony, it bears remarkable similarity as a *ritual form* to the psychosocial modalities that Erikson (1950, 1968) has characterized as "to get" and "to take" (oral sensory kinesthetic) and "to hold on" and "to let go" (anal muscular). These psychosocial modalities are well recognized in psychoanalytic theory as central epigenetic concerns during the first three years of ego development. Letting go of pain and symbolically transmuting it to Mother Earth contains the image of gaining personal strength by the proper release of that which blocks healthy adaption. By letting go of the negative emotion, the cycle of adaptation can become balanced again by a positive change (the growth of the tree = self) which emanates from nurturance of the Mother Earth, the maternal symbol that gives freely of what one needs "to get" to restore psychological and physical equilibrium.

The Sweat Lodge Purification Ritual

As noted above and in Chapter 3, the sweat lodge ritual was used at the conclusion of each day in order to provide an alternative method of releasing the painful and distressing emotions associated with war trauma and its impact on subsequent life-course development.

The Salmon Feast of Thanksgiving

A salmon feast of thanksgiving was held early in the week. A gift of fresh king salmon was donated to the group and provided the basis to celebrate in a meal of thanksgiving for all that is good in life with the fish that is regarded as sacred to many of the native tribes of the Pacific Northwest. There was an abundance of freshly baked salmon, and each participant was asked to fill himself with this special meal and to recognize that life contains many good things to be appreciated and shared with others.

The Mail Call Ritual

The mail call ritual involved a surprise, unexpected delivery of letters to the men each night after dinner. It was prearranged so that every veteran received a letter a day from a friend or family member during the stay at Camp David. The letters were written to encourage the men to continue their efforts to work through their stress disorder and other problems that brought them to the treatment program.

The "Unfinished Business" Ritual

Toward the end of the week, each participant was given two stamped envelopes and stationery in order to write letters to two persons, living or dead, with whom they had "unfinished business." Afterward the letters were mailed if the individual wished to have them sent. The purpose of this ritual was to attempt to bring closure or resolution to a previous and conflicted relationship with someone important in one's life.

The Graduation Ceremony

On the last day, a graduation ceremony was held. Each man received a specially designed diploma which displayed an eaglelike jet aircraft (the Vietnam Freedom Bird) emerging from Lake Crescent and the cedar forests that surround it. After all the diplomas were distributed, a final group session was held at which time expressions of appreciation and gratitude were exchanged.

Summary

In summary, the program utilized many modalities of treatment: (1) individual counseling sessions with different counselors during the six days; (2) group-oriented experiences such as films, lecture, and desensitization exercises; (3) rap group discussions; (4) daily sweat lodge rituals whose focus reflected the treatment objectives of the day; (5) Native American ceremonies for release and healing; (6) a therapeutic milieu of shared responsibility for cooking, washing dishes, cleaning, and living together for a week; and (7) involvement of family and significant others in the treatment plan. Although this brief treatment program bears similarity to other approaches to treating mental disorders, it was eclectic in orientation and took place in a nonclinical environment that was familiar to the men, many of whom had lived in the wilderness of Washington State.

METHOD AND PROCEDURES

Description of the Treatment and Control Groups

All subjects who volunteered for the study were living in the Olympic peninsula of Washington State and were attending weekly "rap" group sessions as part of a Vietnam Veterans Outreach program. Nearly all of the men in the sample had been previously diagnosed as having service-connected PTSD and were involved in group counseling for that reason.

A comparison of the treatment and control group is presented in Table 7.1. This table indicates that the two groups were not significantly different by age, race, nature of military service, educational level, employment, marital status, and levels of psychopathology prior to treatment (see Table 7.2, p. 171). The average age of the sample was 39 years. Over 90% of the men enlisted in the military and were evenly distributed across the branches of service corps, except for the air force. The average age in combat during the Vietnam War was 20, with a range from 16 to 40 years. Approximately half of the men served multiple tours of duty in Vietnam and were also wounded in action. The average level of educational attainment prior to military service was 11th grade; afterward, the majority completed an additional two years of higher education. Approximately two-thirds of the men were unemployed. The modal level of income, from any source, was between $5,000 and $10,000 per year. About half of the men were married at the time of the study; the others were either divorced or single. The overall divorce rate was 33%.

Description of Measures

Symptom Checklist-90 (SCL-90). The SCL-90 is an objective, 90-item, self-report scale that measures general psychiatric symptoms on a four-point Likert scale (Derogatis, 1973, 1977). The nine subscales are: depression, somatization, anxiety, hostility, interpersonal sensitivity (self-consciousness), obsessive-compulsive, paranoia, phobic anxiety, and psychoticism. Three global indices are derived from these scores and include Global Severity Index (GSI), Positive Symptom Distress Index (PSDI), and Positive Symptom Tally. The GSI measures both frequency and intensity of distress across all symptom dimensions. The PSDI measures

TABLE 7.1
Description of the Treatment and Control Groups

VARIABLES	TREATMENT (N=15)	CONTROL (N=11)
Present Age Mean (Years)	39	38.3
Present Age Range (Years)	34-55	35-42
Race		
Caucasian	13	11
Native American	2	0
Military Service		
Enlisted	14	10
Drafted	1	1
Branch:		
Army	5	4
Marines	4	4
Navy	5	3
Air Force	1	0
Mean Age in Vietnam (Years)	20	19.6
Range Age in Vietnam (Years)	16-40	17-24
Multiple Tours	6	
Injured	8	6
Special Operations	9	4
Education (Average Years)		
Prior to Service	11	11
After Service	14	13
Employment Status		
Employed	5	3
Unemployed	10	8
Modal Income	$5,000-$10,000	$5,000-$10,000
Disability Compensation	4	2
Current Marital Status		
Married	6	5
Divorced	3	2
Separated	3	1
Single	3	3
Divorce Rate	33%	33%

Notes: (1) All of the men in counseling at present at Outreach Center.
    (2) With the exception of the measures of depression and anger on the VESI-PTSD, both controls and treatment group had similar levels of psychopathology on the SCL-90 and IES prior to brief psychotherapy. We believe these differences were attributable to the controls knowledge that they were only being tested for purposes of experimental research.

the intensity of the symptoms reported. Cronbach's alpha was reported at .97 (Murphy, 1986).

Impact of Event Scale. The IES, or the intrusion-avoidance scale, was selected as a generic measure of stress response syndrome. It consists of 16 statements assessing post-traumatic symptoms of intrusive reexperiencing or tendencies toward avoidance and denial. Seven items assess intrusive imagery and nine items assess avoidance tendencies. The mean of the intrusion subscale is 21.4, with a standard deviation of 9.6 and a range of 0–35. The mean of the avoidance subscale is 18.2, with a standard deviation of 10.8 and a range of 0–45. Zilberg, Weiss, and Horowitz (1982) found that Cronbach's alphas ranged from .79 to .92. Test-retest reliability time ranged from .86 to .90.

Vietnam Era Stress Inventory. The VESI (Wilson & Krauss, 1985) was included as a measure of post-traumatic stress disorder for Vietnam veterans (Appendix A).

Description of measures of involvement in atrocities. Following the work on abusive violence by Laufer, Frey-Wouters, and Gallops (1985), the *Witnessing Atrocity Scale* measures *indirect* involvement as an observer in the killing, hurting, or mutilating of Vietnamese or seeing American GI's injured or killed and/or mutilated bodies. The *Participating Atrocity Scale* measures *direct* involvement in killing, hurting, or mutilating Vietnamese. Median splits were used to distinguish high and low levels on each atrocity scale in order to assess possible differential effects of these dimensions on the intrusion and avoidance dimensions of PTSD. The comparisons were conducted in order to:

1. determine whether a difference in symptomatology exists between high and low levels of each atrocity dimension;
2. determine the degree of symptom reduction over time within each level of atrocity dimension;
3. assess the pattern of symptomatology present in each atrocity dimension and level; and
4. determine whether a difference in symptomatology exists between atrocity dimensions within levels.

EVALUATION OF THE PROGRAM

On the last day of the program the participants and staff were asked to evaluate the program in order to obtain a measure of the perceived effectiveness of the six-day intensive-treatment program. A 25-item questionnaire with four five-point Likert subscales which ranged from *Disagree Strongly* to *Agree Strongly* was constructed to evaluate the program. The subscale and sample items are as follows:

1. *Overall Appraisal of the Program* (seven items): Items include #1—I found the Intensive to be a valuable experience for me; #17—I feel dissatisfied with what I got out of the Intensive; #22—I believe that I had enough opportunities to talk with the staff about my problems and concerns in living.
2. *Emotional Well-Being* (seven items): Representative items include #3—I feel significantly less emotionally upset than prior to the time of the Intensive; #6—I found the sweat lodge ritual to be helpful to me in emotionally releasing pent-up pain and difficult feelings; #13—I believe that I will be able to cope more effectively with stress in my daily life because of the Intensive; #24—I feel better about myself as a person at this time.
3. *Feelings of Integration* (six items): #4—The Intensive has helped me to put my Vietnam War experiences into a better, more healthy perspective; #12—I feel a greater sense of personal peace and inner harmony because of the Intensive; #25—I believe that this Intensive experience has helped me to heal old wounds that have troubled me.
4. *Interpersonal Relations* (five items): #5—I think that I will be better able to relate to people I care about because of the Intensive; #14—I would like to continue being involved with the participants of the Intensive experience; #23—As a result of the Intensive experience, it will be easier for me to open up to others in the future.

The results of the analysis indicated very strong positive evaluation of the program on each of the subscales (M = Overall Appraisal = 4.81; Emotional Well-Being = 4.43; Integration = 4.52; Interpersonal Relationships = 4.57). No significant differences were found between the staff and the participants in the evaluation of the program. Thus, there was a strong consensus that the program was a valuable experience. Additionally, two free-response items asked the participants to "Please describe what this experience has meant to you" and "If you could change any aspect of the Intensive, what would you like to change?" The results indicated that the participants reported being more able to express feelings in an environment in which there was support, "feelings of connectedness" and bonding. A second theme centered around enhanced feelings of self-worth and self-insight (e.g., "a real man can feel his pain"). Others reported the experience as "spiritual healing" and "emotional fulfillment." In regard to desired changes in the program, the common themes included a request for a longer treatment program with even greater intensity, more opportunities to gain a sense of self-awareness, and more time on termination concerns and decompression.

RESULTS OF THE INTENSIVE TREATMENT PROGRAM

Measures of Psychopathology

Tables 7.2 and 7.3 show the comparison of mean scores on the SCL-90, IES, and VESI-PTSD scales between pretreatment and follow-ups done at one and three months posttreatment. As demonstrated by the t-tests, there is a significant reduction of symptomatology for nearly every measure of psychopathology regardless of income or educational level ($t's_{11} > 2.15$, $p < .05$). Examination of the SCL-90 data indicates that every measure of symptomatology was significantly reduced one month posttreatment except the positive symptom distress index, which showed only a marginal directional change. There is almost no change between the one- and three-month follow-up scores, but the trend seems to be in a direction of symptom reduction. Among the subscales, hostility was most greatly reduced ($t_{11} = 4.45$, $p < .001$), while interpersonal sensitivity appeared resistant to change ($t_{11} = 2.15$, $p < .05$). Interestingly, the global severity index reflecting both the number and intensity of symptoms was significantly reduced at the one- and three-month follow-ups ($t's_{11} > 3.02$, $p < .01$), while the positive symptom distress index reflecting only the intensity of reported symptoms remained relatively unchanged ($t's_{11} > 2.56$, $p < .10$). Closer inspection of these phenomena revealed consistent reduction of the standard deviation for these measures between time intervals, which, when considered along with the significant reduction in the number of symptoms reported, suggests less variability in the remaining symptoms reported.

Scores on the IES also showed a marked reduction in symptomatology. Avoidance is reported at a marginally lower level than intrusion and decreases at a slower rate which does not show a significant change

TABLE 7.2
Outcome of Brief Intensive Psychotherapy Using Sweat Lodge for 15 Vietnam Veterans with Post-Traumatic Stress Disorder

MEASURE OF PSYCHOPATHOLOGY	MEAN SCORES			
	Pre-Treatment	Control[a]	Post-Treatment	
			1-month Follow-Up[b]	3-month Follow-Up
	(n = 15)	(n = 11)	(n = 11)	(n = 12)
Symptom Checklist 90/102 (SCL-90)[c]				
Somatization	2.05	1.94	1.24*	1.22**
Obsessive/Compulsive	2.27	2.60	1.38**	1.45**
Interpersonal Sensitivity	2.01	2.40	1.42+	1.49*
Depression	2.33	2.45	1.40**	1.49**
Anxiety	2.11	2.30	1.20**	1.35*
Hostility	2.16	2.22	1.00**	1.07***
Phobic Anxiety	1.49	2.05	.77*	.88*
Paranoid Ideation	1.68	2.39	1.18+	1.13*
Psychoticism	1.47	1.88	.77*	.83*
Additional Items	2.30	2.40	1.55**	1.69*
PTSD-Cincinnati Scale	2.06	2.37	1.09**	1.26**
Grand Total	2.02	2.26	1.20**	1.27***
Global Severity Index	2.02	2.26	1.20**	1.27**
Positive Symptom Distress Index	.767		.64	.617

+p < .10; *p < .05; **p < .01; ***p < .001

[a]The control scores as compared to pre-treatment.
[b]The 1 and 3-month follow-up scores as compared to pre-treatment scores.
[c]Subscale mean scores as computed by Derogatis et al. 1973.

TABLE 7.3

Changes in PTSD Symptoms as Outcome Measures of Brief Intensive Psychotherapy Using Sweat Lodge for 15 Vietnam Veterans with Post-Traumatic Stress Disorder

MEASURE OF PSYCHOPATHOLOGY		MEAN SCORES		
	Pre-Treatment	Control[a]	1-month[b] Follow-Up	3-month Follow-Up
Impact of Event Scale (IES)				
Intrusion	2.88	3.14	1.90*	1.83**
Avoidance	2.48	2.73	1.93	1.86+
Vietnam Era Stress Inventory (PTSD)				
Depression, Search for Meaning, Identity Diffusion	1.76	2.62*	1.44*	1.48*
Physical Symptoms	1.73	1.95	1.37	1.38+
Stigmatization/Alienation	2.34	2.73	1.95*	1.91*
Sensation Seeking	1.64	1.69	.97*	1.08**
Anger	1.41	2.23*	.92*	.97***
Intrusive Imagery	1.80	1.94	1.29	1.26*
Intimacy Conflict	1.50	2.13	1.43	1.42
Total	1.78	2.29	1.41*	1.42**

+p < .10; *p <.05; **p <.01; ***p <.001
[a]The control scores as compared to pre-treatment.
[b]The 1 and 3-month follow-up scores as compared to pre-treatment scores.

until the three-month follow-up ($t_{11} = 1.84$, $p < .10$). Intrusion shows significant reduction by one month posttreatment ($t_{12} = 2.64$, $p < .05$) and continues in a direction of symptom reduction at three months posttreatment ($t_{11} = 3.11$, $p < .01$).

Results from the VESI-PTSD scale indicate a significant decrease in all measures of psychopathology by three months posttreatment with the exception of intimacy conflict, which showed no significant change across time ($ts_{11} > 1.85$, $p < .10$).

Similar to the hostility scale on the SCL-90, reported anger was greatly reduced ($t_{11} = 3.18$, $p < .01$) as was intrusive imagery ($t_{11} = 2.19$, $p < .05$), a finding consistent with the IES intrusion measure. Of all the VESI-PTSD subscales, sensation seeking was most greatly reduced ($t_{11} = 3.54$, $p < .01$).

Figure 7.1 illustrates the SCL-90 profile and pattern of symptom reduction for our sample of combat veterans. A 37% decrease in overall distress is noted at three-month follow-up. However, the *profile config-uration* remains relatively unchanged from that reported at pretreatment, with two noteworthy distinctions. Interpersonal sensitivity decreased disproportionately slower than the other subscales, showing only a 26% reduction. Hostility decreased disproportionately faster than the other subscales, showing a 50% reduction. Three-month follow-up scores show a slight increase on measures of obsession-compulsion, interpersonal sensitivity, depression, anxiety, hostility, and psychoticism.

COMPARISONS TO OTHER PSYCHIATRIC POPULATIONS

SCL-90

Figure 7.2 presents a comparison of Vietnam veterans with PTSD who participated in the treatment program with other patient populations (general psychiatric outpatients, emergency service psychiatric outpatients, alcoholics) and normative data reported by Derogatis (1973). Pretreatment scores for Vietnam veterans show a greater distress level than any other cohort. In comparison to other patient populations, the Vietnam veterans in our sample show disproportionately higher levels of somatization, obsession-compulsion, hostility, and phobic anxiety. On the average, these scores are 35% higher than those of emergency

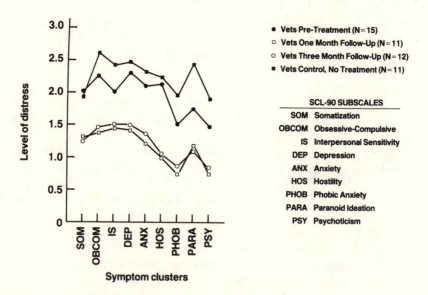

Figure 7.1. SCL-90 profile of subscale scores of Vietnam veterans with PTSD before and after brief intensive psychotherapy.

service psychiatric outpatients, 40% higher than those of general psychiatric outpatients, and 65% higher than Derogatis' normative sample. The three-month follow-up scores show symptom levels comparable to those of general psychiatric outpatients and alcoholics. Interestingly, the veterans' scores are 36% higher than those of alcoholics on interpersonal sensitivity but are similar to those of psychiatric outpatients. On the depression subscale, the scores of the veterans are nearly equivalent to those of alcoholics but lower than those of psychiatric outpatients.

IES

Figure 7.3 graphs the IES subscale scores on intrusion and avoidance for our veteran patients compared to other trauma victims and normative data as reported by Wilson, Smith, and Johnson (1985) and Horowitz (1986). Pretreatment intrusion scores for the veterans were found to be approximately 60% higher than normative data and very similar to data for other trauma victims. The three-month follow-up scores show a 36% decrease in intrusion. Pretreatment avoidance scores for our sample were twice as high as the normative group and slightly higher

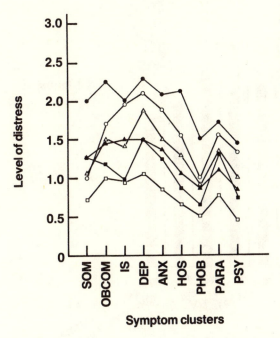

• Vets Pre-Treatment (N=15)
▲ Vets Post-Treatment (N=12)
○ Emergency Service (N=26)*
△ General Psychiatric (N=100)*
■ Alcoholics (N=44)*
□ Control (N=45)*

Figure 7.2. SCL-90 profile of subscale scores of Vietnam veterans with PTSD as compared to other psychiatric populations.

than comparison trauma populations, with the exception of rape victims. The three-month follow-up scores show a 25% overall decrease in avoidance.

VESI

Figure 7.4 presents the VESI-PTSD profile and pattern of symptom reduction for our sample of veterans. A 20% decrease in overall PTSD symptomatology is noted, similar to the result of the SCL-90, and the profile is relatively unchanged from that reported at pretreatment, with one noteworthy distinction. Intimacy conflict was extremely resistant to change and decreased in severity by only 5%. The three-month follow-up showed only a small fractional increase on the subscales of depression, physical symptoms, sensation seeking, and anger, while a slight decrease was found on measures of stigmatization, intrusive imagery, and intimacy conflict.

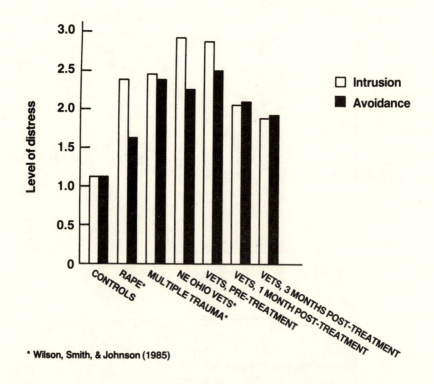

* Wilson, Smith, & Johnson (1985)

Figure 7.3. Comparison of subscale scores on Impact of Event Scale (IES) for Vietnam veteran patients with other trauma victims and controls.

Figure 7.5 shows a comparison of VESI-PTSD profiles for our sample with other trauma victims (northeast Ohio Vietnam veterans and rape victims) and normative data. Veterans who participated in the intensive treatment program have pretreatment distress levels well below those reported by northeast Ohio Vietnam veterans. This difference may be caused by the small sample size and/or differences between the two groups as related to the amount of therapy received at the time of study. However, our veterans' pretreatment scores are comparable to those of rape victims with the exception that rape victims report less stigmatization and more anger. However, inspection of the profiles indicates that in comparison to our veterans three months *after* treatment, the rape victims had higher scores on all of the VESI subscales except intrusive imagery and stigmatization, which reflects war-related unbidden imagery and alienation.

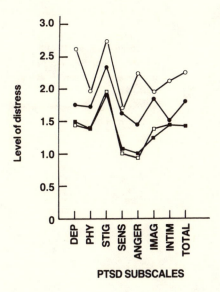

Figure 7.4. VESI-PTSD profile of subscale scores of Vietnam veterans before and after brief intensive psychotherapy.

ATROCITY MEASURES AND PSYCHOPATHOLOGY

Table 7.4 presents a summary analysis of mean scores on the IES subscales of intrusion and avoidance before and after brief intensive psychotherapy for veterans who witnessed or participated in atrocities, as measured by the VESI atrocity scales. The results of the t-tests revealed significantly less intrusion for those in the low-witness category ($M = 12.67$) as opposed to those in the high-witness category ($M = 20.00$) at pretreatment ($t_9 = 33.66$, $p < .01$). However, this finding is *not* repeated at the one- and three-month follow-ups due, in part, to the significant decrease in intrusion across time for those in the high-witness category ($t's_{12} > 6.06$, $p > .001$) as compared to only a directional change in the low-witness group. Comparisons of the mean avoidance scores between high- and low-witness groups demonstrated similar patterns of symptomatology and reduction. Low-witness veterans ($M = 12.33$) reported significantly less avoidance than did high-witness

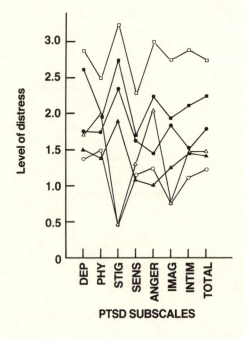

Figure 7.5. VESI-PTSD profile of subscale scores of Vietnam veterans with PTSD and compared to other trauma victims.

veterans ($M = 23.75$) at pretreatment ($t's_9 = 4.3$, $p < .01$) and continue to report less avoidance tendencies over time ($t's_6 > 2.17$, $p < .10$). High-witness veterans also show a significant decrease in avoidance symptoms over time ($t's_{12} > 3.25$, $p < .01$) although the rate of reduction is less than that observed for intrusion. On the other hand, low-witness veterans show only directional change over time.

No significant differences were found between high and low participants in atrocities on intrusion or avoidance measures. Intrusion scores for high-atrocity participants did decrease significantly over time ($t's_5 > 2.66$, $p < .05$), but the avoidance scores were more resistant to change and did not show a significant decrease until the three-month follow-up ($t_5 = 2.09$, $p < .10$). Low-atrocity participants generally did not show any decrease in intrusion or avoidance over time.

The total atrocity scores show a pattern of symptom reduction similar to that found for participants in atrocities. However, veterans with low involvement in atrocities do have significantly less avoidance tendencies at pretreatment than do veterans with higher levels of atrocity involvement.

Table 7.5 presents a summary analysis of the global severity index (GSI) on the SCL-90 before and after the intensive treatment program for veterans who witnessed or participated in atrocities. Median splits were used to distinguish high and low levels of each atrocity dimension to assess possible differential effects on global severity of reported symptoms. Comparisons similar to those presented in Table 7.5 were conducted and the results were nearly analogous.

At the pretreatment level t-tests revealed significantly less global severity for those in the low-witness category ($M = 1.16$) as opposed to those in the high-witness category ($M = 1.83$), ($t_9 = 3.56$, $p < .01$). However, this finding was not repeated at the one- and three-month follow-ups due, in part, to the dramatic decrease in GSI over time in the high-witness group ($t's_{12} > 9.39$, $p < .001$) as compared to only an insignificant directional change for the low-witness group.

Low-atrocity participants consistently reported higher levels of global severity than did high-atrocity participants across time intervals ($t's_5 > 3.18$, $p < .05$). *High-atrocity* participants demonstrated a significant decrease in global severity over time ($t's_5 > 4.37$, $p < .01$), while *low-atrocity* participants reported an insignificant change in the direction of symptom reduction.

Veterans who report low-total-atrocity involvement show less global severity than those who report high-total-atrocity involvement at pretreatment ($t_9 = 1.87$, $p < .10$). Distress levels on the GSI for high-total-atrocity involvement veterans decrease significantly over time ($t's_{10} > 8.22$, $p < .001$) while levels of global severity for low-total-atrocity involvement veterans show only an insignificant change in the direction of symptom reduction.

Table 7.6 presents a summary analysis of the VESI-PTSD scale before and after the intensive treatment program for veterans who witnessed or participated in atrocities. Analysis was conducted in the same manner as shown in Tables 7.7 and 7.8.

At the pretreatment, *low-witness* veterans reported approximately half as much PTSD symptomatology as high-witness veterans ($t_9 = 5.17$, $p < .001$) and slightly less than half at one month posttreatment ($t_6 = 3.66$, $p < .05$). Both groups showed an insignificant change in the direction of symptom reduction over time, with the exception of the high-witness group, who showed a prominent decrease in reported distress levels by three months posttreatment ($t_{12} = 7.03$, $p < .001$).

TABLE 7.4
Summary Analysis of Intrusion and Avoidance Scores on the Impact of Event Scale Before and After Brief Psychotherapy for Patients Who Witnessed or Participated in Atrocities

Impact of Event Scale Time Interval	ATROCITY SCALE					
	Witness		Participant		Total	
	Hi	Low	Hi	Low	Hi	Low
INTRUSION SCALE						
Pre-Treatment	20.00	12.67**	20.00	21.67	19.57	17.25
One-month Follow-up	13.17[d]	10.50	13.33[b]	16.25[a]	11.60[d]	13.33
Three-month Follow-up	10.33[d]	6.50	13.00[b]	18.40	10.00[d]	12.00
AVOIDANCE SCALE						
Pre-Treatment	23.75	12.33**	22.00	20.33	24.00	15.00**
One-month Follow-up	18.33[c]	13.50+	17.33	20.00	17.00[c]	15.00
Three-month Follow-up	16.33[c]	9.50+	14.33[a]	20.60	15.80[c]	12.33+

$+ p < .10; * p < .05; ** p < .01; *** p < .001;$
$a\ p < .10; b\ p < .05; c\ p < .01; d\ p < .001$

Note: Significance levels for comparisons between Hi-Low groups for each atrocity scale within time intervals are reported by $+$, $*$, $**$, $***$, as indicated above, and are read horizontally across the table. Significance levels for comparisons between time intervals (one and three month follow-up scores as compared to pre-treatment scores) for each group and level of the atrocity scale within intrusion and avoidance respectively, are reported by a, b, c, d, as indicated above, and are read vertically down the table.

TABLE 7.5

Summary Analysis of the Global Severity Index
on the Symptom Checklist-90 Before and After Brief Psychotherapy
for Patients Who Witnessed or Participated in Atrocities

SCL-90 Time Interval	Witness		Participant		Total	
	Hi	Low	Hi	Low	Hi	Low
GLOBAL SEVERITY INDEX (GSI)						
Pre-Treatment	1.83	1.16**	1.28	2.02*	1.82	1.46 +
One-month Follow-up	1.00^d	.74	.72^c	1.69*	.90^d	1.13
Three-month Follow-up	.95^d	.65	.65^c	1.77**	.81^d	.96

+ p < .10; *p < .05; **p < .01; ***p < .001;
a p < .10; b p < .05; c p < .01; d p < .001

Note: Significance levels for comparisons between levels of each atrocity scale group, respectively, within time intervals are reported by +, *, **, ***, as indicated above, and are read horizontally across the table. Significance levels for comparisons between time intervals (one and three month follow-up scores as compared to pre-treatment) for each group and level of the atrocity scale are reported by a, b, c, d, as indicated above, and are read vertically down the table.

Low-total-atrocity participants reported significantly higher levels of PTSD than those reported by high-atrocity participants consistently across time ($t's_5 > 2.3$, $p < .05$). Generally, both groups showed only an insignificant reduction in symptoms over time.

Low-total-atrocity involvement veterans reported significantly less PTSD symptomatology than that reported by veterans with high-total-atrocity involvement ($t_9 = 2.33$, $p < .10$). High-total-atrocity involvement veterans reported a significant decrease in PTSD symptoms over time ($t_{10} = 6.15$, $p < .001$), while levels of PTSD reported by low-total-atrocity veterans remained relatively unchanged over time.

Intrusion and Avoidance Aspects of PTSD and Psychopathology

Table 7.7 shows a summary analysis of the severity of psychopathology measured by the global severity index on the SCL-90 and the total VESI-PTSD score as related to the intrusion and avoidance dimensions of PTSD measured by the IES. Median splits were used to distinguish high and low levels of intrusion and avoidance to assess possible differential effects of these dimensions on the severity of psychopathology. Consistent with the model of stress recovery presented by Horowitz (1979), we assert that intrusion and avoidance are not mutually exclusive dimensions of PTSD. It is possible for the trauma victim to experience high levels of both intrusion and avoidance during the stress recovery process.

Comparisons were done to: (1) determine whether a difference in the level of psychopathology exists between high and low levels of intrusion and avoidance, respectively, and; (2) determine whether a difference in the level of psychopathology exists between high levels of intrusion and avoidance and low levels of both dimensions, respectively.

T-tests revealed extremely lower levels of global severity for both low-intrusion and low-avoidance groups as compared to the corresponding high groups ($t_{10} = 11.72$, $p < .001$; $t_7 = 12.15$, $p < .001$; $t = 14.05$, $p < .001$; $t_7 = 13.36$, $p < .001$, respectively). Comparisons done between the high-intrusion and high-avoidance groups revealed no significant difference in levels of global severity or PTSD; however, the low-intrusion group reported slightly higher levels of global severity and PTSD than did the low-avoidance group ($t_5 = 2.06$, $p < .05$).

In recognition of the fact that individuals may have varying or similar levels of intrusion and avoidance not accounted for by Table 7.7, further

TABLE 7.6
Summary Analysis of the VESI-PTSD Index
Before and After Brief Psychotherapy
for Patients Who Witnessed or Participated in Atrocities

VESI-PTSD SCALE Time Interval	Witness		Participant		Total	
	Hi	Low	Hi	Low	Hi	Low
PTSD TOTAL SCORE						
Pre-Treatment	183.63	92.33**	129.25	204.33	180.71	136.40 +
One-month Follow-up	151.25	79.50*	105.33	167.25 + b	142.90 b	134.67
Three-month Follow-up	114.25 d	85.00	99.00	200.40**	105.00 c	130.33

+p < .10; *p < .05; **p <.01; ***p <.001;
a p < .10; b p < .05; c p < .01; d p < .001

Note: Significance levels for comparisons between levels of each atrocity scale group, respectively, within time intervals are reported by +, *, **, ***, as indicated above, and are read horizontally across the table. Significance levels for comparisons between time intervals (one and three month follow-up scores as compared to pre-treatment) for each group and level of the atrocity scale are reported by a, b, c, d, as indicated above, and are read vertically down the table.

TABLE 7.7
Summary Analysis of Severity of Psychopathology
as Related to Avoidance and Intrusion Dimension of PTSD
for Vietnam Veterans Prior to Brief Psychotherapy

	IMPACT OF EVENT SCALE			
	INTRUSION		AVOIDANCE	
	High	Low	High	Low
Measure of Psychopathology				
GSI — SCL-90	2.42	.87***	2.51	.487***
PTSD-VESI	248.13	70.00***	252.00	34.33***

+p < .10; *p < .05; **p <.01; ***p <.001;

comparisons were conducted to address the possible confounding effects of multigroup membership. Table 7.8 presents a summary analysis of comparisons done between the finer distinctions of intrusion and avoidance levels (high levels of both [HH], high-intrusion/low-avoidance [HL], low-intrusion/high-avoidance [LH], low levels of both [LL] as related to the severity of psychopathology reported at pretreatment and three months posttreatment. Given our small sample size, a comparison of this type is difficult. However, several important distinctions are illustrated. Overall, taking into consideration the small cell size of the HL and LH groups, the general pattern appears to be one of no change in symptom severity within groups over time. However, the obvious shift in distribution from the high range to the low is noteworthy. Of the eight individuals high on both intrusion and avoidance at pretreatment, data available at three months posttreatment show that four veterans shift to other groups: one to HL, one to LH, and two to LL. Clearly, while the reported severity of psychopathology within respective groups remains relatively unchanged across time, the data are suggestive of a directional change toward less intrusion and avoidance. Levels of global severity for the LL group as compared to the HH group remain significantly lower at pre- and posttreatment (t_{10} = 10.20, p < .001; t_8 = 6.77, p < .001, respectively), as is the case for levels of PTSD (t_{10} = 12.32, p < .001).

DISCUSSION

*Treatment Outcome: One- and Three-Month
Follow-Up*

The results for the one- and three-month follow-up on the effects of the intensive treatment program indicate a significant reduction in

TABLE 7.8

Summary Analysis of Psychopathology as Classified by Impact of Event Scales for Vietnam Veterans in Brief Psychotherapy

IMPACT OF EVENT SCALE	Pre-Treatment Measure of Psychopathology			Post-Treatment Measure of Psychopathology			Directional Change in Symptom Expression	
	GSI	PTSD	N	GSI	PTSD	N	N	
Level of Intrusion/ Avoidance								
HH*	2.34	240	8	2.44	262.67	3	−62.5%
HL	1.91	204	1	1.50	221.00	1	0.0%
LH	3.09	212.5	2	.89	113.00	1	−50.0%
LL	.87	70	4	1.14	98.14	7	+75.0%

*H = high on IES subscale
L = low

symptoms on all three measures of psychopathology. All of the subscales on the SCL-90 showed decreases at the one- and three-month follow-ups. Noteworthy is the large decrease in hostility, suggesting that the men felt less angry. The global severity index (GSI), which measures both the number and intensity of symptoms, also showed a decrease at the follow-up intervals. However, the positive symptom distress measure (PSD) indicated that for the symptoms that remained distressing, their level was about equal since the item variance was small. Inspection of the individual items that made up the PSD scores indicated the distressing problems largely concerned interpersonal relationships.

A similar set of findings was obtained from IES and VESI measures of PTSD. The results indicate that there was a significant reduction in intrusive imagery associated with the Vietnam War as well as a decrease in avoidance behaviors associated with war stress. Interestingly, however, the avoidance measure did not reach significance until the three-month follow-up, a fact which may indicate that avoidance as a coping strategy is resistant to change. Thus, while the veteran may experience fewer episodes of intrusive imagery, the tendency to avoid thinking about war trauma or the more active, purposive avoidance of trauma-related stimuli remained relatively strong; e.g., "I stayed away from reminders of it."

The results on the VESI also indicate a significant decrease in PTSD symptom clusters: depression, stigmatization, sensation seeking, anger, intrusive imagery, and total PTSD symptoms. Two symptom groups showed relatively little change at the follow-up intervals. The mean scores on the intimacy conflict subscale, which did not change across intervals, indicate that there is an area of disturbance in interpersonal relations. Similarly, the physical symptoms subscale only reached marginal significance at the three-month follow-up. Taken together, the results from the VESI indicate that although the overall severity was significantly reduced and the men felt much *less* depressed, confused, stigmatized, alienated, angry, and sensation seeking, they still had physical expressions of anxiety and difficulty in intimate relations. When these findings are combined with those from the SCL-90 and the IES, there is strong support for the therapeutic efficacy of the intensive treatment program. Yet, change in some symptom clusters was either slow (e.g., avoidance tendencies) or nonexistent (e.g., intimacy conflict). As a general conclusion, it appears that as a result of the treatment program the men felt higher in self-esteem, less depressed, calmer, and far less distressed emotionally as compared to their emotional well-being prior to the program.

COMPARISON OF VIETNAM VETERANS
WITH PTSD AND OTHER PSYCHIATRIC
POPULATIONS

In order to obtain a clearer picture of the level of psychopathology present in the Vietnam veterans suffering from PTSD, comparisons were made on the subscale scores with those found in other psychiatric populations. On the SCL-90 three major differences were found in the comparative analysis. First, the pretreatment profile scores of Vietnam veterans are remarkably higher than those of the comparison populations: general psychiatric outpatients, psychiatric emergency service, and alcoholics (Derogatis, 1973). Second, on the specific subscales the Vietnam veteran sample reported higher scores on somatization, obsession-compulsion, hostility, and phobic anxiety, all symptom clusters consistent with PTSD. However, at the three-month follow-up the subscales for the veterans are significantly less extreme and tend to resemble those of general psychiatric outpatients. Their depression scores, although significantly reduced, remain at a level comparable to that found in alcoholics. Thus, the three-month follow-up data indicate a profile similar to that of outpatients in psychotherapy, a fact that further validates the usefulness of the intensive treatment program.

On the other hand, the mean SCL-90 profile scores for the veterans in the treatment program are elevated enough to suggest the need for additional treatment.*

Comparative analysis of the veterans' scores on the IES shows a configuration similar to that obtained on the SCL-90. As compared to a normative sample without trauma, the Vietnam veterans' pretreatment scores are 60% higher on the intrusion dimension. However, the mean scores on intrusion and avoidance are on an average quite similar to those found for other trauma groups (e.g., rape, multiple trauma). At the three-month follow-up, there was a decrease of 36% in intrusion and 25% in the avoidance dimension of PTSD as assessed by the IES. Similar results were found on the VESI in that there was a 20% decrease in the total PTSD symptomatology. As noted previously, the intimacy conflict dimension of PTSD only decreased in severity by 5%, a nonsignificant change.

In summary, the level of psychopathology of Vietnam veterans with PTSD appears to be very severe prior to the intensive treatment program,

---

* Of the 15 participants in the program, five were later accepted to the American Lake VA PTSD Unit for inpatient treatment.

especially in comparison with other treatment-seeking psychiatric populations. At the three-month follow-up interval the severity of psychopathology resembles that of a general outpatient population, with
significant decreases in PTSD, especially in the level of intrusive imagery.
And, while the anxiety and depressive components of PTSD appear to
have been positively affected by the treatment program, relatively little,
if any, change was seen in the severity of intimacy conflict. Clearly,
there are many possible explanations of this finding, which range from
changed role relations, codependency issues, and difficulties on the part
of the veteran to change patterns of coping and emotional expressiveness. Ultimately, of course, true intimacy requires trust and moments
of vulnerability. If nothing else, PTSD is a profound stress response to
moments of genuine threat and vulnerability. To become vulnerable
again requires the dropping of defenses that have, to a large extent,
ensured survival, even if it is an existence that is numbed and problematic.

THE EXPOSURE TO AND PARTICIPATION
IN WAR ATROCITY

It is probable that all wars have levels of violence that exceed whatever
rules govern the battlefield. The Vietnam War was no exception, and
recent research points to the involvement in episodes of "abusive
violence," more commonly called atrocities, as a significant determinant
of the severity and nature of PTSD (Laufer, Frey-Wouters, & Gallops,
1985). Partly for this reason, the relationship between witnessing and
participating in war atrocities, and psychopathology was examined. As
in previous research (Wilson & Krauss, 1985), the distinction between
witnessing and participating in an atrocity is important because they
involve different types of psychological involvement. The person who
witnesses an atrocity is more often than not involved indirectly in the
event. For example, a platoon of men may enter a village and inad-
vertently come across the grotesque remains of fellow soldiers who
were tortured and mutilated by the enemy. In the Vietnam War there
were many events of this type in which a soldier might be exposed to
the brutal aftermath of violence carried to the extreme. For such a
person, the images and smells form an imprint which usually over-
whelms moral sensibility and conception of a just world. For most the
imprint is indelible and ultimately taxes the survivor's ability to place
it into some perspective of understanding. The difficulty of this task is

that some acts of evil cannot easily be placed into a perspective that ensures that the memory will be made any less painful (see Lifton, 1986, for further discussion in regard to this phenomenon in Holocaust survivors).

The participant in committing an atrocity is placed into a different role than one who witnesses such an act. The participant actively chooses to commit an act of violence against another human being. The person who does such acts may well have formulated a rationalization for the act, such as giving the enemy "an eye for an eye" or expressing feelings of "payback." In some cases the individual seems to cross the line between being a soldier at war and an automaton who kills instinctively, hunting, stalking, and destroying in the most savage manner possible. After the war, the person who was the agent of abusive violence is just as likely as one who witnesses an atrocity to face the impact of such an experience. Recently, Laufer (1988) has proposed that such persons may develop a "serial self" or a kind of second identity by which to insulate the prewar self from that which was involved in the atrocity. This idea is similar to Lifton's (1986) concept of doubling, in which a second self, a double, is formed to cope with extremely traumatic situations, especially when placed into situations that require behavior so radically different from the normal values of a healthy ego. The serial self and the concept of doubling both suggest that the commission of acts of violence that radically alter and oppose the minimal condition of humaneness may, in turn, alter the perpetrator's self-structure in pathological ways that range from severe character deformation to unconscious numbing and self-punishment mechanisms.

What do the results of the analyses of involvement with atrocities reveal in terms of psychopathology? On the IES, the men who scored low on the witnessing of atrocities had significantly less intrusion and avoidance symptoms than did those who had high levels of witnessing abusive violence. Further, for the low-witness group, the mean scores did not decrease significantly from the pretreatment levels. Thus, the low-witness group was less severely affected initially and during the follow-up intervals in comparison to the men who had witnessed many more episodes of atrocities. Interestingly, however, the high-witness group did have significant decreases in intrusion and avoidance symptoms at the follow-up intervals, a fact which suggests that as a result of treatment they were less troubled by what they had witnessed than before the psychotherapy.

But what about the participants in atrocities? As implied earlier, the participation in atrocities would seem to involve different and perhaps more complex psychological dimensions. Contrary to expectation, men who reported low participation in atrocities had significantly *higher* symptoms of intrusion and avoidance at all three intervals. In both groups, however, there was very little change in symptom level over time.

How is one to interpret such findings in such a small sample of treatment-seeking individuals with PTSD? Several alternative explanations readily come to mind. First, men with low participation in atrocities may be more intrapsychically conflicted and preoccupied with having committed an act of abusive violence. If so, one would expect the results we obtained: high levels of intrusion and avoidance symptoms. Thus, episodes of intrusive reliving would contain imagery of atrocities, which in turn would lead to attempts to avoid such imagery and affect. In contrast, men with high participation in atrocity may have developed ways to rationalize, numb, deny, or seal over the atrocity experience. Thus, if the involvement with atrocity led to doubling, a serial self-structure, or some other form of adaptation, then one would expect such persons to deny the involvement by denying to consciousness thoughts or images connected to their responsibility for the acts. By this logic, such persons should tend to self-report less intrusion and avoidance, as found. On the other hand, the measures of PTSD, such as physiological measures of arousal, might reveal more severe PTSD, despite self-reports to the contrary.

This interesting configuration of results found on the IES was also obtained on the SCL-90 and VESI measures of psychopathology. As expected, men with high witness scores had more global severity of symptoms on the SCL-90 and PTSD than did veterans with low witness exposure. However, there was a significant reduction in symptoms at the one- and three-month follow-up for the high-witness group. In fact, the mean scores dropped by half on both the SCL-90 and the PTSD scales, which suggests a powerful therapeutic outcome.

The results for the participants in atrocity parallel those obtained on the IES. Paradoxically, men with low levels of participation in atrocities reported more global severity of symptoms and total PTSD than did veterans with high levels of involvement in atrocities. Although there are several plausible explanations of these findings, it may be that men with only one or two experiences as a participant in atrocities are more conflicted and troubled by such actions than are men with greater degrees of participation. For the latter group, multiple involvement in atrocities may be associated with more successful techniques of avoidance of atrocity-related imagery and affect. As noted above, the concepts of doubling, serial self, splitting off, and sealing over have been used to explain adaptation to grotesque death, killing, and mutilation in situations of brutality. While the specific nature of the mechanisms that might underlie such psychic phenomena as doubling (Lifton, 1986) are not well understood at this time, it is clearly an important area for future research.

CONCLUSION

In evaluating the success of the treatment program, a number of things must be kept in perspective before any conclusions are drawn about the efficacy and applicability of this technique of treatment of PTSD. First, the location of the program was felt to be important. Lake Crescent in the Olympic National Park is a beautiful and picturesque setting. It is a secluded wilderness, shrouded by fir-and-cedar-lined mountains, factors that we felt were especially important and relevant for Vietnam Veterans with PTSD because of the parallels to terrain in Vietnam and because of the sheer physical beauty of the Olympic forest. It was felt that by being together for a week in a remote, "bushlike" spot, without the intrusions or the daily stresses of more urban settings, the men could once again form a "platoon" and rebond in both old and new ways. The "old way," of course, was the style of being a combat unit in Vietnam, replete with military deportment. Indeed, Bruce and I found ourselves being referred to as "Doc" or the commanding officers (CO's) in charge of the program. On the other hand, a new form of bonding became evident and emerged from the "mission" of the treatment program: to heal the scars from the war. And in this way the bonding no longer centered on fighting the enemy, but instead focused on letting go of the pain of war trauma, self-destructiveness, guilt, anger, and feelings of stigmatization and persecution.

It may well be that for Vietnam veterans with severe PTSD, the opportunity to reestablish trust, bonding, and the permission to relinquish pain in order to reformulate the meaning of traumatic experiences may necessitate a safe and naturalistic setting that removes the institutional stigmatization of being a sick patient in need of care. Clearly, careful selection and screening of the participants is important, and not all veterans with PTSD may be ready for such an experience. In the program presented here, all of the men were self-selected volunteers who were motivated to participate in the intensive treatment plan, an eclectic approach which utilized a therapeutic community, group and individual counseling, and Native American rituals (i.e., the homecoming welcome and feast, the planting of a fir sapling, the ceremonial fires, the potlatch, and the daily sweat lodge). Thus, when considering the results of the follow-up testing, it is essential that the treatment program be viewed as a holistic experience in which the sweat lodge was only one of a series of powerful therapeutic endeavors. Yet, its effects cannot be underestimated. Moreover, as originally intended by Native Americans, the sweat lodge is part of tribal customs embedded in a meaningful ecological and cultural context. In this case the cultural context was the current social status of Vietnam veterans with PTSD who possess a unique perspective of themselves and society which was born from their war experiences.

Inside the sweat lodge that common social reality could be shared in a new way which not only validated the difficult realities of the war in their lives, but involved them in an inner search to transform themselves in healthier directions. For most men in the program it was a time of deep soul searching.

When looking at the configuration of the results from the follow-up assessment, it is clear that the intensive treatment program produced significant reductions in post-traumatic symptoms, which remained at a lowered level from the baseline measures. The data indicate that the men felt less depressed, angry, alienated, anxious, and prone to somaticize. The global level of severity of their symptoms was also significantly reduced. But, as noted earlier, intimacy conflict remained problematic, as did avoidance tendencies in terms of dealing with war trauma.

There are several plausible explanations why intimate relations remained conflicted and relatively unaffected by the treatment program. First, we observed that when the spouses and significant others returned to Camp David on Lake Crescent at the end of the week, some of them were suspicious of the overt behavioral change in their partners. Men who had previously been angry, isolated, and constricted were now open, calm, expressive, and affectionate. A few of the women adopted a "wait-and-see attitude," perhaps an expectable reaction after years of interpersonal turmoil. Further, some of the women appeared threatened by the positive changes in appearance and behavior that were self-evident. As we understand it, the threat seemed to revolve around issues of control, since many of the women were used to the role of being the strong, controlling, and dominant partner who was the central, stable person in the family or relationship. Now, however, the veteran seemed to want, and perhaps need, a different relationship.

It is quite possible therefore that previously formed role patterns were out of balance and thus created a new source of conflict.

In other cases, several of the participants later terminated love relationships and began new ones with partners with whom they felt more intimate. In yet another case, the veteran resumed relations with an ex-wife after he came to the realization that because of his PTSD and drug and alcohol abuse, he had acted in ways that contributed to the breakdown of the marriage. Finally, when we assume a more psychiatric perspective of PTSD, it seems reasonable to expect that the symptoms most easily ameliorated are those directly associated with the disorder's hyperarousability, intrusion, reexperiencing and reenactment, anxiety, and depression. These symptoms are psychobiological in nature and the products of extreme stress. Intimate relations, while effected by PTSD, are social in nature and dynamically affected by both partners' needs, motives, and family background factors.

Clearly, it would be interesting to examine the factors that affect successful versus unsuccessful intimate relations where one of the partners suffers from PTSD. Needless to say, any illness has an impact on a family system or attachment process. Perhaps PTSD, like alcoholism, causes the formation of particular kinds of role relationships which range from codependency and enabling to protective nurturance and shielding behaviors.

In conclusion, it can be stated unequivocally that the intensive, one-week treatment program in a naturalistic setting that utilized an eclectic approach combined with Native American rituals for healing and purification was an extraordinary experience. From the initial apprehension and anxiety felt by the participants and the staff, there gradually emerged a profound bonding, caring, and open sharing of lives in pain and fragmentation. During the first nights few men slept very much and many were reliant on VA-prescribed medication to sleep or to feel less anxious. By the end of the week the staff was keeping a grocery bag full of various medications prescribed to reduce the symptoms of PTSD. Moreover, the men had to be awakened for the day's activities because they were sleeping so soundly. Likewise, initially some of the men had to be encouraged to eat during the meals. By the end of the week, however, the very large supply of food had run out. It was not uncommon for men to make two or three trips to the kitchen for additional food and drink.

Appearances, too, changed quite dramatically in a short week. Tired-looking, haggard, and tense faces without much emotional expression transformed to the opposite. By the end there was joking, teasing, laughter, smiles, and a calm, rested appearance. The men spontaneously joined in small groups, clasped hands with the 'Nam handshake and spoke from the heart without fear of judgment. When it was time to leave the camp, everyone seemed ambivalent about leaving their friends, a sentiment most had experienced years before in Vietnam.

PERSONAL COMMENTARY AND CONCLUSION

On the last day there was a long session of picture taking after lunch. It seemed as if everyone wanted to take the experience home in a special way. I was given a special gift of appreciation by the entire group: A Viet Cong flag captured 30 kilometers above the demilitarized zone by a former Navy Seal Team member, which was signed by all the men.

Before dismantling the camp, everyone exchanged addresses and telephone numbers in order to maintain contact. At the end everyone left the camp at the same time and drove down the "homecoming road" which wound its way along a ridge line that overlooked Lake Crescent. Bruce and I wondered if the men felt different on their way back home this time as compared to the jet airplane ride years ago upon return from Vietnam. For our parts, we had mixed feelings about leaving the camp. It had been an incredible week, unlike anything we had ever experienced before as clinicians. Clearly, there was a part of us that wanted to continue the program for another week. We had seen so much healing and recovery from stress take place that we wanted it to continue. On the other hand, we were very tired after working 20-hour days filled with much responsibility. The idea of a relaxing weekend felt good, and we talked about preparing a dinner of fresh king salmon for the staff.

By now it was midafternoon, and while we were driving along the ridgeline, the sun streaked brilliantly through the tall fir trees that thickly populated the gently sloping hillsides. As sparkles of sunlight danced on the lake below, the air felt cool and had the soft and faint aroma of a camp fire which signaled the coming of dusk in the Pacific Northwest. It was one of those rare and transcendent moments in which time seemed suspended and everything was as it should be in a natural order.

As we drove down the highway along Lake Crescent, I looked back at Camp David with its rustic lodges and thought about the week's activities. It was September 1985, and only four months earlier I had experienced my first sweat lodge on the Sisseton-Wahpeton Sioux reservation in South Dakota. I remembered that during that sweat lodge I had asked the Grandfathers to help me find new ways of understanding PTSD and of helping Vietnam veterans and other traumatized persons. Upon reflection at that moment, I felt that I had been taught a great deal in a short amount of time. I recalled, too, the words of a Sacred Pipe carrier of the Sioux tribe who spoke that we would learn to see more of what is "out there" (physical reality) and more of what is "in here" (personal knowledge) each time the entrance to the sweat lodge was opened. And as Bruce and I drove toward his home in Port Angeles, I felt that I was beginning to understand what Crazy Buffalo really meant and laughed inside at my culturally limited view of reality.

It is my belief that the approach we used in the intensive treatment program can be expanded and improved upon in many directions. These include longer treatment programs, careful screening and testing to determine the ideal candidate for this type of experience, and the use of bona fide medicine persons of Native American tribes to assist with certain rituals, such as the sweat lodge. *We do not recommend that anyone attempt to replicate our experience or adapt Native American rituals without the utmost care, respect, knowledge, consultation, and approval of experienced medicine persons. It is also imperative to respect the fact that these rituals are embedded in the culture and cannot be extricated for reasons of expediency or personal gain.* Finally, given the dearth of programs to adequately treat Vietnam veterans and other victims suffering from extreme stress experiences, the evolution and development of innovative approaches to stress recovery and the healing of distressing emotions is a timely and important task for our time.

8

Intervention and Principles of Treatment

Traumatically stressful life events inevitably disrupt the physical and psychological equilibrium of the individual. As noted in Chapter 2, the psychobiology of stress response syndromes is becoming well understood and includes state-dependent learning which occurs in the context of excessive antonomous nervous system arousal, especially in the production and depletion of neurotransmitters. In severe cases of post-traumatic stress disorder (PTSD), the physical disequilibrium may be prolonged and directly associated with episodes of intrusive imagery and reliving which often alternate with periods of depression, isolation, withdrawal, emotional constriction, and detachment. In this regard, it is proper to speak of a complex mind-body relationship, since there is a disruption of the steady state of the autonomic nervous system. This physical disequilibrium is, in fact, the biological substrate of post-traumatic stress disorder and may warrant pharmacological intervention (Roth, 1988). However, the intervention and treatment of post-traumatic stress disorder require more than medication for the alteration of symptoms. To heal from the emotional effects of trauma involves the re-establishment of continuity and cohesion in the self which integrates the core identity processes of the person.

Generally, victims of extremely stressful life events are aware that the trauma has changed them in ways that are not immediately understandable but acutely distressing and often confusing. Initially, many individuals experience shock, numbing, anger, rage, denial, disavowal, grief, tension, mistrust, and symptoms of hyperarousal, such as sleep disturbances. Figure 8.1 summarizes the core set of symptoms associated with post-traumatic stress disorder which eventually becomes the focus

196

of intervention and treatment for persons seeking professional help to work through the psychic residue of their traumatic experiences.

Moreover, it is also common for victims of trauma to be reluctant to talk about their experiences for several reasons. First, they fear that the mental health professional will not understand what they have "gone through" since "they were not there" and therefore cannot possibly understand "what it was like." Second, upon becoming symptomatic, especially with episodes of involuntary, unbidden intrusive imagery,

Traumatic Event

↓

Physical and Psychological Disequilibrium

↓

(Psychological Substrate)

↓

Psychobiological

↓

PTSD Cyclical Alternation

Intrusion/Reexperience[B] (Catecholinergic/Ergotropic)	←——————→	**Avoidance/Numbing** [C] (Cholinergic/Trophotropic)

Intrusion/Reexperience[B]
(Catecholinergic/Ergotropic)

1. Intrusive imagery w/ or w/out affect
2. Affective flooding w/ or w/out imagery
3. Hallucination w/trauma-related imagery
4. Dissociation (flashbacks)
5. Anniversary reactions; emotional lability
6. Unconscious behavioral reenactment
7. Intensification by exposure to stimuli or ideation

Avoidance/Numbing [C]
(Cholinergic/Trophotropic)

1. Restricted affect
2. Detachment, isolation, withdrawal, estrangement
3. Amnesia, impaired concentration and cognition
4. Loss of interest in meaningful activities
5. Developmental arrestation
6. Sense of foreshortened future
7. Depressed affect trauma related

Physiological Hyperarousal (ANS) [D]

1. Exaggerated startle response
2. Affective hyperarousal
3. Frenetic overactivity
4. Sleep disturbance
5. Hypervigilance and scanning
6. Sensation seeking (action addict)
7. Pronounced ANS activity to stimuli w/trauma association

Figure 8.1. Core symptoms associated with post-traumatic stress disorder reactions which are the focus of intervention and treatment. B, C, D = DSM-III-R criteria.

the person typically fears he is "going crazy." Such anxiety may motivate entrance into treatment, but it is more typical for the person to isolate himself, avoid talking about his inner concerns, and, perhaps, engage in self-medication with alcohol or drugs. For treatment to begin, these initial forms of resistance must be overcome in order to establish rapport and trust. It is also important for the clinician to acknowledge these concerns of the victim, which are well founded and defensive in nature. Thus, although it is true that the therapist was not present during the trauma, the reluctance of the client to discuss what happened stems from the need to protect against feelings of vulnerability, helplessness, and further victimization.

As will be discussed later in the section on principles of treatment, the establishment of trust born from an empathic and nonjudgmental stance by the therapist is imperative in order to achieve a working alliance that will permit a successful working through of the victimization. Acknowledging the reality of the individual's fear of not being understood and the apprehension over going crazy is the beginning of validating that the traumatic experience was terrifying, threatening, and produced distressing effects which have interfered with adaptive functioning. Stated simply, this validates that the trauma was real and the probable cause of the present level of emotional distress.

POST-TRAUMATIC THERAPY

The rapid emergence of traumatic stress studies (Figley, 1985, 1986) in the last decade has given birth to a form of treatment known as post-traumatic therapy (PTT) (Ochberg, 1988). In describing the central tenets of PTT, Ochberg writes:

A second clinical approach (cf. PTT) concentrates far more on the recent events, the coping skills and strengths of the victim, the realistic available options, and the correctable misconceptions or self-defeating thoughts that interfere with rapid emotional healing. I prefer the second approach as a place to start, and I prefer related approaches that presuppose no preexisting psychopathology, unless a client clearly indicates that post-traumatic adjustment is not the issue but pre-traumatic problems, perhaps brought to the fore in stressful circumstances, are the prevailing reasons for help. The advantages in what I call post-traumatic therapy (PTT) are its assumption of psychological health, its fundamental assertion that the victim is not to blame, its ability to facilitate a working relationship between victim and therapist through partnership and parity in respect and power. (pp. 9–10)

Ochberg goes on to propose that in post-traumatic adjustment there are five central paradigms that encompass the range of stress reactions in victims: (1) bereavement or a psychological sense of loss; (2) victimization, humiliation, and subjugation; (3) excessive autonomic nervous system arousal; (4) death imagery and the specter of death itself; and (5) negative intimacy or feelings of defilement, subjugation, and humiliation caused by the perpetrator of the victimization. These five clusters of attributes indigenous to post-traumatic adjustment are not new and have been discussed by other clinicians and researchers (e.g., Appley and Trumbull, 1986; Figley, 1985; Horowitz, 1986; Lifton, 1979; Lindy, 1986, 1988; Raphael, 1987; Scurfield, 1985; Wilson, 1988b). However, what is important to the understanding of techniques of intervention and treatment is that these core issues are viewed as the direct consequence of traumatization and not the result of premorbidity or preexisting personality dimensions.

Persons who have been victimized present for treatment with distress and concern about what happened in the trauma, not what happened in childhood.* In most cases, the victim is preoccupied in near-obsessional ways with the events that occurred in the trauma as well as his role in it. In post-traumatic stress disorder, particularly in very severe cases, the psychic residue of trauma *permeates all levels* of psychological functioning and consciousness. For this reason I and my colleagues have written (Wilson et al., 1985) that the individual feels *trapped in the trauma* and fearful that he or she will not be able to overcome the painful affect and imagery which dominates most of his existence.

In severe cases of PTSD, there is a loss of self-continuity and self-sameness, a loss of a coherent and cohesive sense of self, and feelings of narcissistic injury and fragmentation in the ego and identity processes (Horowitz, 1986, Lifton, 1976, 1979; Lindy, 1986; Parson, 1988; Wilson, 1988a). Moreover, the victim also feels highly vulnerable as a consequence of traumatization and is vigilant to potential threats or situations that might render him vulnerable once again, including sessions in the therapist's office. Perhaps for this reason, persons with PTSD are especially prone to testing the therapist's ability or willingness to hear

---

* For persons abused during childhood, their concerns will reflect early traumatization.

the trauma story. If the client believes that the therapist is either unwilling to listen or too distressed by the trauma story, the therapeutic alliance will not be formed to facilitate post-traumatic therapy.

Approaches to the treatment of PTSD are often based on explicit or implicit conceptions of traumatic events and their effect on psychological functioning. In Freud's writings, for example, he defined a traumatic neurosis as a response to excessive stimulation in a brief period of time which overwhelmed the person's ego defenses and coping resources. As a result, the individual became symptomatic in a neurotic-like way in which thoughts and feelings appeared fixated to the event. Freud (1957) wrote:

> The traumatic neuroses demonstrated very clearly that a fixation to the moment of the traumatic occurrence lies at their root. These patients regularly produce the traumatic situation in dreams; in cases showing attacks of an hysterical type in which analysis is possible, it appears that the attack constitutes a complete reproduction of the situation. It is as though these persons had not yet dealt adequately with the situation, as if the task were still actually before them unaccomplished. . . . An experience which we call traumatic is one which within a very short space of time subjects the mind to such a high degree of stimulation that assimilation or elaboration of it can no longer be effected by normal means, so that lasting disturbances must result in the distribution of the energy in the id. (p. 243)

It was Freud's view that the traumatized ego contracted from normal reality-oriented secondary process thinking because attention was directed inwardly to imagery and affect associated with the trauma. A traumatic neurosis was thus characterized by anxiety, depression, nightmares, and persistent concerns about the trauma itself.

As noted by Horowitz (1986), the traditional psychoanalytical approach to treating a traumatic neurosis involved three major principles: abreaction, catharsis, and working through the painful aspects of the stressful event. However, from the perspective of psychoanalysis, the failure to recover from a traumatic event was viewed as a weakness in the ego caused by repressed, instinctual conflicts that were the product of psychosexual development prior to the stressful experience. The *persistence* of symptoms was seen by Freud and others as the result of a character flaw since the neurotic symptoms were simply unleashed by the traumatic blow to ego defenses. Although Freud's model of traumatic neurosis was logically consistent with his instinctual paradigm of neurosis, it clearly fails to recognize the imminence and magnitude of traumatic stressors and their power to produce prolonged stress responses in a person at any age in the lifespan.

I believe that it is especially important for clinicians engaging in post-traumatic therapy to understand just how influential Freud's psychodynamic model of trauma has been because it shifts emphasis away from the magnitude of traumatic stressors on the psychological and physical equilibrium of the person to a focus of premorbidity, character structure, and psychosexual development. As noted by Ochberg (1988), modern post-traumatic therapy regards the issues of premorbidity and preexisting personality structure as relevant *only if* the client raises questions about them during the course of treatment. The potential danger of traditional analytical approaches to treating trauma victims is that it often places far too much emphasis on early psychosexual development and not enough on what happened during and after the traumatic event. Practitioners of post-traumatic therapy recognize that extremely stressful life events can produce *psychic scarring* and PTSD at any point in the life-cycle, from infancy and childhood to the waning years of life.

PHASE-ORIENTED POST-TRAUMATIC THERAPY

In recent years Mardi Horowitz and his associates have developed a conceptual model of stress response syndromes and techniques of psychotherapy that are closely related to the conceptual paradigm itself (Horowitz, 1976, 1979, 1986; Marmar & Horowitz, 1988). Horowitz's model combines many of the principles of psychodynamic theory with an information-processing model of stressful life events. This model proposes that there is a natural sequence of stages to the stress recovery process, which begins with the initial outcry or reaction to the trauma and moves on through a series of distinct stages of: (1) denial/avoidance, (2) intrusive phenomena in affect and imagery, (3) working through, and (4) completion. It is my belief that recovery from trauma is viewed as nearly complete when the individual is capable of integrating the memory and feelings attached to the trauma into the self-structure and ego identity. Psychopathology or PTSD occurs when the individual fixates at one of the stages of stress response (e.g., avoidance); oscillates in a pendulumlike fashion between the avoidance and intrusion cycles; or regresses during the working-through stage.

Clinically, of course, one sign of trauma resolution is when the victim can discuss what happened without distressing affect, avoidance, numbing, or intrusive overloading. At this point, the individual's cognitive reappraisal and reformulation of the trauma are such that reequilibration is established and excessive autonomic nervous system arousal is greatly reduced and at a level similar to the pre-trauma baseline (see Figure 8.1 and Chapters 2 and 3). As a capsule summary of phase-oriented post-traumatic therapy, Horowitz (1986) writes:

> Modifying excessive controls, altering pathological defensive stances, and supporting weak regulatory capacities all are part of the treatment of stress response syndrome. These coping and defensive conditions are set in motion by the impact of stressor events; yet they are also a product of a longstanding personality style. The patient's character also includes enduring schemata of self, others and relationships, as well as persistent life agenda encompassing unconscious scenarios of how the person hopes life will turn out. The treatment invariably involves work with coping and defensism strategies, as well as with the repertoire mentioned above, whether or not these intermediate levels or immediate reaction or personality are interpreted. Then the treatment is both specific and general. (p. 42)

In phase-oriented post-traumatic therapy, Horowitz (1986) has suggested specific treatment objectives for the denial-avoidance and intrusion phases of recovery from extreme stress. In the denial/avoidance phase, he lists seven features of treatment that are designed to facilitate movement through the stages of recovery and to put the person back "on track" of the normal sequence of processing stressful events. These seven treatment objectives are: (1) reduce excessive controls by interpreting defenses and behaviors that are maladaptive; (2) and (3) encourage abreaction and catharsis; (4) facilitate a detailed description of the stressors through association, speech, visual images, role playing, artwork, or reenactments; (5) reconstruct what happened in the trauma; (6) explore emotional dimensions of relationships to others during the event; and (7) encourage emotional relationships with others to counteract psychic numbing and isolation.

Such general principles of treatment during the denial/avoidance phase will help to facilitate a reduction of the seven major symptoms listed in Figure 8.1. Thus, adequate support, a reduction of maladaptive avoidance (e.g., alcohol abuse), catharsis, and active reconstruction of the trauma will work *against* all seven symptoms of post-traumatic avoidance and denial tendencies. For example, (a) affect will be expressed; (b) support and a therapeutic alliance will be formed; (c) amnesia will be lessened; (d) interest in meaningful activities can resume; (e) developmental arrestation can be reduced or eliminated; (f) a greater sense of personal control can be established; and (g) feelings of helplessness and victimization associated with depressive reactions can be explored and placed in perspective.

In the stage of intrusive reexperiencing of trauma, Horowitz (1986) lists 12 techniques of treatment to facilitate the working through of distressing episodes of affective flooding, visual imagery, and thinking. These techniques are as follows: (1) structure events and organize information; (2) reduce the number of external demands; (3) structure periods of rest and recuperation; (4) provide a model for identification and permit temporary dependency and idealization; (5) facilitate cognitive reappraisal and interpret in educative ways; (6) facilitate the differentiation between past and present self-schemata; (7) reduce exposure to stimuli or situations that trigger associations with the trauma; (8) teach "dosing" technique to deal with trauma memories; (9) provide support; (10) evoke positive emotions that are different from negative affect associated with the trauma; (11) employ desensitization and stress-reducing measures; and (12) use antianxiety or other drugs when necessary to attenuate severe symptoms that interfere with psychotherapy.

When successfully employed, these techniques can greatly reduce the debilitating effects of the symptoms of adaptive behavior. Although the *patterning* of episodes of intrusion varies from patient to patient, the central goal of treatment in this stage is to develop enough support and management of daily stressors so that the nature and content of the intrusive material can be interpreted, cognitively reappraised by the client, and worked through to the point that he or she no longer feels vulnerable, fearful, mistrustful, angry, sad, confused as to why it had to happen, and living in a fight-flight modality of nervous system functioning.

As noted earlier, most victims of trauma suffer from a form of narcissistic scarring to their ego and their images of a cohesive and coherent self. The successful working through of distressing affect and imagery restores a sense of integration, coherence, and cohesion to a previously fragmented self that was not only badly injured by the events of the trauma, but very likely *deillusioned* about the meaning of life, the goodness of humankind, and the quality of life in the future.

ISSUES OF COUNTERTRANSFERENCE IN POST-TRAUMATIC THERAPY

Clinicians who work with victims of extreme stress sooner or later come face to face with the reality that some experiences in life are unjust, unfair, brutal, cruel, and deliberately evil. Beyond a doubt, it is difficult to listen empathically and nonjudgmentally to the story of trauma without it generating powerful feelings in the therapist. And the more naturally empathic is the therapist, the greater is the countertransference potential for pain and distress. Individuals suffering from post-traumatic stress disorder have, by definition, endured some of the most life-threatening and terrorizing experiences imaginable. When they come to a mental health professional for help, they often present with a unique combination of reticence and affective intensity. Moreover, as the trauma story unfolds and the deeper, more painful aspects of the experience emerge and intrude in distressing ways upon consciousness, it typically presents the therapist with many challenges to their values and personal conceptions of a just and decent world.

Victims of trauma, especially man-made violence and terrorism, teach us about vulnerability and psychological insecurity. However, effective post-traumatic therapy must recognize and confront the issues of countertransference reactions. Indeed, Danieli (1988), Parson (1988), and Haley (1978, 1985) have all suggested that confronting countertransference is the essential cornerstone of post-traumatic therapy. The diverse range of countertransference reactions all potentially interfere with the creation of a strong therapeutic alliance which will enable bonding, support, trust, and the necessary safe "holding" environment to work through the problems associated with the denial/avoidance and intrusion phases of post-traumatic stress reactions.

Table 8.1 lists common countertransference themes in post-traumatic therapy. The themes are organized into two groupings. The first group includes 11 emotional countertransference reactions and the second group identifies 10 cognitive attributions and interpersonal strategies. These are discussed below.

TABLE 8.1
Common Countertransference Themes
in Post-Traumatic Therapy

Emotional Countertransference Issues
Anger at the source of victimization
Anger at client because of the intensity of affect
Anger at society for failure to help victim
Fear of affective intensity in client
Fear of personal vulnerability and potential for victimization
Anxiety over ability to help the victim
Guilt over being exempted and not suffering
Empathic sadness and grief reactions upon hearing the trauma
   story
Feelings of dread, horror, disgust, shame and revulsion upon
   hearing the trauma story
Numbing of responsiveness in response to psychic overloading
   induced by the trauma story
Deliberate avoidance of the trauma story which may be conscious
   or unconscious

Cognitive Countertransference and Interpersonal Strategies
Belief that "therapeutic blank" screen approach is appropriate
   stance (false neutrality)
Over-identification with the victim
Overcommitment to helping victim
Excessive belief in personal responsibility to shoulder burden of therapy
Ideological and clinical disillusionment produced by the trauma story
Conception of self as rescuer, savior, gifted healer (narcissism)
Form image of client as weak, pitiful and capable of overcoming
   traumatization
Belief that medication will alleviate affective intensity and
   give therapist control
Belief that post-traumatic stress disorder does not exist
Belief that stress symptoms are pre-morbid in origin

EMOTIONAL COUNTERTRANSFERENCE ISSUES

Affective Intensity: Anger/Rage

Individuals suffering from victimization are typically emotionally distressed and unusually intense. Their struggle to move from being a
victim to being a survivor is the heart of what post-traumatic therapy
is about: to transform trauma and to heal. Therapists who work with
persons with post-traumatic reactions experience empathically the distress of their clients, which, in turn, can lead to many different emotional
reactions. Among the most common countertransference reactions in
therapists inexperienced with post-traumatic stress reaction is the sense

of feeling overwhelmed by the trauma story. As noted earlier, traumatically stressful life events are at the extreme end of the stress continuum, and the human account of these difficult events may lead to disillusionment, astonishment, and feelings of being overwhelmed by the patient's story. It is also true that part of feeling overwhelmed arouses issues of vulnerability. The trauma story nearly always contains the message that what happened to the client could just as readily happen to the therapist since human beings are similarly vulnerable to extreme stress experiences.

In response to feeling overwhelmed, vulnerable, or astonished at what happened to the client, the therapist may develop anger at the perpetrator or the source of victimization or, alternatively, at the society's lack of responsiveness to the victim's condition and life circumstances. Anger may also be felt toward the client for telling the trauma story and requesting help from the therapist to get through it. Anger felt toward the patient is particularly hindering in the therapeutic process because the therapist is reluctant or resistant to acknowledge that such an emotion exists. As with most countertransference reactions, the unprocessed reaction suppresses the client's willingness to work through the difficult and conflicted aspects of the traumatic experience.

Fear

Closely related to anger countertransference issues are reactions of fear in the therapist, which usually stems from two sources. First, many traumatized persons are angry to the point of rage and homicidal fantasies of retaliation and "payback." The intensity of the anger and rage is so pronounced that it frightens some therapists who are not accustomed to such reactions. The affective intensity of the client may elicit fear responses in the therapist. Ironically, of course, the affective intensity of rage actually corresponds to the level of *subjective vulnerability*. Thus, countertransference feelings of fear and vulnerability are also closely related to one another. This, then, is the second source of fear, which grows out of the empathic awareness that victimization can lead to states of helplessness, belittlement, humiliation, degradation, and the destruction of will.

Anxiety and Guilt

Guilt and anxiety are also common emotional reactions that are part of countertransference. Anxiety can emanate from many sources and issues in therapy, but primarily it has to do with feelings of uncertainty in the therapist in regard to his ability to "bind" his own emotional state in order to help the client. Stated simply, the therapist has mixed thoughts about whether or not he can cope with what is "going on" in the patient.

Many forms of guilt can arise in post-traumatic therapy. One common reaction is feeling guilty over being exempted from the kinds of trauma that the client has endured. A related form is what Danieli (1988) has termed bystander guilt in which the therapist is self-condemning for failing to take steps to prevent the traumatic event or to somehow rescue the victim from the hands of fate. A third type of self-condemning guilt relates to anxiety and vulnerability in the therapeutic process. Here the therapist feels guilty that the client is not progressing in the stress recovery process and the reason is incompetence or failure on the part of the therapist to fully comprehend the deeper, unresolved issues of the trauma story. If such guilt reactions are sufficiently strong, they may lead to strong avoidance tendencies and shifting focus to pre-trauma personality functioning, to the exclusion of phase-related issues associated with post-traumatic functioning, i.e., the symptoms associated with denial, intrusion, and hyperarousal as they affect work and interpersonal relations.

Empathic Distress

Empathic distress refers to the general category of countertransference reactions, including states of sadness, grief, dread, horror, disgust, shame, or revulsion at what has been disclosed in the trauma story. Sadness and grief reactions in the therapist are natural products of empathic listening but may also be manifestations of issues of personal loss and prolonged grief responses. Reactions of dread, horror, disgust, revulsion, and shame are also experienced by clinicians working with traumatized individuals. It is important to remember that traumatic stressors include such events as rape, torture, war atrocity (e.g., mutilation), disfiguring injuries, and burns, as well as exposure to grotesque situations. These kinds of events, as related through the trauma story, often pose challenges to our conceptions of morality, aggression, and ability to understand the forces that compel individuals to do what they had to do in order to survive. It is precisely for this reason that a genuine, nonjudgmental attitude of acceptance be conveyed to the victim so that he can experience the safety and freedom of the "holding" environment to let go of the pain and to formulate a new perspective of the distressing memories and feelings of the trauma.

Moreover, as with the other forms of emotional reactions in countertransference, the reactions of disgust, dread, horror, and revulsion tap the therapist's human vulnerability, anxiety, and fear. If so, such responses may lead to psychic numbing, deliberate avoidance, or ineffectiveness caused by psychic overloading or the closure of openness and tolerance in regard to the patient's emotional difficulties.

Psychic Numbing and Avoidance Reactions

The last two forms of common countertransference reactions in post-traumatic therapy are mechanisms of avoidance. As stated earlier, it is often painful and distressing to hear the complete trauma story or to treat many persons with post-traumatic stress disorder or other symptoms of affective distress. When the therapist reaches a point of saturation and psychic overload in response to the trauma story, he may experience some degree of psychic numbing or emotional anesthesia. Numbing of the therapist's emotional sensitivity and empathy clearly impedes the course of treatment since the inability to feel and intuit the nature of the issues confronting the patient is associated with ineffective integration and understanding.

Deliberate avoidance, on the other hand, refers to a state in which the therapist consciously or unconsciously avoids the content of the trauma story. Among the classic evasive maneuvers in avoidance reactions is to shift the focus of treatment to pre-trauma personality functioning or to superficial analysis of current behavioral functioning and relationships. Since most victims of trauma are especially sensitive to such issues as trust, honesty, integrity, dignity, and caring, avoidance operations by the therapist will be met by resistance and testing for their willingness to create a positive therapeutic alliance. When the patient tests the limits, it may take many forms, including regression, a dramatic intensification of symptoms, or a reversion to the use of hyperaroused forms of survivor mode functioning. Failure on the part of the therapist to become aware of psychic numbing or deliberate avoidance will likely lead the patient to prematurely terminate therapy.

COGNITIVE COUNTERTRANSFERENCE ATTRIBUTIONS AND INTERPERSONAL STRATEGIES

The emotional countertransference reactions that occur naturally in the therapist are expectable and provide information to the clinician about himself and about issues confronting the client. Cognitive countertransference attributions and interpersonal strategies refer to some of the ways that the therapist formulates his emotional reactions in the treatment process. In a sense, the cognitive attribution process is the flip side of the coin, a schema of enactment vis-à-vis the patient (see also Chapter 1 for a discussion of schemas of enactment). Clearly, of course, there are different types of schemas for enactment that commonly occur in post-traumatic therapy, and which one predominates for a given therapist depends to a large extent on his personality processes, cognitive style, and previous experience in working with victimized individuals. Further, some schemas for enactment may be associated with therapeutic efficacy whereas others are clearly detrimental to post-traumatic therapy. As with many other therapeutic phenomena, the goodness-of-fit between the patient and the clinician must be carefully considered when evaluating the outcome of psychotherapy.

In an overly simplified way it is possible to identify two major subcategories of countertransference schemas for enactment: (1) prosocial overcommitment and (2) emotionally distancing and detached reactions. In the first form the therapist's psychic energies are mobilized and activate strong prosocial identification with the victim. The schema for enactment typically leads to philosophical and moral advocacy on behalf of the victim or his group. The second form, distance and detachment, typically leads to schemas for enactment that attempt to bolster the therapist's sense of conventional control and reliance on traditional psychotherapeutic techniques. I am proposing that these schemas (distance and detachment) are closely related to strong levels of fear, anxiety, and empathic distress that give rise to deliberate avoidance mechanisms which are largely unconscious but expressed intellectually in the therapist's schema for enactment. Stated differently, where negative affect and empathic distress are appraised as unmanageable and therefore threatening to the self-concept of the therapist, the schema for enactment of the therapeutic process is a form of cognitive reappraisal that enables the individual to establish a sense of control and predictability through detachment and distancing.

Prosocial, Positive, Overcommitted Countertransference Schemas for Enactment

The prosocial countertransference reaction as a cognitive attribution process involves the development of schemas for enactment in which the therapist moves beyond the normal role boundaries of therapist to client. There are several ways in which this can occur. For example, the therapist may overidentify with the victim out of a sensitive and deep empathic understating of how the person was psychically injured by the trauma. This level of empathic caring may then lead to being overly committed to helping the client, which, in turn, may potentially facilitate excessive dependency and overidealization of the therapist. Alternatively, however, such prosocial behavior, even if it is a form of overidentification, may be perceived by the client as genuine and lead to trust, bonding, and a fostering of the therapeutic alliance. This is especially likely to happen where the victim has had negative experiences with other mental health professionals who were unknowledgable or inexperienced in post-traumatic therapy.

However, a potential therapeutic trap occurs when the therapeutic alliance does result in success, stabilization, and reequilibration such that the victim transforms the trauma and resumes healthy functioning. The risk to the therapist in terms of countertransference is the development of a schema of enactment as a rescuer, savior, gifted healer, or clinician with special skills in post-traumatic therapy. These self-images and attributions are a form of narcissistic self-representation born out of the therapist's struggle with the empathic distress emanating from the process of treatment. As with other forms of narcissistic functioning, such a schema for enactment contains both grandiosity and distortion which can potentially interfere with the progress of therapy when the therapist's desires for admiration and recognition need to be reinforced through the process of psychotherapy.

Thus, in order to sustain narcissistic gratification, the countertransference reaction may also include a belief that the clinician has a special personal obligation to shoulder the responsibility for the stress recovery process. However, when failures occur in therapy, the narcissistic schema for enactment may lead to ideological and clinical disillusionment generated in response to the trauma story since the therapist's self-esteem may be injured by the failure itself. When this occurs, there are three basic alternatives in terms of cognitive countertransference: first, to defensively bolster the image of being a specially gifted healer and practitioner of post-traumatic therapy and continue with zealous commitment and overidentification; second, to reappraise what has happened and to accept the faulty quality of the narcissistically infused schema for enactment; third, to detach and emotionally distance from the client as a means of resolving the anxiety and cognitive dissonance produced by the failure.

*Emotional Distance and Detachment as a
Schema for Enactment*

The power of the trauma story in a person victimized by an extremely stressful life event may pose a threatening challenge to the therapist attempting to help the person. The threat often takes the form of feeling discomfort with the level of affective intensity and the profound emotional scarring to the self-structure of the victim. Thus, as the degree of empathic distress increases in the therapist, attempts are made to establish a sense of control in the process of psychotherapy. The need to establish a sense of conventional therapeutic control is directly associated with conscious or unconscious attributions of uncertainty as to the ability to render effective assistance to the client.

The schemas for enactment that develop as countertransference reactions are representations of the need for control created by an inner sense of vulnerability and uncertainty as to one's efficacy in the therapeutic process. Among the most common forms of establishing emotional distance is to overemphasize the value of the "blank screen" approach in the process of interaction. By maintaining the "blank screen" and a guarded level of personal disclosure, the therapist attempts to control the degree of affective intensity associated with the client's story of the trauma and its aftermath. In post-traumatic therapy the "blank screen" is a form of false neutrality because it severely limits the depth of the therapeutic alliance and the willingness of the client to reveal the most painful aspects of the traumatic experience.

In other forms of emotional distancing and detachment, the countertransference schema for enactment may include the belief that post-traumatic stress disorder does not exist and that the current psychological difficulties of the client are premorbid in origin. In this case, the focus of therapy shifts to a safer ground, one which deliberately avoids discussing the trauma story and its impact on the victim. This countertransference reaction clearly impedes post-traumatic therapy since it limits the ability of the patient to develop insight into the state of victimization.

Moreover, where the affective intensity of the client is exceptionally strong, the countertransference may include the belief that medication will alleviate the symptom expression and let the patient experience greater feelings of control. Clearly, of course, medication can attenuate the symptoms of post-traumatic stress reactions (Roth, 1988). *However, when the countertransference reaction seeks to enhance the therapist's need for control, the use of medication may simply be a way of controlling the level of fear, vulnerability, and uncertainty in the person responsible for treatment.* Finally, if the client seems trapped in the trauma and unable to progress, the countertransference reaction may include an attribution of the person as weak, pitiful, and capable of overcoming his problems if only he would not defensively resist the therapeutic process.

In conclusion, it can be said that therapeutic work with victims of trauma can produce a wide range of countertransference reactions. These expectable responses in clinicians include different forms of empathic distress (emotional countertransference issues) and the development of cognitive schemas of enactment associated with levels of empathic distress. Successful post-traumatic therapy requires an awareness of these reactions and the willingness to disclose them to other professionals familiar with post-traumatic stress syndromes in order to place them into a healthy perspective. The power of the trauma story can never be underestimated in terms of its ability to generate countertransference reactions in those capable of helping. It must be recognized, too, that not all therapists are suited to engage in post-traumatic therapy. However, those who do have the strength, stamina, and ego resiliency to practice post-traumatic therapy also need the courage to experience their own vulnerability through empathic, nonjudgmental acceptance of the victim. In the process of *being with* the victim, the therapist will experience trauma vicariously through empathic distress which sets in motion the mechanisms of countertransference. Understanding countertransference thus provides one of the essential elements of effective healing.

GENERAL PRINCIPLES OF TREATMENT IN POST-TRAUMATIC THERAPY

The treatment of victims of traumatically stressful life experiences involves a core set of general principles that can facilitate effective post-traumatic therapy. These principles, listed below, are a set of ideas about the central issues that surface in work with trauma victims. They are not meant to be exhaustive, but are reflective of our current collective knowledge about helping victimized individuals to heal.

1. Nonjudgmental Acceptance of the Victim

Victims of psychic trauma feel diminished and overwhelmed by their experiences. They are reluctant to discuss what has happened and often feel stigmatized, tainted, and altered by the stressful event. They tend to believe that no one understands their inner turmoil of feeling trapped in the trauma. It is especially important for the therapist to convey an empathic, nonjudgmental attitude toward the person and what happened to him in the trauma. The clinician needs to be open-minded and prepared to hear the trauma story with all of its distressing qualities, many of which confront our moral attitudes and values.

2. Rapid Intervention and the Establishment of Support Aids the Stress Recovery Process

Following a traumatic life event, it is important to intervene as rapidly as possible to create what Lindy (1986) has termed a trauma membrane around the victim. The trauma membrane protects and cushions the person and serves as a stress buffer against further life stresses which would further tax an already psychically overwhelmed ego. The greater the creation of social, emotional, and economic support for the person, the more rapid will be the stress recovery process.

3. Expectation for Powerful Countertransference Reactions

The treatment of victimized persons typically leads to powerful countertransference reactions which involve empathic distress and the development of schemas for enactment in the therapeutic process. Understanding the nature and vicissitudes of countertransference reactions is the cornerstone of effective psychotherapy.

4. The Willingness to be Tested

Victims of psychic trauma are reluctant to trust others and are especially cautious about revealing the most painful and distressing aspects of their experiences. The therapist can expect to be tested by the client. The clinician treating trauma victims needs to be open, honest, and appropriately self-disclosing without becoming enmeshed in one of the many problems of countertransference.

5. Transference Is a Process of Rebonding and Is Trauma Related

In the transference process the therapist is bonded by the client in *trauma-associated ways*. The transference process, including the creation of a therapeutic alliance, is the essential condition for development of deeper levels of trust which are necessary to work through the most painful aspects of the trauma.

6. The Assumption That Post-Trauma Stress Syndromes Are Caused by the Traumatic Event

Post-traumatic therapy assumes that the patient's current emotional problems are caused by the traumatic event rather than by preexisting psychopathology. Until a complete reconstruction of the person's psychosocial history can be obtained, the assumption of trauma-induced symptomatology facilitates the therapeutic process. A corollary of this principle is that the assumption of premorbidity in post-traumatic reactions will be counterproductive and resisted by the patient.

7. Education About the Nature and Dynamics of Stress Response Syndromes Is Therapeutic

Post-traumatic stress reactions are normal, expectable patterns of adaptation to extremely stressful life events. Educating the client about the nature and dynamics of stress response syndromes is therapeutic; it reduces a sense of isolation and fear of mental illness and restores a sense of personal control over symptom manifestation.

8. Traumatic Stressors Impact on Predominant Stages of Ego Development in the Life-Cycle

Traumatic events can intensify, disrupt, compound, and aggravate the normatively occurring stages of ego development (identity) anywhere in the lifespan. As a consequence of traumatization, the person may fixate, arrest, regress, or accelerate in psychosocial development, depending on the nature of the trauma, age, and constitutional makeup.

9. Traumatic Stress Causes Narcissistic Scarring

Traumatically stressful life events can alter the form and quality of identity in the life-cycle. It is common for the victim to experience a loss of cohesion and continuity in the self after the trauma. There is almost always a form of narcissistic injury to the sense of integrity and cohesiveness of the self as experienced subjectively by the person.

10. Disavowal, Splitting, and Forms of Dissociation Are Major Defense Modalities Following Psychic Trauma

Post-traumatic stress reactions are often very complex and involve defensive attempts to ward off traumatic imagery and affect. These defensive attempts involve forms of dissociation, splitting, disavowal, denial, doubling, and the alteration of personality.

11. Self-Medication Is Common in PTSD

The intensity of traumatic stress responses often leads to self-medication with alcohol or drugs to reduce levels of autonomic nervous system arousal. Excessive or abusive self-medication blocks the individual's ability to feel the psychic pain necessary to successfully work through the stress reactions. Treatment for alcoholism may be a necessary adjunct to other types of therapy.

12. Transformation of the Trauma May Result in Positive Character Traits

The struggle to reformulate and transform the trauma may result in the development of positive traits, including honesty, integrity, sensitivity to others, and strong concerns with equity, justice, truth, spirituality, and a nonmaterialistic value orientation. It is therapeutically beneficial to make the client aware of these virtues, which are often clouded by the absorption in trauma material.

13. Prosocial Action and Self-Disclosure Facilitate the Stress Recovery Process

Research evidence (Gleser et al., 1981; Kahana, Harel, & Kahana, 1988) has shown that prosocial actions and self-disclosure are associated with positive mental health and stress recovery. When victims become survivors, bearing witness to what happened in the trauma is both cathartic and healing in nature. Helping others has a stress-buffering effect and enhances feelings of self-efficacy.

14. Transformation of Trauma Is a Lifelong Process

Massive psychic trauma may leave a psychic legacy that may require years of transformation, even after successful resolution and integration produced by therapy or other means of coping. The residue of the trauma may be reactivated by normal life crises, stages of ego development, and the aging process itself. Therapists working with victims need to be sensitive to the subtle unconscious expression and return of trauma-related symptoms since their onset may make the individual feel vulnerable and anxious that he could be psychically injured once again, just as he was years ago. Reassurances that the episode was probably associated with a stressor of daily living will help to restore equilibrium and a sense of well-being.

The treatment of post-traumatic stress reactions poses a challenging task to the mental health professional. At present, our knowledge of methods of intervention and principles of treatment is growing and becoming more refined as the dynamics and progressions of stress response syndromes are better understood. However, unlike the more biologically based mental disorders, post-traumatic stress disorder is probably the most environmentally caused syndrome. As is now recognized quite clearly, post-traumatic stress disorder is the expectable human pattern of adaptation to extremely stressful life events which are traumatic in nature. As such, one can come to understand the phases and subtype manifestations of the way in which individuals cope with states of victimization or traumatization. Techniques of intervention and treatment reflect the level of understanding these processes of adaptation. In the course of treatment, both the client and the therapist are allied in facilitating a safe and supportive milieu in which the process of organismically based healing can occur. When successful, the victim transforms the trauma and heals—there is restoration of a steady state; deconditioning of hyperarousal neurophysiological mechanisms; and restoration of psychological integration, cohesion, and continuity in personal identity. Ultimately, healing restores human dignity and living with vitality, a sense of meaning, and peace with oneself and nature.

9

In the Arms of Justice

with ALICE J. WALKER

In the last decade post-traumatic stress disorder (PTSD) has emerged as an interesting and important phenomenon in the legal system. Several factors account for this growth of interest in PTSD by attorneys, judges, and mental health experts involved in the forensic process. First, the high prevalence of PTSD among Vietnam veterans has resulted in the use of PTSD as a legal defense in criminal cases (Erlinder, 1984). Second, there has been an expanding awareness and acceptance of PTSD as a unique mental disorder which afflicts a broad cross-section of victimized individuals in our society. As a consequence of traumatization, those who suffer inevitably fall into the arms of justice for one reason or another. For example, children who have been abused or violated by their parents may become the subject of custody suits. Persons who are the victims of job-related injuries may be unable to work and may seek social security benefits, pension claims, or compensation for personal injuries. Similarly, individuals who are the victim of man-made or natural disasters may litigate to get financial compensation for the psychological damages that have impaired their ability to live a normal and productive life.

Among the best examples of successful litigation for negligence in a man-made disaster was the award of 13.5 million dollars to the survivors of the Buffalo Creek Dam disaster in 1979 (Gleser, Green, & Winget, 1981). This case is especially interesting since the defendant (the Pittston Corporation) argued that the post-disaster symptoms of the survivor-litigants was caused by preexisting emotional problems or was simply factitious in nature. However, clinical and empirical research by experts for both sides involved in the lawsuit revealed that the psychopathology of the litigants was the direct result of the devastating flood which killed over 125 persons and displaced thousands of the Appalachian residents whose homes were washed away by the ravaging wall of water that careened down the 16-mile hollow known as Buffalo Creek in Logan County, West Virginia, in 1972 (Erikson, 1976; Gleser, Green, & Winget, 1981).

Today, post-traumatic stress reactions are of concern in the forensic process in four major areas: (1) in criminal litigation by prosecutors and defense attorneys; (2) in civil litigation wherein traumatized or victimized persons seek compensation for damages resulting from unusually stressful life events; (3) in disability claims filed with federal, state, and private organizations (e.g., military service-connected disability from the Veterans Administration, social security benefits, or medical pensions from unions); and (4) in domestic-relations court involving child custody disputes or marital relations where physical, emotional, or sexual abuse is alleged.

This chapter is organized into three sections which address different aspects of PTSD in the forensic process. The first section contains an analysis of PTSD as a legal defense in the criminal justice system and includes a discussion of its relationship to criminal responsibility, mitigation, and the disposition to criminal behavior. The second section contains a discussion of the differential diagnosis and forensic assessment of PTSD. Included here are a set of guidelines for use in preparing a forensic or clinical report. The chapter concludes with a presentation of the psychometric profiles of PTSD in forensic cases using the Minnesota Multiphasic Personality Inventory (MMPI), Impact of Event Scale (IES), Symptom Checklist-90 (SCL-90) scales of psychopathology, and the 16-Personality Factor Questionnaire (16-PF) measure of personality. This research has produced data on the "trauma profile" of victimized individuals. It is our hope that the final section will be of special benefit to clinicians and attorneys who seek to understand normative psychological profiles of traumatized persons.

PTSD AS A LEGAL DEFENSE

Since PTSD is classified as a major mental disorder, it holds the *logical status* of any other mental disorder (e.g., schizophrenia) in terms of explaining the relation of a psychological state of being to a specific criminal act. From our perspective, PTSD *potentially* could affect a person's action in a number of ways that could result in either violent or nonviolent behavior that could be criminal in nature. Indeed, PTSD has been used successfully as an insanity defense in both federal and state jurisdictions using the McNaughten, American Law Institute (ALI), and American Bar Association definitions of insanity.

Table 9.1 summarizes some of the major cases where PTSD has been used as a legal defense. For example, in *State* v. *Heads* (1981) a Vietnam veteran and former Marine reconnaissance point man who walked 38 missions was found not guilty by reason of insanity (NGRI) in the fatal shooting of his brother-in-law during a flashback episode (dissociative state) on a hot, humid August night in Louisiana, under environmental conditions directly parallel to those of his Vietnam combat experiences. Similar verdicts regarding violent behavior involving attempted murder and assault have been rendered in other cases and include: *State* v. *Nghia* (1981), *State* v. *Stein/Hale* (1987), *People* v. *Woods* (1982), *State* v. *Pard* (1980), *State* v. *Mann* (1981), *Commonwealth* v. *Mulchay* (1979), and *State* v. *Goodman* (1987). In these cases it was argued that the defendants were reenacting a traumatic event and, in the process, were misconstruing reality in ways that prevented them from knowing right from wrong, appreciating the wrongfulness of their conduct, and conforming their conduct to the requirements of the law.

In terms of nonviolent crimes, PTSD has also been used as a criminal defense to exculpate criminal responsibility in several cases. For example, in a federal case (*United States* v. *Tindall*, 1980) involving conspiracy to smuggle illicit drugs into the country, the defendant was found not guilty by reason of insanity by a unanimous jury in Boston who believed that this highly decorated former attack helicopter pilot was compelled to recreate another "mission" by smuggling about 7,000 pounds of inert hashish from Morocco to the United States with former members of his helicopter crew in Vietnam. As we discuss below, this case represents a complex form of *unconscious reenactment* of the traumatic events that Tindall and his fellow pilots experienced during the Vietnam War. In the trial, expert witnesses testified that Tindall and his buddies from Vietnam had psychologically recreated their military unit that flew helicopter gunship attacks during the war. The experts believed that because of their PTSD, the mental state of the men compelled them to unconsciously have another mission together (reenactment) against a common enemy—the U.S. government—toward whom they felt angry, alienated, and exploited for their role in the Vietnam War (see Erlinder, 1984, for a discussion of this case).

TABLE 9.1
Selected Criminal Cases Utilizing PTSD as a Defense

CASE CITATION	CRIMINAL CHARGE	FORM OF SURVIVOR MODE RE-ENACTMENT
VIOLENT		
State v. Goodman (1987)	Murder	Dissociation
State v. Heads (1981)	Murder	Dissociation
State v. Verketis (1987)	Murder	Dissociation
U.S. v. Jensen (1985)	Murder	Dissociation
Commonwealth v. Mulchay (1979)	Murder	Dissociation
State v. Mann (1981)	Murder	Dissociation
State v. Felde (1980)	Murder	Dissociation
State v. Marshall (1984)	Murder	Dissociation
State v. Place (1984)	Murder	Dissociation
State v. Luoma (1987)	Murder	Dissociation
People v. Woods (1982)	Attempted Murder	Dissociation
State v. Nghia (1981)	Attempted Murder	Dissociation
State v. Dobbs (1983)	Attempted Murder	Dissociation
State v. Pard (1980)	Attempted Murder	Depression/Suicide
U.S. v. Valdez (1980)	Robbery	Depression/Suicide
State v. Gregory (1979)	Attempted Robbery	Dissociation
State v. Stein/Hale (1987)	Assault	Dissociation
NON-VIOLENT		
U.S. v. Early (1981)	Conspiracy	Sensation Seeking/ Unconscious Reenactment
U.S. v. Tindall (1980)	Conspiracy	Sensation Seeking/ Unconscious Reenactment
U.S. v. Krutchewski (1980)	Conspiracy	Sensation Seeking/ Unconscious Reenactment
U.S. v. Larson (1982)	Conspiracy	Sensation Seeking/ Unconscious Reenactment
U.S. v. Tombs (1981)	Conspiracy	Sensation Seeking/ Unconscious Reenactment
U.S. v. Kidder (1987)	Conspiracy	Sensation Seeking/ Unconscious Reenactment
U.S. v. Rhodes (1987)	Conspiracy	Sensation Seeking/ Unconscious Reenactment
U.S. v. Kessi (1987)	Commodities Fraud	Survivor Guilt/ Unconscious Reenactment

PTSD as Mitigation and as a Basis for Alternative Sentencing

In yet other cases PTSD has been used to mitigate criminal responsibility or to provide the basis of alternative sentencing. In *State v. Gregory* (1979), a former Marine with extensive traumatic combat exposure during the Vietnam War received probation in order to receive treatment of his stress disorder, which caused him to hold hostages for five hours in a bank in Silver Springs, Maryland. Inside the bank, Gregory fired many rounds of ammunition at inanimate objects during a flashback episode to his combat experiences.

In *United States* v. *Valdez* (1982) a highly decorated former crew chief of a helicopter gunship in the Vietnam War robbed seven banks in a *two-week* period of time in San Diego County, California. Expert witnesses testified that Valdez suffered from PTSD, was suicidal, and was depressed due to his physical disabilities which resulted from the crash of his helicopter in Vietnam. Valdez was the sole survivor of his unit and successfully fought off enemy forces until he was rescued. As a result of the crash, Valdez sustained many injuries and lost his arm and eye. The experts testified that psychologically he never recovered from the experience since his dreams of a career in the military were shattered. During the bank robberies, Valdez looked directly at the monitoring cameras and flashed his shiny hooked prosthesis, hidden in his sleeve, at the bank guards in the banks. He had hoped that the rapid exposure of the hook would be seen as a gun and caused him to get shot. Under an arrangement worked out in court, Valdez attended the PTSD treatment program at the Menlo Park Veterans Administration Hospital in California. Interestingly, Valdez twice admitted himself to the VA Hospital during the two-week period of time when he robbed the banks. He was depressed and suicidal and sought help for his PTSD. Similar outcomes in which the defendant was sentenced to treatment rather than incarceration may be found in the cases of *United States* v. *Larson* (1982), *State* v. *Dobbs* (1983), and *United States* v. *Rhodes* (1987).

PTSD and the Disposition to Criminal Behavior

As noted in other chapters, the *Diagnostic and Statistical Manual of Mental Disorders* (DSM-III-R) (APA, 1987) contains four major categories which comprise the diagnostic criteria for PTSD. These categories are: (A) exposure to or direct involvement with a traumatic event; (B) persistent reexperiencing of the trauma in a variety of ways; (C) persistent attempts at avoidance of stimuli that are associated with the trauma; and, (D) persistent symptoms of increased physiological arousal (hyperarousal) that were not present before the trauma. This revised set of diagnostic criteria is useful because it adds both specificity and clarity to the necessary minimal number of criteria required to establish a diagnosis of PTSD.

In terms of understanding how PTSD can predispose an individual to criminal behavior, these categories of symptoms point to more complex psychological processes that may lead to such diverse criminal acts as bank robbery, homicide, drug smuggling, or even commodities fraud. As implausible as this may seem on the surface, we believe that it is possible to understand PTSD as a dynamic *survivor mode* that has unique properties that may result in criminal behavior. The survivor mode of functioning can be conceptualized as involving complex and often subtle forms of behavior that *relive, reenact,* or *compulsively repeat* elements of the traumatic event. Furthermore, these different forms of reenactment can occur at different levels of consciousness or express themselves in highly symbolic forms.

Forms of Reenactment and Reexperience of
Trauma in PTSD

Persons with PTSD can reexperience the distressing aspects of traumatic life events in several ways, including: (1) intrusive or unbidden imagery present during the day or night (Horowitz, 1986); (2) affective (emotional) flooding either with or without trauma-associated intrusive imagery; (3) flashback or dissociative episodes in which the trauma is directly, partially, or symbolically relived or reenacted in behavior; (4) hallucinations that contain *trauma-related* cognitive material or affect; (5) anniversary reactions, which can be conscious or unconscious; (6) intensification of various syndrome symptoms by exposure to events that in some way resemble the traumatic event; and (7) unconscious behavioral reenactments that have a parallel psychological structure to behavior during the trauma. One implication of these forms of reenactment is that the person in such a mental state could distort or misperceive reality and believe that he or she is once again in a life-threatening or traumatically stressful situation. Under the proper environmental cues the person may react to this destortion of reality in a way that leads to a criminal act. As reenactment behavior pertains to disability claims, the person may become so impaired by the avoidance intrusion cycle of PTSD as to be unable to work or meet personal responsibilities. In cases of personal-injury lawsuits, the level of impairment or injury is often a central issue in terms of financial settlements.

The Dynamics of the Survivor Mode of
Functioning

The way in which someone with PTSD reexperiences his or her traumatic episodes varies from subtle and unconscious expressions such as restlessness, irritability, sleeplessness, and hyperalertness to distressing "flashback" images and upsetting feelings of "being back there again." Upon reexperiencing the traumatic event in dreams, distressing intrusive imagery, affective flooding, physiological hyperactivity, or in other ways, the individuals may feel *trapped in the trauma*, helpless and fearful that it is recurring, psychically overloaded, and briefly disoriented as to time and space. In response to this distressing mental state, the individual typically attempts to remove the painful thoughts from conscious or unconscious awareness by avoidance mechanisms. Generally, avoidance is a defensive operation that involves repression, denial, blocking of the intrusive imagery, perceptual distortion, and projection. When successful, the avoidance mechanism returns the unassimilated imagery to unconscious memory. However, when the threshold of effective coping is weakened by demands that exceed the person's capacity to modulate the distressing thoughts, the unbidden imagery returns. Furthermore, as observed by van der Kolk (1987), the person with PTSD is especially vulnerable to a broad range of stimuli that can intensify the symptoms of PTSD and trigger episodes of reexperiencing.

In clinical and forensic work with survivors of profoundly stressful life events, we have observed that because of an ideational or environmental stimulus, the individual with a stress disorder may enter into a *survivor mode* of functioning (Wilson & Zigelbaum, 1983), which is characterized by some or all of the following qualities: an altered state of consciousness, hyperalertness, hypervigilance, excessive autonomic nervous system arousal, frenetic behavior, paranoid ideation, mistrust, and the use of survivor skills and cognitive capacities learned during the period of the traumatic episode. *In addition, depending on the particular personality characteristics of the individual and the situational stressors that trigger the onset of the survivor mode, the person may experience an oscillation between the survivor mode of functioning and normal personality functioning.* Typically, this occurs in a dissociative reaction, but it can occur in nondissociative survivor modalities.

Forms of Dissociation in PTSD and Their Relevance in Legal Issues

Complete Dissociation. In a full dissociative episode the person suffering from PTSD will probably reenact in a direct or symbolic form elements of what occurred during the trauma. For war veterans this might include the reliving of a combat episode or the witnessing of a particularly difficult incident (e.g., torture, mutilation). For example, a Vietnam combat veteran, almost fatally wounded at point blank range on an armored personnel carrier (APC) by a rocket-propelled grenade, 10 years later drove his car off the road into a grassy field nearly 100 miles away from his metropolitan home in a dissociated state in which he thought he was driving the APC in the Vietnam War. The car was stuck and stationed across a railroad track. When a police officer approached the veteran to see if he needed help, he responded by saying, "Just a minute sir and I'll have the 'trac' off the tracks and onto Highway 1 (in Vietnam)." He was arrested for reckless operation and later given treatment for PTSD instead of a fine or punishment. This abbreviated vignette illustrates that regardless of the nature of the precipitating trauma, when a person is completely dissociated he typically experiences an alteration in consciousness, time confusion, a change from his normal personality, and may have only partial recall of his behavior during the dissociative episode.

Partial Dissociation. In other forms of dissociation the person may experience a change in identity, consciousness, or behavior in less extreme forms. In partial dissociation the person may only briefly experience the alteration in consciousness and report varying degrees of awareness of the dissociative state. In other cases the individual may experience a very rapid *oscillation* between the dissociative state and contact with reality. For example, some veterans who saw the movie *Platoon* stated that there were times when they actually believed that they were in Vietnam, which, in turn, alternated with a sense of being "grounded" in a seat at the theater. In a rarer form of dissociation some victims report "micro" flashbacks in which they experience in microseconds the fleeting image or affect associated with the traumatic event.

Blank's Criteria for Dissociative States in Vietnam Veterans and Other Traumatized Persons

In a lucid and well-reasoned article, Blank (1985) has proposed 11 criteria for flashback episodes in war veterans. It is our belief that these criteria also apply to many other persons with PTSD and are especially germane to understanding the relationship of PTSD to the criminal process.

*Characteristics of unconscious dissociative states (flashbacks)**

1. The person has a history of a trauma.
2. The dissociative episode is uncharacteristic of normal personality functioning.
3. The dissociative episode is a reenactment of the trauma.
4. The individual's explanation of the dissociative episode is not a convincing rationalization.
5. The person may appear indifferent to the episode.
6. There is partial or complete amnesia for the episode.
7. The episode may have a psychological structure and process similar to recurrent nightmares.
8. Environmental stimuli may parallel those that existed in the trauma.
9. The episode may be a condensation of many facets of the trauma.
10. The person is not fully aware of the reenactment of the trauma.
11. The person has symptoms of post-traumatic stress disorder.

Blank's criteria of dissociative reactions are useful because they aid in the process of determining the link between a mental state and an alleged crime or other forms of behaviors that would come to the attention of the court. In cases where a legal defense of insanity is being raised, the diagnosis of an unconscious dissociative episode (flashback) is especially important since it bears directly on the test of insanity itself. For example, if a person is reenacting some aspect of a traumatic event and distorting or misperceiving reality at the time he acts in an illegal way, he can be viewed as lacking rational control, the substantial ability to conform his conduct to the requirements of the law, and an inability to appreciate the wrongfulness of his actions. An unconscious dissociative episode, especially in a person suffering from PTSD, is symptomatic of the mental disorder which may have produced the aberrant behavior.

Furthermore, recent research (van der Kolk, 1987) has indicated that although PTSD is caused by an external, environmental event, it has a strong biological component which includes changes in the neuro-

---

* Adapted from Blank, A. S., Jr. (1985). The unconscious flashback to the war in Vietnam veterans. In Stephen M. Sonnenberg, Arthur S. Blank, Jr., and John A. Talbott (Eds.), *The trauma of war: Stress and recovery in Vietnam veterans.* Washington, DC: American Psychiatric Press.

physiology of the brain that are associated with induction of a dissociative state (see Chapter 2 for a discussion). Considered from this
perspective, an unconscious dissociative episode is analogous to aberrant,
irrational behavior that could result from a tumor in the limbic system
and lead to violent, assaultive behavior (Johnson, 1972). In both instances there are neurological abnormalities associated with actions that
might result in criminal behavior. What differs between the conditions
(e.g., PTSD vs. brain tumor) is the etiology of the disorder. Nevertheless,
both conditions could potentially affect behavior in ways that meet the
criteria of insanity.

Three Major Subtypes of Survivor Mode
Functioning: Variations on Reenactment

Dissociation Syndrome. At least three major forms of behavior can be
identified as part of the "survivor mode" of adaptation. First, the survivor
mode of functioning may lead to violent behavior if there exists an
actual or perceived threat that produces conflict with the self-concept,
sense of morality, role obligations, and commitments to significant
others. In such a situation, a *dissociative reaction* may occur as a response
to the approach avoidance conflict dilemma that is present in the
situation. In the dissociative state of consciousness, the survivor is likely
to act similarly to that mode of coping which was employed during
the trauma. Among combat veterans, a dissociative reaction to situational
stress or environmental stimuli may lead to assaultive and violent actions
(e.g., Erlinder, 1984; Wilson & Zigelbaum, 1983; 1986).

Sensation seeking: The action addict syndrome. A second way in which
the survivor mode affects the disposition to criminal action is the *"action
addict"* syndrome. In this mode of coping with PTSD the individual
manifests many of the characteristics of the sensation-seeking motive
(Zuckerman, 1979; also see Chapter 2 for a discussion). We have found
this syndrome to be quite paradoxical in nature since the person appears
to maintain control over the degree to which intrusive imagery is
experienced by *actively* seeking out situations that provide a level of
arousal similar to that experienced in the original trauma. In this survivor
mode, the individual reports feeling an optimal level of arousal that is
experienced subjectively as exciting, exhilarating, and stimulating because it increases the inner state of alertness in much the same way
as did the precipitating trauma. We have found that these individuals
typically seek out vocations or events that can provide this kind of

dangerous, risky, thrilling, adventuresome, and challenging activity (e.g., parachute jumping, flying, scuba diving, gambling, free-style skiing, police and fire work, ocean kyacking, emergency medical service, etc.).

This mode of functioning appears to result in *decreased* levels of reexperiencing, which is in direct contrast to dissociation, in which increased stimulation and arousal may result in alterations in consciousness. Psychodynamically, sensation seeking seems to achieve at least two aims. First, the motivational pattern generates an optimal level of arousal, which enhances the personal sense of being fully alive and animated by "living on the edge of experience." A second, interrelated function is ego-defensive since *the action-seeking behavioral syndrome can be viewed as a complex form of repetition compulsion (Freud, 1959) that actually blocks the onset of intrusive imagery and affective flooding.* In this regard, the sensation-seeking activity can be considered as a defense against PTSD since intense, action-oriented enterprise has a physiological basis and functions as a natural antidepressant. If high levels of action-oriented activity increase neuropeptide secretion in the brain, their existence may provide a powerful neurological reward for the behavior itself and set up an addiction cycle (Janowsky, Risch, & Neborsky, 1986; see Chapter 2 for a discussion).

When the survivor–victim is prevented from engaging in thrill-seeking behavior, the full PTSD symptom pattern emerges. It is theoretically plausible that the sensation-seeking syndrome recreates the psychological elements experienced in the trauma and enables the person to continue striving to master the trauma residue by responding with self-initiated competencies that lead to successful outcomes (i.e., positive emotional arousal and avoidance of intrusive imagery). In essence, the syndrome confirms to the individual that he or she is still alive. This is especially significant since many of these persons fear, at the deepest levels of consciousness, that to cease behaving in this mode will lead to an actual or symbolic death (see Lifton, 1979, for an extended discussion of symbolic death and psychoformative disintegration).

Depression Suicide Syndrome. A third way the survivor mode of functioning can motivate criminal behavior may be seen in the *Depression Suicide Syndrome of PTSD.* In this syndrome the person feels trapped in the trauma, flooded with painful intrusive imagery, hopeless, despondent, and often reports that he or she is simply "a walking shell of his former self that should have died." In addition, the individual may show impacted grief (Shatan, 1974), survivor guilt, sadness, fear of repeating the trauma, a fear of or desire to merge with the dead, and psychic numbing. In this state the person is low in energy and drive, self-recriminating, lacks meaningful goals, and exhibits the classic symptoms of depression. Furthermore, these persons are likely to believe that they are the victims of fate and mere pawns of the events that caused their psychic and physical wounds. Thus, when the individual experiences intrusive thoughts, he often fears that he will again become vulnerable to unpredictable and uncontrollable forces in his life, just as in the trauma.

Indeed, what eventually may lead to a suicide attempt is *profound* despair, survivor guilt, severe anxiety associated with feelings of helplessness, and the belief that there is nothing to live for (Seligman & Garber, 1980). At this point, especially if the individual is subjected to other stresses in life that cannot be easily managed, suicide may seem to be the only way to end the psychic pain and feelings of worthlessness and despair. *In some cases involving the death of a loved one, the person may symbolically wish to reunite with the deceased. Among some survivors such a suicidal wish may be an unacceptable alternative because they would then relinquish their survivor "status." Therefore, this conflicted "will to survive" and "wish to die" may then give rise to criminal action if the individual unconsciously acts out his anger and depression in an attempt to get killed.* Specifically, the actions leading to a criminal act may include pseudoassault (e.g., threatening or shooting at a police officer with no intent to kill), attempted robbery with the hope of getting shot in the act, and purposeful verbal abuse of others who are prone to violence.

In our forensic work we have found that these types of criminal acts are poorly planned and executed. Further, upon completion of the illegal act, the individual does not enjoy having done it and thus it appears that the goal is much more unconscious and multifaceted. First, there is an attempt to get killed or to attack and vent rage at the perceived source of the anguish and suffering. Second, the illegal act may be a form of acting-out or a way of "getting caught" in order to receive help for the PTSD and in the *process* enable the person to bear witness as a survivor–victim of a profound event by revealing an ultimate personal horror (Lifton, 1967). Finally, in some instances the act(s) may be an unconscious reenactment of the original trauma (see also Niederland, 1964, for examples of this tendency among victims of the Nazi persecution).

In summary, we are proposing that all three forms of the survivor mode can potentially constitute variations of reenactment of prior traumatic events. What differentiates the three survivor modes, in part, is the level of consciousness attached to the behavior in question. Nevertheless, each survivor mode can lead to criminal behavior. Research evidence for this position may be found in Wilson and Zigelbaum (1983), whose results showed that PTSD was a strong predictor of criminal behavior among Vietnam veterans. Whether or not such behavior meets the requirement of insanity or some other legal statute must be determined on a case-to-case basis.

THE DIFFERENTIAL DIAGNOSIS OF PTSD

In the courtroom and at different points in the criminal justice system, it is important to employ a set of assessment procedures that will produce a valid and reliable diagnosis of the personality structure of the client. In terms of PTSD, the issue of differential diagnosis is especially important since it is a relatively new diagnostic category (APA, 1980) and commonly *misdiagnosed* by practitioners who are unfamiliar with or inexperienced in working with survivor–victim syndromes (Wilson, 1988a). Indeed, DSM-III-R (APA, 1987) makes explicit the need to differentiate PTSD from adjustment, anxiety, and depressive disorders as well as organic brain syndromes and other forms of psychopathology. Therefore, in this chapter an attempt is made to present a set of procedures that we have used in clinical and forensic work to reach a differential diagnosis of PTSD and to determine whether or not the disorder is related to a particular criminal act or set of behaviors. It is important to emphasize that many valid alternative methods are currently in use for clinical assessment. The focus here is primarily on the assessment of PTSD and its relation to criminal behavior, personal injury, and disability compensation.

The Criteria for the Application of PTSD

The four diagnostic criteria for PTSD listed in DSM-III-R make clear two major concepts that are extremely important in terms of assessing a person's mental state in relation to a criminal act. First, the person must have been exposed to a "stressor that would evoke significant symptoms of distress in almost everyone." Second, there must exist in the person "persistent symptoms of increased arousal that were not present before the trauma" (p. 250). Thus, these criteria indicate that *after* the trauma the person's adaptive functioning and personality traits were changed in ways that can be measured by psychological assessment (e.g., sleep difficulties, problems concentrating, depression, somatization).

It is useful to view the behavioral functioning of a survivor in terms of a *matrix concept*, which assesses the individual's attitudes, emotions, and behavior at three intervals: before, during, and after the traumatic event. The purpose of this technique of assessment is to (1) determine changes in psychosocial functioning, personality dynamics, and adaptive behavior relative to the time of the trauma; (2) determine whether or not these changes in personality can be attributed to the traumatic event, particularly if PTSD is found to exist; and (3) determine whether or not there is a relationship between PTSD and a criminal act. Table 9.2 summarizes the matrix concept.

The Simple Case

In the simple forensic case, the individual's history shows excellent premorbid functioning prior to the traumatic event. As culled from school records and interviews with a cross-section of family, peers, authority figures, and significant others, the individual manifests average or above-average adaptive behavior. However, following the traumatic event there is a discernible change in the level of psychosocial functioning, personality, and adaptive behavior. Among individuals with PTSD, this typically is manifest as isolation and withdrawal, emotional constriction, sleep disturbance, depression, hyperalertness, self-medication with alcohol, and a loss of friendships and intimate relations. In addition, there may be a dramatic ideological change in world view

TABLE 9.2

The Matrix Concept: The Assessment of Cognitive Style, Affect, Identity, and Interpersonal Functioning of Victims/Survivors Before, During, and After a Traumatic Event

Individual Personality	Level of Psychosocial Functioning (Observable changes in level of adaptive behavior)		
	Pre-trauma Characteristics	Traumatic event	Post-trauma
Cognitive style intellectual functioning		(Stressors	*
Affective and motivational states		experienced)	*
Interpersonal behavior and intimate relations			*
Self-concept and identity			*

*Expected changes indicating PTSD symptoms (DSM-III-R criteria)

(e.g., loss of faith in God) and significant changes in personality and personal interests (e.g., loss of interest in hobbies, sports, and previously enjoyed activities). In the simple case the assessment process frequently reveals that the traumatic event was the major life event that occurred between the premorbid personality and the post-traumatic adaptive behavior.

The Complex Case

When a careful psychiatric and forensic assessment establishes a principal diagnosis of PTSD, the "ideal case" presents a clear psychodynamic chain of events that led to the legal circumstances. In these cases, the stressors that precipitated the PTSD and the post-traumatic problems of adaptation are readily discernible and recognized by the defendant and significant others. However, in more complex cases there may be either some evidence of a premorbid character disorder or a specific vulnerability that may make an accurate diagnosis of the client's mental state more difficult.

As noted earlier, in *State of Louisiana* v. *Charles Heads* (1980) the defendant was acquitted of murdering his brother-in-law by reason of insanity caused by his PTSD. Charles Heads was a former Marine who walked point-man on 38 long-range reconnaissance patrols in Vietnam. In a dissociative state of consciousness, Heads killed his best friend and brother-in-law using search-and-destroy ambush tactics without much conscious recollection of what happened. Immediately prior to the fatal shooting Heads was under much stress because his wife had left him with their children and fled to the victim's home. This stressful event caused Heads to experience a vulnerable mental state since his wife and family constituted the only source of emotional support for him after Vietnam. Moreover, Heads' strong need for emotional support was intensified since at age nine he had witnessed his father shoot and kill his mother in an argument. Subsequently, Heads was raised by a grandmother until joining the Marine Corps, where he experienced many combat episodes, including being wounded in a surprise Viet Cong ambush. Interestingly, as noted earlier, Heads' shooting of his brother-in-law occurred on a hot, humid August night after several days of rain in weather conditions that directly paralleled the night in which he was wounded after surviving nearly a year of elite reconnaissance work.

In this case, the expert witnesses believed Heads possessed a premorbid vulnerability to a dissociative reaction and the survivor mode of functioning because of the twin stressor events, which occurred nearly 10 years apart. Thus, when threatened by his brother-in-law, who simply wanted "no trouble at his house" but who unfortunately brandished an unloaded pistol, Heads reacted to the combined set of stressors (heat, humidity, loss of children, weapon) by reverting to combat-trained survival skills. He mistook his brother-in-law for a Viet Cong terrorist and proceeded to "search" his "hootch" after fatally shooting him with a rifle.

In other complex cases, we have found that there is a full range of premorbid experiences that can either confound or be secondarily associated with a post-traumatic stress disorder. These prior experiences include organic brain damage caused by a forceps delivery at birth or other head trauma; child abuse; feelings of inferiority and inadequacy; acts of delinquency; and, psychosocial development in a dysfunctional family. In each case, it is important to determine, as far as possible, the precise way in which the premorbid factor has affected the adaptive functioning of the survivor prior to *and* after the traumatic event. For example, if there is a clear history of antisocial behavior across time intervals in the matrix, it is unlikely that the current legal or psychological problem can be attributed *solely* to PTSD as the major causal variable. In other cases, the exposure to stressors in the trauma may seriously aggravate an underlying disposition or character trait. Finally, it is also possible that a premorbid history may exert very little or no influence on the survivor's current behavior. This is most likely to occur when one can document a strong relationship between the PTSD symptoms, the antecedent stressor events, and the behavior in question. For example, Charles Heads' childhood rendered him vulnerable; he needed loving and caring persons in his life. However, his actions in the shooting were those of a combat soldier, which, in turn, could be directly connected to a 10-year history of undiagnosed and untreated PTSD.

Factitious PTSD

It is inevitable, perhaps, that with the successful employment of PTSD as a legal defense and in civil litigation, factitious cases will arise. Recently, Sparr and Atkinson (1986) and Lynn and Belze (1984) have reviewed cases of factitious PTSD that have occurred in the courts. These cases underscore the need to gather a broad database of objective information to document the nature of the traumatic event and the person's role in it. For example, for Vietnam veterans, the examiner can access and review the daily unit reports of combat activity in Vietnam. These records present a detailed account of a unit's combat activities and provide a means to verify the nature of the war stressors. Thus, if a veteran facing a criminal charge claims he was in heavy combat, these records will generally indicate whether or not the claim is valid. Similarly, other steps can be taken to document the nature of the stressors that would produce PTSD. These include such things as *collaborative interviews* with others involved in the traumatic event (e.g., other victims, survivors, or witnesses), *objective records* of the event (e.g., photographs of a disaster, hospital/medical records, newspaper articles), and *forensic evidence* (e.g., blood samples, ballistic results). By reviewing all of the objective psychohistorical material gathered on the client, one is able discern whether or not the individual was subjected to a stressful life event that might produce PTSD. However, the mere existence of the mental disorder does not presuppose a direct causal link to a criminal act or the level of psychological damage in a litigant.

Assessing the Linkage Between PTSD and Current Behavior

The matrix concept of assessing PTSD enables the clinician to gather information pertinent to a differential diagnosis of PTSD. However, the central forensic issue concerns the *causal link* between the defendant's mental state and the alleged crime or the damages produced to the victim by the trauma. Thus, assuming that a diagnosis of PTSD has been made, the next task is to demonstrate as scientifically as possible its relation or nonrelation to the criminal act or the level of personal injury that resulted from the trauma. To determine this, it is important to gather as comprehensive a set of documents as possible. In cases involving criminal or civil litigation, it is especially important to analyze information from the following sources: (1) all relevant legal documents (e.g., arrest records, police investigations, criminal indictment, laboratory tests); (2) direct psychiatric interviews and the results of biomedical and psychological testing (e.g., MMPI, blood alcohol level); (3) affidavits and statements made by significant others and witnesses that pertain to significant changes following the traumatic event(s) and specific criminal charges; (4) other records (e.g., medical records, military records, VA records, academic records, employment records); and (5) any other documents deemed pertinent to understanding the defendant or litigant.

The information obtained from the above-mentioned sources provides a wealth of material for use in rendering a diagnosis based on the matrix concept presented earlier. Taken as a set, these sources of data help the examiner to gain a clear picture of childhood and adolescent development; the nature and dynamics of the family; academic and intellectual growth; the adaptive competencies and areas of vulnerability and insecurity; motivational and career goals; sexual development and adjustment; personal health; work performance; and the self-concept of the survivor. Elsewhere we have described how the matrix concept aids in preparing a comprehensive forensic or clinical report (Wilson & Zigelbaum, 1986).

THE PSYCHOLOGICAL ASSESSMENT OF PTSD IN FORENSIC AND CLINICAL REPORTS

In cases involving criminal defense, civil litigation, or disability compensation, the psychological assessment of PTSD is often an important aspect of the larger forensic process or treatment plan. At present, the body of research on the psychological assessment of PTSD is not large, and normative test data on subgroups of traumatized persons are very limited.

Traditionally, psychological testing using objective and projective techniques of assessment has permitted the clinician to evaluate areas of convergence and divergence in intrapsychic functioning and to aid in the formulation of personality dynamics. In this section research data will be presented which compare the profiles of PTSD for Vietnam veterans with legal difficulties and persons traumatized in other life-threatening ways (e.g., severe industrial accidents resulting in burns and extensive physical damage). As part of our ongoing research, we have selected three standard tests (MMPI, 16-PF, and SCL-90) and one PTSD-specific measure (IES) in order to explore similarities and differences in the test profiles.

Description of Measures of Psychopathology and Stress

Minnesota Multiphasic Personality Inventory. In addition to the traditional validity and clinical scales of the MMPI, several research scales and subscales were used. As commonly used in clinical settings, the Research Scales include Anxiety, Repression, Ego Strength, and MacAndrews Alcoholism Scale. Limited empirical information on cross-validation is available, and absolute cutoff scores have not been determined (Graham, 1987). However, these scales can add further depth to profile interpretation. Generally, standardized *T*-scores above 70 or below 40 are considered to be extreme and suggestive of psychopathology.

The Anxiety Scale developed by Welsh (1956) contains 39 items and measures apprehension, negative affect, dysphoria, lack of energy, pessimism, and impaired thought processes (Graham, 1977). Reported reliability coefficients include a split-half of .88 and test-retest of .70. Internal consistency has been reported as a Kuder-Richardson 21 value of .94.

The Repression Scale (Welsh, 1956) contains 40 items which cluster as follows: health and physical symptoms; emotionality, violence, and activity; reactions to other people in social situations; social dominance, feelings of personal adequacy, and personal appearance; and personal and vocational interests. Split-half reliability is .48 and test-retest is .74. Kuder-Richardson's 21 measure of internal consistency is .72 (Graham, 1987).

The 68-item Ego Strength Scale as described by Barron (1953) is a measure of physical functioning, seclusiveness, attitude toward religion, moral posture, personal adequacy and ability to cope, phobias, and anxieties. The odd-even reliability is .76, test-retest is .72; Kuder-Richardson 21 value is .78 (Graham, 1977).

Major content areas of the 51-item MacAndrews Alcoholism Scale are cognitive impairment, school maladjustment, interpersonal competence, risk taking, extroversion and exhibitionism, and moral indignation (Graham, 1987). Reported test-retest reliabilities range from .75 to .82 (Moreland, 1985). A cutoff score of 24 has been shown to correctly identify 84% of individuals.

Goldberg (1965) utilized a linear regression equation to develop an index to discriminate between neurotic and psychotic profiles. A cutoff score of 45 on the Goldberg Index correctly classified 70% of individuals. In addition, the scale is an indication of the level of maladjustment such that higher scores indicate more severe psychopathology.

Wiggins Content Scales consist of 13 mutually exclusive, internally consistent, moderately independent scales that represent major content areas of the MMPI. The obtained Cronbach's alphas range from .54 to .89. Few validity studies are available, but general agreement with other measures of the corresponding characteristics has been demonstrated (Taylor, Ptacek, Carithers, Griffin, & Coyne, 1972).

Harris and Lingoes (1955, 1968) developed a set of supplemental scales for each of the clinical scales (2, 3, 4, 6, 8, 9) based on their clinical evaluation of content areas. Caution should be used when interpreting these supplemental scales since there is a large item overlap between them. Kuder-Richardson's 21 measure of internal consistency for the scales ranges from .04 (Authority Problems) to .85 (Lassitude-Malaise and Persecutory Ideas). Little empirical research is available regarding the validity of these scales.

Similarly, Serkownek (1975) developed a set of supplemental subscales for clinical scales 5 (Masculinity-Femininity) and 0 (Social Introversion). Test-retest reliability coefficients range from .58 to .89.

Symptom-Checklist 90. The SCL-90 is an objective, 90-item, self-report scale that measures general psychiatric symptoms on a five-point Likert scale (range 0–4). The subscales are: (1) depression, (2) somatization, (3) anxiety, (4) hostility, (5) interpersonal sensitivity (self-consciousness), (6) obsessive-compulsive, (7) paranoia, (8) phobic, (9) anxiety, and (10) psychoticism. Three global indices are derived from these scores: a Global Severity Index (GSI), Positive Symptom Distress Index (PSDI), and Positive Symptom Tally (PST). The GSI measures both frequency and intensity of distress across all symptom dimensions. The PSDI measures the intensity of the symptoms reported. Cronbach's alpha was found to be .97 (Murphy, 1986).

Impact of Event Scale. The IES is a generic measure of the avoidance and intrusion dimensions of stress response syndromes, including PTSD. It consists of 16 statements assessing the subject's feelings of denial and the occurrence within the past seven days of intrusive thoughts in regard to stressful life events. Seven items assess intrusive imagery and nine items assess avoidance tendencies. The mean of the intrusion subscale is 21.4, with a standard deviation of 9.6 and a range of 0–35 (mean item score = 3.06). The mean of the avoidance subscale is 18.2, with a standard deviation of 10.8 and a range of 0–45 (mean item score = 2.02). Zilberg, Weiss, and Horowitz (1982) found that Cronbach's alphas were high and ranged from .79 to .92. Reliability across time ranged from .86 to .90.

Sixteen Personality Factor. The Sixteen Personality Factor (16-PF) is a multidimensional inventory that measures primary personality factors based on a large body of research on unitary personality traits. The scales were derived through factor analysis and were later validated with normal and abnormal populations. Each of the 16 factors is a unidimensional source trait, and they are relatively independent from one another. Profiles are generated using standard sten scores with a range of 1–10, a mean of 5.5, and a standard deviation of 2. Sten scores of 1 or 10 are considered extreme scores and indicate opposite characteristics. Sten scores of 2–3 or 8–9 are considered significantly deviant from the norm. The reliability of Form A ranges from .21 to .71, with a median of .49. Complex factor analysis has confirmed the concept validity of the measure and indicates that the scales are strongly related to the corresponding pure personality factors they are measuring (Cattell, Eber, & Tatsuoka, 1970).

The Second-Order Factors are derived from the primary 16 scales and attempt to identify specific symptoms based on broader personality characteristics. In addition to the five Second-Order Factors (Extroversion, Anxiety, Tough Practicality, Independence, and Self-Control), three other composite scores were included in our analysis. These include Leadership, Creativity, and Achievement (Croom, Schuerger, DeMuth, & Watterson, 1985).

The Need Estimates are based on correlations between Edwards Personal Preference Schedule and the 16-PF variables (Croom, Schuerger, DeMuth, & Watterson, 1985). Whereas the 16 primary scales are relatively stable factors, the Need Estimates are regarded as motives that will change in their strength as individuals receive gratification of a particular motive.

Description of Sample

The sample consisted of 16 individuals who had experienced a traumatic experience in a military or civilian setting. All stressor events were verified by objective records (e.g., medical records, police reports, military records, daily unit reports, etc.). Seven persons were involved in civil litigation directly related to their traumatic experience. The military sample consisted of nine veterans who participated in heavy combat during the Vietnam War. These individuals were involved in criminal litigation. All of the subjects in the forensic sample had a primary diagnosis of post-traumatic stress disorder and secondary diagnoses which included depression (72%), substance abuse (33%), and dysthymia (22%). A few subjects had Axis II diagnoses of personality disorders (antisocial, paranoid, and mixed-type).

Results

MMPI comparison and scale elevations. Table 9.3 presents the results of a one-way analysis of variance conducted with mean *T*-scores on the MMPI Clinical and Research Scales and Goldberg Indices for the civilian and veteran groups. Scale 5 was excluded from the analyses because the sample included both males and females. Overall, the veteran group obtained elevated mean *T*-scores (above 70) on all the clinical scales, with the exception of Scale 9 (Hypomania). Elevated scores were also evidenced on the *F* Scale (Faking Bad) and the research scale for Anxiety. The civilian sample obtained elevated scores on Scales 2, 4, 6, 7, and 8 (Depression, Psychopathic Deviance, Paranoia, Psychasthenia, and Schizophrenia). The Welsh Code for the entire sample is 28* 764" 13' 50- F' KL:. In terms of the Goldberg Index, both groups were well above the cutoff score and may be characterized as experiencing a great deal of psychological distress of a pathological nature and in need of some form of intervention. Table 9.3 reveals several noteworthy statistically significant differences between the groups. The veteran sample showed a significantly higher level of distress on the clinical scales Depression ($p < .0001$); Paranoia ($p < .05$); Psychasthenia ($p < .001$); and Schizophrenia ($p < .05$). In addition, the research scale Anxiety and the Goldberg Index "Deviant" were significantly higher for the veteran sample ($p < .01$). Overall, in terms of differential diagnosis, it is noteworthy that while both groups were clearly symptomatic as demonstrated by their elevated scores, the veterans generally displayed a higher level of symptom distress.

MMPI subscale comparisons and elevations. Table 9.4 presents the results of a one-way analysis of variance conducted with mean *T*-scores on the Wiggins Content Scales derived from the MMPI for the two groups. As illustrated in the table, the groups present similar profiles, except that the veterans were significantly more depressed ($p < .01$). The scores for the civilian group were within normal limits on all subscales. However, the veterans displayed more symptomatology as exemplified by elevated scores on the following scales: Social Maladjustment, Depression, Psychoticism, Organic Symptoms, and Poor Health.

The results of a one-way analysis of variance conducted with mean *T*-scores on the Harris-Lingoes and Serkownek Sub-Scales derived from the MMPI Clinical and Research Scales are presented in Table 9.5 for the two samples. Inspection of the table indicates that the veterans scored significantly higher on the subscales encompassing Depression,

TABLE 9.3
One-Way Analysis of Variance for Mean MMPI *T*-Scores for Civilian and Vietnam-Related Trauma in a Forensic Sample

	Civilian (N = 7)	Vietnam Veterans (N = 9)	Group (N = 16)
MMPI Clinical Scales			
Lie Scale	49.71	50.00	49.88
Faking Bad	66.71	84.89*	76.94
Faking Good	48.00	46.00	46.88
Hypochondriasis	68.00	83.11	76.50
Depression	80.14	106.44****	94.94
Hysteria	68.57	77.67	73.69
Psychopathic Deviant	72.86	86.00	80.25
Masculinity-Femininity	(59.29)	66.22	63.19
Paranoia	74.57	93.56*	82.25
Psychasthenia	72.00	96.22***	85.63
Schizophrenia	80.14	101.33*	92.06
Hypomania	64.71	61.55	62.94
Social Introversion	63.86	73.78	69.44
F Minus K Index	-1.14	8.00*	4.00
Welsh Code (combined sample)		28* 764" 13' 50- F' KL:	
Research Scales			
Anxiety	61.00	73.22**	68.86
Repression	59.40	64.22	62.50
Ego Strength	37.40	32.22	34.07
McAndrew's Alcoholism (Raw Score)	22.71	22.11	22.38
Goldberg Indices			
Deviant vs. Normal (Cutoff = 123)	146.00	202.29**	178.33
Pathological vs. Characterological (10)	-2.20	-8.86	-6.08
Psychotic vs. Neurotic (Cutoff = 45)	63.86	72.78	68.88

*$p < .05$; **$p < .01$; ***$p < .001$; ****$p < .0001$

Hysteria, Schizophrenia, Psychopathic Deviance, Paranoia, Social Introversion, and Mania. Moreover, the veteran profile consisted of elevations of 22 of the subscales, whereas the civilian profile consisted of only eight. Specifically, the veterans had elevated *T*-scores for *all* five subscales for Depression and *all* six of the Schizophrenia subscales. Additionally, elevations were present for three of the five subscales for Psychopathic Deviance (Social Imperturbability, Social Alienation, Self-Alienation); two of the three Paranoia subscales (Persecutory Ideas and Poignancy); three of the six Social Introversion subscales (Inferiority/ Personal Discomfort, Discomfort with Others, and Physical Concerns);

TABLE 9.4

One-Way Analysis of Variance for Mean MMPI *T*-Scores for
Civilian and Vietnam-Related Trauma in a Forensic Sample

	Civilian (N = 7)	Vietnam Veterans (N = 9)	Group (N = 16)
Wiggins Content Scales			
Social Maladjustment	65.43	76.00	71.38
Depression	65.29	82.44**	71.38
Feminine Interests	48.71	47.11	47.81
Poor Morale	57.00	69.33	63.94
Religious Fundamentalism	49.14	51.89	50.69
Authority Conflict	54.00	51.00	52.31
Psychoticism	61.43	74.11	68.56
Organic Symptoms	66.57	78.33	73.19
Family Problems	57.00	61.22	59.38
Manifest Hostility	56.57	54.11	55.19
Phobias	60.71	63.56	62.31
Hypomania	51.57	53.67	52.75
Poor Health	64.29	72.78	69.63

*p <.05; **p <.01; ***p <.001; ****p <.0001

as well as one each of the subscales for Hysteria, Masculinity-Femininity, and Hypomania (Lassitude/Malaise, Narcissism, and Psychomotor Acceleration).

Especially noteworthy is the fact that the most elevated subscales are those closely associated with the symptoms of PTSD, including Discomfort with Others, Lack of Ego Mastery, Self-Alienation, Persecutory Ideas, Malaise, Mental Dullness, and Subjective Depression. Elevated mean *T*-scores for the civilian sample were limited to two of the Depression subscales (Subjective Depression and Mental Dullness); two Schizophrenia subscales (Lack of Ego Mastery: Cognitive and Conative); two Social Introversion subscales (Inferiority/Personal Discomfort and Physical Concerns); as well as one Hysteria and one Masculinity-Femininity subscale (Lassitude-Malaise and Narcissism). In the area of convergence in the two samples, there are other PTSD-related symptoms such as Physical Concern, Social Alienation, and Physical Malfunctioning. Clearly, the elevation in these different subscales gives a more detailed picture of the expression of PTSD on the MMPI subscale items and therefore may be useful in the process of a differential diagnosis.

MMPI scales and DSM-III-R PTSD classification. Table 9.6 illustrates the pattern of symptomatology related to PTSD as measured by the

TABLE 9.5
One-Way Analysis of Variance for Mean MMPI *T*-Scores for Civilian and Vietnam-Related Trauma in a Forensic Sample

	Civilian (N = 7)	Vietnam Veterans (N = 9)	Group (N = 16)
Harris-Lingoes/Serkownek Sub-Scales			
Subjective Depression	76.00	98.22**	88.50
Psychomotor Retardation	57.86	77.67***	69.00
Physical Malfunctioning	65.86	73.11	69.94
Mental Dullness	76.86	100.00**	89.88
Brooding	62.57	78.67**	71.63
Denial of Social Anxiety	46.00	38.78	41.94
Need for Affection	53.29	50.00	51.44
Lassitude-Malaise	73.14	94.00***	84.88
Somatic Complaints	62.00	69.22	66.06
Inhibition of Aggression	51.00	51.44	51.25
Family Discord	56.00	63.33	60.13
Authority Problems	60.29	57.22	58.56
Social Imperturbability	56.14	76.67	67.69
Social Alienation	65.14	74.00	70.13
Self-Alienation	69.86	80.44	75.81
Narcissism	73.29	85.67	80.25
Feminine Interests	46.29	44.56	45.31
Denial of Masculine Interests	63.14	56.44	59.38
Heterosexual Discomfort	51.43	55.33	53.63
Introspective	51.14	56.00	53.88
Socially Retiring	51.71	57.56	55.00
Persecutory Ideas	61.57	82.00*	73.06
Poignancy	63.00	80.56	72.88
Naivete	55.00	55.44	55.25
Social Alienation	61.14	74.56	68.69
Emotional Alienation	61.00	78.44*	70.81
Lack of Ego Mastery:			
Cognitive	73.14	83.78	79.13
Conative	76.29	94.33**	86.44
Defective Inhibition	63.14	71.22	67.69
Bizarre Sensory Experience	68.86	74.78	72.19
Amorality	51.29	44.67	47.56
Psychomotor Acceleration	71.14	73.00	72.19
Imperturbability	45.14	39.11	41.75
Ego Inflation	61.71	59.00	60.19
Inferiority	73.14	97.78*	87.00
Discomfort with Others	57.71	74.00	66.88
Staid — Personal Rigidity	57.71	63.78	61.13
Hypersensitivity	47.29	65.44**	57.50
Distrust	59.29	66.56	63.38
Physical Concerns	78.43	83.78	81.44

*p <.05; **p <.01; ***p <.001; ****p <.0001

MMPI. As discussed in Chapter 5, the Depression scale (2) detects PTSD symptoms of avoidance, such as numbing, restricted affect, and detachment from others. Additionally, feelings of agitation, tension, and irritability characteristic of hyperarousal are also common. The Psychopathic Deviance scale (4) identifies some of the associated features of PTSD, including excessive use of alcohol and/or drugs, impulsivity, problems in interpersonal relations, limited frustration tolerance, risk taking, and aggressive outbursts. An elevated Paranoia scale generally indicates an individual who is suspicious, guarded, hostile, and overly sensitive. These traits may be considered manifestations of a specific type of post-traumatic symptom related to hypervigilance and excessive autonomic nervous system arousal. Similarly, the Psychasthenia scale (7) often detects symptoms of obsessive rumination. In terms of PTSD, this scale may discern intrusive recollections, distressing levels of anxiety and tension, difficulties concentrating, and psychosomatic expressions such as gastrointestinal complaints, fatigue, and insomnia.

Since the Schizophrenia scale (8) is known to assess thought disturbances, it is highly likely that it is also assessing the more florid aspects of intrusive imagery in PTSD. Clearly, this might include confused, disorganized, and disoriented thought patterns, especially if the individual with PTSD has difficulty distinguishing intrusive thoughts and dissociative tendencies from their current environmental circumstances. *Taken together, these five clinical scales suggest a profile of post-traumatic symptomatology encompassing the major DSM-III-R criteria of reexperiencing, avoidance, and physiological hyperarousal, as well as associated features of depression, somatization, anger, mistrust, and isolation.*

In terms of Harris-Lingoes and Serkownek subscale scores, 75 to 100% of our combined sample obtained elevated scores on the following measures: Subjective Depression, Mental Dullness, Lassitude-Malaise, Self-Alienation, Lack of Ego Mastery (Conative), and Inferiority. Considered collectively, these scales appear to assess feelings of apathy, anhedonia, despair, isolation, stigmatization, and states of hyperarousal. Table 9.6 classifies these symptoms by the DSM-III-R diagnostic categories.

Table 9.7 presents a summary analysis of the MMPI scales and subscales that were elevated above a *T*-score of 100 for *any* subject in the sample, classified according to the DSM-III-R PTSD symptom cluster. This summary further helps to identify the possible MMPI items that are related to the major symptom clusters of post-traumatic stress syndrome.

TABLE 9.6
DSM-III-R Classification of Mean MMPI *T*-Scores for Civilian and Vietnam-Related Trauma (PTSD) in a Forensic Sample (N = 16)

SCALE	PTSD DIMENSION-DSM-III-R
MMPI Clinical Scales[a]	
Depression*	Numbing, Detachment, Hyperarousal
Psychopathic Deviant*	Re-experiencing
Paranoia*	Re-experiencing, Hypervigilence
Psychasthenia*	Re-experiencing, Hyperarousal
Schizophrenia*	Re-experiencing
Harris-Lingoes/Serkownek Scales	
Subjective Depression*	Avoidance, Hyperarousal
Psychomotor Retardation	Avoidance
Physical Malfunctioning	Hyperarousal
Mental Dullness*	Hyperarousal, Numbing
Brooding	Re-experiencing
Lassitude-Malaise*	Hyperarousal
Social Alienation	Detachment
Self-Alienation*	Re-experiencing, Hyperarousal
Persecutory Ideas	Re-experiencing, Hypervigilence
Poignancy	Re-experiencing, Hyperarousal, Detachment
Social Alienation	Re-experiencing, Avoidance Detachment
Emotional Alienation	Re-experiencing, Numbing
Lack of Ego Mastery: Cognitive	Re-experiencing, Hyperarousal
Lack of Ego Mastery: Conative*	Numbing, Avoidance
Psychomotor Acceleration	Hyperarousal
Inferiority*	Detachment
Distrust	Detachment, Re-experiencing
Physical Concerns	Detachment, Re-experiencing, Avoidance

[a]A strong trend (75-100% of sample score in indicated direction) is noted with an "*". All other trends are moderate (50-74%).

SCL-90 and IES: Comparisons and elevations. Table 9.8 presents the results of a one-way analysis of variance conducted with mean item scores for the IES (ranged 1–5) and SCL-90 (range 0–4). Overall, the civilian and veteran samples obtained similar profiles on both questionnaires. Elevations on both the Intrusion and Avoidance scales were obtained on the IES. SCL-90 profile peaks consisted of elevations on the Obsessive/Compulsive and Depression scales. The Positive Symptom Distress Index, and indication of symptom intensity, was also elevated. The only significant difference between the two groups was noted on the SCL-90 Additional Items scale. The veteran sample reported a significantly greater level of sleep disturbance ($p < .05$). It is diag-

TABLE 9.7
MMPI *T*-Scores Above 100 for Civilian and
Military-Related Trauma

SCALE	PTSD DIMENSION (DSM-III-R)
MMPI Clinical Scales	
Hypochondriasis	Somatization
Depression	Depression
Psychopathic Deviant	Anger
Paranoia	Mistrust
Psychasthenia	Obsession/Rumination
Schizophrenia	Intrusion
Wigging Content Scales	
Organic Symptoms	Hyperarousal
	Concentration/Memory Problems
Harris-Lingoes/Serkownek Sub-Scales	
Subjective Depression	Depression
Mental Dullness	Concentration/Memory Problems
Lassitude-Malaise	Somatic, Concentration,
	Sleep Disturbance
Social Imperturbability	Hypervigilence, Detachment
Narcissism	Re-Experiencing, Intrusion
Social Retiring	Isolation
Poignancy	Irritable, Sensation Seeking
Emotional Alienation	Depression
Lack of Ego Mastery: Cognitive	Intrusion, Concentration/Memory
	Problems
Lack of Ego Mastery: Conative	Depression, Rumination
Bizarre Sensory Experience	Intrusion
Inferiority	Isolation

nostically interesting that 100% of the sample reported *low* levels of psychoticism and *high* levels of depression. In addition, nearly 90% of the entire sample reported moderate to extreme distress related to Interpersonal Sensitivity and Anxiety. On the SCL-90, *all* subjects reported experiencing moderate levels of distress across the 10 symptom clusters as well as the specific indices of psychopathology (e.g., PSDI) (see also Chapter 8 for a discussion of the SCL-90 and IES profile).

SCL-90 and DSM-III-R PTSD classification. In terms of the differential diagnosis of PTSD utilizing the SCL-90, four scales emerged as strong indicators of DSM-III-R symptomatology: Interpersonal Sensitivity, Depression, Anxiety, and Additional Items. Table 9.9 summarizes the results. The Interpersonal Sensitivity scale measures feelings of personal inadequacy and inferiority. This scale also discerns feelings of uneasiness and marked discomfort during interpersonal interactions characteristic of traumatized individuals who detach from others, perhaps owing to emotional constriction or feelings of alienation and stigmatization. The SCL-90 Depression scale measures the clinical correlates of major depres-

TABLE 9.8

One-Way Analysis of Variance for Mean IES and SCL-90 Mean Item Scores for Civilian and Vietnam-Related Trauma in a Forensic Population

	Civilian (N = 7)	Vietnam Veterans (N = 5)	Group (N = 12)
Impact of Events Scale (IES)			
Intrusion	3.47	4.00	3.69
Avoidance	2.97	3.53	3.20

	Civilian (N = 5)	Vietnam Veterans (N = 4)	Group (N = 9)
Symptom Checklist-90 (SCL-90)			
Somatization	1.16	1.86	1.47
Obsessive/Compulsive	2.02	2.75	2.34
Interpersonal Sensitivity	1.58	2.11	1.82
Depression	2.08	2.54	2.28
Anxiety	1.86	2.05	1.94
Hostility	1.53	1.58	1.56
Phobic Anxiety	1.32	.93	1.14
Paranoid Ideation	1.27	1.67	1.45
Psychoticism	.94	1.43	1.16
Additional Items	1.94	2.66*	2.26
Global Severity Index	1.59	2.01	1.78
Positive Symptom Distress Index	2.07	2.34	2.19
Positive Symptom Tally	68.00	78.00	72.44

*p <.05; **p <.01; ***p <.001; ****p <.0001

sion and dysthymia as well as suicidal ideation. These symptoms include loss of energy, dysphoric mood and affect, withdrawal, anhedonia, feelings of hopelessness and futility, and a lack of motivation. In terms of DSM-III-R criteria, these symptoms may be indicators of avoidance, denial, numbing, and restricted affect. The Anxiety scale measures characteristic symptoms of anxiety, including free-floating anxiety, panic attacks, high manifest anxiety characteristic of reexperiencing, and hyperarousal. The Additional Items scale may discern additional PTSD symptoms, including disturbed sleep patterns, feelings of guilt, and intrusive affect and imagery associated with the trauma.

Comparisons and elevations on the 16-PF scales. Table 9.10 presents the results of a one-way analysis of variance conducted with mean sten scores on the 16-PF Clinical Scales and Second Order Factors for the two comparison groups. Examination of extreme scores (below 3.00 or above 7.00) reveals that as a group, these traumatized persons were

TABLE 9.9
DSM-III-R Classification of Mean SCL-90 Item Scores for Civilian and Vietnam-Related Trauma (PTSD) in a Forensic Sample (N = 16)

SCALE	PTSD DIMENSION (DSM-III-R)
SCL-90 Clinical Scales[a]	
Interpersonal Sensitivity*	Detachment
Depression*	Avoidance
Anxiety*	Re-experiencing, Hyperarousal
Hostility	Re-experiencing
Additional Items*	Re-experiencing, Hyperarousal

[a]A strong trend (75-100% of sample score in indicated direction) is noted with an *. All other trends are moderate (50-74%).

characterized by the 16-PF as Reserved, Shy, Self-Sufficient, and Tense. In addition, the civilian sample can be further described as being intellectually abstract. On the other hand, the veteran sample scores high on the traits Emotional, Serious, Suspicious, and Apprehensive, perhaps an indication of the strong avoidance and withdrawal components of PTSD. Nevertheless, the two profiles are remarkably similar in their configuration despite two significant differences. The veteran sample was significantly more serious and shy ($p < .05$). In terms of the Second Order Factors, the civilian sample was characterized by *low* levels of Extroversion and *high* levels of Anxiety. The veteran sample was characterized by significantly lower levels of Extroversion ($p < .05$) as well as Leadership, but higher levels of Creativity.

Table 9.11 indicates the results of a one-way analysis of variance conducted with mean percentages on the Murray Need Estimates derived from the 16-PF Clinical Scales for the civilian and veteran groups. Examination of the profiles reveals no significant differences between the two groups. Inspection of the extreme scores (below 30% or above 70%) indicates that as a group, the forensic sample manifested high levels of Autonomy and Abasement and low levels of Dominance. In addition, the civilian sample displayed high levels of Succorance, whereas the military sample exhibited low levels of Exhibition and Affiliation and high levels of Endurance and Aggression. Overall, as related to the symptom clusters of PTSD, the 16-PF suggests a profile in which the extreme stress scores are those for the personality dimensions of Reserved, Emotional, Shy, Self-Sufficient, Introverted, Anxious, and Independent. For the Murray Need Estimates, the sample scored *low* on the scales of Dominance, Affiliation, Exhibitionism, but manifested *higher* scores for Endurance, Change, Abasement, Aggression, and Autonomy. Taken as a set, these personality traits are consistent with

TABLE 9.10

One-Way Analysis of Variance for Mean 16-PF Sten Scores for Civilian and Vietnam-Related Trauma in a Forensic Sample

	Civilian (N = 7)	Vietnam Veterans (N = 9)	Group (N = 16)
16-PF Clinical Scales			
Reserved vs. Warm	3.00	2.56	2.75
Concrete vs. Abstract	7.14	6.22	6.62
Emotional vs. Calm	3.14	2.67	2.88
Adaptive vs. Assertive	4.14	4.00	4.06
Serious vs. Enthusiastic	4.43	2.56*	3.38
Expedient vs. Conscientious	4.43	4.56	4.50
Shy vs. Bold	2.86	1.44*	
2.06			
Tough-Minded vs. Sensitive	4.29	3.78	4.00
Trusting vs. Suspicious	5.71	7.00	6.44
Practical vs. Imaginative	4.43	4.89	4.69
Forthright vs. Socially Aware	5.57	5.89	5.75
Composed vs. Apprehensive	6.71	8.33	7.63
Conservative vs. Critical	5.43	6.22	5.88
Group Oriented vs. Self-Sufficient	8.43	8.78	8.63
Impulsive vs. Meticulous	4.57	4.33	4.44
Relaxed vs. Tense	7.00	7.56	7.31
16-PF Second Order Factors			
Extroversion	2.83	1.23*	
1.93			
Anxiety	7.03	8.06	7.62
Practicality	6.31	6.11	6.20
Independence	4.10	4.42	4.28
Self-Control	4.05	4.16	4.11
Leadership	3.78	2.35	2.98
Creativity	6.90	7.24	7.09
Achievment	5.83	5.67	5.74

*p <.05; **p <.01; ***p <.001; ***p <.0001

dynamics of PTSD, especially in the *avoidance* tendencies of being isolated, withdrawn, low in feelings of self-worth, self-sufficient, mistrustful, anxious, and angry. Although these results are based on a small sample of persons suffering from PTSD, they may provide a clue as to post-traumatic personality alteration, a phenomenon that is not well understood at this time.

The 16-PF and DSM-III-R PTSD classification. Based on our sample, Tables 9.12 and 9.13 further summarize these findings of the 16-PF factors to identify the PTSD dimensions that are most likely being reflected in the personality measures.

TABLE 9.11
One-Way Analysis of Variance for Mean 16-PF Murray Need Estimate Percentages for Civilian and Vietnam-Related Trauma in a Forensic Sample

	Civilian (N = 7)	Vietnam Veterans (N = 9)	Group (N = 16)
16-PF Murray Need Estimates			
Achievement	65.14	61.56	63.13
Deference	41.29	45.44	43.63
Order	52.29	60.44	56.88
Exhibition	31.86	19.78	25.06
Autonomy	73.43	76.89	75.38
Affiliation	38.29	20.89	28.50
Intraception	32.57	39.67	36.56
Succorance	70.43	64.56	67.13
Dominance	13.86	3.89	8.25
Abasement	82.57	88.56	85.94
Nurturance	53.71	45.44	49.06
Change	51.86	44.78	47.88
Endurance	66.14	85.11	76.81
Heterosexuality	68.43	54.44	60.56
Aggression	62.57	77.33	70.88

TABLE 9.12
DSM-III-R Classification of 16-PF Sten Scores for Civilian and Vietnam-Related Trauma (PTSD) in a Forensic Sample (N = 16)

SCALE	PTSD DIMENSION (DSM-III-R)
16-PF Clinical Scales[a]	
Reserved*	Isolation, Mistrust
Emotional	Hyperarousal, Irritability
Adaptive	Depression, Withdrawal
Serious	Depression, Isolation
Shy*	Emotional Constriction, Isolation, Overactive Sympathetic Nervous System
Self-Sufficient*	Detachment
16-PF Second Order Factors	
Introversion*	Isolation, Alienation
Anxiety	Intrusion, Hyperarousal
Practicality	Sense of Foreshortened Future
Independence	Detachment
Creativity	Divergent Thinking

[a]A strong trend (75-100% of sample score in indicated direction) is noted with an "*". All other trends are moderate (50-74%).

TABLE 9.13

Trend Analysis of Mean 16-PF Percentiles of Murray Need Estimates for Civilian and Vietnam-Related Trauma (PTSD) in a Forensic Sample (N = 16)

SCALE	PTSD DIMENSION (DSM-III-R)
16-PF Murray Need Estimates[a]	
LOW	
Exhibitionism	Depression, Isolation
Affiliation	Mistrust, Isolation, Detachment
Dominance*	Detachment
HIGH	
Abasement*	Low Self-Esteem, Guilt
Endurance	Hypervigilence
Aggression	Anger, Rage
Autonomy	Detachment

[a]A strong trend (75-100% of sample score in indicated direction) is noted with an "*". All other trends are moderate (50-74%).

As noted in recent research (Aronoff & Wilson, 1985), the tendency to score *high* on the needs of abasement, endurance, autonomy, and aggression and *low* on the motives of dominance, affiliation, and exhibitionism is associated with a mode of social interaction that is generally disaffiliative and concurrent. This mode of social interaction activated by personality processes is typically characterized by low levels of initiation of goal-directed activity, withdrawal, low levels of participation in group activity, and a lack of effectance motivation (White, 1963). *Thus, considered from the perspective of post-traumatic personality alteration, one potential consequence of psychic trauma may be to reorganize the personality functioning of the individual so that both cognitively and emotionally he becomes less proactive in his personal strivings and exhibits less ego mastery in adaptive behavior.* Viewed in this way, the personality alteration could be regarded as more safety-oriented, prone to external attributions of causality, avoidant, and vigilant. The person may see the world as an unpredictable, hostile, and threatening place. If so, then the traumatized individual may attempt to cope either by seclusion, avoidance, isolation, and withdrawal, or alternatively, by forceful, aggressive, excessively vigilant, and active controlling modes of adaptive behavior. In either form of coping, avoidant or hypervigilant-controlling, the function of the behavior is to attempt to increase a sense of security, predictability, and psychological control over events. However, as Kahana, Harel, Kahana, and Rosner (1988) have noted, some victimized persons also cope instrumentally in healthy ways that are not pathological or maladaptive. In such cases the person may not suffer from PTSD or experience an alteration in personality. Clearly, much future research is needed to elucidate the complex interactions between personality processes, the appraisal and processing of a traumatic event, and subsequent transformations in the organization of the self-structure of the survivor. These issues are discussed below.

PTSD Profiles: MMPI, SCL-90, and 16-PF

To conclude our analysis of PTSD profiles and their assessment for forensic and clinical purposes, we have generated four figures which hopefully will be useful to clinicians and others working with traumatized persons who seek to understand their scores on traditional psychometric approaches to assessing levels of psychopathology. Figure 9.1 illustrates three MMPI profiles as reported by Burke and Mayer (1985) and Hyer and O'Leary (1986) for Vietnam veterans seeking psychiatric treatment at VA medical centers, as well as for a random psychiatric population (Burke & Mayer, 1985). These samples are described in Chapter 5.

Figure 9.1 illustrates that the profile configurations for the three groups are quite similar, although Hyer et al.'s (1986) group of 26 veterans shows extremely high elevations on MMPI scales F, 2, and 8. As reviewed in Chapter 5, similar PTSD profile configurations have been reported in several other studies (see p. 118). Thus, it is difficult to know whether or not the individuals were exaggerating their symptoms for purposes of treatment and service-connected disability compensation or were actually manifesting extreme levels of psychic distress. Figure 9.2 presents the findings for the two samples that were described earlier. Again, it is noteworthy when examining the profile to observe that the configurations are the same, except that the Vietnam veteran sample is more elevated on the validity and clinical scales, a finding similar to that obtained by Hyer et al. (1986). However, in our sample the veterans' scores on the Depression, Schizophrenia, Psychasthenia, and Paranoid scales are extremely elevated (*T*-scores = 90–105), which may reflect the fact that *all* of the men were charged with serious felony charges (e.g., first-degree murder). In each case the veteran had a well-documented history of chronic PTSD that was untreated and had resulted in multiple and continual failures in work and intimate relations.

This profile would seem to genuinely reflect the severity of their illness, the stresses associated with incarceration, and the prospect of a major trial which could result in their death or a long prison sentence. With these difficult circumstances, the elevations on Psychasthenia and

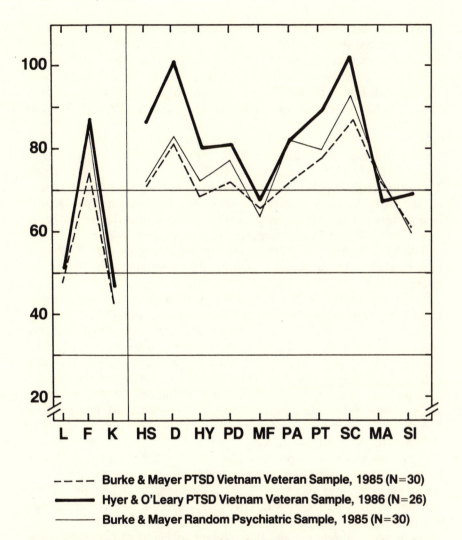

Figure 9.1. Comparative MMPI profiles for Vietnam veterans and psychiatric patient samples.

Paranoia, in addition to Depression and Schizophrenia, probably reflect feelings of persecution, obsessive rumination about the war, as well as their current legal difficulties. In contrast, however, the civilian litigants presented a less extreme 2–8 or 8–2 PTSD MMPI profile. Since these cases typically involved only a single stressor event, as opposed to the multiple stressors encountered during a year of combat duty in Vietnam as well as being incarcerated, it is not surprising that the scores are not as elevated as those of the incarcerated veteran group. Nevertheless, the profile configurations for both the civilian trauma and veteran samples are remarkably similar to that reported by Frederick (1985) for 48 cases of adolescent and adult trauma (e.g., automobile accidents, natural disasters, physical assault), who had *T*-scores above 85 on scales F, 8, and 2.

In recent years the SCL-90 has been used in several studies of war trauma and man-made disaster (e.g., Gleser, Green, & Winget, 1981; Green & Grace, 1988; Kahana, Harel, & Kahana, 1988; Lindy, 1988). These studies provide a basis by which to compare profile configurations on the SCL-90 scales. Figure 9.3 illustrates the comparative data for four groups: (1) Vietnam veterans with PTSD before and after treatment (see Chapter 7); (2) 150 Holocaust survivors studied by Kahana, Harel, and Kahana (1988); (3) normals studied by Derogatis (1973); and (4) nine persons from our forensic sample (data were not available for the entire sample).

As shown in Figure 9.3 the profile configuration for our forensic sample is quite similar to that of the veterans with PTSD *prior* to treatment and to the sample of Holocaust survivors, the majority of whom had never received psychiatric treatment since their internment (Kahana, Harel, & Kahana, 1988). Further, in comparison to the non-pathological sample, the nine subjects in our sample, as well as the veterans and Holocaust survivors, show elevations on the following scales: Somatization, Obsessive/Compulsive (rumination), Interpersonal Sensitivity, Depression, Anxiety, and Hostility. Moderated elevations were also found on Phobic Anxiety, Paranoid Ideation, and Psychoticism. Clearly, the elevations on the scales of Depression, Obsessive/Compulsive, Anxiety, and Interpersonal Sensitivity are quite consistent with the major symptom patterns of PTSD (avoidance and emotional restriction; intrusive imagery and affect; hyperarousal, self-consciousness, and interpersonal sensitivity).

These same symptoms are also evident in Figure 9.4, which shows the 16-PF profile configurations of all 16 of the subjects in our forensic sample. Furthermore, the typical profile for anxiety reactions as discerned in 80 cases by Cattell et al. (1970) is also presented for comparative purposes. As noted earlier, the PTSD forensic sample is characterized as Reserved, Emotional, Shy, Apprehensive, Self-Sufficient, and Tense. The profile configuration is also quite similar to that for persons suffering from anxiety reactions, a fact which supports the classification of PTSD as an anxiety disorder in DSM-III-R. The only apparent differences

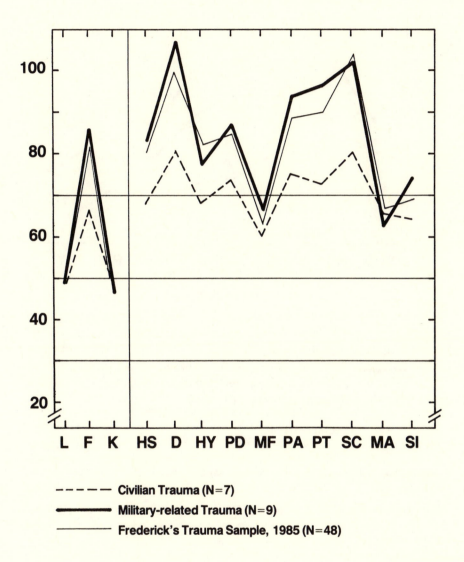

Figure 9.2. MMPI profiles for civilian and military-related trauma compared to Frederick's trauma sample.

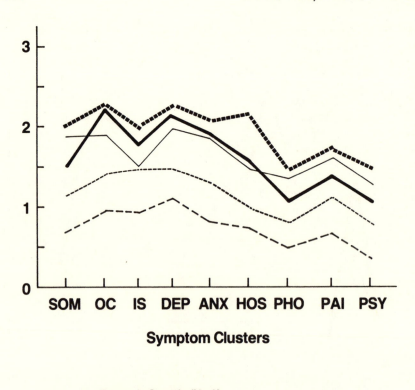

Symptom Clusters

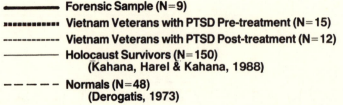

Figure 9.3. SCL-90 profiles for forensic sample, comparative survivor groups, and normals.

appear to be that the forensic sample emerges as more Reserved, Shy, Tough-Minded, and Self-Sufficient.

DISCUSSION

In a society in which there are an increasing number of persons suffering from traumatic life experiences, the interrelated issues of the

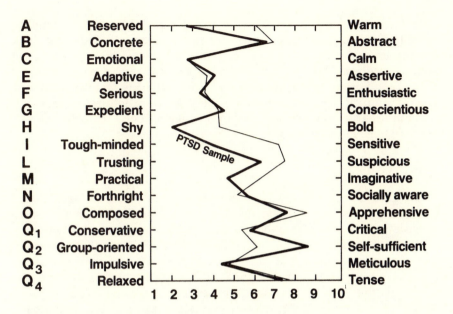

A	Reserved	Warm
B	Concrete	Abstract
C	Emotional	Calm
E	Adaptive	Assertive
F	Serious	Enthusiastic
G	Expedient	Conscientious
H	Shy	Bold
I	Tough-minded	Sensitive
L	Trusting	Suspicious
M	Practical	Imaginative
N	Forthright	Socially aware
O	Composed	Apprehensive
Q_1	Conservative	Critical
Q_2	Group-oriented	Self-sufficient
Q_3	Impulsive	Meticulous
Q_4	Relaxed	Tense

1 2 3 4 5 6 7 8 9 10

Figure 9.4. 16-PF profiles for PTSD forensic sample compared to Cattell's anxiety reaction profile.

diagnosis, treatment, litigation and compensation of post-traumatic stress syndromes will require both greater sophistication and normative profile data to aid in these clinical and forensic processes. In the legal arena, expert witnesses will be called on to explain forms of post-traumatic adaptation and psychopathology as it bears on such issues as criminal responsibility, levels of psychological damage or personal injury, and the determination of disability compensation. On a human and societal level, the latter issues are important because potentially they have enormous impact on the ability of a person, for example, to live without fear and insecurity if a pension for trauma-related disability will enable him to support a family, meet financial obligations, and live with dignity.

On a cultural level, it is also important to understand that victimized persons are often fragile, vulnerable, and humanly diminished by traumatic experiences. It is important to recognize that these persons often require specialized post-traumatic therapy in order to restore a healthy stress recovery process (Ochberg, 1988). How we collectively respond to victimized persons (e.g., war veterans, rape victims, P.O.W.'s, abused children) also reflects our values as a society and the policies that are legislated or developed to meet the needs of traumatized persons.

Moreover, in a world characterized by massive global trauma, we simply cannot afford to assume that the very real and often urgent needs of psychically traumatized persons will be met by existing health care agencies (Wilson, Harel, & Kahana, 1988). For this reason, organizations such as the Society for Traumatic Stress Studies (STSS) and the National Organization of Victims Association (NOVA) were formed to provide a forum for advocacy and research in broadening our knowledge about traumatic stress syndromes.

CONCLUSION

The goals in this chapter were threefold: (1) to present a conceptual framework by which to understand stress response syndromes in the forensic process; (2) to highlight some of the major considerations in arriving at an accurate differential diagnosis of PTSD; and (3) to present research evidence on actual forensic cases that involved both military- and civilian-related trauma. In terms of the latter consideration, it was noted that the paucity of normative psychometric data on PTSD profiles for trauma victims often results in misdiagnosis, confusion, and frustration in legal matters regarding the issues of criminal responsibility and disability compensation, especially with agencies such as the Social Security Administration and the Veterans Administration. Among the reasons this happens is that psychological tests, such as the MMPI, are frequently relied upon as valid "yardsticks" of psychopathology, and the typical profile for trauma victims (extreme elevations on scales F, 2, and 8) is often mistaken for malingering or exaggeration of symptoms for purposes of compensation. Precisely for this reason, clinicians and researchers must have normative data on individuals traumatized by different stressor events in order to understand the range, severity, and patterning of post-traumatic adaptation and personality functioning.

The result of the study presented in the third section of this chapter represents an initial step in the direction of understanding the expression of PTSD on such standardized personality measures as the MMPI, SCL-90, 16-PF, and IES scales. What do the results indicate from this small sample of individuals involved in the legal system in terms of either facing a criminal charge or seeking compensation for trauma-induced psychological damage?

MMPI

On the MMPI, the forensic sample ($N = 16$) had T-score elevations above 70 on the following scales (arranged from highest, 92, to lowest,

74): Schizophrenia, Psychasthenia, Paranoia, Psychopathic Deviance, Fake Bad, Hypochondriasis, and Hysteria. Additionally, the Goldberg Index was also elevated (178.33), indicating a direction of pathological deviance. Furthermore, it was noted that the scores for the Vietnam veterans were significantly higher on the following scales: Faking Bad (84), Depression (106), Paranoia (94), Psychasthenia (96), Schizophrenia (101), and the Goldberg Index (203). Clearly, given the multiple stressor experiences of combat in Vietnam, these scores seem to reflect the severity of their psychopathology. As noted in Chapter 6, these MMPI clinical scales (2, 8, 7, 6) appear to be assessing the DSM-III-R symptom clusters of intrusion, avoidance, and physiological hyperarousal.

MMPI Subscales

The standard MMPI subscales typically employed in clinical assessment (Harris/Lingoes, Serkownek, and Wiggins) also produced findings consistent with the accumulated body of research on PTSD. In addition to assessing some of the core symptom features of PTSD, these subscales also seem to discern some of the associated features of the stress syndrome. Specifically, in the sample, the subjects had elevated *T*-scores on the following subscales: subjective depression; social maladjustment; organic symptoms; mental dullness; lassitude-malaise; social, emotional, and self-alienation; narcissism; persecution; poignancy; lack of ego mastery; bizarre sensory experience; inferiority; and physical concerns. Similar findings were obtained on the SCL-90, 16-PF, and IES scales, which showed profile elevations on depression, anxiety, hostility, psychoticism, intrusion, and avoidance symptoms.

In terms of the nonpathological traits measured by the 16-PF, the forensic sample was characterized as strongly reserved, emotional, shy, apprehensive, self-sufficient, introverted, anxious, low on leadership initiative, and high on creativity, autonomy, abasement, aggressiveness, and endurance. Moreover, the sample scored low on the personality dimensions of dominance, affiliation, and exhibitionism. The aggregate of personality characteristics measured by the 16-PF is consistent with personality processes associated with a disaffiliative (withdrawn) and concurrent (submissive) style of social interaction (Aronoff & Wilson, 1985; Bales, 1970; Leary, 1957). It was suggested that this personality profile for individuals with PTSD may reflect an alteration in personality structure caused by the traumatic event.

As noted in Chapter 1, the personality processes of the person may then organize a coping style that is either avoidant or hypervigilant-controlling in nature. In avoidant coping, the person is seclusive, isolated, withdrawn, passive, dependent, and lacks proactive mastery and initiative in adaptive behavior. In the hypervigilant-controlling mode, the individual is aggressive, intrusive, forceful, controlling and autonomous. In both forms of post-traumatic coping organized by personality processes, the goal of the behavior is to reduce unpredictability and uncertainty in the environment in an attempt to enhance feelings of safety, security, and personal control. In this regard, we referred to these forms of coping as safety-oriented (Aronoff & Wilson, 1985) because they concern "security operations" that emanate from a core of anxiety and mistrust which grew out of the traumatic event.

As noted in Chapter 1, these forms of coping can also be considered as part of the cognitive style of the individual who either reduces or augments the acquisition and processing of information in situations. The avoidant form of coping is characterized by information reduction, a narrowing of attention, rigidity in the search of the stimulus field, and low persistence in acquisition of data relevant to problem solving. On the other hand, the hypervigilant-controlling form of coping is far more likely to excessively scan the stimulus field and actively persist in acquiring information about persons, events, and situations in order to maintain a sense of control and prediction. What is significant about these disparate forms of coping is that: (1) they reflect an alteration in personality processes; and (2) they are *trauma-specific* forms of cognitive processing. By this we mean that the person tends to perceive the world through the lens of a trauma. Thus, the cognitive style, whether avoidant or hypervigilant, is to a large extent organized around the traumatic experience, a point Horowitz (1976) has made as well.

In conclusion, the results of the study of psychometric markers of PTSD on the MMPI, 16-PF, and IES scales in the forensic sample have produced many interesting results that are useful in differential diagnosis. Several implications of these results warrant consideration. *First, the elevations found on the validity, clinical, and subscales of the MMPI may be identifying a global PTSD profile that overlaps with other affective and anxiety disorders.* In the sample, the two most elevated clinical scales were 8–2/2–8. Consistent with our interpretation of these findings in terms of PTSD and personality alteration, Graham (1987) has summarized much of the research on the two-point 8–2 code as follows:

> Persons with the 28/82 code report feeling anxious, agitated, tense, and jumpy. Sleep disturbance, inability to concentrate, confused thinking, and forgetfulness also are characteristic of 28/82

people. Such persons are quite inefficient in carrying out their responsibilities, and they tend to be unoriginal in their thinking and stereotyped in problem solving. They are likely to present themselves as physically ill, and somatic complaints include dizziness, blackout spells, nausea, and vomiting. They resist psychological interpretations of their problems, and they are resistant to change. They underestimate the seriousness of their problems, and they tend to be unrealistic about their own capabilities.

28/82 individuals are basically dependent and ineffective, and they have problems in being assertive. They are irritable and resentful much of the time; they fear loss of control and do not express themselves directly. They attempt to deny undesirable impulses, and cognitive dissociative periods during which they act out may occur. Such periods are followed by guilt and depression. 28/82 persons are rather sensitive to the reactions of others, and they are quite suspicious of the motivations of others. They may have a history of being hurt emotionally, and they fear being hurt more. They avoid close interpersonal relationships, and they keep people at a distance emotionally. This lack of meaningful involvement with other people increases their feelings of despair and worthlessness. (p. 104)

Clearly, this description is an accurate, if global, characterization of post-traumatic stress disorder but without the trauma-specific quality of intrusive imagery. However, when the psychasthenia scale (7) is also elevated, as in our sample and others reviewed in Chapter 6, the tendency to ruminate about the trauma and experience episodes of intrusive imagery may be picked up by the questionnaire. As Graham (1987) notes, the 278/728 three-point code is characterized as follows:

Persons with this code often present a mixed-picture diagnostically. They are experiencing a great deal of emotional turmoil, and they tend to have a rather schizoid life-style. Brief, acute psychotic episodes may occur. They tend to feel tense, nervous, and fearful, and they have problems in concentrating and attending. They feel depressed, despondent, and hopeless, and they often ruminate about suicide. Affect appears blunted or otherwise inappropriate. These persons lack basic social skills and are shy, withdrawn, introverted, and socially isolated. They feel inadequate and inferior. They tend to set high standards for themselves and to feel guilty when the standards are not met. They tend to show interest in obscure, esoteric subjects. (p. 114)

This elevated three-point code, particularly the tendency "to show interest in obscure, esoteric subjects," suggests obsessive rumination about trauma-related imagery and affect in persons suffering from PTSD.

Trauma and Personality Alteration

The results of the 16-PF also raise the possibility that traumatic life events may produce significant alteration in personality functioning. Although we have no pre-trauma measures on the 16-PF by which to discern changes in profile configurations, the pattern that was obtained may point the way for future studies to examine both pathological and nonpathological forms of personality alteration associated with trauma. As I have written elsewhere (Wilson, 1988a), extremely stressful life events may alter personality propensities in ways that are theoretically predictable depending on the organization of the self-structure of the individual prior to the trauma. For example, a person who was active, dominant, assertive, and forceful prior to a traumatic event may develop an aggressive, hypervigilant-controlling mode of adaptation afterward. Similarly, a person who was passive, dependent, and unassertive prior to a trauma may manifest an avoidant-isolation mode of coping post-trauma. By extending the logic of a person by situation (trauma) interaction paradigm to the analysis of post-traumatic personality alteration, it is conceptually possible to specify different forms of: (1) pathological and nonpathological adaptation; (2) reorganization of ego structure; and, (3) coping and defensive style that are employed to manage distressing affect and imagery resulting from the trauma.

Finally, the results of the present study also discerned profile configurations on the MMPI, SCL-90, and 16-PF which are remarkably similar to those found by other researchers not studying a forensic sample per se. As Figures 9.1 to 9.4 clearly demonstrate, the forensic sample matches closely those obtained for treatment-seeking Vietnam veterans, victims of diverse adult traumatic events, and survivors of the Nazi Holocaust. The similarity in profile configuration supports the ecological validity of our findings and measures of post-traumatic stress syndromes. A comparative analysis of stress response syndromes is especially valuable since it affords the opportunity to determine the interactive effects of personal resource variables, the nature of the stressor dimensions in a particular traumatic event, and the recovery environment as they codetermine the cognitive processing of the stressful life event and subsequent adaptation.

Epilogue

The field of traumatic stress is presently on the verge of unprecedented growth as a discipline. In the 20th century, the study of victimization and survivorship has been limited to episodic inquiries following major disasters, wars, or traumas that stimulated the medical and psychological study of those who became survivors. During the last 50 years, however, the level of massive global trauma is unparalleled in human history: the Nazi Holocaust, World War II, the atomic bomb at Hiroshima, the Korean War, the Vietnam War, the Cambodian Holocaust, and continuing warfare, terrorism, disaster, torture, and famine in many parts of the world. This fact is not meant as a doomsday statement but simply a recognition that traumatic events, at both the societal and individual level, are now a part of our collective consciousness which brings with it the emerging awareness that these experiences can profoundly alter human adaptive functioning in a variety of ways that we are just beginning to understand in depth.

During the last decade the study and treatment of post-traumatic stress disorder has become an increasingly important, if controversial, area in the medical and behavioral sciences. Undoubtedly, the recognition of PTSD in DSM-III as a unique mental disorder was extraordinarily useful in advancing knowledge in the field of traumatic stress studies. First, the acknowledgment of PTSD as a mental disorder validated its existence for many mental health professionals. It permitted clinicians and researchers to "see" a syndrome that had its own unique properties and dynamics and previously was diagnosed under different psychiatric rubrics. Second, the study of PTSD has posed major challenges to existing theories of personality and psychopathology. Today we are rethinking psychodynamic, biological, and cultural explanations of mental disorders. Moreover, it is my belief that the full understanding of post-traumatic stress syndromes, both pathological and nonpathological, will require an integrated, holistic theory that can account for the complex interrelationships between neurophysiological responses to

261

stress, psychological modalities of coping and defense, and cultural mechanisms of healing and reintegration. In his historical review of the concept of traumatic neuroses, Trimble (1981) noted that since the 19th century the attempts to explain post-traumatic stress reactions have alternated between *external* causality (e.g., psychic stressor) and *internal* causality (e.g., cerebral concussion). This finding is heuristically valuable because today we have the methodological and technical ability to systematically explore competing hypotheses which will permit researchers to evolve higher-order explanations of traumatic stress syndromes.

Third, the classification of PTSD in DSM-III also spurred new research into the diagnostic criteria themselves. In DSM-III-R we have an expanded and revised set of diagnostic criteria which reflect, to a degree, current advances in the field (Brett, Spitzer, & Williams, in press). Clearly, not all clinicians or researchers are in agreement with these diagnostic criteria or their classification as an anxiety disorder. Nevertheless, such debate is both healthy and productive since it should generate research that will: (1) help to resolve questions regarding the essential core symptoms of the disorder; (2) establish the proper classification as a syndrome; (3) identify the types of events and persons most vulnerable to pathological manifestations of the disorder; and (4) differentiate nonpathological and subclinical forms of adaptation to extreme stress.

Fourth, I believe that in our commitment to understanding PTSD and helping distressed victims, we have overemphasized the psychopathology of survivors. I do not wish to minimize the very real suffering of many persons with traumatic stress syndromes, but it is also the case that many victimized persons resume life, raise children, hold a job, and manage their daily affairs in a reasonable manner. Furthermore, even in cases of severe PTSD, the patients often have many positive character traits, shaped and colored by the trauma, that we need to understand. Above and beyond the pathological symptoms are often found deeply human attributes of empathy, integrity, a concern with justice, equality, fairness, ethics, and dignity. In other ways, many survivors possess a wisdom about life and are often grounded in the ability to discern the genuine from the fake; the sincere from the manipulative; the nurturing from the exploitative; the spiritual from the spiritually impacted; the altruistic from the egocentric; the animated from the stagnant; the integrated from the disconnected; the self-determined from the socially conforming; and the loving from the hateful.

It may be that most of these higher qualities and values have their origin in the trauma in which the possibility or specter of death brings into awareness the existential meaning of nonbeing. To face the possibility of one's own death and the profound sense of vulnerability to the limits of one's life-cycle may alter forever an individual's sense of being in the world. Clearly, we know that the death encounter or its symbolic equivalent can affect psychoformative processes at many levels of consciousness and functioning (Lifton, 1988). Survivors frequently experience massive disillusionment and profound changes in ideology, beliefs, attitudes, and values. But how is it possible that many individuals transform and overcome psychic trauma? What are the forms of personality alteration produced by traumatic events? What are the mechanisms of the healthy transformation, adaptation, and recovery from extreme psychic trauma? What does it mean to be a "survivor?"

It seems clear to me that the study of traumatic stress will continue unabated into the 21st century. The questions raised above, and the many that are yet to be formulated, will ultimately become the subject of inquiry for future generations who will work in the field of traumatic stress studies. At this point in our collective knowledge, we have learned that psychic trauma never occurs in a vacuum. As Figley has noted (1985), trauma produces a wake which extends its effects into the fabric of society, the lives of ordinary people, and the generations of children which follow along the common pathway of humanity. To study traumatic stress is to learn a great deal about the extremes of human nature in terms of life, death, and the transformation of the spirit.

Appendix A:
Vietnam Era Stress Inventory

Name   Telephone (area code and number)

Address (Street, City, State, Zip Code)

The Vietnam Era Stress Inventory (VESI) contains a set of questionnaires which are primarily designed to assess the experiences of the men and women who served in the military during the Vietnam Era, 1962–1975. The VESI contains a number of different parts which include (I) Biographical; (II) Combat experiences in Vietnam; (III) Exposure to specific stressors in the Vietnam War; (IV) Post-Vietnam stress assessment; (V) Post-Vietnam "homecoming" experiences; (VI) Post-Vietnam legal problems. Each part of the inventory contains self-explanatory instructions. To complete the entire questionnaire takes between 1–1½ hours. Most individuals completing the VESI questionnaire find it interesting and valuable as a learning experience about themselves and report benefitting from doing it. If it is convenient for you, you may choose to complete the questionnaire one part at a time. Please complete all of the items on the VESI questionnaire.

At the present time the VESI instrument is being used as part of a large-scale study to learn more about the special concerns of Vietnam era veterans. If you wish to participate in this project, please return the questionnaire to the address listed below. All information is kept strictly confidential and will be used only to learn about the post-Vietnam stress problems of comparative groups of Vietnam Era veterans. Your cooperation is greatly appreciated. Mail completed questionnaires to:

> Dr. John P. Wilson, Director,
> Forgotten Warrior Research Project on Vietnam Era Veterans
> The Department of Psychology
> Cleveland State University
> Cleveland, Ohio 44115

All participants will receive, free of charge, a series of reports on the findings which will be mailed to the address listed above at the first available date.

PART I BIOGRAPHY QUESTIONNAIRE—SECTION A
INSTRUCTIONS

The following list of questions concern background information prior to your military service. Please read each question carefully and answer as accurately as you can remember. Do not skip any questions.

1. Present age: _____

2. Date of Birth _____ / _____ / _____
               Mo   Day   Yr

3. Where were you born?

   _____
   City and State or Country

4. Race or ethnicity

   _____ American Indian or Alaskan Native
   _____ Asian or Pacific-Island American
   _____ Mexican-American
   _____ Black
   _____ White

5. How many children were there in your family including yourself? _____

6. How many brothers and sisters did you have? (If you were an only child, check none.)

   Brothers _____
   Sisters _____
   None _____

7. Were you the oldest child, youngest child, or in between?

   Oldest child? _____
   The _____ oldest child of _____ .
   Youngest child? _____

8. What was the size of the city, town or village in which you lived?

   _____ Under 2,500
   _____ 2,500—9,999
   _____ 10,000—49,000
   _____ 50,000—249,000
   _____ 250,000—One Million
   _____ Over One Million

9. How much schooling have you had?

   _____ Completed grade school or less
   _____ Some high school
   _____ Completed high school
   _____ Some college/trade school
   _____ Completed college/trade school
   _____ Some post-graduate work
   _____ Completed Ph.D.

10. Through your high school years, how many different towns or cities did you live in? _____

11. What course or program were you taking at that time?

High School ____
College (Liberal Arts) ____
College (Vocationally oriented—e.g., engineering, pre-med) ____
SPECIFY: _____
Graduate school for M.A. ____
Graduate school for Ph.D., M.D., D.D.S. ____
Employed ____
SPECIFY: _____
Can't recall ____

12. Present employment status.

Employed full-time ____
Employed part-time (and want it this way) ____
Employed part-time (but don't like it this way) ____
Unemployed (but actively looking for a job) ____
Unemployed (and not looking for a job) ____
Laid-off ____

13. What is your approximate annual gross (before taxes) income?

0—$5,000 ____
$5,001—$10,000 ____
$10,001—$15,000 ____
$15,001—$20,000 ____
$20,001 or more ____

14. Were you married at the time you entered the military?

Yes ____   No ____

15. (IF YES to #14) How long had you been married? ____

16. (IF NO to #14) Were you:

Single ____
Separated ____
Divorced ____
Widowed ____

17. Did you have any children at the time you entered the military?

Yes ____   No ____

(IF YES) How many? ____

18. Present marital status.

Married (never divorced) ____
Married (previously divorced) ____
Married (previously widowed) ____
Separated ____
Divorced and still single ____
Divorced (living with "lover") ____
Living with "lover" ____
Common law marriage ____
Single ____

19. If divorced, in what year(s) were you divorced? ____

20. Present number of children. ____

21. Did you register for the draft?
Yes ____   No ____

22. Did you ever do anything to try to change your draft status—like seeing a doctor or lawyer, getting married and having children, seeing a draft counselor, etc?

Yes ____   No ____

268

23. How did your mother feel about your going into the military?

Very positive _____
Somewhat positive _____
Neutral, indifferent _____
Somewhat negative _____
Very negative _____
Mother deceased _____

24. How did your father feel?

Very positive _____
Somewhat positive _____
Neutral, indifferent _____
Somewhat negative _____
Very negative _____
Father deceased _____

25. (IF MARRIED) How did your wife feel?

Very positive _____
Somewhat positive _____
Neutral, indifferent _____
Somewhat negative _____
Very negative _____

26. What branch of the service did you serve in?

Marines _____
Army _____
Air Force _____
Navy _____
Coast Guard _____

27. How did you get into the military?

Drafted _____   Enlisted _____

28. Active service dates.

From: _____ To: _____
        Mo/Day/Yr   Mo/Day/Yr

29. Inactive service, Reserves, or National Guard.

From: _____ To: _____
        Mo/Day/Yr   Mo/Day/Yr

30. Final date of Discharge including completion of any Reserve/National Guard service.

Final Discharge: _____
                     Mo/Day/Yr

31. Type of Discharge:

1. _____

2. _____

32. Did you ever re-enlist?

Yes _____   No _____

33. How were you sent to Vietnam?

Routine transfer _____
Volunteered _____
Other (Specify) _____

34. Did you do more than one tour in Vietnam?

Yes _____   No _____

35. (IF YES to #34) How did that happen? _____

36. Dates of service in Vietnam.
                  Mo/Yr

From: _____ To: _____
        Mo/Yr   Mo/Yr

From: _____ To: _____
        Mo/Yr   Mo/Yr

37. In general, how did you feel about going to Vietnam?

Very positive _____
Somewhat positive _____
Neutral _____
Somewhat negative _____
Very negative _____
Not sure/don't remember _____

38. How adequately do you feel you were trained for your military assignment in Vietnam?

Badly trained and not ready _____
Undertrained and not ready _____
Needed some more training but ready _____
Fairly well trained and ready _____
Don't know _____

39. Did you correspond with anyone back home continuously during your tour in Vietnam?

Yes _____ No _____

40. (IF YES to #39) Who?

Mother _____
Father _____
Brother(s) _____
Sister(s) _____
Wife _____
Relative _____
Girlfriend _____
Friend _____
Other _____

41. Did you experience your first sexual intercourse while stationed in Vietnam?

Yes _____ No _____

42. (IF YES to #41) Do you think this experience has affected your current attitudes about your sexuality?

Yes _____ No _____

43. How do you feel concerning your current attitudes about your sexuality?

Very positive _____
Somewhat positive _____
Neutral _____
Somewhat negative _____
Very negative _____
Not sure _____

270

PART I BIOGRAPHY QUESTIONNAIRE—SECTION B

The following list of problems have been reported by some veterans as having happened to them before military service. Check (✓) those problems (if any) which happened to you PRIOR TO MILITARY SERVICE.

____ Truancy ("cutting" school more than 5 days a year and occurring in more than one year)

____ Expulsion or suspension (getting kicked out) from school

____ Delinquency (arrested or appeared in Juvenile Court)

____ Running away from home on more than one occasion for at least overnight

____ Persistent lying (lying frequently)

____ Repeated sexual intercourse in a casual relationship

____ Getting drunk often or using drugs regularly

____ Thefts (stealing for fun)

____ Vandalism (destroying property for fun)

____ Poor grades in school

____ Frequent violations of rules at home, school, or work

____ Initiation of fights (getting into fights fairly often)

____ Walking off jobs because you got angry

____ Being negligent as a parent (not taking care of your responsibilities as a parent)

____ Engaging in illegal occupations (pimp, "fencing goods," selling drugs, etc.)

____ Being "reckless" and getting into trouble because of it

____ Moving frequently without planning where you would live

____ Persistent "dealing others" (conning, manipulating, exploiting other people) for personal gain

____ Experiencing many hassles with authority figures (e.g., boss, teacher, police, etc.)

____ Expectation of trickery or harm (being suspicious) from other people

____ Continually being on the lookout for signs of threat, or taking unneeded precautions to feel secure

____ A need to be guarded or secretive in your affairs

____ Tendency to avoid accepting blame when warranted

____ Tendency to question the loyalty of other people

____ Tendency to show that you really know the truth about situations

____ Tendency to be overconcerned with people's hidden motives and the special meanings of their words

____ Tendency to be overly jealous

____ Tendency to be easily slighted and quick to take offense and strike back

271

_____ Tendency to exaggerate problems (making mountains out of molehills)

_____ Tendency to be ready to counterattack when a threat was perceived

_____ Often found yourself unable to relax

_____ Tendency to give the appearance to others as being "cold" and unemotional

_____ Tendency to take pride in being objective, rational, and unemotional

_____ Tendency to lack a true sense of humor

_____ Found it hard to experience passive, soft, tender, and sentimental feelings

_____ Feeling that you were a person of unusual importance and uniqueness and capable of doing truly great things in life

_____ Often feeling or thinking that you could achieve unlimited success, power, accomplishment, beauty, and wealth

_____ Tendency to feel that your "looks" or appearance was especially important and that people secretly admired the way you carried yourself in the world

_____ Tendency to be "cool" or "really outraged" when you felt criticized or ignored by others

_____ Tendency to feel that people really should do special favors for you

_____ Tendency to find it "hard" or "stupid" to sympathize with others when they were in periods of distress

_____ Tendency to feel that it was okay to take advantage of others if it was in your interest and personal gain

PART II COMBAT EXPERIENCES IN VIETNAM

INSTRUCTIONS

Below is a list of 21 different combatant roles in the Vietnam War. Place a (✓) next to the role(s) which describe a combat experience you had during your tour of duty. You may, of course, check as many roles as appropriate to your experience. After you have checked a role, please circle the number which best represents the degree of stressfulness you felt in that combatant role.

Degree of Stressfulness of Combat Roles

0. None—No real concern over death or injury
1. Little—Generally apprehensive over what might happen
2. Moderate—Fear of contacting enemy
3. Quite a bit—Worried about getting injured and/or shot
4. Extreme—Feared might die in the situation

EXAMPLE

__✓__ 1. Flying as an observer on a Forward Air Control mission.

    0 (1) 2 3 4

_____ 1. Forward observation post on ground.

    0 1 2 3 4

_____ 2. Flying reconnaissance observation and taking fire.

    0 1 2 3 4

_____ 3. Flying reconnaissance observation and getting shot down.

    0 1 2 3 4

_____ 4. Standing (pulling) perimeter guard duty with no incoming or sapper fire.

    0 1 2 3 4

_____ 5. Standing (pulling) perimeter guard duty and receiving incoming mortar or rocket fire or sapper attack.

    0 1 2 3 4

_____ 6. Being part of a convoy and receiving enemy fire.

    0 1 2 3 4

_____ 7. Being a part of unit patrols which encountered antipersonnel weapons (land mines, booby-traps, trip wires, etc.).

    0   1   2   3   4

_____ 8. Being a part of a unit patrol which was ambushed.

    0   1   2   3   4

_____ 9. Being a part of a unit patrol which engaged Viet Cong or North Vietnamese in a firefight.

    0   1   2   3   4

_____ 10. Being a part of a unit patrol which received sniper fire or sapper fire.

    0   1   2   3   4

_____ 11. Being a part of a unit patrol which received incoming mortar fire, artillery, or rockets from the enemy.

    0   1   2   3   4

_____ 12. Being at a base camp which received incoming mortar fire, artillery, or rockets from the enemy.

    0   1   2   3   4

_____ 13. Flying helicopter attack gunships.

    0   1   2   3   4

_____ 14. Flying helicopter slicks and receiving enemy fire.

    0   1   2   3   4

_____ 15. Flying helicopters and not receiving enemy fire.

    0   1   2   3   4

_____ 16. Performing LRPP.

    0   1   2   3   4

_____ 17. Being a "tunnel rat" and checking enemy base camps.

    0   1   2   3   4

_____ 18. Being a part of a river patrol or gunboat.

    0   1   2   3   4

_____ 19. Being a demolitions expert.

    0   1   2   3   4

_____ 20. Being assigned to Graves and Registration to retrieve dead bodies from the field of combat.

    0   1   2   3   4

_____ 21. Being a medic in combat.

    0   1   2   3   4

_____ 22. Other (If you experienced a combatant role not listed above, please feel free to describe it here and place a number which indicates the stressfulness you felt in that combatant role.)

Perceived Control Over Events in Combat Roles

For the combatant roles checked above please indicate in which of them did you feel most helpless and out of control of your own fate. For example, some men report that pulling perimeter guard duty led them to greater feelings of helplessness than a firefight in the "bush."

Based on your experiences please write down the roles which represent those situations in which you felt most helpless. Using the number which identifies the combatant role checked, rank order the checked roles in which you felt *most* helpless (not in control of your fate) to those in which you felt least helpless (most in control of your fate).

ROLES: _____
Most   Least

For the roles you checked above, how many weeks total were you in these combatant roles? Note, it is possible that you may have performed more than one role during the same period of time. Please indicate the sum total of weeks that you were actually in these roles, even if they overlapped.

_____ Sum total number of weeks

PART III SPECIFIC STRESSORS IN VIETNAM

INSTRUCTIONS

Below is a list of questions that are about your experiences in Vietnam and what you have thought about them. Please read each one carefully. After you have done so, circle one of the numbered spaces to the right that best describes the frequency that experience happened to you. Circle only one numbered space for each question and do not skip any items.

Frequency for Numbered Spaces

Never—Experience did not occur
Rarely—Experience occurred one time every month
Occasionally—Experience occurred one time every two weeks
Often—Experience occurred one or two times each week
Very Often—Experience occurred three or more times each week

EXAMPLE

	Never	Rarely	Occasionally	Often	Very Often
1. How often do you have backaches?	0	(1)	2	3	4

	Never	Rarely	Occasionally	Often	Very Often
1. How often did you fire your weapon at the enemy?	0	1	2	3	4
2. How often did you kill the enemy?	0	1	2	3	4

276

3. How often did you see someone killed? 0 1 2 3 4

4. How often did you see enemy wounded? 0 1 2 3 4

5. How often did you see our guys wounded? 0 1 2 3 4

6. How often did you see dead enemy? 0 1 2 3 4

7. How often did you see dead Vietnamese? 0 1 2 3 4

8. How often did you see our own dead? 0 1 2 3 4

9. How often did you find yourself in a combat situation in which you thought you would never survive? 0 1 2 3 4

10. How often were you directly involved as a participant in hurting Vietnamese? 0 1 2 3 4

11. How often were you indirectly involved as an observer in killing Vietnamese? 0 1 2 3 4

12. In your opinion, how often were you in danger of being killed or wounded in Vietnam? 0 1 2 3 4

13. How often were you unable to identify the enemy upon engaging Vietnamese? 0 1 2 3 4

14. How often were you adequately briefed of military objectives before participation on maneuvers? 0 1 2 3 4

15. How often did you experience frustration over repetitive capture and loss of terrain objectives? 0 1 2 3 4

16. How often did not tactical briefings coincide with your experiences in operations? 0 1 2 3 4

17. How often did you feel that the ARVN were not committed to the defense of South Vietnam? 0 1 2 3 4

	Never	Rarely	Occasionally	Often	Very Often
18. How often did you participate in a body count of enemy dead?	0	1	2	3	4
19. In your opinion, how often was the military objective dependent upon the body count?	0	1	2	3	4
20. How often did you see our guys wounded by anti-personnel devices (booby traps, trip wires, etc.)?	0	1	2	3	4
21. How often did you not find yourself in a safe area (e.g. Saigon, Unit HQ)?	0	1	2	3	4
22. How often did you find yourself in a combat situation in which the enemy attack was unpredictable?	0	1	2	3	4

	Never	Rarely	Occasionally	Often	Very Often
23. How often did you hear statements made by guys with less than 30 days left in-country (short-timers) which mentioned the loss of a buddy while in Vietnam?	0	1	2	3	4
24. How often did you hear statements made by guys (short-timers) which indicated he saw himself as a survivor within his unit?	0	1	2	3	4
25. How often were you bothered by bad climate?	0	1	2	3	4
26. How often were you bothered by bad food?	0	1	2	3	4
27. How often were you bothered by separation from family?	0	1	2	3	4

28. How often were you bothered by separation from friends? 0 1 2 3 4

29. In your opinion, how often were you aware of the controversy the Vietnam War was creating in the U.S.? 0 1 2 3 4

30. In your opinion, how often were you aware of the controversy the Vietnam War was creating in your home community? 0 1 2 3 4

31. How often were you bothered by the insects and filth? 0 1 2 3 4

32. How often were you bothered by the sight and sound of dying people? 0 1 2 3 4

33. How often were you bothered by loss of freedom of movement? 0 1 2 3 4

34. How often were you bothered by not having any girls or sex for one year? 0 1 2 3 4

35. How often were you bothered by lack of privacy? 0 1 2 3 4

36. How often were you bothered by fatigue? 0 1 2 3 4

37. How often were you bothered by long periods of boredom? 0 1 2 3 4

38. How often were you bothered by the threat of disease? 0 1 2 3 4

39. How often were you directly involved as a participant in killing Vietnamese? 0 1 2 3 4

40. How often were you indirectly involved as an observer in hurting Vietnamese? 0 1 2 3 4

41. How often were you aware that guys with less than 30 days left in Vietnam acted differently because they were survivors who were going home? 0 1 2 3 4

42. How often were you bothered by the threat of injury? 0 1 2 3 4

43. How often were you bothered by not counting as an individual? 0 1 2 3 4

279

	Never	Rarely	Occasionally	Often	Very Often
44. How often were you directly involved in mutilating bodies of Vietnamese? (e.g., cutting off ears, putting heads on sticks, placing bodies in grotesque positions)	0	1	2	3	4
45. How often were you indirectly involved as an observer of the mutilation of bodies of Vietnamese?	0	1	2	3	4

	Never	Rarely	Occasionally	Often	Very Often
46. Were there any specific events during your tour in Vietnam that were especially difficult for you to cope with emotionally? (Please describe) _____					

280

PART IV VPTSD STRESS ASSESSMENT QUESTIONNAIRE—SECTION A

INSTRUCTIONS

Below is a list of problems and complaints that some Vietnam Era veterans sometimes have. Please read each one carefully. After you have done so, please circle one of the numbered spaces to the right that best describes HOW MUCH THAT PROBLEM HAS BOTHERED OR DISTRESSED YOU DURING THE PAST SIX (6) MONTHS INCLUDING TODAY. Circle only one numbered space for each problem keeping in mind the definition of frequency for each numbered space. Do not skip any items.

Frequency for Numbered Spaces

Not at all—Problem does not occur
A little bit—1 to 9 times a month
Moderately—10 to 14 times a month
Quite a bit—15 to 20 times a month
Extremely—21 to 30 times a month

EXAMPLE

HOW MUCH WERE YOU BOTHERED BY:	Not at all	A little bit	Moderately	Quite a bit	Extremely
1. Backaches	0	(1)	2	3	4

HOW MUCH WERE YOU BOTHERED BY:	Not at all	A little bit	Moderately	Quite a bit	Extremely
1. Feeling anxious or nervous	0	1	2	3	4
2. Suicidal thoughts	0	1	2	3	4

281

		Not at all	A little bit	Moderately	Quite a bit	Extremely
3.	Problems of concentration	0	1	2	3	4
4.	Feeling depressed (down, bummed out)	0	1	2	3	4
5.	Thoughts of a buddy killed in Vietnam	0	1	2	3	4
6.	Asking yourself why a buddy was killed in Vietnam and not you	0	1	2	3	4
7.	Feeling guilt that a buddy was killed in Vietnam and not you	0	1	2	3	4
8.	Feeling like isolating or withdrawing yourself from others	0	1	2	3	4
9.	Having problems going to sleep	0	1	2	3	4
10.	Experiencing nightmares of the war	0	1	2	3	4
11.	Experiencing anger	0	1	2	3	4
12.	Experiencing rage	0	1	2	3	4
13.	Experiencing explosive anger	0	1	2	3	4
14.	Experiencing sadness over lost buddies that you cannot express	0	1	2	3	4
15.	Getting rid of unpleasant thoughts about Vietnam when they come into your head	0	1	2	3	4
16.	Feeling numb or nothing inside	0	1	2	3	4

17.	Feeling that all of your problems are caused by other people doing things to you	0	1	2	3	4
18.	The fear of losing control of your impulses (e.g., feelings, emotions)	0	1	2	3	4
19.	Mistrusting what others say or do	0	1	2	3	4
20.	Memories of Vietnam which just seemed to pop into your head in an unpredictable way	0	1	2	3	4
21.	Using alcohol to help you feel better	0	1	2	3	4
22.	Using hard drugs to help you feel better (e.g., speed, heroin)	0	1	2	3	4
23.	Using military-like self-defense tactics when under stress	0	1	2	3	4
24.	War-related thoughts (i.e., memories of Vietnam)	0	1	2	3	4
25.	Taking drugs prescribed by a doctor for your emotional upset	0	1	2	3	4
26.	Feeling an inability to be close to someone you care about	0	1	2	3	4
27.	Feeling that you treat women like sexual objects (i.e., just someone to fuck)	0	1	2	3	4
28.	Experiencing sexual problems	0	1	2	3	4
29.	Feeling alienated from other people	0	1	2	3	4

	Not at all	A little bit	Moderately	Quite a bit	Extremely
30. An inability to talk about the war	0	1	2	3	4
31. Experiencing a fear of losing loved ones	0	1	2	3	4
32. Feeling like you lost your romantic, sexual sensitivity in Vietnam	0	1	2	3	4
33. Getting into fights or conflicts with loved ones	0	1	2	3	4
34. Getting into fights with others	0	1	2	3	4
35. Feeling unable to express your real feeling to others	0	1	2	3	4
36. "Flying off the handle" in frustration when things don't go right	0		2	3	4
37. Losing your temper and getting out of control	0	1	2	3	4
38. Experiencing problems with your wife or lover	0	1	2	3	4
39. Arguing with your wife or lover	0	1	2	3	4
40. Having a problem trusting others for fear of something bad happening to you	0	1	2	3	4
41. Getting nervous around other people who are *not* Vietnam veterans	0	1	2	3	4

		0	1	2	3	4
42.	Experiencing problems being close to your mother	0	1	2	3	4
43.	Experiencing problems being close to your father	0	1	2	3	4
44.	Your wife or lover complaining that Vietnam has messed-up your relationship with her	0	1	2	3	4
45.	Worrying that Vietnam is affecting the way you relate to your children	0	1	2	3	4
46.	Feeling that you are no good and worthless	0	1	2	3	4
47.	Problems remembering things you know you should remember	0	1	2	3	4
48.	Feeling that you have no real goals that matter	0	1	2	3	4
49.	Feeling that you are different than you were before going to Vietnam (i.e., that your sense of identity just won't come together in the right way)	0	1	2		
50.	Feeling self-conscious as a Vietnam veteran	0	1	2	3	4
51.	Experiencing self-doubt and uncertainty	0	1	2	3	4
52.	Feeling that you cannot control the important events in your life	0	1	2	3	4

	Not at all	A little bit	Moderately	Quite a bit	Extremely
53. Feeling like you really died in Vietnam and are just a walking "shell" of your old self	0	1	2	3	4
54. Not feeling really satisfied with yourself	0	1	2	3	4
55. Not feeling proud of the kind of person you are	0	1	2	3	4
56. Feeling that you are not a person of worth	0	1	2	3	4
57. Feeling that Vietnam took away your "soul" (i.e., dehumanized you)	0	1	2	3	4
58. Feeling that you just cannot get a hold on things	0	1	2	3	4
59. Feeling like you are still searching for something in your life but just cannot seem to find it	0	1	2	3	4
60. Feeling like you've been a failure since leaving military service	0	1	2	3	4
61. Feeling like you would like to "kick some ass" for what happened to you in Vietnam	0	1	2	3	4

62. Having fantasies of retaliation for what happened to you in Vietnam (e.g., blowing up buildings, "flying choppers loaded with weapons," "wasting" government officials) 0 1 2 3 4

63. Feeling out of touch (alienated) from the government 0 1 2 3 4

64. The feeling that you are stigmatized for being a Vietnam (Era) veteran 0 1 2 3 4

65. Feeling cynical about governmental processes and policies 0 1 2 3 4

66. Feeling like you lost your faith in people after Vietnam 0 1 2 3 4

67. The feeling that you were used by the government for serving in Vietnam 0 1 2 3 4

68. Having problems with persons in authority positions 0 1 2 3 4

69. Feeling that your work is menial and below your capabilities 0 1 2 3 4

70. The wish that you could work in a job that did good for others (i.e., mankind or society) 0 1 2 3 4

71. Feeling uneasy in a crowd such as at a party or movie 0 1 2 3 4

72. Experiencing conflicts with co-workers 0 1 2 3 4

287

	Not at all	A little bit	Moderately	Quite a bit	Extremely
73. Legal problems	0	1	2	3	4
74. The feeling of quitting your job because the work was less than you could do	0	1	2	3	4
75. Feeling that life has no meaning for you	0	1	2	3	4
76. Feeling the need to find more purpose in life	0	1	2	3	4
77. Feeling jumpy or jittery, especially when sudden noises occur	0	1	2	3	4
78. Feeling nervous when you hear a helicopter	0	1	2	3	4
79. Driving down the highway and finding yourself searching for ambush spots	0	1	2	3	4
80. Walking in the woods and listening carefully to the sounds around you	0	1	2	3	4
81. Thoughts that it is hard to really believe that Vietnam happened to you	0	1	2	3	4
82. Thoughts that Vietnam is something you still cannot accept in your life	0	1	2	3	4
83. Thoughts that Vietnam was just one great big nightmare	0	1	2	3	4

		0	1	2	3	4
84.	Feeling the need to have a weapon on or near you	0	1	2	3	4
85.	Feeling you drive recklessly	0	1	2	3	4
86.	The need to engage yourself in dangerous or highly risky adventures in which you feel that you "live on the edge"	0	1	2	3	4
87.	The need to seek out high degrees of "sensation" that are inherently risky	0	1	2	3	4
88.	The feeling that you are not free to make your own choices important to your life	0	1	2	3	4
89.	The feeling that your personal existence (life) is without meaning	0	1	2	3	4
90.	The feeling that you should be achieving something but you don't know what	0	1	2	3	4
91.	Headaches	0	1	2	3	4
92.	Nervousness or shakiness inside	0	1	2	3	4
93.	Faintness or dizziness	0	1	2	3	4
94.	Pains in heart or chest	0	1	2	3	4
95.	Feeling low in energy or slowed down	0	1	2	3	4
96.	Trembling	0	1	2	3	4
97.	Poor appetite	0	1	2	3	4
98.	Heart pounding or racing	0	1	2	3	4
99.	Nausea or upset stomach	0	1	2	3	4

	Not at all	A little bit	Moderately	Quite a bit	Extremely
100. Trouble getting your breath	0	1	2	3	4
101. Hot or cold spells	0	1	2	3	4
102. Numbness or tingling in parts of your body	0	1	2	3	4
103. A lump in your throat	0	1	2	3	4
104. Feeling weak in parts of your body	0	1	2	3	4
105. Awakening in the early morning	0	1	2	3	4
106. Feeling that nothing matters anymore	0	1	2	3	4

PART IV VPTSD STRESS ASSESSMENT QUESTIONNAIRE—SECTION B

INSTRUCTIONS

The following list contains symptoms that are associated with Post-Traumatic Stress Disorder. Read each symptom and if you experienced it, place a check (√) in the year after Vietnam when you felt it first began. Then place a second check (√) to indicate at what year after Vietnam you feel the symptom no longer bothered you or was evident in your life, or place a check (√) if you consider the symptom still present today. Finally, keep in mind that the Homecoming is the first six months after Vietnam.

EXAMPLE

	Home-coming	One Year	Two Years	Three Years	Four Years	Five Years	Six Years	Seven Years	Eight Years	Nine Years	Ten Years	Still Present
1. Crying easily		√			√							
2. Frequent sleeping	√											√

	Home-coming	One Year	Two Years	Three Years	Four Years	Five Years	Six Years	Seven Years	Eight Years	Nine Years	Ten Years	Still Present
1. Psychic or emotional numbing												
2. Depression—feelings of helplessness, hopelessness, apathy, dejection												
3. Anger—rage, hostility (feeling like a walking time bomb)												

291

	Home-coming	One Year	Two Years	Three Years	Four Years	Five Years	Six Years	Seven Years	Eight Years	Nine Years	Ten Years	Still Present
4. Anxiety—nervousness												
5. Fear—specific fears associated with combat experiences												
6. Emotional constriction and unresponsiveness to self and others												
7. Tendency to react under stress with "survival tactics"												
8. Sleep disturbances and recurring nightmares of combat												
9. Loss of interest in work and activities; fatigue, lethargy												
10. Hyperalertness, startles easily												
11. Avoidance of activities that arouse memories of trauma in war zone												
12. Seeking out experiences that are risky, dangerous and exciting in ways similar to Vietnam												

292

13. Suicidal feelings and thoughts; self-destructive behavior tendencies

14. Survivor guilt—wondering why you survived and a buddy died

15. Flashbacks to traumatic events experienced in war; intrusive thoughts

16. Guilt feelings associated with acts done in Vietnam

17. Fantasies of retaliation and destruction; ideological changes and confusion in value system

18. Cynicism and mistrust of government and authority

19. Alienation—feeling estranged

20. Existential malaise and meaninglessness; search for meaning in life

21. Negative self-image; low self-esteem

293

	Home-coming	One Year	Two Years	Three Years	Four Years	Five Years	Six Years	Seven Years	Eight Years	Nine Years	Ten Years	Still Present
22. Memory impairment especially during times of stress	—	—	—	—	—	—	—	—	—	—	—	—
23. Hypersensitivity to issues of equity, justice, fairness, equality and legitimacy	—	—	—	—	—	—	—	—	—	—	—	—
24. Impulsive—abrupt changes (quick) in lifestyle (job, relocation)	—	—	—	—	—	—	—	—	—	—	—	—
25. Problems in establishing or maintaining intimate relationships	—	—	—	—	—	—	—	—	—	—	—	—
26. Tendency to have difficulty with authoritative figures (challenging and testing authority, rules and regulations)	—	—	—	—	—	—	—	—	—	—	—	—
27. Emotional distance from children and concern about anger alienating children, wife and others	—	—	—	—	—	—	—	—	—	—	—	—
28. Inability to talk about war experiences and personal emotions	—	—	—	—	—	—	—	—	—	—	—	—

294

29. Fears of loss of others, rage, losing control

30. Wanting to secretly return to Vietnam

31. Tendency to explode in fits of rage and anger; especially when disinhibited by drugs/alcohol

32. Withdrawal from others; isolation

33. Mistrust of others

PART V HOMECOMING
QUESTIONNAIRE—SECTION A

INSTRUCTIONS

The following list of questions concern those events which happened to you at DEROS through the first six months after your return from Vietnam. Please read each question carefully and answer as accurately as you can remember. Keep in mind that these questions concern the FIRST SIX MONTHS AFTER VIETNAM.

---

1. At DEROS, how long did it take you to go from Vietnam to a military base in the U.S. (CONUS)? (Write in number of hours or days) _____

2. At DEROS, how did you feel about leaving Vietnam?

   Very positive   _____
   Somewhat positive   _____
   Neutral, indifferent _____
   Somewhat negative   _____
   Very negative   _____

3. At DEROS, did you feel like a short-timer who survived?

   Yes _____   No _____

4. When you arrived from Vietnam to a stateside military base, did anything significant (unusual) happen during outprocessing?

   Yes _____   No _____

   (IF YES) Please describe) _____
   _____
   _____

5. How long did outprocessing take at CONUS? (Number of hours) _____

6. After outprocessing and leaving base, what was the first thing you did?
   _____
   _____

7. After outprocessing, how long was it in hours or days until you went home to your spouse or parents' house?

   Days _____   Hours _____

8. Once home, how long was it until you contacted a friend?

   Days _____   or   Hours _____

9. At DEROS and return to CONUS on the plane from Vietnam, how many buddies went with you? _____

10. At DEROS and return to CONUS on the plane from Vietnam, how many men from your unit went with you? _____

11. At what stateside base (airport) did you land? _____

12. Was there anyone there to greet you?

    Yes _____   No _____

    (IF YES) Who? (e.g., mother and/or father, wife, girlfriend)

13. After outprocessing were you discharged from the military or on leave and still in the service?

    Discharged _____ On leave _____

14. During the first 6 months after being back from Vietnam, did you meet anyone with whom you had been in Vietnam?

    Yes _____   No _____

15. If you didn't go home after being outprocessed at CONUS, what did you do? _____
    _____
    _____

16. During homecoming, did you feel like isolating yourself (e.g. continuously staying in a basement, room, attic, etc.)?

    Yes _____   No _____

17. Did you join a traditional service organization (e.g., VFW, DAV)?

    Yes _____   No _____

    (IF YES) Which one? _____

    Are you still an active member?

    Yes _____   No _____

    (IF NO) What year were you last active? _____

18. After discharge, did you try to get a job but failed because you were told you were not qualified either by lack of education or training or experience?

    Yes _____   No _____

19. After discharge, what was the length of time to your first job (specify if weeks or months)? _____

20. If you went to school (technical or college) after discharge, what was the length of time to your first attendance (specify weeks or months) ? _____

21. How did things work out regarding your plans in the first six months after Vietnam? (Please explain)

    _____

    _____

22. Did things go the way you wanted?

    Yes _____   No _____

23. With whom did you spend the most time?

    Mother   _____
    Father   _____
    Brother(s)   _____
    Sister(s)   _____
    Wife   _____
    Relative(s)   _____
    Girlfriend   _____
    Friend   _____
    Lover   _____
    Other   _____

24. Are you now or have you within the past year seen a psychiatrist or psychologist, either private or VA staff, for the purpose of psychoanalysis?

    Yes _____   No _____

PART V HOMECOMING
QUESTIONNAIRE—SECTION B

INSTRUCTIONS

The following list of items have been reported by some veterans as happening to them during Homecoming (THE FIRST SIX MONTHS AFTER VIETNAM). Please read each item carefully and circle the number appropriate to the frequency of your experience for that item. Do not skip any items.

Frequency for Numbered Spaces

Not at all—Problem does not occur
A little bit—1 to 9 times a month
Moderately—10 to 14 times a month
Quite a bit—15 to 20 times a month
Extremely—21 to 30 times a month

EXAMPLE

AS A VIETNAM VETERAN:	Not at all	A little bit	Moderately	Quite a bit	Extremely
1. How often did you have backaches?	0	(1)	2	3	4

AS A VIETNAM VETERAN:	Not at all	A little bit	Moderately	Quite a bit	Extremely
1. How often did you feel rejected by family?	0	1	2	3	4
2. How often did you feel rejected by friends?	0	1	2	3	4
3. How often did you feel rejected by relatives?	0	1	2	3	4
4. How often did you feel stigmatized (e.g., baby killer, doper, crazy)?	0	1	2	3	4

AS A VIETNAM VETERAN:	Not at all	A little bit	Moderately	Quite a bit	Extremely
5. How often did you feel mistrust of authority?	0	1	2	3	4
6. How often did you feel angered over being used or exploited for serving in the military?	0	1	2	3	4
7. How often did you experience problems with authority figures?	0	1	2	3	4
8. How often did you feel you were not appreciated by others for serving your country?	0	1	2	3	4
9. How often did you feel like isolating yourself (e.g., continuously staying in a basement, room, or attic)?	0	1	2	3	4
10. How often did you feel cynical about political leaders?	0	1	2	3	4
11. How often did you feel cynical about war-related decisions by political leaders?	0	1	2	3	4
12. How often did you need to smoke pot (marijuana) after coming home from Vietnam or release from active service?	0	1	2	3	4
13. How often did you need to use hallucinogens (LSD, acid, mescaline, etc.)?	0	1	2	3	4
14. How often did you need to use hard drugs (heroin, smack, horse, opium)?	0	1	2	3	4
15. How often did you need to use amphetamines (speed)?	0	1	2	3	4

AS A VIETNAM VETERAN:	Not at all	A little bit	Moderately	Quite a bit	Extremely
16. How often did you need to use downers (Darvon, seconal, "soapers," angel dust, barbiturates)?	0	1	2	3	4
17. How often did you need to use cocaine?	0	1	2	3	4
18. How often did you need to use alcohol?	0	1	2	3	4
19. How often did you exercise regularly (e.g., jogging, swimming, weightlifting)?	0	1	2	3	4
20. How often did you worry about your physical health and well-being?	0	1	2	3	4
21. How often did you find yourself unable to go to sleep at night?	0	1	2	3	4
22. How often did you keep irregular hours?	0	1	2	3	4
23. How often did you keep an irregular diet?	0	1	2	3	4
24. How often did you feel like discussing your Vietnam experiences?	0	1	2	3	4
25. How often did you use the services of the Veterans Administration during Homecoming?	0	1	2	3	4
26. How often *to date* have you used the services of the Veterans Administration?	0	1	2	3	4

	Not at all	A little bit	Moderately	Quite a bit	Extremely
AS A VIETNAM VETERAN:					
27. How often *to date* have you used to services of a private social worker, psychologist, or psychiatrist for war-related personal problems?	0	1	2	3	4
28. How often *to date* have you used the services of the clergy (e.g., minister, priest, rabbi) for war-related personal problems?	0	1	2	3	4
29. How often have you *ever* talked about Vietnam since you came home?	0	1	2	3	4

PART V HOMECOMING QUESTIONNAIRE—SECTION C

INSTRUCTIONS

The following list of items have been reported by veterans concerning their physical well-being. Please read each item carefully and check (✓) those items which you experienced *during Homecoming*. After you have checked an item, please circle the number which best represents the number of times the item was experienced during *the first six months after Vietnam*. Do not skip any items.

Frequency for Numbered Spaces

Not at all—Problem does not occur
A little bit—1 to 9 times a month
Moderately—10 to 14 times a month
Quite a bit—15 to 20 times a month
Extremely—21 to 30 times a month

EXAMPLE

	Not at all	A little bit	Moderately	Quite a bit	Extremely
1. Backaches	0	(1)	2	3	4

	Not at all	A little bit	Moderately	Quite a bit	Extremely
1. High blood pressure	0	1	2	3	4
2. Irregular heart beat	0	1	2	3	4
3. Diarrhea	0	1	2	3	4
4. Headaches	0	1	2	3	4
5. Trembling	0	1	2	3	4

		0	1	2	3	4
6.	Poor appetite	0	1	2	3	4
7.	Cold extremities (fingers, toes, etc.)	0	1	2	3	4
8.	Physical pain in your body	0	1	2	3	4
9.	Shortness of breath	0	1	2	3	4
10.	Low energy level	0	1	2	3	4
11.	Chest pains	0	1	2	3	4
12.	Nervousness	0	1	2	3	4
13.	Stomach pains	0	1	2	3	4
14.	Loss of memory	0	1	2	3	4
15.	Difficulty concentrating	0	1	2	3	4
16.	Overly stimulated/ hyped up	0	1	2	3	4
17.	Difficulty with bowel movements	0	1	2	3	4
18.	Ulcers	0	1	2	3	4
19.	Inflammation of the colon	0	1	2	3	4
20.	Inflammation of the stomach (gastritis)	0	1	2	3	4
21.	Inflammation of the pancreas	0	1	2	3	4
22.	Rectal bleeding	0	1	2	3	4
23.	Numbness in parts of body	0	1	2	3	4
24.	Tingling in extremities of the body	0	1	2	3	4
25.	The air smelling Oriental	0	1	2	3	4
26.	Rapid breathing	0	1	2	3	4
27.	Loss of muscle strength	0	1	2	3	4
28.	Loss of coordination	0	1	2	3	4
29.	Uncontrolled muscle contraction	0	1	2	3	4
30.	Hemorrhoids	0	1	2	3	4
31.	Inability to eat food	0	1	2	3	4
32.	Grinding teeth	0	1	2	3	4

PART V HOMECOMING QUESTIONNAIRE—SECTION D

INSTRUCTIONS

The following list is made up of organizations and support networks some Vietnam veterans have joined as members after their return from Vietnam. Read each item and if you joined the listed organization, place a check (√) by it. Then check (√) the time interval (i.e., Homecoming, One Year, Three Years, Five Years, Ten Years) at which you joined that organization *after Vietnam*. Finally, please check (√) if you are still an active member. The Homecoming is the first six months after Vietnam.

EXAMPLE

	Home-coming	One Year	Three Years	Five Years	Ten Years	Still Active
√ 1. Firemen's Club	√	√	√	—	—	√
√ 2. Book Club	√	—	—	—	—	—

	Home-coming	One Year	Three Years	Five Years	Ten Years	Still Active
__ 1. Attend Church	—	—	—	—	—	—
__ 2. Recreation Group (e.g., softball team, bowling team)	—	—	—	—	—	—
__ 3. Veterans' Organizations (e.g., VFW, American Legion)	—	—	—	—	—	—
__ 4. Civic Group (e.g., Kiwanis, Rotary, Lions Club)	— —	— —	— —	—	— —	— —
__ 5. P.T.A.	—	—	—	—	—	—
__ 6. Boy Scouts	—	—	—	—	—	—
__ 7. Big Brothers	—	—	—	—	—	—

304

8.	Military Reserves							
9.	Membership in Professional Organizations (e.g., Am. Metallurgist)							
10.	Volunteer for Community Service (e.g. aid to the elderly, solicitor for foundations)							
11.	Political Activity (e.g., Republican, Democratic, other)							
12.	Fraternal Organizations (e.g., Shriners, Masons, Elks)							
13.	Neighborhood Organizations (e.g., Block Watch, Cleveland Hts. Community Congress)							
14.	Ethnic Unity Groups (e.g., Danish Brotherhood)							
15.	Unions or Trade Membership							
16.	College or School Clubs or Organizations							
17.	Other (Please specify) _____							

PART VI POST-VIETNAM LEGAL PROBLEMS

INSTRUCTIONS

The following is a list of some legal problems veterans have had since Vietnam. If you have had one of these legal problems, please circle the number which indicates the number of times you have been arrested, convicted, and/or acquitted for that problem.

EXAMPLE

1. Driving without a license

Arrested	1	2	③	4	5	6+
Convicted	1	②	3	4	5	6+
Acquitted	①	2	3	4	5	6+

1. Driving Under the Influence (DUI)

Arrested	1	2	3	4	5	6+
Convicted	1	2	3	4	5	6+
Acquitted	1	2	3	4	5	6+

2. Disorderly Conduct

Arrested	1	2	3	4	5	6+
Convicted	1	2	3	4	5	6+
Acquitted	1	2	3	4	5	6+

3. Assault

Arrested	1	2	3	4	5	6+
Convicted	1	2	3	4	5	6+
Acquitted	1	2	3	4	5	6+

4. Weapons Charge

Arrested	1	2	3	4	5	6+
Convicted	1	2	3	4	5	6+
Acquitted	1	2	3	4	5	6+

5. Breaking and Entering

Arrested	1	2	3	4	5	6+
Convicted	1	2	3	4	5	6+
Acquitted	1	2	3	4	5	6+

6. Theft

Arrested	1	2	3	4	5	6+
Convicted	1	2	3	4	5	6+
Acquitted	1	2	3	4	5	6+

7. Drug-related

Arrested	1	2	3	4	5	6+
Convicted	1	2	3	4	5	6+
Acquitted	1	2	3	4	5	6+

8. Rape

Arrested	1	2	3	4	5	6+
Convicted	1	2	3	4	5	6+
Acquitted	1	2	3	4	5	6+

9. Manslaughter (Homicide)

Arrested	1	2	3	4	5	6+
Convicted	1	2	3	4	5	6+
Acquitted	1	2	3	4	5	6+

10. Failure to pay alimony

Arrested	1	2	3	4	5	6+
Convicted	1	2	3	4	5	6+
Acquitted	1	2	3	4	5	6+

11. Non-support of children

Arrested	1	2	3	4	5	6+
Convicted	1	2	3	4	5	6+
Acquitted	1	2	3	4	5	6+

12. Child(ren) custody

Arrested	1	2	3	4	5	6+
Convicted	1	2	3	4	5	6+
Acquitted	1	2	3	4	5	6+

13. Vagrancy

Arrested	1	2	3	4	5	6+
Convicted	1	2	3	4	5	6+
Acquitted	1	2	3	4	5	6+

14. Other (Specify)

Arrested	1	2	3	4	5	6+
Convicted	1	2	3	4	5	6+
Acquitted	1	2	3	4	5	6+

15. Number of times on probation

    1 2 3 4 5 6+

    Total number of months on probation _____

16. Number of times sentenced to county jail

    1 2 3 4 5 6+

17. Total number of months spent in county jail _____

18. Number of times sent to prison

    1 2 3 4 5 6+

19. Total number of months spent in prison _____

FEEDBACK OF VIETNAM ERA STRESS
INVENTORY

Please feel free to comment on any part of this questionnaire or tell
us about any feelings you may have that may not have been covered
by the questionnaire.

Appendix B:
Pearl Harbor Research Questionnaire

Developed by: The Center of Applied Gerontology and the Department of Psychology, Cleveland State University, Cleveland, Ohio, in conjunction with the National Pearl Harbor Survivors Association. (216) 687–2543, 687–2541, or 687–4570.

THE SURVIVORS OF PEARL HARBOR
AND WORLD WAR II: THE 45TH
ANNIVERSARY REUNION—1986

This survey contains questions designed to understand *your experiences at Pearl Harbor on December 7, 1941 and during World War II.* The primary purpose of the survey is to gather your perceptions of these experiences and learn about their effect on the course of your life and the aging process. We are interested in learning how individuals adapt to difficult and stressful war-time experiences. All information is confidential. Most persons find that completing the questionnaire is useful and interesting. We sincerely appreciate your cooperation. We believe that it is important to have your testimony of Pearl Harbor, World War II and its aftermath for future generations. Thank you for your participation.

Your Name: _____

Address: _____

City, State, Zipcode: _____

Telephone: (Area Code) _____

All information is strictly confidential

PART I—COMBAT AND MILITARY SERVICE
IN WORLD WAR II

Below is a list of questions about your experiences on December 7, 1941 at Pearl Harbor *and* in World War II.

Section A—General Military

1. When did you enter and leave the military service for the first time? Please give year and month, if possible.

    Entered service:
        Year _____ Month _____
    How old were you at that time? _____

    Discharged:
        Year _____ Month _____

2. Your branch of service? Please list your military occupational specialty (M.O.S.) next to your branch of service.

    1. Army _____
    2. Navy _____

　　3.　Coast Guard _____

　　4.　Marines _____

　　5.　Air Corps _____

3.　Were you drafted into the armed forces (at first entry) or did you enlist? (Please circle)

　　1.　Drafted　　　　　2.　Enlisted　　　　　3.　Entered from ROTC

4.　What was your rank at:

　　Entry _____

　　Discharge: (Year) 19 _____　　Rank _____

Section B—Pearl Harbor Dec. 7, 1941:
Your Experience of the Day

5.　Please tell us what you recall about your Pearl Harbor experiences. When were you assigned to Pearl Harbor prior to the Japanese attack on December 7, 1941?

5B.　What was your duty assignment and location at Pearl Harbor or on the island on December 7, 1941?

5C.　Beginning with the early morning of December 7, 1941, please tell us what you *saw* and what you *did* throughout the day.

_____

_____

_____

_____

_____

_____

_____

_____

_____

_____

_____

5D.　How long (months & years) did you stay at Pearl Harbor before being assigned to other duty? _____

_____

Section C

6. Please list the significant locations where you were during your military career: Circle how stressful your experiences were at each one of these locations.

    Pacific Theater (list)
    Location(s) _____

    Year(s) _____ How long? (# of months) _____

      Overall, how stressful was it?

1	2	3	4
Not at all	Mildly stressful	Stressful	Extremely stressful

    European Theater (list)
    Location(s) _____

    Year(s) _____ How long? (# of months) _____

      Overall, how stressful was it?

1	2	3	4
Not at all	Mildly stressful	Stressful	Extremely stressful

    U.S.A. and other (list)
    Location(s) _____

    Year(s) _____ How long? (# of months) _____

      Overall, how stressful was it?

1	2	3	4
Not at all	Mildly stressful	Stressful	Extremely stressful

6A. Were you a P.O.W. during W.W. II? 1. No   2. Yes
    Location(s) _____

    Year(s) _____ How long? (# of months) _____

      Overall, how stressful was it?

1	2	3	4
Not at all	Mildly stressful	Stressful	Extremely stressful

6B. If you were a P.O.W., have you ever gone back to the location of the camp? Describe _____
_____

7. After *Discharge,* did you find your training experiences in the military helpful in your subsequent work career?

   1. No
   2. Yes, to some extent. Explain _____
   3. Yes, very much. Explain _____

8. How did your military experience affect your adjustment to aging? (Circle)

1	2	3	4	5
Very negative	Negative	No effect	Positive	Very positive

Section D—Combat Experiences

During the *last year* (1986) please indicate if you have had any of the following recollections about the Japanese attack and what happened at Pearl Harbor, December 7, 1941.

Please circle.

1. I have had, at times, recurring thoughts about "the Day of Infamy" (December 7, 1941) and what happened at Pearl Harbor.　Yes　No

2. I have had, at times, dreams of the attack on Pearl Harbor.　Yes　No

3. On December 7, I have special feelings about the attack on Pearl Harbor.　Yes　No

4. Thoughts about the attack at Pearl Harbor sometimes just pop into my mind.　Yes　No

5. I have, at times, bad feelings towards Japanese people and avoid them when I can.　Yes　No

6. I sometimes find it difficult to express my feelings about what happened at Pearl Harbor.　Yes　No

7. I cannot remember much of what happened at Pearl Harbor.　Yes　No

8. After the attack at Pearl Harbor, I found it difficult to be real close to people.　Yes　No

9. Sometimes I wonder why I survived the Japanese attack and my buddies died.　Yes　No

10. When I hear the sounds of certain engine noises, it reminds me of the Pearl Harbor attack.　Yes　No

11. I have, at times, difficulty going to sleep or staying asleep.　Yes　No

12. I am easily startled or made "jumpy" by loud or   Yes   No
    unexpected noises.

13. Even today I still have, at times, anger at the   Yes   No
    Japanese for the attack on Pearl Harbor.

14. Looking back, I believe that the Pearl Harbor   Yes   No
    experience had a deep influence on the course of
    my life.

15. I have had, at times, memories of the bombed   Yes   No
    ships and airfields at Pearl Harbor.

16. I have had, at times, memories of the   Yes   No
    explosions, screaming and confusion at Pearl
    Harbor on the Day of Infamy.

17. How many times have you returned to Hawaii
    to visit Pearl Harbor?

    Number of times _____

    List years _____

Section E—World War II—Military Duty and the Theater of War After Pearl Harbor

Please indicate if you had the following experiences in W.W. II:

1. Did you fire a weapon against the enemy? (Circle)

   1. No   2. Yes

2. Did you kill or think you killed anyone?

   1. No   2. Yes

3. Were you under enemy fire?

   1. No   2. Yes

4. Were you wounded by enemy action?

   1. No   2. Yes. How were you wounded? _____

---

5. If wounded: circle all of the following which apply:

   1. I was hospitalized   2. My wound was life threatening
   3. My wound left me impaired   4. My wound led to my discharge

6. Were any members of your unit killed or wounded by the enemy?

   1. No   2. Yes, wounded
   3. Yes, killed   4. Both wounded and killed

6A. Were any family members, friends or relatives killed in W.W. II?

    1. No   2. Yes, wounded
    3. Yes, killed   4. Both wounded and killed

7. Were any *Americans or Allies* killed or wounded in your presence?

    1. No   2. Yes, wounded
    3. Yes, killed   4. Both wounded and killed

8. Were any *enemy* killed or wounded in your presence?

    1. No   2. Yes, wounded
    3. Yes, killed   4. Both wounded and killed

9. Did you see or witness an *American or Allied* soldier who was tortured or mutilated by the enemy?

    1. No   2. Yes, tortured
    3. Yes, mutilated   4. Both tortured and mutilated

10. Did you ever witness or participate in atrocities against enemy soldiers by American or Allied forces?

    1. No   2. Yes, witnessed
    3. Yes, participated   4. Both witnessed and participated

11. Did you ever see or witness the destruction of towns or geographical areas as a result of combat warfare?

    1. No   2. Yes

12. Did you see or witness the injury or death of *civilians* caught up in warfare?

    1. No   2. Yes, injury of civilians
    3. Yes, death of civilians   4. Yes, both injury and death of civilians

12A. Were you ever directly exposed to attack by the enemy (i.e., bombing, mortar attacks, infantry attack)?

    1. No   2. Yes, once or twice
    3. Yes, sometimes   4. Yes, many times

13. Did you ever experience a combat or war-related incident that was so awful, upsetting or grotesque that it changed your views of life?

    1. No   2. Yes. Describe the experience _____

_____

_____

14. During W.W. II, did you ever find yourself in life-death ("close-call") survival situations?

    1. No   2. Yes. Describe your reaction _____

_____

_____

15. Did you ever experience combat or operational fatigue so bad that you thought you would not make it through the war?

    1. No   2. Yes. Describe your reaction _____

PART II—POST WORLD WAR II: REENTRY INTO CIVILIAN LIFE
Section A

1. Thinking back to your discharge, what feelings did you have about your military service after being discharged? (Circle)

1. Very positive	2. Generally positive	3. Both positive and negative	4. Generally negative	5. Very negative

2. Over the years, have you been a member of any of the following veterans organizations? *Circle* all that apply.

    1. VFW or American Legion
    2. DAV
    3. AMVETS
    4. USO
    5. Other veteran organizations. List _____

3. After W.W. II were you in a national guard or reserve unit?

    1. No _____   2. Yes. # of years _____

4. Are there any friends from your service days that you keep in touch with on a regular basis? (Circle)

    1. No _____   2. If yes, how many? _____

5. Over the *past year* (1986) have you had any of the following contacts with friends that date back to your military service? Circle yes or no. (Received or sent):

    1. Greeting cards   Yes   No
    2. Letters   Yes   No
    3. Phone calls   Yes   No
    4. Actual visits   Yes   No
    5. Reunions   Yes   No

6. Have you had a *previous* reunion with men/women from your service unit other than now in 1986?

    1. No _____   2. Yes, reunion year(s) _____

7. What does it mean to you to belong and/or attend the meeting of the Pearl Harbor Survivors Association?

_____

_____

_____

Section B—Present Health Appraisal

1. To what extent do you feel that *your* experiences in *Work War II* affected your *present* physical health? (Circle)
   1. Very little   2. Some   3. Much   4. A great deal

2. To what extent do you feel your World War II experiences affect your *present* emotional state? (Circle)
   1. Very little   2. Some   3. Much   4. A great deal

3. Do you consider your current *physical* health to be:
   1. Excellent   2. Good   3. Fair   4. Poor

4. Do you consider your current *mental* health to be:
   1. Excellent   2. Good   3. Fair   4. Poor

5. During the *past* few weeks did you ever feel: (Circle)

Pleased about having accomplished something?	Yes	No
That things were going your way?	Yes	No

   During the *past* few weeks did you ever feel: (Circle)

Proud because someone complimented you on something you had done?	Yes	No
Particularly excited or interested in something?	Yes	No
On top of the world?	Yes	No
So restless that you couldn't sit long in a chair?	Yes	No
Bored?	Yes	No
Depressed or unhappy?	Yes	No
Very lonely or remote from other people?	Yes	No
Upset because someone criticized you?	Yes	No

6. Please *circle* whether you agree or disagree with each of the following statements.

Most persons have a lot of control over what happens to them in life	Agree	Disagree
If a person tries hard enough, he will reach his goals	Agree	Disagree
There is little one can do to alter his fate in life	Agree	Disagree
Most people don't have much influence over what happens to them	Agree	Disagree

Our success in life is outside of our own control

                                                    Agree   Disagree

The average person is largely a master of his own fate

                                                    Agree   Disagree

7. Please *circle* whether you agree or disagree with the following statements.

I come first and should not have to care so much for others

                                                    Agree   Disagree

I enjoy doing things for others

                                                    Agree   Disagree

In this day and age it doesn't make sense to stop and help out someone
in trouble

                                                    Agree   Disagree

I can't imagine a situation in which I would risk my own life to help
someone else

                                                    Agree   Disagree

I try to help others, even if they do not help me

                                                    Agree   Disagree

8. Have you received medical treatment for health problems that resulted
    from military service in W.W. II?
    1. No
    2. Yes. Describe. _____

    _____

9. Have you ever received service-connected disability benefits?
    1. No   2. Yes, but no longer   3. Yes, still receive benefits

10. Some veterans believe that their military experience was "the *best* time
    of their lives". Others say it was the *"worst* of times"; still others believe
    it was both good and bad. How do you feel?

My military experience was:

Circle: Very Good   Good   Good & Bad   Bad   Very Bad
                1   2   3   4   5

11. Considering the most influential events in your life, where would you
    place "military service" in W.W. II as an influence on the person you
    are *now*? Circle *number* on the scale below:

Military experience on my life had:

0	1 2 3	4 5 6	7 8 9
No influence	Least influence	Moderate influence	Most influence

11A. In what ways have your W.W. II military experiences affected your ability to deal with stresses and setbacks in later life? _____

_____

_____

_____

12. To what extent have you shared your W.W. II experiences with each of the following persons: Please circle one answer for each line.

Degree of sharing W.W. II experiences

Persons	*Not at all*	*Little*	*Some*	*Much*	*Very much*
Spouse	1	2	3	4	5
Children	1	2	3	4	5
Mother	1	2	3	4	5
Father	1	2	3	4	5
Grandchildren	1	2	3	4	5
Other family	1	2	3	4	5
Close friends	1	2	3	4	5
Co-worker(s)	1	2	3	4	5
Counselor(s)	1	2	3	4	5
Clergy	1	2	3	4	5

13. Have there been times when you wanted to block out and forget your military experiences? (Circle)

1. Never
2. Yes, at one time, but it is no longer difficult to think and talk about
3. Yes, and it continues to be a difficult experience

13A. Was W.W. II the most intense and meaningful experience in your life?

1. No   2. Yes

14. Have you revisited the geographic places of your service in W.W. II?

1. No, and I do not care to
2. No, but I hope to in the near future

  3. No, but I have always wanted to
  4. Yes, please list where and when? _____

15. Why was it important to revisit this location? _____

_____

16. Listed below are some experiences and problems that some veterans
    reported during *reentry* into civilian life and at the *present time* (1986).

    Please indicate your experiences both at *reentry* and during the past year
    (1986) by circling Yes or No.

		At reentry after W.W. II		During the last year (1986)	
1.	Nightmares in which I relive my W.W. II experiences	Yes	No	Yes	No
2.	Startled easily	Yes	No	Yes	No
3.	Drinking problem	Yes	No	Yes	No
4.	Difficulty in sleeping	Yes	No	Yes	No
5.	Felt depressed	Yes	No	Yes	No
6.	Recurrent upsetting thoughts about the war	Yes	No	Yes	No
7.	Felt guilt about surviving	Yes	No	Yes	No
8.	Felt emotionally overcharged (extremely "hyped up")	Yes	No	Yes	No
9.	Felt numb, or unable to feel emotions	Yes	No	Yes	No
10.	Deliberate avoidance of things that remind me of W.W. II	Yes	No	Yes	No
11.	Drug addiction	Yes	No	Yes	No
12.	Problems remembering what happened during the war	Yes	No	Yes	No
13.	Felt distant or estranged from people	Yes	No	Yes	No
14.	Difficulty in concentrating	Yes	No	Yes	No
15.	Felt upset when things remind me of my W.W. II experiences	Yes	No	Yes	No
16.	Felt angry at what actually happened in the war	Yes	No	Yes	No
17.	Easily irritated	Yes	No	Yes	No
18.	Felt nervous, anxious	Yes	No	Yes	No
19.	Hard to express my feelings	Yes	No	Yes	No
20.	Avoided talking about the war	Yes	No	Yes	No
21.	Felt isolated	Yes	No	Yes	No
22.	Felt mistrustful of people	Yes	No	Yes	No
23.	Hard to settle down, get "feet on the ground"	Yes	No	Yes	No

24. Problems at work   Yes   No   Yes   No
25. Marital difficulties   Yes   No   Yes   No
26. An urge to catch-up on living   Yes   No   Yes   No

17. How did your military service in W.W. II affect your post-war life? Describe some of the desirable and undesirable aspects of this experience.

_____

_____

_____

_____

_____

_____

_____

18. Considering all of your experiences in W.W. II and at Pearl Harbor, what would you like to say about this to future generations?

_____

_____

_____

_____

_____

_____

_____

_____

_____

_____

_____

_____

_____

_____

_____

_____

_____

_____

PART III—BACKGROUND INFORMATION

The following list of questions concern background information. Please read each question and answer as accurately as you can.

1. Your age (now) _____ Date of birth _____
   _____   Month Day Year

   Your sex:
   1. Male _____   2. Female _____

2. Your marital status (Circle appropriate answer)

   1. Married   4. Widowed and not remarried
   2. Remarried after divorce   5. Remarried from widowhood
   3. Divorced and not remarried   6. Never married

3. How many children do you have? _____ # Sons _____ # Daughters_____

4. Your religious affiliation (Circle)

   1. Catholic   3. Jewish
   2. Protestant   4. Other, specify _____

5. Are you currently? (Circle all that apply)

   1. Retired   2. Working full time   3. Working part time
   4. Unemployed   5. Would like to work   6. Self-employed

6. What was the highest grade in school that you completed *before* W.W. II? (Circle)

   1 2 3 4 5 6 7 8   9 10 11 12   13 14 15 16   17 18 19 20
   Elementary   High   College   Graduate
     school   school   or
                                                        professional
                                                          school

6A. What was the highest grade in school that you completed *after* W.W. II? (Circle)

   1 2 3 4 5 6 7 8   9 10 11 12   13 14 15 16   17 18 19 20
   Elementary   High   College   Graduate
     school   school   or
                                                        professional
                                                          school

6B. Did you use the G.I. bill to get further education or vocational training?   1. No   2. Yes

7. What have been your major life occupation(s)?

Thank you!

References

Achterberg, J. (1985). *Imagery in healing: Shamanism and modern medicine*. Boston: New Science Library.

American Psychiatric Association (1980). *Diagnostic and statistical manual of mental disorders* (3rd ed.). Washington, DC: American Psychiatric Association.

American Psychiatric Association (1987). *Diagnostic and statistical manual of mental disorders* (3rd ed., rev.). Washington, DC: American Psychiatric Press.

Andreasen, N. (1984). *The broken brain*. New York: Harper & Row.

Anisman, H. (1978). Neurochemical changes elicited by stress: Behavioral correlates. In H. Anisman & G. Bignami (Eds.), *Psychopharmacology of aversively motivated behavior*. New York: Plenum Press.

Anisman, H., Kokkinidis, L., & Sklar, L. S. (1985). Neurochemical consequences of stress: Contributions of adaptive processes. In S. R. Burchfield (Ed.), *Psychological and physiological interactions*. Washington DC: Hemishpere.

Anisman, H. L., Ritch, M., & Sklar, L. S. (1981). Noradrenergic and dopaminergic interactions in escape behavior: Analysis of uncontrollable stress effects. *Psychopharmacological Bulletin, 74,* 263–268.

Anisman, H. L., & Sklar, L. S. (1979). Catecholamine depletion in mice upon reexposure to stress: Mediation of the escape deficits produced by inescapable shock. *Journal of Comparative Physiological Psychology, 93,* 610–625.

Anthony, E. J., & Koupernick, C. (Eds.) (1974). *The child in his family: Children at psychiatric risk* (vol. 3). New York: Wiley.

Antonovsky, A. (1979). *Health, stress, and coping*. San Francisco: Jossey-Bass.

Appley, M. H. (1962). Motivation, threat perception, and the induction of psychological stress. *Proceedings, Sixteenth International Congress of Psychology, Bonn 1960* (pp. 880–881). Amsterdam: North Hollard.

Appley, M. H., & Trumbull, R. (1967). *Psychological stress: Issues in research*. New York: Appleton-Century-Crofts.

Appley, M. H., & Trumbull, R. (1986). *Dynamics of stress: Physiological, psychological, and social perspectives*. New York: Plenum Press.

Archibald, R. C., Long, D. M., Miller, C. & Tuddenham, R. D. (1962). Gross stress reactions in combat—A 15-year follow-up. *American Journal of Psychiatry, 119,* 317–322.

Archibald, R. C., & Tuddenham, R. D. (1965). Persistent stress reaction after combat: A 20-year follow-up. *Archives of General Psychiatry, 12,* 475–481.

Aronoff, J., & Wilson, J. P. (1985). *Personality in the social process*. Hillsdale, NJ: Lawrence Erlbaum.

Atkinson, R. M., Reaves, M. E., & Maxwell, M. J. (1988). Complicated post-combat disorders in Vietnam veterans: Comprehensive diagnosis and treatment in the VA system. In J. P. Wilson, Z. Harel, & B. Kahana (Eds.), *Human adaptation to extreme stress: From the Holocaust to Vietnam*. New York: Plenum Press.

323

Bales, R. F. (1970). *Personality and interpersonal behavior.* New York: Holt, Rinehart, & Winston.

Barron, F. (1953). An ego-strength scale which predicts response to psychotherapy. *Journal of Consulting Psychology, 17,* 327–333.

Beck, A. (1976). *Cognitive therapy and the emotional disorders.* New York: International Universities Press.

Beck, A. T., Ward, C. H., Mendelsohn, M., Mock, J., & Erbaugh, J. (1961). An inventory measuring depression. *Archives of General Psychiatry, 4,* 561–571.

Blank, A. S., Jr. (1985). The unconscious flashback to the war in Vietnam veterans: Clinical mystery, legal defense, and community problem. In S. M. Sonnenberg, A. S. Blank, Jr., & J. A. Talbott (Eds.), *The trauma of war: Stress and recovery in Vietnam veterans.* Washington, DC: American Psychiatric Press.

Block, J. H., & Block, J. (1980). The role of ego control and ego-resiliency in the organization of behavior. In W. A. Collins (Ed.), *Development of cognition, affect and social relationships.* The Minnesota Symposium on Child Psychology (vol. 13). Hillsdale, NJ: Lawrence Erlbaum.

Bradburn, N. M. (1969). *The structure of psychological well-being.* Chicago: Aldine.

Braun, B. G. (1984). Multiple personality and other dissociative phenomena. *Psychiatric Clinics of North America, 7*(1), 171–193.

Braun, B. (1986). *Treatment of multiple personality disorder.* Washington, DC: American Psychiatric Press.

Brende, J. D. (1984). The psychophysiological manifestations of dissociation. *Psychiatric Clinics of North America, 7*(1), 41–50.

Brett, B., Spitzer, R., & Williams, J. (in press). The DSM-III-R diagnostic criteria for Post-Traumatic Stress Disorder. *American Journal of Psychiatry.*

Brett, E. A., & Ostroff, R. (1985). Imagery and post-traumatic stress disorder: An overview. *American Journal of Psychiatry, 142*(4), 417–424.

Britton, K. T. (1986). The neurobiology of anxiety. In L. L. Judd and P. M. Groves (Eds.), *Psychobiological foundations of clinical psychiatry* (pp. 79–93). New York: Basic Books.

Brown, J. E. (1986). *The sacred pipe.* Baltimore: Penguin Books.

Burke, H. R., & Mayer, S. (1985). The MMPI and the post-traumatic stress syndrome in Vietnam era veterans. *Journal of Clinical Psychology, 41*(2), 152–156.

Byrne, D. (1961). The repression-sensitization scale. *Journal of Personality, 29,* 334–349.

Cannon, W. B. (1932). *The wisdom of the body.* New York: Norton.

Cattell, R. B., Eber, H. W., & Tatsuoka, M. M. (1970). *Handbook for the 16-PF.* Champaign, IL: Institute for Personality and Ability Testing.

Chaney, H. S., Williams, S. G., Cohn, C. K., & Vincent, K. R. (1984). MMPI results: A comparison of trauma victims, psychogenic pain, and patients with organic disease. *Journal of Clinical Psychology, 40*(6), 1450–1453.

Chelune, G. J. (1979). *Self-disclosure.* San Francisco: Jossey-Bass.

Ciaranello, R. D. (1983). Neurochemical aspects of stress. In N. Garmezy & M. Rutter, (Eds.), *Stress, coping, and development in children.* New York: McGraw-Hill.

Coelho, G. V., Hamburg, D. A., & Adams, J. E. (Eds.) (1974). *Coping and adaptation.* New York: Basic Books.

Cohen, J., & Cohen, P. (1975). *Applied multiple regression/correlation for the behavioral sciences.* New York: Halsted.

Costa, E. (1985). Benzodiazepine-GABA interactions: A model to investigate the neurobiology of anxiety. In A. H. Tuma and J. Maser (Eds.), *Anxiety and the anxiety disorders* (pp. 27–57). Hillsdale, NJ: Lawrence Erlbaum.

Coyne, J., & Lazarus, R. (1980). Cognitive style, stress perception, and coping. In L. Kutash and L. B. Schlesinger (Eds.), *Handbook of stress and anxiety.* San Francisco: Jossey-Bass.

Croom, B., Schuerger, J. M., DeMuth, P., & Watterson, D. G. (1985). *An occupational interpretation system: Manual for companion software to the 16-PF questionnaire.* Unpublished manuscript. Cleveland State University, Cleveland, Ohio.

Danieli, Y. (1985). The treatment and prevention of long term effects and intergenerational transmission of victimization: A lesson from Holocaust survivors and their children. In C. R. Figley (Ed.), *Trauma and its wake: The study and treatment of post-traumatic stress disorder* (pp. 295–314). New York: Brunner/Mazel.

Danieli, Y. (1988). Treating survivors and children of survivors of the Nazi Holocaust. In F. Ochberg (Ed.), *Post-traumatic therapy and victims of violence* (pp. 278–295). New York: Brunner/Mazel.

Davidson, L. M., Fleming, I., & Baum, A. (1986). Post-traumatic stress as a function of chronic stress and toxic exposure. In C. R. Figley (Ed.), *Trauma and its wake, Vol. II: Traumatic stress theory, research, and intervention.* New York: Brunner/Mazel.

Dean, R. S. (1986). Lateralization of cerebral functions. In D. Wedding, A. M. Horton, & Webster, J. (Eds.), *The neuropsychology handbook: Behavioral and clinical perspectives.* New York: Springer.

DeFazio, V. J. , Rustin, S., & Diamond, A. (1975). Symptom development in Vietnam era veterans. *American Journal of Orthopsychiatry, 45*(1), 158–163.

Delaney, R., Tussi, D., & Gold, P. E. (1983). Long-term potentiation as a neurophysiological analog of memory. *Pharmacological and Biochemical Behavior, 18,* 137–139.

Denny, N., Robinowitz, R., & Penk, W. (1987). Conducting applied research on Vietnam combat-related post-traumatic stress disorder. *Journal of Clinical Psychology, 43*(1), 56–66.

Derogatis, L. R. (1973). SCL-90: An outpatient psychiatric rating scale—Preliminary report. *Psychopharmacology Bulletin, 9,* 13–28.

Derogatis, L. R. (1977). Confirmation of the dimensional structure of the SCL-90: A study in construct validation. *Journal of Clinical Psychology, 33*(4), 981–989.

Dobbs, D., & Wilson, W. P. (1960). Observations on the persistance of war neurosis. *Diseases of the Nervous System, 21,* 40–46.

Dohrenwend, B. S., & Dohrenwend, B. P. (1974). *Stressful life events: Their nature and effects.* New York: Wiley.

Dohrenwend, B. P., & Shrout, P. E. (1984). "Hassels" in the conceptualization and measurement of life-stress variables. *American Psychologist, 40,* 780–786.

Eitinger, L., & Strom, A. (1973). *Mortality and morbidity after excessive stress.* New York: Humanities Press.

Elder, G. A., & Clipp, E. C. (1988). Combat experience, comradeship, and psychological health. In J. P. Wilson, Z. Harel, B. Kahana (Eds.), *Human adaptation to extreme stress: From the Holocaust to Vietnam.* New York: Plenum Press.

Ellison, G. D. (1977). Animal modes of psychopathology: The low-norepinephrine and low-serotonin rats. *American Psychologist, 32,* 1036–1045.

Erdoes, R., & Ortiz, A. (1987). *American Indian myths and legends.* New York: Pantheon Books.

Erikson, E. (1950). *Childhood and society.* New York: Norton.

Erikson, E. (1968). *Identity, youth and crisis.* New York: Norton.

Erikson, E. (1982). *The life-cycle completed.* New York: Norton.

Erikson, K. (1976). *Everything in its path: Destruction of community in the Buffalo Creek Flood.* New York: Simon & Schuster.

Erlinder, C. P. (1984). Paying the price for Vietnam: Post-traumatic stress disorder and criminal behavior. *Boston College Law Review, 25*(2), 305–347.

Fairbank, J. A., Keane, T. M., & Malloy, P. F. (1983). Some preliminary data on the psychological characteristics of Vietnam veterans with post-traumatic stress disorder. *Journal of Consulting and Clinical Psychology, 51*(6), 912–919.

Figley, C. R. (1978). *Stress disorders among Vietnam veterans.* New York: Brunner/Mazel.

Figley, C. R. (Ed.) (1985). *Trauma and its wake: The study and treatment of post-traumatic stress disorder.* New York: Brunner/Mazel.

Figley, C. R., & Leventman, S. (Eds.) (1980). *Strangers at home: Vietnam veterans since the war.* New York: Praeger.

Figley, C. R., & McCubbin, H. I. (Eds.) (1983). *Stress in the family. Vol. II: Coping with catastrophe.* New York: Brunner/Mazel.

Foy, D. W., Sipprelle, R. C., Rueger, D. B., & Carroll, E. M. (1984). Etiology of post-traumatic stress disorder in Vietnam veterans: Analysis of premilitary, military, and combat exposure influences. *Journal of Consulting and Clinical Psychology, 52*(1), 79–87.

Frankenhaeuser, M. (1986). A psychobiological framework for research on human stress and coping. In M. H. Appley & R. Trumbull (Eds.), *Dynamics of stress: Physiological, psychological and social perspectives.* New York: Plenum Press.

Frederick, C. J. (1985). Children traumatized by catastrophic situations. In S. Eth & R. S. Pynoos (Eds.), *Post-traumatic stress disorder in children.* Washington, DC: American Psychiatric Press.

Freud, S. (1917). Mourning and melancholia. In J. Strachey (Ed.), *Standard edition* (vol. 14, pp. 237–259). London: Hogarth Press.

Freud, S. (1920). Beyond the pleasure principle. In J. Strachey (Ed.), *Complete psychological works, standard edition* (vol. 18). London: Hogarth Press, 1953.

Freud, S. (1957). *A general introduction to psychoanalysis.* New York: Liveright.

Freud, S. (1959). *Standard edition.* J. Strachey (Ed.). London: Hogarth Press.

Freud, S. (1957, 1966). *Introductory lectures on psychoanalysis.* New York: Liveright.

Frye, J. S., & Stockton, R. A. (1982). Discriminant analysis of post-traumatic stress disorder among a group of Vietnam veterans. *American Journal of Psychiatry, 139*(1), 52–56.

Gardner, R. W., Jackson, D. N., & Messick, S. J. (Eds.) (1960). Personality organization and cognitive controls in intellectual ability. *Psychological Issues, 2*(4), 8.

Garmezy, N. (1981). Children under stress: Perspectives on the antecedents and correlates of vulnerability and resistance to psychopathology. In A. I. Rabin, J. Aronoff, A. A. Barclay, and R. A. Zucker (Eds.), *Further explorations in personality.* New York: Wiley Interscience.

Garmezy, N., & Rutter, M. (Eds.) (1983). *Stress, coping, and development in children.* New York: McGraw-Hill.

Gayton, W. F., Burchstead, G. N., & Matthews, G. R. (1986). An investigation of the utility of an MMPI post-traumatic stress disorder subscale. *Journal of Clinical Psychology, 42*(6), 916–917.

Gellhorn, E., & Kiely, W. F. (1972). Mystical states of consciousness: Neurophysiological and clinical aspects. *Journal of Nervous and Mental Disease, 154*(6), 399–405.

Gleser, G. C., Green, B. L., & Winget, C. (1981). *Prolonged psychosocial effects of disaster: A study of Buffalo Creek.* New York: Academic Press.

Goldberg, L. R. (1965). Diagnosticians vs. diagnostic signs: The diagnosis of psychosis vs. neurosis for the MMPI. *Psychological Monographs, 79* (9, Whole No. 602).

Goldstein, K. M. (1963). *The organism.* New York: Boston Beacon Press.

Goldstein, K. M., & Blackman, S. (1978). *Cognitive style.* New York: Wiley.

Graham, J. R. (1977). *The MMPI: A practical guide.* New York: Oxford University Press.

Graham, J. R. (1987). *The MMPI* (2nd ed.). New York: Oxford University Press.

Gray, J. A. (1985). Issues in neuropsychology of anxiety. In A. H. Tuma & J. Maser (Eds.), *Anxiety and the anxiety disorders* (pp. 5–27). Hillsdale, NJ: Lawrence Erlbaum.

Green, B. L., & Grace, M. C. (1988). Conceptual issues in research with survivors and illustrations from a follow-up study. In J. P. Wilson, Z. Harel, & B. Kahana (Eds.), *Human adaptation to extreme stress: From the Holocaust to Vietnam.* New York: Plenum Press.

Green, B., Wilson, J. P., & Lindy, J. (1985). Conceptualizing post-traumatic stress disorder: A psychosocial framework. In C. R. Figley (Ed.), *Trauma and its wake: The study and treatment of post-traumatic stress disorder.* New York: Brunner/Mazel.

Grinker, R. R., & Spiegel, J. P. (1945). *Men under stress.* Philadelphia: Blakiston.

Groves, P. M., & Young, S. J. (1986). Neurons, networks, and behavior: An introduction. In L. L. Judd and P. M. Groves (Eds.), *Pscyhobiological foundations of clinical psychology* (vol. 4, pp. 1–21). New York: Basic Books.

Haley, S. (1985). Some of my best friends are dead. Treatment of the PTSD patient and his family. In W. Kelly (Ed.), *Post-traumatic stress disorder and the war veteran patient.* New York: Brunner/Mazel.

Hall, R. (1985). Distribution of the sweat lodge in alcohol treatment programs. *Current Anthropology, 26,* 134–135.

Hare, R. D. (1970). *Psychopathy: Theory and research.* New York: Wiley.

Harner, M. J. (1980). *The way of the Shaman: A guide to power and healing.* San Francisco: Harper & Row.

Harner, M. (1982). *The way of the Shaman.* New York: Bantam Books.

Harris, R., & Lingoes, J. (1955). *Subscales for the Minnesota Multiphasic Personality Inventory.* Mimeographed materials, Langley Porter Clinic.

Harris, R., & Lingoes, J. (1968). *Subscales of the Minnesota Multiphasic Personality Inventory.* Mimeographed materials, Langley Porter Clinic.

Helzer, H., Robins, L. N., Wish, E., & Hesselbrock, M. (1974). Depression in Vietnam veterans and civilian controls. *Archives of General Psychiatry, 31,* 807–811.

Henry, J. L. (1982). Possible involvement of endorphins in altered states of consciousness. *Ethos, 10*(4), 394–408.

Henshaw, H. W. (1910). *Sweating and sweat houses.* Smithsonian Bureau of American Ethnology (pp. 661–663). Washington, DC: US Government Printing Office.

Hocking, F. (1965). Extreme environmental stress and its significance for psychopathology. *American Journal of Psychotherapy, 24,* 4–26.

Hocking, F. (1970). Psychiatric aspects of extreme environmental stress. *Diseases of the Nervous System, Aug.,* 542–545.

Horowitz, M. J. (1976). *Stress response syndromes.* Northvale, NJ: Jason Aronson.

Horowitz, M. J. (1979). Psychological response to serious life events. In V. Hamilton & D. M. Warburton (Eds.), *Human stress and cognition.* New York: Wiley.

Horowitz, M. J. (1986). *Stress response syndromes* (2nd Ed.). Northvale, NJ: Jason Aronson.

Horowitz, M. J., Wilner, N., & Alvarez, W. (1979). Impact of event scale. A measure of subjective strength. *Psychosomatic Medicine, 41,* 209–218.

Hyer, L., Fallon, J. H., Harrison, W. R., & Boudewyns, P. A. (1987). MMPI overreporting by Vietnam combat veterans. *Journal of Clinical Psychology, 43*(1), 79–83.

Hyer, L., O'Leary, W. C., Saucer, R. T., Blount, J., Harrison, W. R., & Boudewyns, P. A. (1986). Inpatient diagnosis of post-traumatic stress disorder. *Journal of Consulting and Clinical Psychology, 54*(5), 698–702.

Jacobson, E. (1974). *Depression.* New York: International Universities Press.

Jaffe, J. H., & Martin, W. (1980). Narcotic analgesics and antagonists. In L. S. Goodman & A. Gilman (Eds.), *Pharmacological basis of therapeutics* (6th Ed.). Macmillan: New York.

Janoff-Bulman, R. (1985). The aftermath of victimization: Rebuilding shattered assumptions. In C. R. Figley (Ed.), *Trauma and its wake: The study and treatment of post-traumatic stress disorder.* New York: Brunner/Mazel.

Janowsky, D. S., Risch, S. C., & Neborsky, R. (1986). Strategies for studying neurotransmitter hypotheses of affective disorders. In L. L. Judd & P. M. Groves (Eds.), *Psychobiological foundations of clinical psychiatry* (pp. 179–189). New York: Basic Books.

Jilek, W. G. (1982). Altered states of consciousness in North American Indians ceremonials. *Ethos, 10*(4), 326–343.

Johnson, R. (1972). *Aggression in man and animals.* Philadelphia: Saunders.

Kahana, B., Harel, Z., & Kahana, E. (1988). Predictors of psychological well-being among survivors of the Holocaust. In J. P. Wilson, Z. Harel, & B. Kahana (Eds.), *Human adaptation to extreme stress: From the Holocaust to Vietnam.* New York: Plenum Press.

Kahana, B., Harel, Z., Kahana, E., & Rosner, T. (1988). Coping with extreme trauma. In J. P. Wilson, Z. Harel, & B. Kahana (Eds.), *Human adaptation to extreme stress: From the Holocaust to Vietnam.* New York: Plenum Press.

Kardiner, A. (1959). Traumatic neuroses of war. In S. Arieti (Ed.), *American handbook of psychiatry* (Vol. I). New York: Basic Books.

Kardiner, A., & Spiegel, J. (1947). *War stress and neurotic illness.* New York: Hoeber.

Keane, T. M., Fairbank, J. A., Caddell, J. M., Zimering, R. T., & Bender, M. E. (1985). A behavioral approach to assessing and treating post-traumatic stress disorder in Vietnam veterans. In C. R. Figley (Ed.), *Trauma and its wake: The study and treatment of post-traumatic stress disorder.* New York: Brunner/Mazel.

Keane, T. M., Malloy, P. F., & Fairbank, J. A. (1984). Empirical development of an MMPI subscale for the assessment of combat-related post-traumatic stress disorder. *Journal of Consulting and Clinical Psychology, 52*(5), 888–891.

Kelly, D. D. (1982). The role of endorphins in stress-induced analgesia. *Annals of the New York Academy of Sciences, 398,* 260–271.

Kenrick, D. T., & Funder, D. (1988). Profiting from controversy: Lessons from the person-situation debate. *American Psychologist, 43,* 15–23.

Kernberg, O. (1975). *Borderline conditions and pathological narcissism.* New York: Jason Aronson.

Ketwig, J. (1985). . . . *And a hard rain fell.* New York: Macmillan.

Kinzie, D. (1988). The psychiatric effects of massive trauma on Cambodian refugees. In J. P. Wilson, Z. Harel, & B. Kahana (Eds.), *Human adaptation to extreme stress: From the Holocaust to Vietnam.* New York: Plenum Press.

Kobasa, S. C. (1979). Stressful life events, personality, and health: An inquiry into hardiness. *Personality and Social Psychology, 37,* 1–11.

Kobasa, S. C., Maddi, S. R., & Courington, S. (1981). Personality and constitution as mediators in the stress-illness relationship. *Journal of Health and Social Behavior, 22,* 368–378.

Kobasa, S. C., Maddi, S. R., Salvatore, R., & Kahn, S. (1982). Hardiness and health: A prospective study. *Journal of Personality and Social Psychology, 42,* 168–177.

Koenig, W. (1964). Chronic or persisting identity diffusion. *American Journal of Psychiatry, 120,* 1081–1084.

Kohut, H. (1971). *Analysis of the self.* New York: International Universities Press.

Kolb, L. C., & Multipassi, L. R. (1982). The conditioned emotional response: A sub-class of the chronic and delayed post-traumatic stress disorder. *Psychiatric Annals, 12,* 979–987.

Krystal, H. (1968). *Massive psychic trauma.* New York: International Universities Press.

Laufer, R. S. (1988). The serial self: War trauma, identity and adult development. In J. P. Wilson, Z. Harel, & B. Kahana (Eds.), *Human adapatation to extreme stress: From the Holocaust to Vietnam.* New York: Plenum Press.

Laufer, R. S., Frey-Wouters, E., & Gallops, M. S. (1985). Traumatic stressors in the Vietnam War and post-traumatic stress disorder. In C. R. Figley (Ed.), *Trauma and its wake: The study and treatment of post-traumatic stress disorder.* New York: Brunner/Mazel.

Laufer, R. S., Gallops, M. S., & Frey-Wouters, E. (1984). War stress and trauma: The Vietnam veteran experience. *Journal of Health and Social Behavior, 25,* 65–85.

Lazarus, R. S., & Folkman, S. (1984). *Stress, appraisal, and coping.* New York: Springer.

Leary, T. (1957). *Interpersonal diagnosis of personality.* New York: Ronald Press.

Lerner, M. J. (1974). The justice motive: Equity and parity among children. *Journal of Personality and Social Psychology, 29,* 539–550.

Levinson, D. J. (1978). *Seasons of a man's life.* New York: Ballantine Books.

Lex, B. W. (1979). The neurobiology of ritual trance. In E. G. d'Aguili, C. D. Lauflin, & J. MacManis (Eds.), *The spectrum of ritual.* New York: Columbia University Press.

Lidz, T. (1946). Psychiatric casualties from Guadalcanal. *Psychiatry, 9,* 193–215.

Lifton, R. J. (1967). *Death in life: Survivors of Hiroshima.* New York: Simon & Schuster.

Lifton, R. J. (1976). *The life of the self.* New York: Simon & Schuster.

Lifton, R. J. (1979). *The broken connection.* New York: Simon & Schuster.

Lifton, R. J. (1983). *The broken connection.* New York: Basic Books.

Lifton, R. J. (1986). *The Nazi doctors.* New York: Basic Books.

Lifton, R. J. (1988). Understanding the traumatized self: Imagery, symbolization, and transformation. In J. P. Wilson, Z. Harel, & B. Kahana (Eds.), *Human adaptation to extreme stress: From the Holocaust to Vietnam.* New York: Plenum Press.

Lindy, J. D. (1986). An outline for the psychoanalytic psychotherapy of post-traumatic stress disorder. In C. R. Figley (Ed.), *Trauma and its wake* (vol. II). New York: Brunner/ Mazel.

Lindy, J. D. (1988). *Vietnam: A casebook.* New York: Brunner/Mazel.

Lindy, J. D., Grace, M. C., & Green, B. L. (1981). Suvivors: Outreach to a reluctant population. *American Journal of Orthopsychiatry, 51,* 468–478.

Lopatin, I. A. (1960). Origin of the Native American steam bath. *American Anthopologist, 62,* 977–993.

Ludwig, A. M. (1966). Altered states of consciousness. *Archives of General Psychiatry, 15,* 225–234.

Lynn, E. J., & Belze, M. (1984). Factitious post-traumatic stress disorder: The veteran who never got to Vietnam. *Hospital and Community Psychiatry, 35(7),* 697–701.

Maier, S. F. & Seligman, M. P. (1976). Learned helplessness: Theory and evidence. *Journal of Experimental Psychology, 105,* 3–46.

Maier, S. F., Sherman, J. E., Lewis, J. W., et al. (1983). The opioid/non-opioid nature of stress induced analgesia and learned helplessness. *Journal of Experimental Psychology, 9,* 80–90.

Mails, T. (1972). *Mystic warrior of the plains.* New York: Doubleday.

Mains, R. E., Eipper, B. A., & Ling, N. (1977). Common precursor to corticotropins and endorphins. *Proceedings of the National Academy of Sciences, 74,* 3014–3018.

Mangold, T., & Penycate, J. (1985). *The tunnels of Cu Chi.* New York: Berkeley Books.

Marmar, C. R., & Horowitz, M. J. (1988). Diagnosis and phase-oriented treatment of post-traumatic stress disorder. In J. P. Wilson, Z. Harel, & B. Kahana (Eds.), *Human adaptation to extreme stress: From the Holocaust to Vietnam.* New York: Plenum Press.

Maslow, A. H. (1970). *Motivation and personality.* New York: Harper & Row.

Mason, J. (1975). Emotion as reflected in patterns of endocrine integration. In L. Levi (Ed.), *Emotions: Their parameters and measurement.* New York: Raven Press.

McClelland, D. C. (1974). *Power: The inner experience.* New York: Irvington Press.

Merbaum, M., & Hefez, A. (1976). Some personality characteristics of soldiers exposed to extreme war stress. *Journal of Consulting and Clinical Psychology, 1,* 1–6.

Meyeroff, B. (1974). *The Peyote hunt.* New York: International Universities Press.

Moreland, K. L. (1985). *Test-retest reliability 80 MMPI scales.* Unpublished materials. (Available from NCD Professional Assessment Services, P.O. Box 1416, Minneapolis, MN 55440).

Morrison, A. (1986). *Essential papers of narcissism.* New York: New York University Press.

Murphy, S. A. (1986). Health and recovery status of victims one and three years following a natural disaster. In C. R. Figley (Ed.), *Trauma and its wake: Traumatic stress theory, research, and intervention.* New York: Brunner/Mazel.

Nace, E. P., O'Brian, C. P., Mintz, J., Ream, N., & Meyers, A. L. (1978). Adjustment among Vietnam veteran drug users two years post service. In C. R. Figley (Ed.), *Stress disorders among Vietnam veterans.* New York: Brunner/Mazel.

Nefzger, M. D. (1970). Follow-up studies of World War II and Korean war prisoners. I. Study plan and mortality findings. *American Journal of Epidemiology, 91,* 123–138.

Neher, A. (1961). Auditory driving observed with scalp electrodes in normal subjects. *Electroencephalography and Clinical Neurophysiology, 13,* 449–451.

Neher, A. (1962). A physiological explanation of unusual behavior in ceremonies involving drums. *Human Biology, 34,* 154–160.

Niederland, W. (1964). Psychiatric disorders among persecution victims. *Journal of Nervous and Mental Disease, 139,* 458–474.

Niederland, W. (1968). The problem of the survivor. In H. Krystal (Ed.), *Massive psychic trauma.* New York: International Universities Press.

Ochberg, F. (1988). *Post-traumatic therapy and victims of violence.* New York: Brunner/ Mazel.

Parson, E. R. (1988). Post-traumatic self disorders (PTsfD): Theoretical and practical considerations in psychotherapy of Vietnam war veterans. In J. P. Wilson, Z. Harel,

& B. Kahana (Eds.), *Human adaptation to extreme stress: From the Holocaust to Vietnam.* New York: Plenum Press.

Penk, W. E., Robinowitz, R., Roberts, W. R., Paterson, E. T., Dolan, M. P., & Atkinson, R. M. (1981). Adjustment differences among male substance abusers varying in degree of combat experience in Vietnam. *Journal of Consulting and Clinical Psychology, 49,* 426–437.

Prince, R. (1980). Variations in psychotherapeutic procedures. In H. C. Triandis and R. Brislan (Eds.), *Handbook of cross-cultural psychology.* New York: Allyn & Bacon.

Query, W. T., Megran, J., & McDonald, G (1986). Applying post-traumatic stress disorder MMPI subscale to World War II POW veterans. *Journal of Clinical Psychology, 42*(2), 315–317.

Raphael, B. (1987). *When disaster strikes.* New York: Humanities Press.

Redman, D. E., & Krystal, J. H. (1984). Multiple mechanisms of opiate withdrawal. *Annual Review of Neuroscience, 7,* 443–478.

Reid, W. H., Dorr, D., Walker, J. I., & Bonner, J. W. (Eds.) (1986). *Unmasking the psychopath: Antisocial personality and related syndromes.* New York: Norton.

Rose, R. M. (1985). Psychoendocrinology. In R. H. Williams (Ed.), *Textbook of endocrinology* (7th ed.). Philadelphia: Saunders.

Rossi, E. L. (1986). *The psychobiology of healing.* New York: Norton.

Roth, W. T. (1988). The role of medication in post-traumatic therapy. New York: Brunner/ Mazel.

Sachar, E. J. (1975). Neuroendocrine abnormalities in depressive illness. In E. J. Sachar (Ed.), *Topics in psychoendocrinology.* New York: Grune & Stratton.

Schildkraut, J. J., Green, A. I., & Mooney, J. J. (1985). Affective disorders: Biochemical aspects. In H. I. Kaplan & B. J. Sadock (Eds.), *Comprehensive textbook of psychiatry, vol. IV,* Baltimore: Williams & Wilkins.

Schnaier, J. A. (1986). A study of women Vietnam Veterans and their mental health adjustment. In C. R. Figley (Ed.). *Trauma and its wake: Traumatic stress theory, research and intervention.* New York: Brunner/Mazel.

Scurfield, R. M. (1985). Post-trauma stress assessment and treatment: Overview and formulations. In C. R. Figley (Ed.), *Trauma and its wake: The study and treatment of post-traumatic stress disorder.* New York: Brunner/Mazel.

Seligman, M. E. (1974). *Learned helplessness.* San Francisco: Freeman Press.

Seligman, M. E., & Garber, J. (1980). *Human helplessness.* New York: Academic Press.

Selye, H. (1950). *The physiology and pathology of exposure to stress.* Montreal: Acta.

Serkownek, K. (1975). *Subscales for Scales 5 and 0 of the Minnesota Multiphasic Personality Inventory.* Unpublished materials, 3134 Whitehorn Rd., Cleveland Heights, OH.

Shatan, C. F. (1974). Through the membrane of reality: Impacted grief and perceptual dissonance in Vietnam combat veterans. *Psychiatric Opinion, 11,* 6–15.

Shook, J. H. (1986). *One soldier.* New York: Bantam Books.

Silver, S. M. (1986). An inpatient program for post-traumatic stress disorder: Context as treatment. In C. R. Figley (Ed.), *Trauma and its wake: Traumatic stress theory, research, and intervention.* New York: Brunner/Mazel.

Silver, S., & Wilson, J. P. (1988). Native American healing and purification rituals for war stress. In J. P. Wilson, Z. Harel, & B. Kahana (Eds.), *Human adaptation to extreme stress: From the Holocaust to Vietnam.* New York: Plenum Press.

Smith, J. R. (1984). Individual psychotherapy with Vietnam veterans. In S. Sonnenberg, A. Blank, & J. A. Talbot (Eds.), *Stress and recovery in Vietnam veterans* (pp. 125–165). Washington, DC: American Psychiatric Press.

Smith, J. R. (1985). Rap groups and group therapy for Vietnam veterans. In S. M. Sonnenberg, A. S. Blank, and J. A. Talbott (Eds.), *Stress and recovery in Vietnam veterans.* Washington, DC: American Psychiatric Press.

Solkoff, N., Gray, P., & Keill, S. (1986). Which Vietnam veterans develop post-traumatic stress disorder. *Journal of Clinical Psychology, 42,*(5), 687–698.

Sparr, L. F., & Atkinson, R. M. (1986). Post-traumatic stress disorder as an insanity defense: Medicolegal quicksand. *American Journal of Psychiatry, 143*(5), 608–612.

Specter, P. E. (1977). What to do with significant multivariate analysis of variance. *Journal of Applied Psychology, 67,* 158–163.

Stein, L. (1978). Reward transmitters: Catecholamines and opioid peptides. In M. A. Lipton, A. DiMascio, & K. F. Killam (Eds.), *Psychopharmacology: A generation of progress.* New York: Raven Press.

Strober, M., Green, J., & Carlson, G. (1981). Utility of the Beck Depression Inventory with psychiatrically hospitalized adolescents. *Journal of Consulting and Clinical Psychology, 40,* 482–483.

Tart, C. J. (Ed.) (1969). *Altered states of consciousness.* New York: Wiley.

Taylor, J. B., Ptacek, M., Carithers, M., Griffin, C., & Coyne, L. (1972). Rating scales as measures of clinical judgement: III. Judgements of the self on personality inventory scales and direct ratings. *Educational and Psychological Measurement, 32,* 543–557.

Terr, L. C. (1985). Children traumatized in small groups. In S. Eth and R. S. Pynoos (Eds.), *Post-traumatic stress disorder in children.* Washington, DC: American Psychiatric Press.

Trimble, M. R. (1981). *Post-traumatic neurosis.* Chichester: Wiley.

Trimble, M. R. (1985). Post-traumatic stress disorder: History of a concept. In C. R. Figley (Ed.), *Trauma and its wake: The study and treatment of post-traumatic stress disorder* (pp. 5–14). New York: Brunner/Mazel.

van der Hart, O. (1983). *Rituals in psychotherapy: Transition and continuity.* New York: Irvington.

van der Kolk, B. A. (1985). Nightmares and trauma: A comparison of nightmares after combat with lifelong nightmares in veterans. *American Journal of Psychiatry, 141,* 187–190.

van der Kolk, B. A. (Ed.) (1987). *Psychological trauma.* Washington, DC: American Psychiatric Press.

van der Kolk, B. A., & Greenberg, M. S. (1987). The psychobiology of the trauma response: Hyperarousal, constriction and addiction to traumatic reexposure. In B. A. van der Kolk (Ed.), *Psychological trauma.* Washington, DC: American Psychiatric Press.

van der Kolk, B. A., Greenberg, M. S., Boyd, H., et al. (1985). Inescapable shock, neurotransmitters and addiction to trauma: Towards a psychobiology of post-traumatic stress. *Biological Psychiatry, 20,* 314–325.

van der Kolk, B. A., Krystal, H., & Greenberg, M. S. (1984). Post-traumatic stress disorder as a biological based disorder: Implications of the animal model of inescapable shock. In B. A. van der Kolk (Ed.), *Post-traumatic stress disorder: Psychological and biological sequelae.* Washington, DC: American Psychiatric Press.

Vereby, K., Volvavka, J., & Clouet, D. (1978). Endorphins in psychiatry. *Archives of General Psychiatry, 35,* 877–888.

Wallace, A.F.C. (1966). *Religion.* New York: Random House.

Wallin, H. N. (1968). *Pearl Harbor: Why, how, fleet salvage, and final appraisal.* Washington, DC: US Government Printing Office, Naval History Division.

Watson, C. G., Kucala, T., & Manifold, V. (1986). Cross-validation of the Keane and Penk MMPI scales as measures of post-traumatic stress disorder. *Journal of Clinical Psychology, 42* (5), 727–732.

Welsh, G. S. (1956). Factor dimensions A and R. In G. S. Welsh and W. G. Dahlstrom (Eds.), *Basic readings on the MMPI in psychology and medicine* (pp. 264–281). Minneapolis: University of Minnesota Press.

White, R. W. (1959, 1963). *The ego and reality in psychoanalytic theory.* New York: International Universities Press.

Williams, T. (1987). *Post-traumatic stress disorder: A handbook for clinicians.* Washington, DC: Disabled American Veterans.

Wilson, J. P. (1978). *Identity, ideology and crisis: The Vietnam veteran in transition* (Vol. 2). Washington, DC: Disabled American Veterans.

Wilson, J. P. (1980a). Conflict, stress and growth: The effects of war on psychosocial development among Vietnam veterans. In C. R. Figley & S. Leventman (Eds.), *Strangers at home: Vietnam veterans since the war*. New York: Praeger.

Wilson, J. P. (1980b, May). *Towards an understanding of post-traumatic stress disorders among Vietnam veterans*. Testimony before the U.S. Senate Subcommittee on Veteran Affairs.

Wilson, J. P. (1988a). Understanding the Vietnam veteran. In F. Ochberg (Ed.), *Post-traumatic therapy and victims of violence* (pp. 227–254). New York: Brunner/Mazel.

Wilson, J. P. (1988b). Treating the Vietnam veteran. In F. Ochberg (Ed.), *Post-traumatic therapy and victims of violence* (pp. 278–295). New York: Brunner/Mazel.

Wilson, J. P., Harel, Z., & Kahana, B. (Eds.) (1988). *Human adaptation to extreme stress: From the Holocaust to Vietnam*. New York: Plenum Press.

Wilson, J. P., & Krauss, G. E. (1980). *The Vietnam era stress inventory*. Cleveland, OH: Cleveland State University.

Wilson, J. P., & Krauss, G. E. (1982). *The Vietnam era stress inventory*. Cleveland, OH: Cleveland State University.

Wilson, J. P., & Krauss, G. E. (1985). Predicting post-traumatic stress syndromes among Vietnam veterans. In W. Kelly (Ed.), *Post-traumatic stress disorder and the war veteran patient*. New York: Brunner/Mazel.

Wilson, J. P., Smith, W. K., & Johnson, S. K. (1985). A comparative analysis of PTSD among various survivor groups. In C. R. Figley (Ed.), *Trauma and its wake: The study and treatment of post-traumatic stress disorder*. New York: Brunner/Mazel.

Wilson, J. P., & Zigelbaum, S. D. (1983). The Vietnam veteran on trial: The relation of post-traumatic stress disorder to criminal behavior. *Behavioral Sciences and the Law, 4*, 69–84.

Wilson, J. P., & Zigelbaum, S. D. (1986). Post-traumatic stress disorder and the disposition to criminal behavior. In C. R. Figley (Ed.), *Trauma and its wake: Theory, research, and intervention*. New York: Brunner/Mazel.

Winer, B. J. (1971). *Statistical principles in experimental research*. New York: McGraw-Hill.

Winkelman, M. (1986). Trance states. *Ethos, 14*(2), 174–203.

Winnicott, D. W. (1950). Aggression in relation to emotional development. In D. W. Winnicott, *Collected papers: Through paediatrics to psychoanalysis*. London: Tavistock Publications.

Wright, S. (1983). *Meditations in green*. New York: Scribner's.

Zilberg, N., Weiss, D. S., & Horowitz, M. J. (1982). Impact of event scale: A cross validation study and some empirical evidence supporting a conceptual model of stress response syndromes. *Journal of Consulting and Clinical Psychology, 50*(3), 407–414.

Zuckerman, M. (1979). *Sensation seeking*. Hillsdale, NJ: Lawrence Erlbaum.

Zuckerman, M. (1983). A biological theory of sensation seeking. In M. Zuckerman (Ed.), *Biological bases of sensation seeking, impulsivity and anxiety*. Hillsdale, NJ: Lawrence Erlbaum.

Zuckerman, M., Kolin, E. A., Price, L., & Zoob, I. (1964). Development of a sensation seeking scale. *Journal of Consulting and Clinical Psychology, 28* (6), 477–480.

Zuckerman, M., & Linn, K. (1968). Construct validity of the sensation seeking scale. *Journal of Consulting and Clinical Psychology, 32*(4), 420–426.

Name Index

333

Subject Index